THE FLAG REVELATION

Copyright © 2024 Christopher Maddish

All rights reserved. No part of this publication may be reproduced, distributed, or transmitted in any form or by any means, including photocopying, recording, or other electronic or mechanical methods, without the prior written permission of the publisher, except in the case of brief quotations embodied in critical reviews and certain other noncommercial uses permitted by copyright law. For permission requests, write to the publisher, addressed "Attention: Permissions Coordinator," at the address below.

HomonoiaBooks.com
Homonoia Books
PO Box 11
Lansdale, PA 19446

ISBN: 979-8-9893563-0-0 (paperback)
ISBN: 979-8-9893563-1-7 (ebook)
ISBN: 979-8-9893563-2-4 (hardcover)

Ordering Information:
Special discounts are available on quantity purchases by corporations, associations, and others. For details, visit HomonoiaBooks.com.

Publisher's Cataloging-in-Publication Data
Names: Maddish, Christopher, 1974- .
Title: The flag revelation : proof of providence due to the mysterious & uncanny connections of the 50 states of America, synchronicity illustrated / Christopher Maddish.
Description: Lansdale, PA : Homonoia Books, 2024. | Summary: A look at US state flags, revealing an emergent pattern: each state has a look-a-like fraternal flag twin, based upon many uncanny coincidences found between them. This phenomenon is further reinforced by providential alignments of geography, history, culture, and vexillology.
Identifiers: LCCN 2023922949 | ISBN 9798989356324 (hardback) | ISBN 9798989356300 (pbk.) | ISBN 9798989356331 (audio) | ISBN 9798989356317 (ebook)
Subjects: LCSH: Flags – United States – States. | Flags – United States – States – History. | Flags – Research. | Flags – Social aspects. | Coincidence. | BISAC: HISTORY / United States / General. | REFERENCE / Signs & Symbols.
Classification: LCC CR113.2 M33 2024 | DDC 929.9/2/0973 M--dc23
LC record available at https://lccn.loc.gov/2023922949

THE FLAG REVELATION

Proof of Providence due to the Mysterious & Uncanny Connections of the 50 States of America, Synchronicity Illustrated

CHRISTOPHER MADDISH

This book is dedicated to my wife, Trish

TABLE OF CONTENTS

Introduction		1

PART I: A Vast Armada of Navy Blue

chapter 1	Michigan & Pennsylvania	7
	A Keystone of Serendipity Unlocks a Path of Providence	
chapter 2	Wisconsin & Maine	25
	Coincidentally, a Midshipman Merges Along the St. Croix River	
chapter 3	Montana & Kansas	37
	Two Golden Bullets Preserved for Posterity on the Prairie	
chapter 4	Connecticut & Vermont	49
	The Creative Left and Logically Rigorous Right United	
chapter 5	Oregon & Nebraska	67
	The Point of No Return Between the Future Past	
chapter 6	Alaska & Nevada	85
	The Essence of Freemasonry Is Apparent in Their Contours	
chapter 7	Idaho & Minnesota	103
	Everlasting Inner Beauty vs. Fleeting Outer Beauty	
chapter 8	Kentucky & Delaware	131
	The Blue-Eyed Pauper and Blue-Blooded Prince See Eye to Eye	
chapter 9	South Dakota & Oklahoma	151
	The Sacred Center of America Is Sheltered in This Harbor	
chapter 10	Utah & Louisiana	169
	Prayers of Different Feathers Bring Faith to the Few and Many	

| chapter 11 | South Carolina & Reverse Oregon | 187 |
| | *A Tale of Two States and/or Two Dreams of Janus* | |

PART II: Balance Between a Dark and Light Force

chapter 12	North Dakota & Illinois	217
	A Union of Heaven and Earth	
chapter 13	Indiana & Rhode Island	241
	The Alchemy of Fire and Water Hidden in Plain Sight	
chapter 14	Wyoming & West Virginia	269
	Sacred Synchronicity upon the 50th Year of Jubilee	
chapter 15	New York & New Jersey	295
	The Big Apple and Zesty Tomato	
chapter 16	Virginia & Massachusetts	327
	The Alpha and Omega at the Genesis of America	

Closing Thoughts	369
Selected Bibliography	373
Epilogue	391
About the Author	393

INTRODUCTION

This book presents a new order for the 50 states of America through the lens of syn-chronicity. Essentially, this is a revelation that the states are connected in an unexpected and mysterious manner that can be labeled as synchronicity or Providence.

Providence is a core value of the United States that was held in high esteem by the founding fathers. But the challenge of explaining Providence to the uninitiated can be rather difficult, as synchronicity and Providence are essentially grounded in nonlinear thinking where logic and reason fade. Usually, only when looking back after a long and fruitful life and all its strange and winding turns will the perception of Providence become apparent.

As for this book, the presentation of each state with a particular partner rests on a foundation of synchronicities shared between each pair of states. The core element that binds a state to another is an alignment of designs shared between paired state flags. Since flags are roundly regarded as sacred objects in all cultures, it should be no surprise that something of Providence should find itself associated with the state flags of the United States.

After reading this book, it should be evident that, just as states have official birds, colors, songs, and snacks, each state has what is hereby coined a "fraternal flag partner." Besides the peculiar alignment of having similar flag elements, this relationship is further reinforced by history, geography, politics, and culture. This assignment was not decided by a committee or by vote—rather, it should be regarded as an organic association.

Synchronicity is a notoriously difficult word to describe because it's grounded to the inherent bias of personal perception. A technical definition would be "the occurrence of meaningful coincidences that seem to have no cause." On the basic level, it can be described as a random alignment of a situation that causes a profound emotional response. It's also associated with a chance meeting of a long-lost friend and having just thought about them beforehand.

The semi-fictional story concerning the origin of the very word "synchronicity" dates to the mid-1900s when Dr. Carl Jung coined the term after a therapy session when a patient told him about a dreaded beetle that haunted her dreams. At the very moment she finished her confession, there was a tapping at the window. Would you believe it was a beetle? She apparently went into an apoplectic frenzy, and Dr. Jung went to great lengths to calm her down. True or not, it's the official origin story of synchronicity, a strong emotional response to an out of the ordinary, statistically rare, chance event.

Another example caked with several layers of synchronicity is the story of six college friends who decide to throw a college reunion a decade after graduation. The plan was to also bring gifts since it was the winter holidays. However, they forgot "on purpose" to invite the one friend who was more or less a roommate of convenience. She had only been a part of the circle of friends as a means to cover the rent. When the organizer went to the bookstore to purchase a book about the South Pacific, a book about tree frogs fell off the shelf, crashing into her face and breaking her $500 sunglasses. Someone brought a newspaper to the party, and there on the front cover was the uninvited friend of the group. The article featured how she had just been granted a prestigious six-figure grant and was doing research in the Amazon forest on poisonous tree frogs to collect their toxic secretions in order to combat cancer. The roommate of convenience was wearing the exact same pair of sunglasses as the ones that were broken a mere hour earlier when a random book assaulted the organizer at the bookstore. Just then, one of the friends received a text that her husband had been diagnosed with skin cancer. Mere coincidence? Fact or fiction? Regardless, this is a remarkable multilayered whammy of synchronicity.

With that basic 101 introduction of synchronicity out of the way, the following chapters will be filled with facts and stories that align in a similar serendipitous fashion. Although flags are created in a random order, a pattern has emerged from a chaotic process.

The primary difference is that Providence has spiritual overtones, while synchronicity, at least officially speaking, lacks any religious connotation and is respected by academia. But if you read anything about Dr. Jung, he was deeply concerned about the nature and destiny of the soul and pondered endlessly on things of a spiritual and sacred matter.

The revolutionary concept of this book is that every state has a flag twin. Not an identical twin per se, but rather a fraternal twin. Put another way, the various 50 state flags pair up the same way you can tell two people are related by their physical resemblance, which can be described as a wingman, soulmate, partner in crime, guardian angel, sister state, or simply as the buddy system. Everyone gets a buddy.

This is not a traditional reference book but can be used in such a manner. Great effort has been made to keep the stories interesting and to stay away from a stuffy and dry academic reference style. For those who want to explore further, a selected bibliography is located at the back of the book, with a QR code link for detailed notes online.

This is the first book of a trilogy. This book covers the state flags that follow the simple pattern of state seals centered on a background. The states that use this basic design are mostly northern states, with a few exceptions. The second book will focus on the state flags that have sharp abstract designs, which are mostly southern states. The final book will include the external territories of the U.S. and other extraordinary flags related to the U.S.

PART I

A VAST ARMADA OF NAVY BLUE

one

MICHIGAN & PENNSYLVANIA

A Keystone of Serendipity Unlocks a Path of Providence

THE FLAG REVELATION

MICHIGAN

The regal flags of Pennsylvania and Michigan use a heraldic coat of arms centered on a navy-blue background. Heraldry is an art form with a civic purpose from medieval Europe. It's the ancestor of the modern logo and was regulated by the royal offices to indicate the rank, ownership, and territories within and of a kingdom. Previously, only members of the nobility were entitled to use a heraldic coat of arms.

The centrally placed coat of arms traces its origins to the state seals, and using the state seal as the primary design element in the state flag is a frequent occurrence. But a curious kind of harmony becomes apparent when these flags are placed side by side. The two black horses of Pennsylvania harmoniously align with the brown elk and moose of Michigan. Both sets of hoofed ungulates are standing on their hind legs, supporting the central shield with their front legs. On Michigan's flag, the elk is on the left hoist-side of the flag, while the moose is on the right fly-side.

A wild kindred spirit is echoed with the free-roaming deer of Michigan, while civilized domestication is apparent with the work horses of Pennsylvania. The "naked" unharnessed and bare-hoofed antlered deer of Michigan exem-

PENNSYLVANIA

plify an organic state of being. The "clothed" fancy red-and-silver-harnessed, horseshoed, "antlerless" horses of Pennsylvania express a domestic tranquility manufactured by human hands.

The bald eagle in the crest is a key linking point, as both states honor the national bird at an honor point—the crest on a coat of arms. The state mottos appear in the compartment. Pennsylvania's motto is written on a red scroll. Michigan's is written on a white interconnected strip.

Both shields feature scenes by the water. Pennsylvania has a colonial schooner on a body of water, which many assume to be the Delaware River. On the other hand, Michigan has a man in a Daniel Boone–style outfit standing by the shoreline, waving and holding a long gun in the other hand. We don't know which lake the man is supposed to be standing by, but it's commonly believed to be Lake Michigan. Overall, the shields have balanced portions of yellow, sky blue, green, white, and brown, but in different configurations. Sky blue represents the water in Michigan, but in Pennsylvania, sky blue is used for the heavens. Conversely, the color yellow dominates the sky in Michigan, but a solid yellow field has a plow resting in its center for Pennsylvania. Concordance occurs with the color green, which is used to represent the land on both flags.

Federal symbols of the national seal are present in the talons of Michigan's bald eagle—a bundle of arrows for war in the fly-ward talon and an olive branch for peace in the hoist-ward talon. But for Pennsylvania, objects of balanced duality appear below the shield of arms—a stalk of corn and an olive branch. Officially, the olive branch is a symbol of peace. But when crossed with a stalk of corn, these deliciously edible plants incidentally reflect a union of two hemispheres, representing the New and Old Worlds.

Corn was domesticated by Native Americans thousands of years before the arrival of Christopher Columbus, while olives were domesticated in the Old World thousands of years before the Vikings intermittently explored North America at the dawn of the first millennium. Also note that olives are associated with the spiritual and divine within Judaism, Christianity, and Islam. Concordantly, corn has a deeply spiritual connection with Native Americans. The holiness of the olive tree is also tied to the ancient stories associated with Zeus on Mount Olympus; likewise, there are countless Native American traditions that expound about the divine origins of corn. Thus, on the flag of Pennsylvania, two sacred plants make a harmonious whole, yet they originate from opposite sides of the Earth—the Western and Eastern Hemispheres.

Geography

Pennsylvania and Michigan also share opposite shorelines on Lake Erie, and ironically Pennsylvania has a larger Lake Erie shoreline. As Michigan has one of the Great Lakes corresponding to her own name via Lake Michigan, so too in a local sense does Pennsylvania, with Lake Erie matching with the city of Erie in Pennsylvania.

Flint, Michigan, and Allentown, Pennsylvania, make a pair of spunky sister cities that were once thriving industrial centers and have had to reinvent themselves after their suffering of woes captured the attention of the nation. Like yin and yang, Pennsylvania is divided into a dominant eastern and secondary western half separated by the great mountains of Appalachia, while Michigan is divided into a secondary northern and dominant southern half separated by lakes that are great.

Since Pennsylvania is considered the Keystone State in between the six southern states of the South and six states of the North of the original 13, Michigan is the secondary Keystone State of the second batch of 13 states. Reason being, Michigan has territory due north and south of Canada, she has a keystone arch that is set on Indiana and Ohio, and most importantly, Michigan is the fraternal flag partner of Pennsylvania, the original Keystone State.

History

Coincidentally, the colonial foundations of Michigan and Pennsylvania were built upon the hostile displacement of Whites on Whites. Pennsylvania's first colonial settlers landed under a Swedish flag, while Michigan's first permanent settlers originated under a French flag. The equivalent "Swedish Mayflower" landed in the Delaware Bay in late March 1638. But it was two ships instead of one—the *Kalmar Nyckel* and *Fogel Grip*. This historic landing wasn't in Pennsylvania, but rather in Delaware. Thus, the first settlement in Pennsylvania was an outgrowth of this Swedish colony initially planted in Delaware. Five years after the landing of the "Swedish Mayflowers" at Wilmington, these Scandinavian immigrants settled in what was destined to become Pennsylvania in 1643. Almost 40 years passed after the settlement of this Swedish colony, which eventually became an English colony. But before the inhabitants of the Delaware Valley were obligated to speak English instead of Swedish, the Dutch invaded the area in a hostile merger, mostly to increase their profit margins in the lucrative fur trade. In 1655, the Netherlands conquered New Sweden. The Dutch allowed the various Scandinavian colonists—mostly Finnish and Swedish—to stay. Eleven years later, the British conquered the Dutch in 1664, assuring that future peoples living in the Delaware Valley were to speak English. But Pennsylvania was not yet Pennsylvania. The English conquistadors attached the settled area to New York Colony, so for a short 17 years, people living and born in what was to become eastern Pennsylvania were in some fashion a part of the colony of New York.

Pennsylvania's start as a separate English colony was the proverbial story of the little fish getting eaten by the bigger fish that later got eaten by a biggest fish that was later sold at market to pay off a debt. In 1681, the biggest fish in England, King Charles II, sold this coveted slice of American pie to a Quaker named William Penn as payment for a debt, and the rest has been traditional Pennsylvania English history since 1681.

Michigan was also an outgrowth of a non-British colony that was later obliged to speak English. Again, like the story of the *Mayflower*, the first European settlers of Michigan crossed a body of water—the St. Mary's River—from Ontario, Canada, to the upper peninsula of Michigan. But in this case, it only took a few minutes or hours instead of a few months. The names of the boats that brought Michigan its first permanent settlers have been lost in the annals of time, if the boats were even named. Instead, the name Marquette has become well remembered for Michigan in much of the same manner William Penn is for Pennsylvania. Marquette, though, was not a Quaker but rather a Catholic missionary. The first settlement in Michigan was set up by Father Marquette in 1668 as a mission for Native Americans on the Upper Peninsula at St. Sault Marie. Also note that St. Sault Marie, Michigan, was an outgrowth of Quebec, which was first settled in 1608. Sixty years later, expanding from Quebec, Michigan, it was finally settled by the French in 1668. For the next 95 years, the land that became Michigan was under the firm grip of the City of Lights until 1763. In 1763, Paris lost all of its colonial claims on the mainland to the United Kingdom in the aftermath of the last French and Indian War.

By synchronicity, both states had mini interstate wars. During Pennsylvania's colonial period, Connecticut became a deadly rival in a land dispute, while Michigan became engaged in a bitter conflict with Ohio over Toledo. The land claims dispute between Pennsylvania and Connecticut lasted several decades and had a death toll, prisoners of war, and a 60-mile death march. The mini interstate war erupted over the ownership of the Wyoming Valley. The northern part of Pennsylvania was initially chartered to Connecticut in 1662 under King Charles II, but then, in a boneheaded move, King Charles II assigned the area to William Penn in 1681. Oopsie on the sovereign!

This misunderstanding in claims became known as the Pennamite-Yankee Wars, which intermittently flared for 30 years, from 1769 until President Washington settled the issue. Trouble started when people from Connecticut attempted to expand in the Wyoming Valley. However, Pennsylvania did not welcome these Yankee immigrants and tried to forcibly dislodge these unwelcome settlers. Eventually, Washington decided that the Wyoming Valley belonged to Pennsylvania and that the Connecticut settlers could stay on the condition that they become Pennsylvanian citizens.

Michigan and Ohio's heated and terse standoff over a land claim error became known as the Toledo War. The area in dispute was first given to Ohio in 1802, when its state borders were being decided. Three years later, when Michigan Territory was created in 1805, its southern border was set to the southern edge of Lake Michigan. The whoopsie part was that people assumed that the southern border of Lake Michigan was north of Toledo. It wasn't. When Michigan was about to become a state, the 1835 Michigan-Ohio War erupted under President Andrew Jackson. Although historians call this confrontation a war, no battles officially took place. It was settled peacefully in 1836 in Ohio's favor. Michigan lost Toledo, but she was given a consolation prize—the entire Upper Peninsula.

Pennsylvania and Michigan are two of the few states that were invaded and had their original capital cities occupied by Mother Britannia. During the early part of the American Revolution, Philadelphia was occupied. In the aftermath of the disastrous Battle of Brandywine on September 11, 1777, Loyalist forces were able to occupy Philadelphia. The British Loyalist occupation forced the evacuation of the pre-constitutional U.S. Congress westward to York, Pennsylvania, where the first Constitution was written, the Articles of Confederation. British forces finally left Philadelphia in 1778 in order to defend New York City, as the new Rebel-French alliance worried the British.

In Michigan, the British invading army came from the north during the War of 1812. The British Army, under the command of General Isaac Brock with the original Native American Tecumseh, marched into Michigan and successfully captured Detroit. The fall of Detroit led to the deadliest and most tragic loss of U.S. forces from Canada at the Battle of Frenchtown on January 18-23, 1813. Frenchtown started out as an easy win for the United States, but Canadian forces rallied with fresh troops from occupied Detroit. Of the 1,000 U.S. defenders at Frenchtown, nearly half lost their lives that day. But it didn't end there. Nearly 100 of the injured U.S. troops who surrendered were murdered by Native American allies of the British when transporting them north was deemed too difficult a task.

The Civil War reached a climactic height at Gettysburg, Pennsylvania. It was the largest battle of the war and is considered the turning point, in favor of the Union. Michiganders played a critical role as defensive wingmen repulsing this most mighty of Confederate advances, arguably saving the day. Also of note, a short list of Michigan defenders at the Battle of Gettysburg included the Chief of Artillery Henry Jackson Hunt of Detroit, General Elon J. Farnsworth, and one of the most important U.S. cavalry units to roll thunder, The Michigan Cavalry Brigade. The Michigan Cavalry was better known as the Michigan Wolverines and was under the command of Colonel Armstrong Custer. Henry Jackson Hunt was the chief of artillery who was responsible for decimating and debilitating the Southern charge into Northern lines. A loss in Pennsylvania of this magnitude on the eve of a 4th of July after two years of bloody conflict would have certainly broken Union morale and most likely would have led to the independence of the Confederate States of America.

Michigan and Pennsylvania also gave America two real Indiana Jones–caliber heroes at the turn of the 20th century: Charles Lindbergh and Robert Peary. It may be somewhat of a foggy memory for most Pennsylvanians, but the Keystone State was the birthplace of Robert Peary, the first person to reach the North Pole in 1909. Peary was born in Cresson, Pennsylvania, on May 6, 1856. A few years later, the name *Spirit of St. Louis* became a part of the American vocabulary thanks to Charles Lindbergh in 1927. Charles Lindbergh was born in Detroit, Michigan, and became the first person to fly solo across the Atlantic from New York to Paris, France.

Part of the reason why these Indiana Jones–type figures have lost their luster, unlike their contemporary counterpart Amelia Earhart, is due to their short-sighted points of view, which were quite common in that era. Charles Lindbergh espoused a superior greatness of his ethnic line, while Peary fathered several children with Inuit women in the Arctic, even though he was already married. It seems Peary's potentially embarrassing behavior was ignored by the media so as to maintain a Boy Scout image for publicity dollars.

Even after their accomplishments, they became national drama kings. The murder and kidnapping of Charles Lindbergh's son sent the nation into an uproar in 1932, many calling it *the crime of the century*. As was a common sentiment of the time, Lindbergh was outspokenly proud and convinced of Nordic superiority. Ironically, the man who was eventually convicted of kidnapping and murdering Lindbergh's son—Bruno Richard Hauptmann—was from the country of Germany.

Lindbergh was also an outspoken advocate for noninterference during World War II, and President Franklin D. Roosevelt even thought he was a Nazi sympathizer. Only after the Japanese surprise attack at Pearl Harbor of 1941 did Lindbergh become an advocate for American involvement. Likewise, Peary's claim to have reached the North Pole is cast with a small shadow of doubt, as his rival, Frederick Cook from New York, highlighted the lack of independent validation of Peary's claim, and it is calculated today that Peary may have been off by several miles. Furthermore, Peary did not get to the North Pole all by himself. Peary received critical assistance from Arctic locals and Matthew Henson, who was African American.

From a perpetually changing modern view of history, Lindbergh and Peary were ordinary men who did the extraordinary. They were able to fire up and cultivate the imagination and light of American exploration. Their triumphs once seemed superhuman, but the two were mortal men who played both the part of the sad fool and the epic hero.

The vast majority of wheels that spin across the roads of America originate in Michigan. Detroit, Michigan, is the headquarters of General Motors, Chrysler, and Ford. But before the age of the horseless chariot, ox- and horse-powered wheels of wood were already spinning across the nation. One of the most iconic vehicles of that era was the canvas-covered Conestoga wagon, which was originally developed in Lancaster, Pennsylvania.

The First Amendment of the Constitution guarantees freedom of religion. With great zeal, Pennsylvania and Michigan fully exercised this right, and the result was two famous made-in-the-USA congregations that broke with convention. Jehovah's Witnesses are a native Pennsylvanian sect that formed out of the teachings of Charles Taze Russell, born in Allegheny, Pennsylvania, in 1852. In 1881, Russell effectively founded the Watch Tower Society. Interestingly, Jehovah's Witnesses do not call their houses of worship churches, but rather Kingdom Halls. Another popular point of this community is that their faith keeps them from pledging allegiance to the U.S. flag (or any other flag, for that matter). But holy original matters for Michigan came to light with the Seventh-day Adventist Church. This unique congregation was established at Battle Creek, Michigan, in 1863. One of the particulars that distinguish Seventh-day Adventists is church service on Saturday, as is traditional in Judaism. Also note Jehovah's Witnesses earned a profound measure of respect in Germany since they did not cooperate with the Nazi regime and notably refused to salute the Third Reich's flag. Many perished under "the purple star" in the death camps for their religious beliefs. And on the ethical treatment of animals front, Seventh-day Adventists generally follow a vegetarian diet and totally abstain from pork.

Perhaps the foremost patriotic and religious icon for the United States is the Liberty Bell. Originally made in London, it arrived in Pennsylvania in 1752. This 12-foot musical instrument set to E-flat cracked shortly after it arrived in Pennsylvania. Though the bell was recast and remolded in colonial Pennsylvania, it cracked again sometime after the War of 1812. Attempts to seal the fissure were futile, and the crack became a part of its essential character and a providential footnote that all did not have liberty. Slavery was still a legal institution in the land of the free when the bell changed names from the colonial Pennsylvania State House Bell to the more famous Liberty Bell.

Weighing over 2,000 pounds and more than just a bronze bell, it was originally a public alert system. Today it has transcended its original intention, becoming an iconic symbol for freedom, Philadelphia, and the nation. An Old

Testament verse is inscribed upon it, taken from Leviticus 25:10. The inscription reads, "PROCLAIM **LIBERTY** THROUGHOUT ALL THE LAND UNTO ALL THE INHABITANTS THEREOF." This quote refers to the biblical Year of Jubilee during which slaves are given their freedom. The bell's recasting by colonial Americans and inscription relating to liberty is another illustration of synchronicity at work. The inscription relating to "LIBERTY" as quoted from the Bible is a typeset coincidence that allowed this bell to become an American cultural icon. The original makers and recipients of the Pennsylvania state house bell were oblivious to this object's destiny and future role as a national symbol. As the bell was recast upon its arrival to Philadelphia after it broke, so too would a revolutionary government recast the makings of colonial government in Philadelphia. In Philadelphia the American government was recast for a second time in 1787 via the U.S. Constitution, after the dismal performance of the first government under the Articles of Confederation. Also, imagine if the "state house bell" quoted another part of the Bible that did not mention liberty? What if a biblical inscription about the glorious divine right of kings to rule his subjects or the obligation of a slave's duty to obey his master had been used instead? It's likely the old Pennsylvania state house bell would have been lost to the ages, since it would no longer herald a call to "LIBERTY."

On a semi-parallel note, Detroit also has a like-minded bronze memorial reflective of the city and national ethos. Theirs is called "The Spirit of Detroit." This 26-foot statue was also cast overseas in Oslo, Norway. It features a man holding a golden orb in his left hand that represents the Divine, and in his right hand, he holds a family. The Spirit of Detroit also makes a biblical reference about freedom, but from the New Testament, Corinthians II 3:17: "NOW THE LORD IS THAT SPIRIT AND WHERE THE SPIRIT OF THE LORD IS, THERE IS LIBERTY."

Thus the amazing synchronicity, or mark of Providence, is that old Philadelphia and relatively new Detroit have a pair of bronze guardians as paramount representations of each city, both with biblical inscriptions heralding a call to liberty, uniting the old essence of a sacred testament with the new.

Culture

The cultures of Pennsylvania and Michigan are tuned to a similar range. Each state is dominated by a large metropolitan center, Philadelphia and Detroit, respectively. These mega-cities on the eastern sides of their respective states have wealthy central skyscraper center points and are surrounded by gritty, rough-and-tumble, deep navy, black- and blue-collar neighborhoods balanced with a patchwork of upcoming islands of revitalization and artistic blocks of super creativity. Beyond the city limits is a relatively prosperous ring of suburban communities. Away from the big cities, small, country-style cities and farms dot the inlands yonder far and wide, graciously filled with ample room for hunting and fishing.

As Philadelphia is famous for the all-American cheesesteak, Detroit has a similar tasty pulmonary-paralyzing, protein-packed dish—the Coney Island dog. The Philadelphia cheesesteak is composed of thin slices of beef that are fried like a burger and topped with cheese—the best choice being American. Secondary essential toppings are fried onions and ketchup. The often overlooked and hard-to-get-key ingredient is the perfect steak roll that's soft on the inside and slightly hard on the outside. In a parallel yet distinct flavor is the Detroit Coney Island dog. It's an all-beef hot dog and topped with a meat chili, minus the beans. But this is no ordinary chili dog. The key ingredient is a specially prepared bean-less, secretly spiced meat chili. Toppings include finely chopped raw sweet onions and a glaze of yellow mustard, either one stripe or two. Eating a Coney Island dog with ketchup is taboo, just as it would be an abomination to put mustard on a Philly cheesesteak. The Philly cheesesteak became an American icon in the movie *Rocky* (1976), while the Detroit Coney Island dog appeared in the movie *The Crow* (1994).

Both Philadelphia and Detroit are cities in the big boy club, whereby they support all four of the majors in broadcast sports: baseball, basketball, hockey, and football. Most cities don't have the capacity to hold all four cards. Likewise, the fanatic fandom is ubiquitous in the city and surrounding suburban areas. Since their teams play in different conferences, this book is a permission slip for Philly fans to root for Detroit and vice versa. On the whole, Philadelphia and

Detroit share nearly equivalent blessings and burdens of the modern big city, with similar population sizes and phenotypes/demographics.

In American cinema, Detroit, Michigan, and Philadelphia, Pennsylvania, gave birth to legendary underdogs rising to the top with *Rocky* (1976) and *8 Mile* (2002). These works of art, which are partially autobiographical, became exemplars of the American Dream. In *Rocky*, a small-time boxer with a heart of gold is given a chance to fight in the big leagues, while in *8 Mile*, a dirt-poor nobody is able gain the respect of the urban underworld with heart, soul, and focused determination. Even though Sylvester Stallone suffered an injury during birth that gave him a speech impediment, he did not let this issue handicap his career. Likewise, the story of *8 Mile* is a partial confessional about Marshall Mathers, better known as Eminem. Mathers refused to let low social economic expectations and bullying keep him from chasing his heart's desire and achieving national success.

The Detroit-native Temptations of the 1960s are harmoniously balanced a generation later with the Philadelphia-born Boyz II Men in the 1990s. During the 1970s, as Detroit gave rise to Motown, Philadelphia came up with Philly soul.

The most iconic transgenerational global pop star is Louise Veronica Ciccone, better known as Madonna, who is from suburban Bay City, Michigan. In a similar tone, from suburban Philadelphia, the national girl-power pop star Alecia Beth Moore, more famously known as Pink, is from Doylestown, Pennsylvania. On the glam rock and roll end, from Michigan, we have Alice Cooper, whose band made it big in 1972 with "School's Out." Cooper's hard rocking and shocking melodies match with equal passion with Pennsylvanian hair metal band Poison, whose glam-rock androgynous wardrobe caught the eye of American youth in 1988.

More recently, a contrasting consort of superstars are Taylor Swift and Dej Loaf. Dej Loaf, from Detroit, Michigan, was born 1991 and is a match made in yin-yang heaven with Taylor Swift, who was born in West Reading, Pennsylvania, in 1989.

From the laugh bag, Pennsylvania gave America two of its most famous comedian royals—Kevin Hart and Bill Cosby—both of whom wickedly tickled the funny bone of America. From Michigan, Sinbad would equally spread chummy chuckles across the nation with his rated-PG social family humor. Stars from *Saturday Night Live* who come from these two states include Pennsylvanian practical joke peanut heads Tina Fey and Dennis Miller. They are matched with the merry moon-goobers from Michigan David Spade, Gilda Radner, Tim Meadows, and Tim Robinson.

Besides grinding on America's giggle spot, Michigan and Pennsylvania enchanted and educated the youth of America with a duo of more than wise storytellers in John Hughes and Chris Columbus. John Hughes, from Lansing, Michigan, gave America the Brat Pack. Hughes's work includes *Sixteen Candles* (1984), *The Breakfast Club* (1985), and *Some Kind of Wonderful* (1987). From small town Spangler, Pennsylvania, Chris Columbus told more fanciful stories of wonder and youthful adventure with *The Goonies* (1985), *Gremlins* (1984), and, most recently, as a director for the *Harry Potter* franchise. When Columbus and Hughes combined their powers, they created a solid, sparkling, everlasting jewel for any caste and creed to enjoy, *Home Alone* (1990)—Columbus was the director and Hughes was the writer.

A ghost story that enchanted the public is *The Crow* from 1994. The Michigan native who penned this story is James O'Barr. According to O'Barr, the story of *The Crow* was inspired by a true story of a young couple murdered over a $20 engagement ring in Detroit. O'Barr was also dealing with his own loss, as his fiancée was killed by a drunk driver. His story is set in Detroit and is a tale of a magical crow that resurrects a ghostly version of the protagonist, who is then able to serve supernatural justice. In concordance, *The Sixth Sense* in 1999 became a legendary ghost story in Philadelphia. A ghost by the name of Malcolm (wait for it) Crowe meets a boy with clairvoyant powers played by Haley Joel Osment. Unlike most ghost stories that are created to scare and spook, *The Sixth Sense* also touches on themes of justice and love. Eventually, as Crowe helps the boy, he helps himself. The story ends on the bittersweet fragrance of love, as did the actual events during the filming of *The Crow*, when actor Brandon Lee lost his life on the set.

Coincidentally, Michigan and Pennsylvania were the stages of two, much-adored time travel movies, *Somewhere in Time* (1980) and *12 Monkeys* (1995). Christopher Plummer stars in both cult classic time travel films.

On a keynote, the original grandfather movie to open the floodgates on the topic of zombies was *The Night of the Living Dead*, filmed in Pennsylvania in 1968. Much of the cast was also born in Pennsylvania—including Judith O'Dea and Russell Streiner. A generation later, in 1981, *The Evil Dead* was made—another independent low-budget cult film about the deceased. The director, Samuel Raimi, is from Royal Oak, Michigan, and the movie stars a man and woman from Michigan, Bruce Campbell and Ellen Sandweiss. Both movies touched upon taboo themes and were underdog productions outside the hard-to-get-at and established big-budget studio networks.

Besides entertaining America, Michigan and Pennsylvania are also home to two ubiquitous TV teachers—Mr. Rogers and Ms. Frizzle. Mr. Fred Rogers is from Pittsburgh and taught young children about feelings, imagination, and all the various people in their neighborhoods. Ms. Frizzle, played by Lily Tomlin from Detroit, on the other hand, took the class on amazing adventures that illustrate any number of scientific concepts with humor, drama, and plain old cartoonish fun.

Doubly talented persons connected to both Pennsylvania and Michigan include one of the most influential CEOs of our times, Lee Iacocca, and the author of *Marley and Me* (2008), John Grogan. Iacocca was born in Allentown, Pennsylvania, in 1924. He later rose to the executive offices at Ford and Chrysler and revamped the American auto industry, ensuring Americans had good jobs and drove safe cars. John Grogan was born in Detroit, Michigan, in 1957 but later moved to suburban Pennsylvania. Grogan's golden retriever Marley—who would follow in the paw prints of the all-American dog that included the likes of Rin Tin Tin, Lassie, and Benji—was not a talented wonder dog, but rather a heartwarming, dopey, loveable, punky puppy puff.

Two voices that contrast like the wild elk and moose of Michigan and the domesticated and broken-in black horses of Pennsylvania are Dr. Wayne Dyer from Detroit and Dr. Avram Noam Chomsky from Philadelphia. Their perspectives contrast like opposite poles of a magnet. Dyer set the gold standard as the penultimate spiritual self-help guru, taking a deep dive into the irrational and mystical side of life and becoming a supreme advocate for the law of attraction and the power of synchronicity. He concluded that everything is underscored by a powerful force of divine proportions. At the extreme opposite end of this everywhere-magnet of human consciousness is Chomsky, who took the rational football of hard-nosed, objective, detached, non-emotional thinking and never stopped running or looked back. Dyer and Chomsky were both platformed by PBS and have legions of pupils who contrast like oil and water, yet the two are united along several lines of thought as exemplars of civil discourse. Both men have or had profoundly deep perspectives of contrasting salinities, champion or championed peace between all nations, and are or were fundamentalists of the human spirit in all its songs, whether good, bad, ugly, or beautiful.

Pennsylvania and Michigan coincidentally have marmots in their state ethos that are superficially similar yet so very different. The groundhog is not a hog, but it is Pennsylvania's most celebrated marmot, a shy chubby ground squirrel that wouldn't hurt a fly. The early pioneers were so taken by its cuddly mystique that it resulted in Groundhog Day—an original nondenominational American holiday. Every February 2, the nation turns its attention to the small Central Pennsylvania town of Punxsutawney to deduce the length of winter, if a ground squirrel should see its own shadow. The nation has never much to-do for this yearly winter event, but it did result in a charming cinematic classic *Groundhog Day* in 1993. Across the shore of Lake Erie, another marmot is held with high esteem: the wolverine. But its name is also a misnomer since it is not related to the wolf family. The wolverine is slightly larger than a groundhog, more like a miniature grizzly bear ready to defend its honor with ferocity. But the holiday special centered on Michigan that matches the resounding soulful enchantment of *Groundhog Day* is *Prancer* (1989), a story that expands on one of Santa's lost reindeer and clarifies what is most precious during the holidays. Thus, Three Oaks, Michigan, is a perfect match for Punxsutawney, Pennsylvania.

Coincidentally, each state is associated with a lauded flag maker, and each was able to seize the mysterious, ever-spotty limelight of history. First, we have

Betsy Ross, born in 1752. She became the seamstress associated with the eponymously famous version of the revolutionary flag, the Betsy Ross flag. There's no doubt Betsy Ross knew George Washington since they went to the same church. Some 200 years later, Pennsylvania's guardian angel state gave rise to another semi-legendary flag maker, Robert G. Heft, who was of the first generation to sew the iconic 50-starred flag. Heft sewed the flag for a school project and would claim that the modern U.S. flag was based on his design.

If Ross or Robert would have saved their receipts and other hard evidence of their contribution to the designs of the American flag, their stories would actually garner less curiosity and interest. The hard evidence is that Francis Hopkinson was the chairman of the Continental Navy Board's Middle Department when the U.S. flag resolution was adopted in 1777. At the time, Hopkinson wrote a letter to Congress dated May 25, 1780, requesting booze as compensation for his flag design; Francis Hopkinson wrote a request for a "quarter cask of public wine" as payment. Francis's request was denied, and Hopkinson did not write anything more on his grand contribution to America's identity.

Likewise, the hard evidence for the current 50-starred flag points to a subcommittee in the Defense Department, which established the pattern for adding stars long before Heft would have conceived of a 50-starred flag. Yet Rob was the first American to sew a 50-starred American flag before it became official, rather than just drawing it on paper. This alone is a noteworthy achievement. Similarly, the legacy of Betsy Ross was first to establish a claim with the "Betsy Ross" flag, with a focus on the shape of the stars being five-pointed instead of six. However, Robert's story does not quite add up; likewise, Betsy Ross's story seems to have some extra yarns that do not mesh with the record of history.

The Betsy Ross flag is now an icon immutably associated with its assumed creator. Further her name, Betsy Ross, shouts upon the hilltops of history—the spirit of the American Revolution. Also, it's a fact that she was a patriot, and it is a near certainty she sewed the first generation of American flags since she was a seamstress. These facts alone make her worthy of recognition as a patriotic pioneer and highlight the oft-overlooked contributions of women who aided the cause.

THE FLAG REVELATION

As it is, the element of mystery associated with Betsy Ross is the crowning jewel that adds an enchanted sparkle to her name, as a mystery always has a more magnetic appeal than a stone-cold, undisputed fact. Mystery provides a powerful manna that can create a bridge to span the centuries, which allows life to breathe itself into the past. Coincidentally, by sheer fate, Robert Heft was living in Ohio at the time of his special flag project at Lancaster High School, just outside of Columbus. It's a certain kind of synchronicity that a man from Ohio would later plant a carbon copy of "Robert's Flag" on the moon half a score after a prototype manifested on Earth, in Ohio.

At the moment, Betsy Ross's claim has some serious doubts, and it's quite obvious that Robert Heft by accident (or on purpose) had experienced creative and embellished memories that originated somewhere between reality and a dream. Nonetheless, it's a near certainty that Betsy Ross sewed the first versions of the American flag, and it's a fact that Robert made a 50-starred flag before it was official. Nevertheless and forevermore, Pennsylvania and Michigan were the first to cast a luminous shadow upon two very special versions of the American flag, at the beginning in 1776 and upon the celestial year of jubilee in 1969.

From a certain distance, the flags of Pennsylvania and Michigan can be mistaken as one for the other. Do the structural similarities of these state banners on opposite shores of Lake Erie add up to nothing more than an eerie coincidence? Perhaps, there is a deep power behind profound coincidences. The correlations between certain coincidences are fundamental aspects to learning, as positive and negative connections are perpetually constructed within the mind's eye, which allow for the emergence of pattern recognition. Some types of knowledge must be broken in, as one breaks in a horse, with patience and due diligence as echoed by the supporters of Pennsylvania. However, there are other aspects to knowledge that are grounded to the wild and random matrix of life, which can be associated with the organic, unbroken ungulates of Michigan. This journey begins with a regal sendoff from the Keystone State, where our path begins, at the intersection of synchronicity and Providence.

two

WISCONSIN & MAINE

Coincidentally, a Midshipman Merges Along the St. Croix River

WISCONSIN

A coat of arms that features two male supporters on a blue background connects these state flags. The critical point of alignment is the sailor. They are nearly identical in dress, and there is only the slightest of differences. If you want to spot them before they are pointed out below, now is your last chance to tap the long-lasting sense of discovery.

The states' names are present on each flag, and the one-word state mottos are in the crest position. Wisconsin's is written in black lettering upon an even swallowtail ribbon with the word "Forward." Maine's motto is written in white lettering upon a seesawed red ribbon with the Latin word *Dirgo*, which means "I lead." Together, these mottos echo a similar style as to "Lead Forward."

Fatefully, an endemic species that makes a home in each state appears on each flag. Wisconsin has a badger facing the sailor standing on a heraldic torse (a head band) woven of blue and yellow. Maine has a moose lying on a bed of grass under a pine tree facing the farmer.

The sailors on each flag are nearly identical. But they are standing on opposite sides, and the colors of their hats differ: black for Wisconsin and white for Maine. Finally, Wisconsin's sailor is at attention while Maine's is at ease.

MAINE

A deeper level of harmony exists between the dissimilar supporters of the miner and yeoman farmer. These occupations are connected to the bounty of the earth instead of the bounty of the sea. The miner of Wisconsin works under the earth, while the farmer of Maine works on top of the earth. The miner with a red shirt is wearing an old-style mining hat with a lit candle. Thus, his hat illuminates the darkness. The farmer's hat does the opposite. It blocks out light so he can see better without the glaring sun. In addition, the pickaxe of the miner balances with the scythe of the farmer. Both tools have long handles with strong metallic business ends.

Geography

As far as synchronicities are concerned, if the Richter scale were applied to the common name of the rivers that make up their borders, it would be a solid 10. On the east coast of Maine, the border between Canada and the U.S. is the St. Croix River. Providentially, on the west coast of Wisconsin on the border with Minnesota is another St. Croix River. Wisconsin's St. Croix feeds into the Mississippi River, while Maine's St. Croix flows into the Atlantic Ocean.

Both states are pierced by the 45th parallel north; thus, both are midway between the freezing North Pole and the sultry equator. Consequently, both states have an understanding of climates on par with Toronto, Ottawa, Montreal, and Quebec. Due to the states' northern perspective, immersive water sports are rarely a thing, as the shoreline waters have a hard time heating up in the summer. Sister cities of nearly equal latitude are Bangor, Maine, and Green Bay, Wisconsin. As for brother bays, Green Bay's match is Penobscot Bay, and the scenic Apostle Islands of Wisconsin match the splendor of Maine's Acadia National Park.

Both states are in the snowy CBC, Cold Beach Club, since they're completely north of Canada's most southern point, Point Pelee. This means they can hold their own in a snowball fight against Canada, solo.

The sailors indicate boats are big business and leisure activity for both states. Speaking of lakes, the largest lake totally within Wisconsin is Lake Winnebago. A perfect match for Winnebago is Lake Sebago of Maine. Lake Sebago is the deepest lake in Maine. Although Winnebago covers a larger surface area at 206 square miles, compared to Lake Sebago at 45 square miles, Lake Sebago is much deeper with a maximum depth of 316 feet, in contrast Winnebago's max depth is 21 feet. Lakes Sebago and Winnebago are harmonically matched as the *Deep and Wide Bago Sister Lakes*.

History

The written histories of Wisconsin and Maine begin with France. The two founding fathers are Jean Nicolet, Sieur de Belleborne (1598-1642) for Wisconsin and Pierre Dugua, Sieur de Mons (1558-1628) for Maine. First Pierre Dugua landed on Saint Croix Island in 1604, establishing the first root of Acadia, the proverbial *Virginia of New France*. Acadia first sprouted on U.S. soil, not Canada. A year earlier, in 1603, King Henry IV of France gave Dugua exclusive rights to colonize lands in North America between 40° to 60° north (which included Wisconsin) and a monopoly in the lucrative fur trade. Two interesting men on these early voyages to the equivalent Virginia of New France—Acadia—include Samuel De Champlain and Mathieu da Costa. Samuel de Champlain (1567-1635) was the royal cartographer of the eponymous Lake Champlain, and Mathieu da Costa was a linguist and a free Black person. Note Mathieu's arrival at Maine/Acadia predated the infamous slave ship landing of the *White Lion* in Virginia in 1619.

Much later in Wisconsin, Jean Nicolet (1598-1642) landed at Green Bay in 1634. In fact, Nicolet was sent to the area by de Champlain, the governor of New France, in order to contact the Ho-Chunk Nation, establish trade, and find a route to Asia. Consequently, Nicolet was first to chart Lake Michigan and is thought to have landed at Red Banks, Wisconsin. Nicolet was a part of the generation that believed that China was just around the corner, and he was crossing into Asia. So when Nicolet landed at Green Bay, as to pay homage and honor to the supposed Chinese, he was purported to be wearing fine yellow Chinese robes.

During the Civil War, Wisconsin and Maine were core brothers in arms. Of the many battles when the U.S. was in peril, the men of Maine and Wisconsin answered the call to duty to safeguard the mission of the United States. On the second day of the Battle of Gettysburg, Little Round Top was at the pivot point between victory and defeat. Manning the extreme left-wing position was the 20th Maine, led by native son of Maine Joshua Chamberlain. On the first day, the Union suffered setback after setback as the Southern army pushed them to the breaking point.

By the second day, the Union would halt the Southern advance when it careened into the 20th Maine. After several punishing charges from the Alabama Infantry, Chamberlain's regiments held strong and staved off defeat. Eventually, the 20th Maine's ammunition was exhausted, and the daring decision to lead a bayonet charge was ordered. The gamble paid off, and the Confederate advance was repulsed, and the Union left flank was secured for another day.

Likewise, the limelight of Civil War heroics would shine upon Wisconsin—in particular the Iron Brigade. They were also known as the Black Hats due to their distinguished black 1858 Hardee Hats that contrasted with the more common stubby visor ball cap. The Wisconsin Iron Brigade was originally composed of three Wisconsin regiments and one Indiana regiment. The Iron Brigade earned their name when they stood up to the formerly unstoppable Stonewall Jackson at the Second Battle of Bull Run. It was here that a Union stonewall "partially of iron" was erected of Wisconsin makings, as they held their ground against the fiercest of Southern generals, Thomas Stonewall Jackson. Then, at the Battle of Antietam, the Wisconsin Iron Brigade spearheaded the battle, proving again and again their worth and determination that would shock Southern units. After Antietam, the 24th Michigan joined the Iron Brigade due to a massive loss of life at the bloody cornfield, where bodies piled up to become a virtual layer of topsoil. As it was with the 20th Maine at Gettysburg, the Iron Brigade was thrust into a position as a critical defender of the Union. On the first day of the battle, the Iron Brigade stalled the Confederate advance. As General Lee rolled over the Union army on July 1, the Iron Brigade was a primary component of the force that denied Lee his victory. The Iron Brigade's defensive sacrifice provided critical help that allowed the army to consolidate upon the high ground of Cemetery Ridge. The following day, the 20th Maine was to maintain Union ground at Little Round Top.

The *USS Maine* and *USS Wisconsin* are two ships of the gilded age that made their mark on history in matters concerning war and peace. In their wake, a birth of nations in between North and South America would result; one was Central American, and the other was in the Caribbean. The *USS Maine* was the harbinger of war between Spain and the United States. It was a war between the first of the American Empires with the first of the American Republics. In 1898, the *USS Maine* was sent to Havana, Cuba, to protect American interests in the area as the Cuban War of Independence embattled the isle. Since 1895, Cubans had been struggling to break free from Spanish rule. Previously, the Cubans had made two attempts: the Ten Years' War of 1868 to 1878 and the Little War from 1879 to 1880. However, it was the third try that was successful, and only after the U.S. joined into the fray on behalf of the Cuban rebels. The catalyst that pulled the U.S. into war with Spain was the explosion on the *USS Maine* on February 15, 1898. Two hundred and fifty-one servicemen lost their lives in the explosion, but 94 survived.

As now and then, the cause of the explosion is hotly debated. Some blamed a Spanish mine, while others thought it was simply a careless accident. The fuel used at the time, bituminous coal, was highly flammable and known to spontaneously ignite. Half a year later, war commenced with Spain on April 21, 1898. The public was whipped into a frenzy of excitement by the hyperbolic yellow press of that era. Spain was demonized at the loss of life, as the *USS Maine* became a rally cry in the same way it was with the Alamo: "Remember the Maine!" The Spanish-American War ended on December 10, 1898. In the wake of the lopsided U.S. victory, Spain lost control of the Philippines, Cuba, Puerto Rico, and Guam.

Spain was effectively expelled from the New World. Out of the original kingdoms to colonize the Americas, France, England, and the Netherlands were allowed to retain token territories and tiny islands in this hemisphere. However, the nation that unlocked and awoke the eastern and western halves of the Earth to each other's mutual existence was given no quarter. In the wake of the *USS Maine's* loss, Cuba became independent from the United States on May 20, 1902.

As for the *USS Wisconsin*, her role in nation making is connected to a wake spawned in the aftermath of peace. On November 21, 1902, the *USS Wisconsin* hosted peace negotiations of the warring parties of Colombia's Thousand Days' Civil War, which had started on October 17, 1899. This was one of Colombia's most deadly wars and was fought between conservatives and liberals. The following year, Panama declared independence on November 3, 1903.

Panama's genesis was "peaceful," but the price of war was already paid in advance from previous attempts for independence. The death of Panamanian patriot Victoriano Lorenzo was of key importance. Lorenzo was a hold out on the Liberal faction who kept fighting even after the peace treaty was signed aboard the *USS Wisconsin* in 1902. Lorenzo strongly advocated for liberal reforms such as land rights, representation, and indigenous rights. However, he was captured and executed by a firing squad against a tall seaside wall on the Pacific at the Plaza Francia on May 15, 1903. It was the iconic death of a soon-to-be national

THE FLAG REVELATION

hero beset by the beauty of the seaside jungle. Lorenzo's execution turned him into a martyr, motivating Panamanians—especially those of the Liberal faction—toward secession. Although Panama's birth to freedom was technically bloodless due to U.S. support, Lorenzo's martyrdom is seen as a harbinger of Panama's independence, and a nation he would never have the chance to know.

Many times over, Panama attempted to break away from Colombia, far more than Cuba did from Spain. Panama had 53 revolutions in 57 years before finally achieving independence. From 1838 to 1840, Panama had a secession movement as "Estado Libre." Likewise, the U.S. racked up a long rap sheet of sending troops to Panama many times over—the most expensive was the Panama Crisis of 1885. Panama City was occupied to protect U.S. interests and keep the peace. Thirty years earlier, the U.S. built the Panama Railway in 1855. This was in fact the first transcontinental railroad since it beat the more famous across the U.S. of 1869 by 14 years. Although a much shorter distance, the harsh jungle reaped a five-figure death toll for this trespass of civilization.

With U.S. Naval support, Panama finally broke free on November 3, 1903. The ship that cut the umbilical cord from Bogotá was the *USS Nashville*. As per luck, the captain was Commander John Hubbard from South Berwick, Maine. Hubbard used that delightfully harmless, yet annoying tactic of stalling the Colombian Navy from suppressing the 1903 Panamanian revolutionaries. It worked, and Panama's 1903 birth was bloodless due to U.S. big stick and not so silent "la, la, la, la, la, I can't hear you because my fingers are in my ears," over-talking distractive diplomacy. The cherry on top was that the *USS Nashville* was credited with firing the first shot of the Spanish-American War on April 21, 1898.

As for war and peace, the shock waves of the *USS Maine* were the harbinger of Cuban independence, as the arrows of the U.S. war eagle were aimed at Spain. However, an olive branch was wielded on the deck of the *USS Wisconsin* to end the Colombian Thousand Day Civil War. As a consequence, a chain of events allowed for the birth of a new nation in the Americas: Panama. Poetically, the *USS Wisconsin* would live a long peaceful life, never firing a shot in the war, ending her life as scrap metal in 1924, while the *USS Maine* met the fate of a

Klingon Warrior, assassinated by mysterious forces and exiting history's stage in a blaze of glory, as a battle cry for revenge.

Culture

Writing is something special, and Kovic and King are two mighty pens that cast a spell on the American public. Ron Kovic, from Ladysmith, Wisconsin, was born on the 4th of July, 1946, and his birth date would become both a book and movie, *Born on the Fourth of July* (1989). He was paralyzed and became an iconic anti-war spokesman of the 1960s, whose essence was partially distilled into the character Lieutenant Dan from *Forrest Gump* (1994). Stephen King—born in 1947 in Portland, Maine—became the King of Macabre with a monopoly on horror, as several of his books were destined for Hollywood as cult blockbuster hits—*Carrie* (1976), *The Shining* (1980), *The Green Mile* (1999), and *It* (2017) are just a few.

Two stores that were able to grow seriously deep roots across the nation to impact the everyday styles and keeping every man, woman, and child warm and cozy are Kohl's, which began operations in Brookfield, Wisconsin, and L.L. Bean, which sprouted in Greenwood, Maine.

The winter blasts of Maine and Wisconsin were fundamental in shaping the modern snowmobile. In 1895, William J. Culman and William B. Follis of Brule, Wisconsin, got a patent for front ski and rear tread propulsion. Another key component was built by Alvin Orland Lombard from Springfield, Maine, who invented the track-wheeled vehicle, which was applied to every tank, bulldozer, and snowmobile since.

Two technical wizards of the modern storytelling age who underscored the artistic value in film and cinema are Orson Welles and John Ford. First, there was director John Ford from Cape Elizabeth, Maine, who was born in 1894. He directed *Stagecoach* (1939) and *The Grapes of Wrath* (1940) and would go on to win six Academy Awards. Most of his silent era movies are lost, but he is regarded as the inspiration for latter day directors like Akira Kurosawa and Orson Welles. It just so happens that Welles is the official cinematic wingman of John

Ford. Orson Welles, from Kenosha, Wisconsin, was able to capture that Johnny Ford movie magic and cast his own spell over audiences with films like *Citizen Kane* (1941) and *The Trial* (1962). Welles's gravitas was apparent when he hosted the documentary *The Man Who Saw Tomorrow* (1981) about the prophet Nostradamus and was able to reach into the psyche of Generation X. It may be hard for the modern audience to appreciate these classical works of cinema since movie making has evolved with taste. But it must be noted that Welles and Ford were among the first to bring new cutting-edge cinematic techniques that are now a pedestrian standard.

Two women to kick off the energy of the *Xennials* are Rachel Brosnahan from Milwaukee, Wisconsin (born in 1990), and Anna Kendrick from Portland, Maine (born in 1985). Brosnahan stars in *The Marvelous Mrs. Maisel* (2017-2023) on Amazon Prime, while Anna Kendrick has starred in *The Twilight Saga* (2008-2012) and *Pitch Perfect* series (2012-2017).

Two men who built fundamental devices of the modern age are John Bardeen of Madison, Wisconsin, and Edwin Hall of Gorham, Maine. Bardeen was the co-father of the transistor in 1947, and a generation earlier Edwin Hall discovered the Hall effect after working with magnets and currents. Today, the Hall effect electronics and transistors are everywhere, from modern cars to cell phones.

Two well-known superheroes from the area are Mark Ruffalo from Kenosha, Wisconsin (born 1967), and Patrick Dempsey from Lewiston, Maine (born 1966). Ruffalo is best known for his role as the cinematic Incredible Hulk of Marvel, while Dempsey starred in several hits like *Outbreak* (1995), *Freedom Writers* (2007), and played the dreamy surgeon on *Grey's Anatomy* (since 2005). William Dafoe from Appleton, Wisconsin (born 1955), matches with Charles Rocket from Bangor, Maine (born 1949). Dafoe was the tragic war hero in *Platoon* (1986) and later made top-tier fame as the Green Goblin in the original *Spider-Man* movies (since 2002). Charles Rocket was cast as an excellent bad guy in *Dumb and Dumber* (1994) and *Hocus Pocus* (1993).

Two pioneers of TV's now-ubiquitous female super cop were Tyne Daly and Linda Lavin. Daly is from Madison, Wisconsin. She was born in 1946 and played Detective Mary Beth Lacey in *Cagney & Lacey* during the 1980s. She would later inspire a thousand-fold women to pursue police work. But a decade earlier, there was Detective Janice Wentworth on the TV show *Barney Miller* (1975-1982), played by Linda Lavin from Portland, Maine, who was born in 1937.

Fancy old stars who lit up the stage once upon a time are Don Ameche and James Flavin. James Flavin, from Portland, Maine (born 1906), was a golden age actor who charmed us in the black-and-white era. Don Ameche, from Kenosha, Wisconsin (born in 1908), is another star who was able to shine across the century. His last burst of colorful and joyful radiation was epic in the movie *Trading Places* (1983) opposite Eddie Murphy. But fifty years earlier, Flavin starred in *King Kong* (1933).

From the class of '59, two Boom-Xers are Bradley Whitford from Madison, Wisconsin, and Judd Nelson from Portland, Maine. Whitford appropriately starred in *Billy Madison* (1995) and played chief of staff Josh Lyman on *The West Wing* (1999-2006). Judd Nelson became a super Gen X star with the *Breakfast Club* (1985) and as the king of the essential '80s Brat Pack.

Ultimate action bad guys who were able to move beyond their typecast roles are Kurtwood Smith from New Lisbon, Wisconsin, and Nick Wyman from Portland, Maine—born in 1943 and 1950, respectively. Smith was the ultimate mature bad guy thug in *RoboCop* (1987) but became the top cheese head on *That '70s Show* (1998-2006) as the no-nonsense old-school dad, who was happy to put his "foot up" lazy teenagers' "asses." Nick Wyman was also able to play the bad guy in *Die Hard 3* (1995).

Laura Ingalls Wilder and Theodora R. Jenness were women of America's mid-century who wrote about life on the frontier. Jenness was born in 1847 in Greenwood, Maine, and spent several years on the frontier in Dakota Territory as a missionary. She went on to write *Piokee and Her People,* a Ranch and Tepee Story in 1894 and several other novels that captured the closing frontier. From Pepin County, Wisconsin, Wilder was born in 1867 and had her work picked up in the timeless league of TV as her books inspired the *Little House on the Prairie* (1974-1983) TV series.

THE FLAG REVELATION

Maine and Wisconsin are states with rather humble designs that reflect the vast sea of blue flags that make up the banners of the American Republic. Nearly every blue flag that features the state coat of arms can match either state of *Middle Earth,* who make their hearth and home along 45th north. But there is one distinct element that entangles these sacred banners separated by a space of 1001 miles: the sailor. The midshipman is nearly wearing the same outfit, only to differ by the color of their hat. These sailors cover both sides of the flag and a ship—port and starboard, whether viewed from the front or back. Together their banners collide and reveal a higher ordered motto of "Leading Forward" as it is, was, and shall be, forevermore.

three

MONTANA & KANSAS

Two Golden Bullets Preserved for Posterity on the Prairie

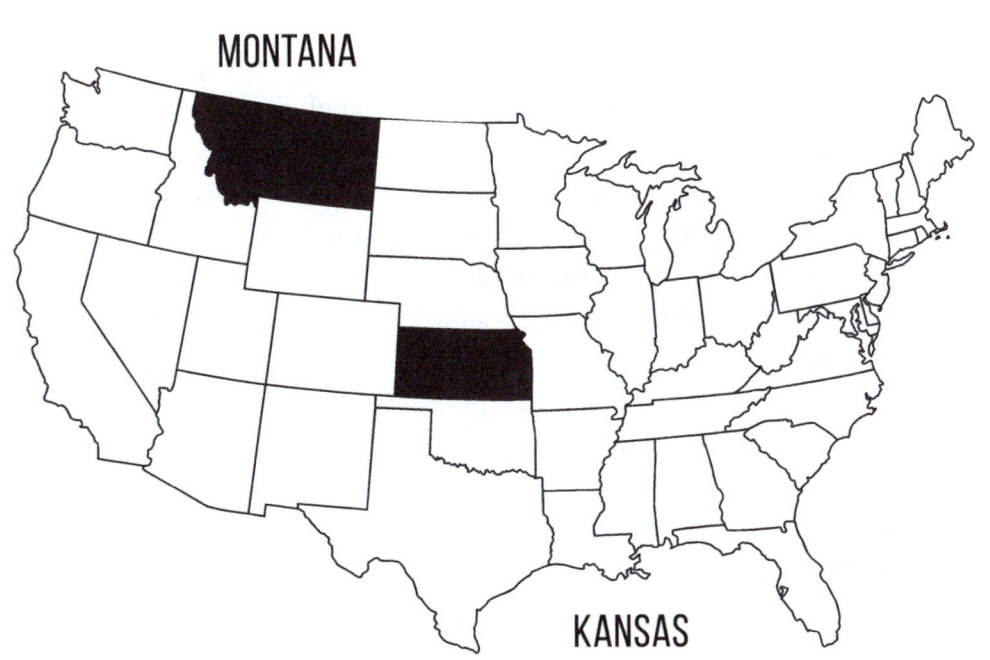

MONTANA

When you put the flag of Montana next to the flag of Kansas the apparent resemblance is obvious.

Each flag has centrally placed circular seals that reveal landscape scenes and create a harmonious bridge of balance: plains in front of the mountains, a river flowing toward the right, and the sun peeking over the horizon through the valleys. Montana and Kansas also use the circularly inscribed official state seal minus the outer ring, which declares it as the state seal.

Furthermore, Montana and Kansas's seals completely abandon the European style of heraldry. Their state seals employ an artistic landscape motif. One exception is a small heraldic wreath of yellow and blue above the seal of Kansas that's crested with the state flower. This tidbit of heraldry is not a part of the official state seal and is only found on the state flag.

The similarly matched block font of their state names are both written in yellow. Kansas has KANSAS below the seal, while MONTANA has his name written above the seal.

Another providential parallel is the placement of their names, which reflects their relative geographies. Typically, the upward position on a map indicates

KANSAS

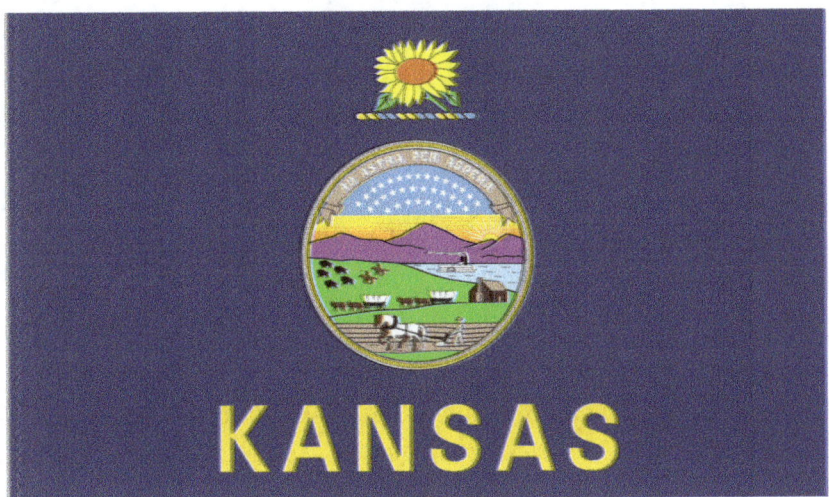

north; likewise, Montana's name is printed above the seal in spatial balance. The down position is usually south, and Kansas's name is in a "southern" position below the seal.

By happenstance the seals harmonize from a scientific point of view, like the difference of kinetic and potential energy. Can you guess which is which? First a quick review about the two standard states of energy. Matter in motion is said to express kinetic energy. But when the same object is lying still, it's said to express potential energy. Consequently, the flag of Montana reflects the quiet stillness of potential energy, while the hustle and bustle of Kansas conveys the dynamic, always-in-motion concept of kinetic energy.

In more familiar terms, Kansas's flag is reflective of the wild commotion of the morning rush. Of all the flags, Kansas has the most going on—including people, animals, cows, horses, and vehicles. More specifically, there are five bison, four cart ox, four horses, two Native Americans, one farmer, and two very hard to see cattle drivers who are apparently in the wagon somewhere, in addition to a ferry boat. Likewise, the Sun is positioned on the right side of the valley, and by normal map convention, right represents the east. Thus, it looks like a veritable busy Kansas morning sunrise. In stunning contrast, Montana's flag is more like the end of the day, as if everyone has gone home and is getting ready for supper after a hard day's work. It has zero people and nothing going on, with only some tools placed in the foreground, set for the next day's duties. Likewise, the Sun is placed on the left side of the valley. Also, by standard map reckoning, left is associated with the west. It looks like a veritable tranquil Montana Big Sky sunset.

Both flags have mottos written on ribbons in the seals. Kansas's motto is written on a red ribbon along the top of the seal. Written in Latin it reads, "Ad Astra Per Aspera," which is usually translated "Unto the Stars Through Difficulties," but in a direct word equivalent translation it reads "Unto Astral-Bodies for Inspiration," meaning to shoot for the stars during hard times. The motto of Montana is written on a white ribbon along the bottom of the seal and reads in Spanish, "Oro Y Plata." Note Montana's flag is the only one in the Union to use Spanish. In a "cognate/cognitive," word to word equivalent translation, this would translate as "Ore and Platinum," but in a proper translation it means gold and silver.

Kansas has one distinction that Montana does not—a sunflower in the crest position on top of a heraldic wreath. Kansas has the most recognizable state flower out of any state. The sunflower is a delightfully happy flower that seems to be smiling and is a native flower to North America. Montana's state flower is the proverbial opposite: the moonflower. Just kidding. It's the bitterroot, but wouldn't that be coy if a moonflower just happened to be the state flower of Montana? It just rolls off the tongue so eloquently—the Montana Moonflower.

The bitterroot is also edible, but not with the seeds. Rather, the root is the consumable part. The bitterroot is an ancient seasoning for Native Americans that was first introduced to Lewis and Clark. Montana does not display the bitterroot on their flag but instead nine pine trees stand at attention—three tall and six short ones. As for specific meaning to this random order, nobody seems to know. And if you were wondering, moonflowers are real. As the name suggests, they bloom during a full moon or at night. Perhaps the most famous moonflowers are the night-blooming cereus.

Geography

The land of Montana and Kansas are vast prairie states of the Great Plains. The North American Great Plains was once a natural rival to the savannah of Africa in the amount and diversity of wild animals. Enormous herds of buffalo, pronghorn antelope, deer, and elk were once closely guarded by packs of wolves, coyotes, bears, and cougars. The most successful animal of the bygone, free-roaming prairie epoch of the Great Plains just happens to have a name that matches the lay of the land, the prairie dog. Inaccurately named a dog, they are more like squirrels. Considered a nuisance by some, prairie squirrels are also survivors to the often-pushy money molding march of man. But nowadays Montana and Kansas have become America's virtual breadbasket. Kansas leads the nation in wheat production and Montana is not far behind.

Ice and grass are fairly ordinary kinds of material, but Montana and Kansas have honored these pedestrian items with national sanctuaries. Glacier National Park in Montana is a virtual slice of Alaska found in the United Forty-Eight. Glaciers are extraordinary bodies of ice. As lakes and rivers have their own mystique, glaciers too exhibit their own glacial presence. It's one of those things you really need to see and experience for yourself, and soon. Due to global warming, the park may need a name change since scientists estimate the glaciers may shortly all melt away. In Kansas, the Tallgrass National Preserve is a particular kind of prairie whereby an original native super grass is allowed to grow. Supergrasses usually grow taller than most men, in the seven-to-nine-foot range, and 10 to 11 foot grass is not unheard of.

History

Montana and Kansas have a key historical alignment of matching caliber by which they were pierced in the heart by an arrow of historic proportions. The events of Bleeding Kansas are considered the opening pregame season of the U.S. Civil War. The Civil War officially started on April 12, 1861, but before then, little bits of terror were breaking out all over from Harpers Ferry, Virginia, to Lawrence, Kansas. While in Montana, the sharpest footnote of the violent struggle between Natives and Newcomers transcends time at Little Bighorn. But before Custer's Last Stand, the debate between ending slavery and letting it expand in the newer territories reached a raucous roar in Kansas. The presidents and congress dodged the buck to the settlers of Kansas. Subsequently, pro-slavery and abolitionist groups raced to Kansas in order to make it in their own image. In the ensuing chaos, the rash of American-on-American political violence became known as Bleeding Kansas.

Pro-slave settlers poured into Kansas Territory from Missouri, while Massachusetts set up a private company to help free-soil settlers move to Kansas. Kansas developed two types of communities: pro-slave and non-slave. Subsequently, Kansas had a difficult time deciding about whether to become a free state or slave state. The first time around, a fraudulently elected pro-slavery government formed in the spring of 1855. Then a free-soil state constitution was issued at Topeka in the fall of 1855, and another pro-slave constitution was issued at Lecompton in 1857. A radical free soil and rights for women Leavenworth Constitution was also issued in 1858. Finally, Kansas was set to free soil in 1859 with the Wyandotte Constitution, minus equal rights for women.

Born in the middle of it all, Kansas was admitted as a free state on January 29, 1861, before the Civil War but after the succession crisis had already begun. When Kansas was born, South Carolina, Mississippi, Florida, Alabama, Louisiana, and Georgia had already dissolved their ties with the U.S. Constitution. Like a child born out of wedlock, Texas was present for Kansas's birth but left shortly afterward, giving Kansas a quick friendly Texan hello-and-goodbye. North Carolina, Tennessee, Arkansas, and Virginia hung around a little longer—about three months—and were able to get a good peek at the new baby.

Although the Civil War officially started April 12, 1861, as far as Kansas was concerned, it started in 1855. Pro-slavery border Ruffians from Missouri clashed with free-soil member Jay Hawkers in a deadly, low-simmering conflict that took over 100 American lives. But when the war officially started after Lincoln called to arms to defend the Union, Kansas was witness to the horrific, savage partisan attacks of a biblical fashion, and the majority of atrocities were committed by the pro-slavery border ruffians. One of the most spiteful acts of terror and vengeance was led by William Quantrill. He oversaw the public execution of over 150 young and old male civilians, many in front of their families, on August 21, 1863 at Lawrence, Kansas.

Less than a generation later, another golden bullet was shot into the heart of America with the tragedy of Armstrong Custer. The general was a dashing, brash, and highly esteemed hero for the Union side of the U.S. Civil War. However, his intuitive, one-man Rambo style of leadership that helped turn the tide at Gettysburg would be less useful with the Plains Indians. Custer's brash leadership resulted in his death and the death of the men under his command at Little Bighorn, Montana. Especially painful was the fact that it happened in late June 1876, on the eve of America's 100th birthday. Eleven years after the madness of the Civil War, the U.S. was steadily recovering and healing from those self-inflicted scars. Feelings of higher hopes were in the air. But news of this lopsided battle put a slight damper on America's Centennial—July 4, 1876.

The tragic story of Custer's Last Stand is the dreamy stuff of Hollywood. In fact, Sitting Bull, who led the party of Native Americans to victory on that fateful day, was given a dreamy vision of the fight. The Battle at Little Bighorn has become the most memorable victory for Native Americans against the U.S. government. Over 300 men surrendered their lives at Little Bighorn, Montana, on June 26, 1876—the majority being on the U.S. side and a minority from the Native American side. Little did this victory accomplish for the Native American, if only a memorable wanderlust moment in history. Eventually all the Plains Indians were forced to adapt to the modern world and abandon their free and nomadic lifestyle.

Custer's Last Stand and Bleeding Kansas are two aces of American history. They are tragic and paradoxically hopeful echoes from the past. The Native American and the Confederate were united in a similar destiny to exile. Both groups saw their ancient and established way of life come to an end under violent restriction from the U.S. government. No longer would America tolerate the right to own another man or the right to roam freely across the plains.

Even today a lingering pain remains on all sides. Likewise, General Custer lost some luster as a hero of the American West. As America grew to maturity, she gained compassion and better insight into her less-than-democratic treatment toward Native Americans.

Today, the limelight of history has shifted from pride to guilt in somber reflection of the lost forlorn ways of the Native American. The fall of Custer and his men challenges us to remember our past. As General Custer risked his life for the Union, from a serendipitous line he also gave up his life so we would not forget the Native American. Forlorn and forsaken are the ways of our ancient ancestors, but perhaps America is ready for a new kind of limelight that sparkles on all sides, where an unlimited range of colors shines upon the past. Where, in time, all men and women can be seen as heroes rather than villains.

Perhaps that place is somewhere above the clouds. The skies of Montana and Kansas are no stranger to men—and two notable heroines—flying amongst the fluffy ridges of the heavens. Amelia Earhart rose to the highest of heights and was an international superstar during her lifetime. Due to her accomplished flying record, Earhart has earned an honored place in every American history book. She overcame the gender prejudices of her time and is a beacon of inspiration to follow one's heart. Amelia made headlines as the first woman to fly solo across the Atlantic Ocean, but she also raised the bar as the first pilot, male or female, to fly across the Pacific from Oakland, California, to Honolulu, Hawaii, in 1935. In 1937, Earhart was planning to fly around the world, and she nearly did. She flew into the Sun on an easterly route starting from Oakland, California, to Florida. She left Miami on June 1, 1937, and flew to Brazil over the Atlantic to Africa, India, Southeast Asia, and Australia. With more than 80% of the flight complete, she disappeared as she approached the tiny South Pacific isle of Howland Island on July 2, 1937. Radio contact was made, but her signal was lost shortly afterward. So close and just out of reach, it was the most tragic of tragedies. Amelia Earhart's mysterious disappearance has haunted pilots and historians to this day.

Montana coincidentally has a forlorn heroine who also rose above the clouds in the pursuit of her dreams, as Evelyn Sharp flew face first against the negative winds of gender conformity. Sharp was born in the small town of Melstone,

Montana, in 1919. She became entangled with aviation through a lucky twist of fate. Her mother gave her up for adoption, and her adopted family moved to Nebraska. Fatefully, a man who rented a room at her family house had trouble paying his rent, and in lieu of rent money he taught the teenage Miss Sharp how to fly. And fly she did. Miss Sharp became a pilot instructor herself and schooled over 300 men in the art of aviation. With the outbreak of World War II Sharp joined the first group of the original military World War II W.A.F.S. pilots (Women's Auxiliary Ferrying Squadron), which later evolved into the more popular W.A.S.P. (Women Airforce Service Pilots) Squadron and used a logo designed by Walt Disney. But like Earhart, tragedy befell Evelyn Sharp during a flight over Cumberland County, Pennsylvania, when her P-38 fighter plane crashed, taking her life on April 3, 1944. Although not as remembered as Amelia Earhart, Sharp was a part of the legendary first generation of female pilots who had the right stuff.

Besides providing the first class of original female pilots, Montana and Kansas were home to womankind's first steps into the political arena. Kansas became the spotlight of the nation and the world when the first female mayor took office. And with that historic move, a quaint town in Kansas became a watershed moment for the political advance for women in 1887. Mayor Susanna Salter was elected town mayor of Argonia more than 30 years before women gained the right to vote on a national level in 1920 with the 19th Amendment. Coincidentally, Montana elected the first woman to U.S. Congress in 1916—a woman by the name of Jeanette Rankin. Elected to the House of Representatives, Representative Rankin was the first federal congresswoman to grace Capitol Hill in Washington, DC. Notably she was a pacifist, voting against going to war with Germany during World War I, and was the only congressperson to vote against going to war with Japan during World War II. Even during the 1960s Rankin became an American stalwart for peace, leading demonstrations to end the war in Vietnam. Rankin and Salter were the first of first women to take the lead and to gracefully go where no woman had gone before.

Culture

Kansas has produced plenty of comforting, soulful, and heartwarming Hollywood starlets. Legendary stars from the black-and-white era include Gary Cooper from Helena, Montana, and Buster Keaton from Piqua, Kansas. Gary Cooper was the original American Joe Cool, winning several academy awards including best actor for *Sergeant York* (1941) and *High Noon* (1952). Buster Keaton also had a kind of stoic grace, but he was a pioneering talent to slapstick and comedy. Keaton was also responsible for one of the greatest films from the silent era—the original action-drama-comedy—*The General* in 1926. It was set in the Civil War Era, and Orson Welles considered it his favorite movie.

A more recent classic American father figure from the 1950s includes the original forest ranger in the television series *Lassie* (1954-1974)—Robert Bray of Kalispell, Montana. Bray starred as Ranger Corey Stewart and was coincidentally a Gary Cooper look-alike. In a similar vein, we have the wise and even-tempered hunky-dory father figure in *Leave it to Beaver* (1957-1963), played by a man from Lawrence, Kansas. Hugh Beaumont starred as Ward Cleaver who became the iconic happy-go-lucky dad of the 1950s. But today's modern family is usually a far cry from the one presented in *Leave it to Beaver.*

Coincidentally, on the sitcom false-reality television mash up *Modern Family* (2009-2020), the fictional gay couple happen to be hometown heroes of Montana and Kansas. Jesse Tyler Ferguson is from Missoula, Montana, and stars as the petite ginger-headed father Mitchell Pritchett. The husky teddy bear Cameron Tucker is brought to life by Eric Stonestreet from Kansas City, Kansas.

Actresses who exude the folksy Kansas friendliness include Annette Bening from Topeka, who starred in *American Beauty* (1999), and the woman who played the adoptive mother of E.T. in *E.T. the Extra-Terrestrial* (1982), Dee Wallace of Kansas City. These women match well with Montana mountain girls, Michelle Williams from Kalispell, who starred in *Brokeback Mountain* (2005), and Constance Towers from Whitefish, Montana. Constance Towers is noted for her soap roles on *General Hospital* (as the villainess Helena Cassadine) and *Capitol* (1982-1987).

Ironically the most famous person from Kansas is a fictional person who was whisked away by a tornado to a magical place somewhere over the rainbow. Dorothy Gale and Toto are legendary characters perpetually tied to Kansas and the imagination of childhood. Dorothy started out as a loveable character in a children's book first published in 1900. But when the story was made into a film for the third time in 1939, it became something more magnificent and magical. "Toto, I've a feeling we're not in Kansas anymore," turned into an iconic American catch phrase, underlining a quantum shift in perception—like when Columbus landed in America, when the first atom was split, or when we discovered there are thousands and thousands of other galaxies besides our own. A similar fictional heroine from *Never-Never Land* but from Montana was Lily from the epic franchise *Star Trek* and the movie *First Contact* (1996). Montana was the setting of this film where aliens make first contact with the human species. The reason for this contact is that earthlings had attained a certain level of technological sophistication. When Lily is finally made aware that she is no longer on Earth but in a spacecraft, Captain Picard reveals this startling situation by opening a cargo bay. Upon its opening, the Earth is visible below and Captain Picard says, "Montana will be up soon, but you may want to hold your breath, it's a long way down." Like Dorothy's keen observation that she is no longer in Kansas, Lily becomes keenly aware that she is no longer in Montana. *The Wizard of Oz* and *Star Trek* represent the two ends of the fantastic realm of imagination from pure fantasy to science fiction. Although completely different stories, Dorothy and Lily represent the revelation of a new realm of reality and learning to have faith in strangers, themselves, and of course, that there is no place like home.

Vast herds of buffalo once roamed the Great Plains from Kansas to Montana. But quiet, now, is that lost wild thunder of the romantic virgin prairie, domesticated today into gentle fields of golden abundance. The wheat harvests of these two sibling states have become the daily bread sustaining and filling the tummies of Americans north, south, east, and west. Their stories, like their

THE FLAG REVELATION

flags, share similar notes and tones, but have their own distinct point of view. It should be apparent that Kansas's wingman is Montana, or rather Montana's wingwoman is Kansas.

four

CONNECTICUT & VERMONT

The Creative Left and Logically Rigorous Right United

CONNECTICUT

Connecticut and Vermont's flags are linked by their exaltation of the plant kingdom. The grapevines and pine trees are the focal point for each state. Additionally, grape leaves decorate the edges of Connecticut's shield at five different points. At each grape leaf cluster, a golden sphere can be found. If you were to connect the clusters of golden dots, it would make a star. Likewise, the branches of a pine tree appear outside Vermont's shield as a crossed laurel—partially acting something like a supporter, bleeding into the compartment. Both fancy framed shields are rimmed in gold, and the state mottos can be found on swallow-tailed cut ribbons.

The flag of Connecticut traces its roots to the seal for Saybrook Colony, which existed from 1635 to 1644. The seal of Saybrook featured the same motto but with the hand of Providence holding the motto near the top. The hand of God/Providence is usually depicted as a hand appearing out of a cloud. Instead of three grapevines, there were 15. When Saybrook Colony was purchased by Connecticut Colony in 1644, the seal was transferred to Connecticut Colony and was used for the next 67 years. Then, on October 25, 1711, the governor and legislature culled the vineyard to three grapevines. The historical concord is

VERMONT

aligned with the three original English colonies that evolved into Connecticut: Saybrook Colony, New Haven Colony, and Connecticut Colony itself.

Finally, the flags are a perfect match for the Christmas tree with a Hanukkah menorah. There are nine clusters of grapes reflective of the nine candles of the lauded holiday candlestick, and the tree of Vermont is just waiting for decorations and presents.

Geography

Connecticut and Vermont share a special kind of geographic resonance. They are both bound by the powerfully outspoken states of New York and Massachusetts. As Vermont is landlocked, Connecticut is also an internally locked state that is blocked off from international waters by New York and Rhode Island. In order to sail out of Connecticut, one must pass through the territorial waters of New York or Rhode Island. Thus, Connecticut is the only state of the 13 original colonies that does not have an international maritime border. Note, Pennsylvania shares a freshwater international maritime border with Ontario. Likewise, Vermont has an international maritime border with Quebec via Lake Champlain.

The river of critical concord is the Connecticut River. The Connecticut River serves as an external interstate border for Vermont, while it is an internal inter-town border within Connecticut.

Two roads that connect Connecticut with Vermont are I-91 and Route 5. A whimsical synchronicity is that these numbers are somewhat patriotic for each state. Vermont became a state in 1791 during the 18th century, and Connecticut was the fifth state in the Union. These roads serve as a concrete braid that connects Newport, Vermont, to New Haven, Connecticut.

History

The creation of Connecticut and Vermont is tied to two opposing pressures from the east and the west. Connecticut was born in a tug of war between the Dutch and English. The western pressure came from the "Dutch" in New Amsterdam, while the eastern pressure was rooted to the "English" of Massachusetts. As the colony of New Netherlands established its center in what is now New York City, it became a fierce rival to the English colonies in the east centered on Boston. The Connecticut River was smack in the middle between these rival spheres of English and Dutch influence. After the Dutch initially planted a colony, House of Hope, in 1633 at what later became Hartford, the English colony at Plymouth responded in kind with their own colony the same year, which became Windsor. Seventeen years later, the ethnic and trading tensions between the Dutch and English were resolved with the Treaty of Hartford in 1650. This treaty set up the border between the English colony of Connecticut and New Netherland, which followed the general shape of modern-day Connecticut along its western border. Essentially, the Dutch were kicked out of Connecticut and back to the borders of modern-day New York.

As for the eastern and western friction for Vermont, it was another tug of war fought between New York and New Hampshire. The situation that led to the creation of Vermont was about the lands west of the Connecticut River. After

Quebec fell to British supremacy, New Hampshire and New York simultaneously started to issue land grants in Vermont. As a consequence, confusion reigned. King George III attempted to resolve the issue in 1764, deciding in favor of New York. A similar situation evolved on the borderlands between Virginia and Pennsylvania, where the disputed region attempted the novel-third option as a new colony called Westsylvania. However, no firebrand *Blue Mountain* "papas militia" ever formed in Pennsylvania. In this way, it was unlike Vermont, where the Green Mountain Boys arose to bolster support for the third option. Further, unlike New York and New Hampshire, Pennsylvania and Virginia were able to find common ground and snuff out the novel-third—neither mine nor yours—option. Westsylvania half-heartedly attempted to become the 14th state, but that seat was reserved for Vermont.

Besides semi-parallel pressures from the east and west, Vermont is fundamentally connected to Connecticut. Many of the founding fathers of Vermont were born in Connecticut. The equivalent George Washington figure for Vermont is Ethan Allen, who was born in Litchfield, Connecticut, in 1738. Although Ethan Allen's early patriot win at Ticonderoga was a bloodless, minor engagement, the cannons and other weapons seized were essential and gave the U.S. the upper hand during the years-long siege at Boston starting on April 19, 1775. It wasn't until Ethan Allen's cannons rolled on top of Dorchester Heights that the standoff was concluded on March 17, 1776, securing a victory and forcing the British to flee from Boston.

Ira Allen, Ethan Allen's younger brother (another founding father of Vermont) was born in Cornwall, Connecticut. He designed the Great Seal of the State of Vermont, which is the basis for the design of Vermont's flag. The first governor for the Republic of Vermont, Thomas Chittenden, was born in East Guilford, Connecticut in 1730. Seth Warner from Roxbury, Connecticut, was born in 1743 and was an officer with the Green Mountain Boys. He was victorious at Crown Point in early May 1775, where several precious cannons were captured.

An important semi-forgotten Green Mountain Boy from Connecticut to surrender his life for Vermont was Remember Baker from Roxbury, Connecticut. He was a first cousin to Ethan Allen and Seth Warner, who was known as the tall, red-headed, and freckle-faced giant, akin to Conan O'Brien. Before the breakout of the American Revolution, Remember Baker fought against New York's claim on Vermont—initially known as the New Hampshire Grants—and joined the Green Mountain Boys with the rank of captain. On March 21, 1771, a force of New Yorkers captured Baker at his mill. During the fight, Remember lost a thumb and his wife broke her arm when jumping from a window. Afterward, the Green Mountain Boys rescued Remember. Later, when war for Independence broke out, Remember Baker was a part of the party that raided Ticonderoga for vital control of America's Rolling Thunder. But on August 22, 1775, while Baker was scouting in Quebec, he was shot and killed by Natives allied to the British. The Indians cut off his head, put it on a pole, and carried it as a trophy when they returned to Quebec City of Saint-Jean-sur-Richelieu.

Perhaps the most essential connection between Vermont and Connecticut is the fact that the original name of Vermont was New Connecticut. Vermont originally proclaimed its independence on January 15, 1777, as the Republic of New Connecticut. For the next five months, New Connecticut fought unofficially on the side of the rebelling 13 colonies. It wasn't until June 1777 that New Connecticut was officially renamed as Vermont, it seems at the behest of Thomas Young, a member of the Sons of Liberty.

Is the pen mightier than the sword? No doubt the sword came first, but whence the ability of solidifying words was mastered by mankind, the sword's monopoly on power was numbered. As powerful words muzzled the power of the sword, Connecticut and Vermont provided two preeminent masters of word-smithery: Joseph Smith from Sharon, Vermont, and Harriet Beecher Stowe from Litchfield, Connecticut. The work of their pens left a permanent mark on the fabric of American society. Their lives are testaments created in the wake of freedom that illustrated the power of the First Amendment.

The First Amendment holds a sacred space for American values. It is the gold standard of American freedoms forged in the furnace of the Enlightenment. The First Amendment prevents the government from making laws that regulate an establishment of a state religion; the passing of laws that would prohibit the free exercise of religion; or abridge the freedom of speech, the freedom of the press, the freedom of assembly, or the right to petition the government for redress of grievances. It's a rather strange amendment that is composed of several laws in one. Nine months after Vermont's birthday into the Union, the First Amendment was adopted on December 15, 1791. The rank of the First Amendment, as first of first rights, is an auspicious position that underscores its value, giving the highest glory to the power of the pen. The founding fathers placed the value of the pen superior to the power of the sword. Not to worry—the power of the sword is enshrined as the second most important of American values via the Second Amendment, which was adopted on the same date with eight other less famous amendments.

Joseph Smith's legacy is a testament to rights articulated in the First Amendment, and in particular, the free exercise of religion. Smith was the founder of Mormonism, a branch of Christianity that arose within the United States. Puritans, Anglicans, Catholics, Baptists, Quakers, Presbyterians, Calvinists, Eastern Orthodox, Lutherans, Amish, Coptic, Armenian, Ethiopian, Anabaptist, Moravian, Dutch Reformed, Church of Sweden, Congregationalists, Oriental Orthodox Churches, and Mennonites are branches of Christianity that formed in the Old World. They were able to thrive by a curious type of Providence that resulted in healthy communities of love and compassion.

However, the 14th state was the garden where the seed of the new Mormon faith blossomed. Mormonism was the first faith to arise in the wake of the First Amendment. It would stretch the spiritual comfort zone of the American public. The groundbreaking and controversial aspect of this branch was the addition of a religious text known as *The Book of Mormon: An Account Written by the Hand of Mormon, Upon Plates Taken from the Plates of Nephi*, first published in 1830. According to Mormon tradition, *The Book of Mormon* was based upon the discovery of ancient golden plates in Manchester, New York. Apparently, Joseph Smith was able to translate an ancient script labeled as "Reformed Egyptian" with special spectacles known as "Urim and Thummim."

Many of the stories presented in *The Book of Mormon*, like many of the stories of the *Bible*, do not conform to the conventional modern view of world history as revealed by scientifically substantiated archaeology. Nevertheless, all stories contain an intangible wisdom that reflects in various degrees an aspect of the divine. Certainly, *The Book of Mormon* is a sacred American treasure that has served its community well. The evidence of this power has resulted in strong interconnected loving communities—not only in the United States, but across the world.

Mormonism was the first big step that expanded the religious panorama of religion in America. Although the First Amendment secured freedom of religion, in practice for much of American history, religions beyond mainline Protestantism were suspect and often reviled. Catholics and Jews were free to worship as Americans, but for the first half of American history they were often subject to scorn and suffered from occasional outbursts of vicious intolerance. Likewise, Mormons paid a heavy toll for their beliefs in the beginning and were persecuted by various institutions and individuals. Two years after publishing his book, Joseph Smith was tarred and feathered in 1832 by an angry mob that beat him unconscious in Ohio. In 1838, the first Mormon War erupted in northwestern Missouri. A few dozen Mormons were killed, and Joseph Smith fled with his flock to Illinois. It was here that Joseph Smith founded his last Mormon colony at Nauvoo. Ironically, the sequence of events that led to his death were tied to rights guaranteed in the First Amendment.

A splinter group that had formed in Nauvoo took issue with some of the doctrines of Smith's teachings—notably polyamory and the concept that man can progress into a divine being. This rival group of Mormons established a paper called the Nauvoo Expositor that was highly critical of the founder. In response, Joseph Smith ordered the destruction of their printing press and the destruction of all printed copies of the slanderous paper. Smith was later arrested on charges of destruction of the press and rioting. However, he was arrested in Nauvoo, where the charges were quickly dismissed as he was the power and purpose behind that city.

To many non-Mormons and members of the Mormon splinter group, Joseph Smith had put himself above the U.S. Constitution. Smith was able to enjoy the rights guaranteed by the First Amendment, yet he denied those same rights to others. This duplicitous exercise of the First Amendment ruffled quite a few feathers across Illinois. The Governor Thomas Ford wrote about the issue, "I now express to you my opinion that your conduct in the destruction of the press was a very gross outrage upon the law and liberties of the people. It [the Nauvoo Expositor] may have been full libels, but this did not authorize you to destroy it. There are many newspapers in the state which have been wrongfully abusing me for more than a year, and yet such is my regard for the liberty of the press and the rights of a free people in a republican government that I would shed the last drop of my blood to protect those presses from any illegal violence."

Another arrest warrant was issued to bring Joseph Smith to court. On June 25, 1844, Joseph Smith along with about a dozen co-defendants peacefully turned themselves in on the charge of inciting a riot. All but two defendants were granted bail on the riot charge; only Joseph and his older brother, Hyrum Smith, were charged with treason against the state of Illinois and transported to Carthage Jail. Carthage is the county opposite of Iowa's little southern nub. While Smith and his co-defendants awaited their trial in Carthage, a mob of about 200 men stormed the building and killed the brothers.

So, what voice from Connecticut can match the founder of a major worldwide congregation? That is certainly a tall order, and that order is fulfilled by Harriet Beecher Stowe. Like Joseph Smith, Harriet Beecher Stowe was touched by a special Providence when her words would awaken the heart of the nation. Her book *Uncle Tom's Cabin* was published in 1852 and had a profound impact on the psyche of the American public. Although a book of fiction, it is based upon fact, and it preached at the soul of America. It opened many eyes to the horrors of slavery and prevailing attitudes toward African Americans. *Uncle Tom's Cabin* was the best-selling novel of the 19th century, and the second best-selling book of that era just behind the Bible. Again, it proves whether a book is fact or fiction, it can still have a profound and spiritual impact on the human heart. Like *The Book of Mormon* in 1830, *Uncle Tom's Cabin* was a polarizing scripture in 1852.

Harriet Beecher Stowe lived to the ripe old age of 85, passing on Canada Day 1896. So beloved and far-reaching was her work that she is venerated within the Anglican Church—also called the Episcopal Church or Church of England. This is the national church of the U.K. whereby the ruling monarch of the British Royal family is regarded as the spiritual head. The Archbishop at Canterbury is the highest-ranking officer of the church, somewhat analogous to the Pope for Rome. Like the Catholic Church, the Episcopal Church has a list of men and women who are venerated as saints. July 1 is reserved for Harriet Beecher Stowe, who is listed as a writer and prophetic witness. Thus, an American woman from Litchfield, Connecticut, is regarded as a saint in some degree by the British royal family and their flock. Coincidentally, St. Stowe's Day happens to fall on Canada Day, and providentially, *St. Stowe* was born on a Flag Day in the U.S., and it was a Nutmegger who was the primary architect of the modern U.S. flag, as we shall see in a later chapter.

Unlike Joseph Smith, Stowe lived a long and fruitful life. The ranking martyr from Connecticut to match with historical and spiritual glory to Joseph Smith is John Brown from Torrington, Connecticut. John Brown was a true-blue centurion, born in the year 1800. Centurions are the privileged, once-in-a-lifetime generation whose birth year is synchronized to the turn of the century. The lives of centurions mark and capture the zeitgeist of the century, as their age is entangled with the age of the century. During the War of 1812, John Brown was 12. When the Missouri Compromise of 1821 took effect, John Brown was 21. Most importantly, when Nat Turner led a slave revolt across Southampton County, Virginia in 1831, John Brown was 31, as was Nat Turner himself.

Right now, the centurions of the 21st century are entering young adulthood. Like all centurions, they have a fleeting sense of the previous century yet are barred from any sort of firsthand memory. When they reach their first ring of royalty in the year 2030, one year of Saturn, they will begin their rule across the generations. Upon their second royal ring at age 60, two cycles of Saturn, their values will set in stone the flavor of the 21st century in the year 2060. In 2080, whence they are to be ignored and forgotten, a new generation of centurions will wait in the womb of their mothers for the start of the 22nd century, and the cycle will reset in the year 2100.

John Brown of Connecticut and Joseph Smith of Vermont claimed their actions were divinely motivated and ordained. Their passing were divisively celebrated or mourned as either something good or something bad. Regardless of one's view, the wake of their souls crashed auspiciously onto the lighthouse of the First and 13th Amendments of the Constitution. The American flag is coincidentally composed of 13 stripes. Although the number of stars has changed, a 13-striped flag was created as the constant in a symbol for freedom and liberty. The flag would finally live up to its name when the 13th Amendment was ratified, putting an end to the most ancient and onerous way of life.

Harriet Beecher Stowe and John Brown's actions via the pen and sword had a deep effect. Their efforts helped to shape public perception about slavery and represented the different manners in which it could be attacked—through words and an uprising. The institution of slavery in the United States of America as ordained by biblical scripture was finally undone after the severest of prices was paid in a heavy sum of blood. John Brown was the first political martyr for the cessation of slavery.

Connecticut and Vermont both existed by themselves, in limbo, before they were officially recognized by the proper authorities. Connecticut is known as the Constitution state because it issued the first legal document to govern an English colony in the Americas. The Fundamental Orders of Connecticut was officially adopted and in legal effect starting on January 24, 1639 (O.S. January 14, 1639). If cities are cells, then the DNA of a city is coded by legal documents like the Fundamental Orders of Connecticut, which articulate how to set up a town's structures and other organelles. The Fundamental Orders of Connecticut were not approved by the king or its parent colony in Massachusetts. It wasn't until 1662 that Connecticut became an official colony recognized by the king and Parliament. Thus, Connecticut Colony had a 23-year period of flying as a quasi-independent colony. Likewise, Vermont declared her independence from the U.K. and New York on January 15, 1777. Vermont also had an independent nation state period, like Texas did, but Vermont's phase lasted five years longer, a total of 14 years, ending when Vermont joined the U.S. on March 4, 1791, becoming the 14th state.

Connecticut and Vermont are a union of the oak with the maple. Oaks and maples can be found all across the U.S., but they retain a special place with these states. For Connecticut, its first constitution was hidden from the authorities on the pre-centennial of the U.S. Constitution. A century before the U.S. Constitution was adopted, King James II united all of the Northeast from New Jersey to Maine into one super colony known as the Dominion of New England. One of the king's orders was to gather up all the previous colonial charters and constitutions and declare them void. However, Connecticut did not comply. As the semi-fact, semi-fiction story goes, the colonial governor of the Dominion of New England met the leaders of Connecticut on a chilly, dark night on Halloween, 1687. Governor Andros expected the Connecticut leaders to surrender the charter, which was initially lying on the table. But then candles were given the happy boo birthday treatment, and when the candles were relit, the charter had magically disappeared. Apparently, Joseph Wadsworth fled the meeting house and hid the charter in an oak tree on the Wyllys estate. As a consequence, the tree became known as the Charter Oak and is now an iconic symbol of Connecticut. For Vermont, the connection with the maple tree does not have such a fantastic story, but like the pre-centennial constitutional surprise, instead of a trick, we get a treat. Maples provide wood, shade, beauty, and most importantly, maple syrup. The maple family tree is just as diverse as the oak family tree, but the sugar maple is at the core of Vermont's symbolism. Humans must suck about 40 gallons of maple tree blood to make one gallon of sweet breakfast nectar. Also, sugar maples make the best baseball bats. So how's that for a "trick or treat" story?

Numbers are important for each of the states. Connecticut holds extra special value because of its fifth position, like five fingers with five golden rings. Connecticut represents the completion of a hand or a thumbs up. If you can convince Connecticut to trust you, you are on your way. Thus, Connecticut holds a key to consistency to the American spirit. This is echoed by the ultimate nuts and bolts Nutmegger, Roger Sherman, who signed five great documents at America's genesis: the Continental Association , Petition to the King, Declaration of Independence, Articles of Confederation, and the Constitution.

Vermont is the 14th state, or rather the first state born within the United

States. Vermont's anti-slavery government was the harbinger of things to come. The founding fathers debated endlessly on the topic of slavery, but Vermont laid down the gauntlet and abolished the ancient right of owning another man as property. The 14th state set the lead tempo, whence a state born free was balanced with a state born in bondage. Eventually, the chorus of the nation was forced to follow Vermont's beat.

Connecticut and Vermont are like the yin and yang of New England. Connecticut represents the fast-paced, industrial, go go, money and dough, winner approach. But Vermont is tuned to the more relaxing, Zen, chill-lax, let things happen on a natural timetable. These reputations are like night and day, organic and artificial, or rest and stress. Healthy amounts of stress and rest are needed for a balanced life, but these states take it to the extreme. The capital of Hartford, Connecticut, is like a buzzing beehive made of concrete and full of big city problems. However, the capital of Montpelier, Vermont, is a soothingly quiet after sunset town where the fresh hijinks of a teen could easily make the papers.

Connecticut was blessed with the *brainiac* "Braintree" power of New England combined with the shrewd, New Amsterdam, Dutch and dime, nickel killer, cutthroat acumen. After all, if bottom lines are not met, the ship will not float, sir. Coincidentally, the insurance industry with its vast mountains of capital makes Connecticut a numbers junkie. But this kind of numerology sinks its teeth into finance. Connecticut is also infected with the tinkering ingenuity of a Dutchman's apprentice—thus technical wizardry is Connecticut's specialty.

The engineering feels of Connecticut was best demonstrated when Christopher Lloyd played the fictional Einstein-like Dr. Emmett Lathrop, or Doc Brown. Lloyd himself is from Stamford, Connecticut. Of authentic tinker jocks that established the Connecticut brand, Samuel Colt from Hartford, born in 1814, revolutionized the arms manufacturing process to make revolvers. John Fitch from Windsor was born in 1743 and designed the first operating steamboat for the U.S. Charles Goodyear from New Haven, born in 1800, was a self-taught chemist whose rubber products launched a company that retains his name on a blimp. Perhaps of lasting fame is David Bushnell from Westbrook. He was born in 1740 and invented the first submarine that was used in battle during the American Revolution. In psychology, Connecticut is what is known as a left brained state, a mind that is inclined to logic, math, and science. Finally, it should be no surprise that Noah Webster is from Hartford, Connecticut. Fed up with the "looks good to me" rules of spelling, he dedicated his life to confining words with logical spelling rules. Webster's first dictionary was published in 1806, called *A Compendious Dictionary for the English Language*, and his legacy continues to influence language today. Many believe that the first Adam named the animals according to ancient tradition, but it is a fact that Noah cast a spell on their names, at least in English.

If Connecticut is left brained, then Vermont is right brained. The right brain is considered the center of the artistic, feeling, intuitive, dreamy side of mind. Maybe there is a mysterious substance in the maple syrup. But when people move to Vermont their right brain seems to become hyperactive. Ben and Jerry's ice cream is the flagship of unconventional and quirky ice cream concoctions. The artistically counter, very real cult band of Phish was formed in Vermont. Bernie Sanders embodies certain Vermont values. Vermont is a welcome home to experimental and creative art colonies, many of which can be found in Burlington. As for the arts and sciences, if art is your pleasure, then Vermont is a treasure, but if science is your call, head directly to the Nutmegger stall.

Culture

Paul Giamatti and Sam Lloyd are known for playing antiheroes. Paul Giamatti, from New Haven, Connecticut (born 1967), slid into the American limelight with the movie *Sideways* (2004). His charm and acting talent have led to a string of hits like *Fred Claus* (2007) and the HBO miniseries *John Adams* (2008). Sam Lloyd, a light and funny spirit from Springfield, Vermont (born 1963), starred in *Scrubs* (2001-2010) and *Cougar Town* (2009-2015).

If music is the extra dimension of space and time that animates prayer, two soulfully stirring singers from Connecticut and Vermont that answer that call are the Carpenters and the von Trapp Family. The Carpenters were a sibling duo of couple's music who reminded the public that modern melodies can be stuffed with a bag full of smiles and sunshine in the 1970s. Richard was born in 1946 and Karen Carpenter in 1950, and they are from New Haven, Connecticut. Their hits include "They Long to Be Close to You" and "We've Only Just Begun." Elisabeth von Trapp was born in Lamoille County, Vermont, in 1955 and is the daughter of the famous Trapp Family singers from Austria, which the musical the *Sound of Music* (1965) is based upon. Thus, the mountains of Vermont are truly filled with rays or drops of golden sun. Elisabeth von Trapp is the Vermont-born von Trapp that performs as a little-known famous folk singer. Maybe if we press it, we can get a duet of Richard Carpenter and Elisabeth von Trapp in order to honor Connecticut and Vermont.

Cartoons are often considered child's play, but that is not always the case. Animated characters are often magnetically hypnotic for children, but this art form can be tailored to more mature audiences. Seth MacFarlane from Kent, Connecticut (born 1973), and Michael D. DiMartino from Shelburne, Vermont (born 1974), are animated artists who were able to cast this media with two contrasting forms of spectacular storytelling. Michael DiMartino is the co-creator of the TV show *Avatar: The Last Airbender* (2005-2008) and *The Legend of Korra* (2012-2014). Michael DiMartino also had a hand in *King of the Hill* (1997-2010) and *Family Guy* (since 1999). And speaking of *Family Guy*, this punch to nuts, *Simpsons* on speed, television show creator is a none too famous Nutmegger, Mr. MacFarlane.

A match of money men, John Pierpont Morgan from Hartford, Connecticut, is the financial wizard to match Henry Wells of Thetford, Vermont. J. P. Morgan was the financial dragon and master wizard with powers far greater and beyond the legendary realm of Oz. J. P. Morgan was tapped by a mysterious force, as he was being able to synergize banking with emerging technologies, namely the railroad and a new-age-alchemy that effectively turned steel into gold. Since then, J. P. Morgan's luminous shadow lives on in communities all across Connecticut. This state has steadfastly spawned several schools of financial wizardry, which can cast spells that can reduce or manipulate payrolls, safely guard taxable income with a spell of invisibility, forecast financial weather patterns, and master the divination of the dividend.

Henry Wells's key to success was his ability to undercut the competition with cheaper and faster express mail. Wells became wise to the ways of the courier and applied this knowledge as a co-founder of American Express, established March 18, 1850. Two business quarters later, California became the 31st state on September 9, 1850. Wells sensed an opportunity to open an express mail route to this furthest corner of America, but his American Express business partners caught the "chicken fecal flu" and refused to follow Wells's lead. Henry Wells, sensing opportunity, held on to his dream of an express route to California. He consequently organized a new company, Wells Fargo, which opened an express mail route to California on March 18, 1852. Taking this calculated risk paid off, and now the descendant of the express company's banking operations, Wells Fargo & Company, is a major, too-big-to-fail financial institution, and hosted a Western television series from 1957 to 1962 based upon the lived experiences of Frederick J. Dodge (1854-1938).

Henry Wells and J. P. Morgan were men who mastered money via careful study and hard-won experience from opposite vectors within the transport industry. Wells became wealthy from the front line, learning the ropes of express delivery, and then later, applying that knowledge to become a financial titan. J. P. Morgan came from the other direction, growing out of the financial control room of money and the bank, and later coming to dominate the transport industry via the railroad. This matches well with the reputation of Connecticut as the first of first techno states in the Union. J. P. Morgan, a native Nutmegger, even courted the audience and employment of Nicholas Tesla. Vermont also has a rugged, naturalist reputation that fits well with Henry Wells, a native Vermonter, who experienced the fun and wild runs across the frontier of America as a courier when it used to be upstate New York and Michigan. Henry Wells is the iconic original Flash of DC comics lore, while J. P. Morgan is the iconic X-Men mutant of amazing strength who could turn into steel: Colossus.

Two men who cast the most powerful sort of magic, enchanting words that solidify on paper, trace their roots to Vermont and Connecticut. Words can move nations, and cause women to heel, to war, to jump, to run, to sell, to buy, and to steal. George Jones from Poultney, Vermont, born in 1811, was the co-founder of *The New York Times*, established in 1851. Coincidentally, as one of the cornerstones of American media was laid, Charles Henry Dow's birth was providentially synchronized to this event. Chuck D was also born in 1851. The ripples of Dow's life are perpetually recanted across the financial world, with talk mundane and shouts profane. Chucky Dow co-founded the *Wall Street Journal* (established in 1889) and the Dow Jones & Company (established in 1882). The wake of Dow's life and his name has permanently embedded itself within the life blood of every American and non-American across the civilized world. Have you ever heard of the Dow Jones Industrial Average? You can thank Mr. Charlie Dow from Sterling, Connecticut, for that phrase. Dow was able to cut across time by avoiding the temptation of reporting opinions and bedding with advertisers, establishing neutral news, with a focus on financial matters. However, during the election of 1900, the *Wall Street Journal* set a precedent by endorsing a political candidate to office, incumbent president William McKinley.

As Georgia and Mississippi are a part of the Deep South, Vermont and Connecticut are a part of the Deep North. Latitude and attitude can have a profound consequence, and the contrasting qualities make up a wholesome whole—like the union of the left and right hemisphere of mind, which allows the collective creative consciousness to soar in arts and sciences. Further, it is union of the scrappy upstart that could, battle born during the American Revolution in 1777, with the elegantly long established hardwood colonial oak of 1639.

As indicated with these flags, Vermont and Connecticut are a conjoined union of the grapevine and the pine tree, as the bouquet of fine wine is appreciated while embers of smoked pinewood crackle their sweet and simple poetry by the fireplace on a snowy starlit winter's night. Together such aromatic scents work in concord to unlock that essential feeling of a rosy and cozy, with roots to Connecticut and Vermont.

five

OREGON & NEBRASKA

The Point of No Return
Between the Future Past

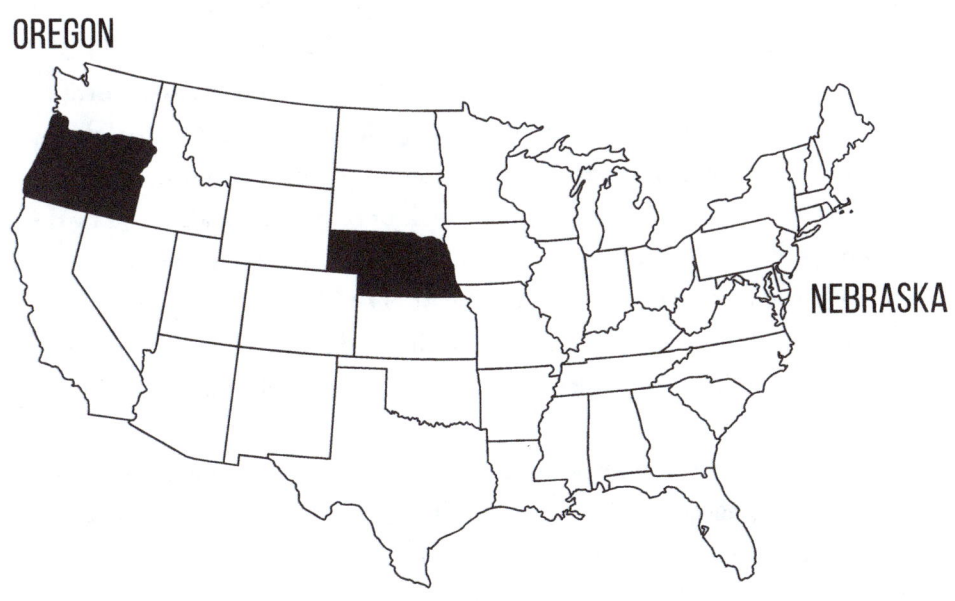

OREGON

Oregon and Nebraska present contrasting worldviews of the past and the present via a comparison of ancient and modern technologies. At the center of Oregon's flag is an ox-powered vehicle, a technology familiar to any pharaoh of the 31st century BC. However, the same pharaohs would be either mystified or horrified by the sail-less and horseless vehicles found on Nebraska's flag. Any spacefaring civilization will recognize that the technological sophistication of a train is a conspicuous tell—a tell that the fundamentals of physics are understood by the proprietors of such devices. Nearly all the princes and clergymen born near the times of ancient revelation would, no doubt, view the steam engine and telegraph as something akin to black magic or the workings of the devil. However, the vehicles found on Nebraska's flags are fruits extracted from nature by the hand of science.

The sailing ship and animal-drawn cart were the original modus operandi for moving long distances. Long ago, astrologers and alchemists held respected positions in society and government. However, by the 1800s sweeping changes flowed across society and technology. As engineered machines replaced the ox and horse, astronomers and chemists replaced the esteemed seats of power once

NEBRASKA

held by court astrologers and alchemists.

By serendipity, key symbols that highlight the contrasting worlds of the ancient and modern era are the ox car of Oregon and the train of Nebraska. It is a comparison of ox power versus the fossil-fueled iron ox. Even today, fossil fuel technology is the dominant form of transportation, which comes in diesel or several standard octanes from 87/regular to 93/premium. The other ancient-modern alignment is the ferry boat of Nebraska and the sailing ship of Oregon. Oregon actually has two boats on its flag, but for this relationship, the ship further left is key. It's a boat powered by sail, a common technology known to all the ancient empires of old and new worlds. However, the boat on Nebraska's flag has forsaken the sail. The modern ferry boat is able to travel across water independent of wind and can even cruise upstream.

Oregon and Nebraska happen to be the temporal guardians of the U.S. Civil War. Oregon was the last state of the Virgin Union, while Nebraska was the first state of the post Virgin Union. The Virgin Union was the time period before the secession crisis, when America was wholly united and unbroken. Only 33 states would bear witness to an American Eden, when no state had yet to make war upon another.

In total, three states were born during the secession crisis: Kansas, Nevada, and West Virginia. When Oregon was born in 1859, slavery was a fundamental aspect of the American Dream. In contrast, when Nebraska was born in 1867, this most ancient and vicious of specters that plagued mankind since the rise of the great pyramids—slavery—was dead in the United States. It truly was the start of a new world order.

Nebraska and Oregon also have complimentary designs that connect. Oregon has a sheaf of wheat at the bottom of her framing heart, while Nebraska has several sheaves of wheat in front of the cabin. Oregon has the silhouettes of pine trees on the right, while Nebraska has leafy trees on the right. And these trees represent the great familial divide among trees, angiosperms versus gymnosperms. Earth is currently divided by these two family trees, but it always hasn't been the case.

Gymnosperms are better known as pine trees, mostly. They don't produce flowers and typically have thin needle-like leaves, as found on Vermont's flag. One can consider the pinecone as a "woody flower." In contrast, angiosperms are flowering plants, and their leaves are often flat and wide. Angiosperm leaves are the common conception of a leaf, as found on Connecticut's and Canada's flags. In a way, one can think of flowers as colored leaves. This is how flowers are thought to have evolved—from modified, colored leaves, which eventually became the fragrant icons of beauty and romance and are basically the genitals of plants. Fatefully there's a well-known, primitive "flowering plant" that's stuck in the middle evolutionary intermediate step between that stage of a colored leaf and being a true flower: the poinsettia, or *Euphorbia pulcherrima*. Next time Christmas rolls around, take a close look at a poinsettia, it's a virtual Neanderthal of flowers. Red leaves mimic the trait of a flower. You can easily search on the Internet for an image, but it's best to see and feel the red leaves for yourself. The red leaves of the poinsettia give us the impression of a flower, but it's not an actual flower.

As Oregon reflects the ancient way of sail and animal power, Nebraska is the harbinger of modern life. The gymnosperms on Oregon's flag are an ancient order of plant-kind that has been around since before the age of dinosaurs. In contrast, the angiosperms on Nebraska's flag are a relatively new age plant-form that came into dominance after the great extinction 66 million years ago when our ancestors were empowered by cosmological happenstance to become the dominant life form, as it was for mammals and flowering plants.

Coincidentally, the date found on Oregon's flag is also the publication date of *On the Origin of Species by Means of Natural Selection*, or *The Preservation of Favoured Races in the Struggle of Life* (1859), written by Charles Darwin (1809-1882). Shortly after the publication of this book, the U.S. Civil War would begin, and the knowledge imparted by this book would lead to virtual civil war of the mind's eye across every religion. Although this theory is readily recognized by scientific communities across nations and several religions, there are segments of society that continue to wage a virtual war against such logically radical ideas.

As the year upon the flag of Oregon is synchronized to a book that changed our place and view of the universe, Nebraska's date of 1867 is aligned to another revolutionary article that changed the practice of medicine. On St. Patrick's Eve, March 16, a proverbial pot of gold more precious than gold itself was handed to the sick and wounded. This medical advance was one small step for a surgeon, one giant leap for the health of humankind. Dr. Joseph Lister of Upton House, England, born on April 5, 1827, published a process for antiseptic surgery in a medical journal called *The Lancet*.

In 1867 a new medicine wheeled from science slowly and steadily flowed from England to the four corners of the world like a luminous force field, banishing deathly, ignorant practices from the shadows. The generations born after 1867 were finally free from the invisible and deadly shackles of microbiological infections.

Take not for granted the light of this knowledge. Who can tally the lives and limbs saved since this most valued and heralded announcement back in 1867? Dr. Lister's now common-sense list of hygienic recommendations for surgery required that surgeons should wash their hands before and after surgery, and medical instruments and the wound were to be treated with an antiseptic solution.

If only this discovery were made just a mere decade earlier in 1857, perhaps a million lives and a million more limbs could have been saved during the War

Between the States. Only divine Providence knows why and when such blessings are bestowed. But in 1867, this revelation allowed souls to traverse the dangerous rapids of surgery more safely.

Joseph Lister performed the world's first antiseptic surgery on August 12, 1865, mere months after the Confederacy capitulated. Dr. Lister's game changing surgery consisted of cleaning an 11-year-old boy's fractured leg with an antiseptic solution. He was amazed to see recovery-patient zero's bones fuse back together.

The solution to this new type of miracle life and limb saving surgery came about in the wake of Louis Pasteur's (1822-1895) research. Joseph Lister came across Pasteur's published articles and applied those ideas with his own. Before his 1867 publication, surgery was a dangerous and often deadly procedure. The medical establishment had yet to connect the dots between the cause of gangrene and microbes. Even in the early days of Joseph Lister's antiseptic surgical procedures, his ideas were mocked. *The Lancet* itself, a year later in 1868, warned the medical establishment against Lister's antiseptic procedures. However, by 1881 Joseph Lister's ideas were legion. Little did Dr. Lister know back in 1867 that he was laying the cornerstone of the germ theory of disease. Previously, the root causes of human diseases were the work of spells, black magic, and evil spirits. Nay, the witch doctor is on permanent hiatus on the account of a Mr. Lister. In 1892, Joseph Lister received a hero's jubilee at the celebration of Louis Pasteur's 70th birthday in Paris. Lister gave a speech that honored Louis Pasteur to a room packed full of pomp, the press, big wigs, and other VIPs of the state. Upon the conclusion of his address, in which he gave much credit to Louis Pasteur, Dr. Lister received a well-earned standing ovation and was kissed by Louis Pasteur himself. Think of the ending of James Cameron's *Titanic*, but only much bigger and with more applause.

Perhaps you're wondering if the popular mouthwash Listerine is connected to Joseph Lister? Well, indeed it is. In 1881 a pharmacist named Jordan Wheat Lambert obtained a formula for an antiseptic mouthwash invented by Dr. Joseph Lawrence, and it was named in honor of Joseph Lister. Listerine was so popular with dentists that by 1914 Listerine became the first over the counter mouthwash sold in the U.S.

Other matching content on the flags are mountains and bodies of water. The body of water for Oregon is the ocean, and the sun is setting. The setting sun alludes to the ending of a cycle—in America's case it serendipitously foreshadows the end of slavery. You might ask if the sun could be rising? Well no, Oregon is on the West Coast. Also note the old-style sailboat is heading west, and west is associated with endings and death. This is why legends and cowboys drift off into the sunset as opposed to drifting off into the sunrise. As the sun falls off the edge of the Earth, it's proverbial lights out. But look closely at the ship heading east. It is a hybrid ship of sail and power paddle. Since the east is associated with the beginning or birth, it portends a changing of a new modern America. The second boat also fulfills a trinity of the three man-made structures to align on both flags. For Oregon, the triplet codon is an ox cart, a sailing ship, and a hybrid sail-steam ship (UAA). For Nebraska, the three are a paddle boat, a train, and a cabin (AUG). If you forgot what triplet codons are, they are a sequence of three nucleotide bases that enable cells to construct proteins. As for UAA and AUG, please enjoy your biology homework, where answers can easily be found on the Internet.

Both states have names and a year present. Mottos reflective of the Civil War themes are also present. Oregon puts it simply with THE UNION, while Nebraska has EQUALITY BEFORE THE LAW written on a ribbon, which directly refers to equity among all the varieties of mankind: male, female, Black, White, and everything else in between.

Lastly, the overall color palette matches harmoniously. Dark blue and yellow dominate as if they are an old library stamp, blue jeans, or blueprints. But Nebraska has a minor addition of gray to represent the mountains and the foreground. Finally, both flags have flags on flags. It's more discernible if you look at an image on a website that focuses clearly on the seal. There is one flag at the front of Nebraska's paddle boat and several flags are just barely visible on the masts and the stern of the sailing vessels. Masts are the "telephone poles" that hold the sails, while the stern is the back bumper of a boat.

THE FLAG REVELATION

Geography

During the Oregon Trail period, Oregon and Nebraska Territories were the flying buttresses of the east and the west, respectively. Although Oregon and Nebraska do not currently share a border, once upon a time when they were young and wild territories, they were neighbors for five and a half years. The great wagon trains that crossed the Oregon Trail from May 30, 1854, until February 14, 1859, crossed directly from Nebraska Territory into Oregon Territory.

Oregon Territory and Nebraska Territory are the cornerstones of the northwest quarter, which includes Washington, Idaho, Montana, Wyoming, and the Dakota twins.

Oregon and Nebraska as territories started out like huge cumulonimbus clouds that took up the entire sky. Typically, territories shrink like a collapsing cloud, and when they condense to the right size, they become a state, as was the case with Oregon. However, as Nebraska shrank, it was also, for a short while, able to expand beyond the Louisiana Purchase. From 1861 until 1863, Nebraska Territory effectively joined the West Coast team. Nebraska ruled over land that was formerly a part of Oregon Territory.

When the northern half of Nebraska that once touched Canada collapsed to its current northern border, Nebraska's nose grew like Pinocchio. You can still see the remnants of Nebraska's west coast nose on the map of America; it's part of the lower corner where Wyoming juts into Utah. Most importantly here, the tip of Nebraska's lost and long nose was cut from Oregon Territory.

But today, this small slice of "*Orbraskgon Territorial Heritage*" belongs to Wyoming. Important places that have Oregon and Nebraska heritage are Eden, Pinedale, Wyoming Peak, and most importantly South Pass, which is the Rocky Mountain Gap that marks a waterfall/rainfall transition between the Atlantic and Pacific Oceans.

Nebraska is nearly shaped like a cannon as if to shoot settlers westward, and indeed that was the case. Of all the westward trails, the Oregon Trail is perhaps the most famous. It was in Nebraska where most westward trails merged. The many trails had different starting points, but in Nebraska they became one. The most notable stopover point was at Fort Kearny, Nebraska. It was here that the

Oregon Trail, Bozeman Trail, Mormon Trail, California Trail, Ox-Bow Trail, and Pony Express were locked and loaded. In this case, wagons could be loaded with fresh supplies and enjoy some wild frontier entertainment. Thus Fort Kearny, Nebraska is the ultimate OG great-great-grandfather father of rest stops of the highway.

Note that Oregon City, Oregon is famous as the official terminus of the Oregon Trail, while Independence, Missouri, is the famous starting point. However, as the official Oregon Trail became congested, other starting points popped up all along Iowa, Missouri, and even Nebraska. One particularly interesting starting off point was in Nebraska herself at Nebraska City. Nebraska City was the beginning of the Ox-Bow Trail that started where the original Fort Kearny resided until it was moved to its current location. This trail became especially popular with freighter wagons. Perhaps Oregon City and Nebraska City deserve a sister city relationship? In the broad view of frontier wagon trails, Oregon City was just one of many important destinations, just as Nebraska City was one of many more staging areas. And note, as railroads expanded across the frontier, white wagon trains became quaint legends of the past. As it is apparent with a comparison of the flags of Nebraska and Oregon, from ox-driven wagon trains to coal-fired trains of steel.

Concordantly both states are home to incredibly beautiful sand dunes. Along the Oregon Coast, the Oregon Dunes National Recreation Area is a perfect collision of the sea, sand dunes, and sky. The dunes of Oregon were part of the inspiration for Frank Herbert's science fiction space opera novel, *Dune* (1965). In the heart of Nebraska there are the Sand Hills. This is where the prairie blends on virgin grassy dunes. The Nebraska dunes were undulating waves of grass, as if a wavy sea were instantly made into grass. But there is sand everywhere and breaks where sand traps appear, which makes it look like a golf course.

Two iconic landmarks that reflect the spirit of their respective states are Crater Lake for Oregon and Chimney Rock for Nebraska. These landmarks offer contrasting beauty. Lakes by a mountain are a dime a dozen in the Rockies, but the rounded nearly perfect circle of Crater Lake seems surreal. The enchantment is an intense, steeply sloped and appropriately named Wizard Island Hill that can put a spell on the observer. In a similar vein, the thrusting skyward spire of Chimney Rock is a stirring example of nature's beauty. This landmark became a literal rite of passage for those upon the Oregon Trail whilst in Nebraska. Later in the golden age of the home PC, Chimney Rock left an imprint on Generation X with one of the few educational video games that was able to balance learning with fun with *The Oregon Trail* (1985). In a way, Chimney Rock is as much an icon of Nebraska as it is for Oregon, due to its association with the Oregon Trail.

Although located at nearly the same latitudes, the weather between these fraternal twin states is like night and day. Oregon is famous for its even keeled, goldilocks weather that is neither too hot nor too cold, but persists in an overcast cool rainy season that seems to last all year. However, Nebraska is subject to bipolar, tripolar, or quadripolar weather. The Nebraska sky has a moody attitude that delights in surprising unsuspecting tourists with a quadruple kick of winter, spring, summer, and fall weather in one day.

History

Two Native American legends who left their warrior's wake in Oregon and Nebraska are Chief Paulina and Crazy Horse. Historians don't know with certainty as to the location of their birth. However, Chief Paulina was born somewhere in Oregon Territory and Crazy Horse was born somewhere in Nebraska Territory.

Crazy Horse is a paramount warrior of the plains, known for his many victories against the Euro-Americans. Some of the highlights of Crazy Horse's resume include the Fetterman Fight of 1866, the Wagon Box Fight of 1867, and Custer's Last Stand of 1876.

Chief Paulina joined that all too familiar pattern of resistant Natives who refused to submit to the U.S. government. He became a famous guerrilla warrior who could evade capture and inflict serious harm on Oregon Country settlers. Chief Paulina also took special aim at Natives who submitted to a muted life on the reservation. Although Crazy Horse and Chief Paulina were skilled resistance fighters, both their lives ended in violent spasms.

Crazy Horse of Nebraska Territory surrendered at the Red Cloud Agency near Fort Robinson, Nebraska, during the first week of May 1877, with about 1,100 followers. Later, when the Nez Perce War was raging to the north, U.S. forces asked if he would join them in subduing the hostile Natives. Here is where things get lost in translation. The interpreter said he agreed to fight "till all the Nez Perce were dead," but it is believed that this is a wrong interpretation, and what he actually said was that they would fight "till no White man is left." The officers in charge assumed the worst and took Crazy Horse into custody, even under the protest that what Crazy Horse said was mistranslated. Somewhere in the miscommunication of orders or perhaps a cover up, Crazy Horse was bayoneted in the back by a guard. Crazy Horse officially died in custody on September 5, 1877, at Fort Robinson, Nebraska, under misunderstood, unclear facts.

In Oregon Territory, the current story of Chief Paulina's death was under the auspices of revenge. After his party of warriors sacked the property of James N. Clark in the John Day River Valley, a posse gathered to extract a reprisal. Sometime in this spring of 1867, vigilantes shot and scalped Chief Paulina near the Klamath Reservation. The leader of the posse, Howard Maupin, took credit for killing Chief Paulina was purported to have taken his scalp.

Two Native leaders who left more romantic closing songs on the settlement of the west include Chief Joseph for Oregon and Red Cloud for Nebraska. Their indigenous nations resisted in the final quarter, a time period from after the U.S. Civil War 1865 to the massacre at Wounded Knee 1890. They would follow the pattern as set back east by Tecumseh and Black Hawk. As rebels of forlorn causes desperately holding on to their sacred lands, they were eventually overcome by insatiable greed and want of modernity.

Red Cloud was born near North Platte, Nebraska, in 1822. But he was destined to have a war of his own namesake, Red Cloud's War. The spark of the war began when Red Cloud's nation expanded upon Crow Territory in Wyoming. The Crow appealed to U.S. forces for help to expel the Red Cloud's allied tribes. Part of the reason Red Cloud's encroachment into Crow Territory was in disregard to a previous agreement was the lack of sufficient game in their own territories. The fact that Crow and Lakota were bitter rivals did not help—it was an all too familiar bitterness that often transcended their mutual resentment toward Whites. Taking advantage of this situation, the army could easily recruit Indians to fight other Indians. No doubt if aliens landed on Earth, they could easily pit any modern nation against other nations in a heartbeat.

Chief Joseph was born in northeastern Oregon in the 1840s. The Nez Perce were at first granted a large reservation around the tristate area of Washington, Oregon, and Idaho by the 1855 Walla Walla Treaty. However, in 1860 gold was discovered on their land, but according to the treaty no Whites were allowed to visit without Nez Perce permission. By 1869, the Nez Perce Indians were coerced into giving up most of their land to satisfy the appetite of the gold diggers.

The Nez Perce who submitted to federal pressure moved to a much smaller reservation in Idaho. But as in many cases, there were holdouts who refused to sign the new treaty. They were given a 30-day notice to move out by June 1877. When June 1877 rolled around, the remaining Nez Perce of Oregon were at war with the U.S. for simply holding on to their birthright lands, originally given to them in the 1855 Treaty of Walla Walla.

Before Red Cloud of Nebraska and Chief Joseph of Oregon surrendered, they were afforded several small victories. Red Cloud's greatest victory was in northern Wyoming, known as the Fetterman Fight. It was here that the plot line of 1984's *Red Dawn* played out in real life. However, it was not a war of underdog White kids in the hills, fighting a superior communist war machine. The underdogs in 1866 were led by Red Cloud, fighting the superior war machine of the United States. At the Fetterman Fight, about 80 soldiers were on guard detail at Fort Phil Kearny. After the Indians gained the attention of the U.S. military, which included Crazy Horse, they were able to lure the pursuing cavalry into a trap. Once separated and surrounded, one thousand braves were able to annihilate the U.S. force of 81 soldiers on December 21, 1866. Eventually Red Cloud's *Red Dawn* hit-and-run tactics shut down traffic all along the Bozeman Trail of Montana. However, the Wagon Box Fight of 1867 demonstrated the superiority of advanced weaponry. The U.S. soldiers were outnumbered approximately 30 to 1 (sources vary). Yet, the servicemen were carrying the new breech-loading Springfield Model. Thus, soldiers didn't have to waste time loading each bullet from the front-muzzle of the gun barrel with a ram rod. The British faced similar odds at the Battle of Ulundi, and their advanced weaponry effectively ended the Zulu War in South Africa on July 4, 1879.

But on June 17, 1877, the Battle of White Bird Canyon was a total victory for the Nez Perce. The Indians were outnumbered two to one, fighting uphill against a technologically superior enemy. The U.S. forces even had Nez Perce scouts on their side, yet they lost the battle. Thirty-four U.S. servicemen lost their lives, while only three men on the Nez Perce side were wounded.

Red Cloud's war included fighters from the Lakota, Cheyenne, and Arapaho tribes. Most of the battles took place in Montana and Wyoming from 1866 until 1868. But the original Nebraskans were not defeated by the sword—rather it was the pen that brought peace. Red Cloud acquiesced according to a new 1868 Fort Laramie Treaty, which created the Great Sioux Reservation. Six years later, General Armstrong Custer would report about the findings of gold on this reservation. Similarly, the Nez Perce of Oregon were not alone in their campaign of resistance; a small band of the Palouse Indians joined their cause.

Although Chief Joseph's war was much shorter, the Nez Perce showed a cunning and intelligence that often outwitted the pursuing U.S. Army. The Red army was used to living in the wild and could easily ferry across rivers with family and all possessions in tow. However, when the White army traversed the river, it was a clunky, time-consuming ordeal. In one instance, when the U.S. Army crossed a river, the Nez Perce band re-crossed, knowing it would take the White army several hours to catch up. After fending off the White army for six months with minor skirmishes and pitched fights, the Red army was exhausted from a one-thousand-mile journey from Idaho in the heart of Montana. The clock ran out for the fighting Nez Perce. They were only 40 miles from the Canadian Border, where they were to meet up with Sitting Bull when U.S. forces finally overpowered them on October 5, 1877. It was here that Chief Joseph gave a most eloquent speech of surrender, lauded by the halls of history.

After the Indian Wars ended, Chief Joseph and Red Cloud continued their fight for equality, but with the power of the pen. They visited Washington DC to seek recompense for their people's sufferings, but often to deaf ears.

Chief Joseph departed for the great council fire in the sky on September 21, 1904. His voice has become an eloquent ember of the collective Native American experience to the bitter and uncompromising will of "progress." Chief Joseph's swan song truly transcends the ages, as an enshrined farewell to arms, foretelling that the future will eventually subsume all our present attachments. Red Cloud became eponymously associated with his name on December 10, 1909, when his spirit became one with the blissful red sunset, when every so often, clouds are eloquently positioned such that they set the sky and themselves ablaze with a stunning red haze. Indeed, the spirit of Red Cloud lives on perpetually with each glowing red sunset, or more aptly, red dawn.

Although Nebraska and Oregon were far from the front of WWII, the ugly specter of war would pay them a visit. As the tide of war turned in favor of the allies, the U.S. was able to bomb Japan with near immunity. Imperial Japan attempted to strike back in the most peculiar way with balloon bombs. In a way, these balloon bombs were precursors to unmanned drones. Although these weapons did not have cameras and a guidance system, they were programmed to release their deadly ballast at certain air pressures.

The pilotless drone bombs looked something like floating jellyfish in the sky, which the Japanese called Fu-Go. The balloons were approximately 33 feet in diameter and could lift 1,000 pounds. The jet stream was used to deliver the bombs, and approximately 10,000 "Japanese Man O' War" were launched, starting in November 1944. About 1,000 balloons crossed the Pacific to North America, landing in Canada and the U.S. It was hoped that the bombs would start forest fires, and perchance hit a city. However, the balloon bombs did little to no damage. Most of the Fu-Go bombs landed in the states of the Nebraska-Oregon Territorial heritage group. Oregon received the mother lode of revenge balloons, while at least four landed in Nebraska. The vast majority of bombs went off harmlessly, but there was one case in Oregon where a Sunday school picnic was hit. On May 5, 1945, a pregnant woman and five children were killed when they investigated a Fu-Go bomb that landed in the forest of Gearhart Mountain, near Bly, Oregon. The Sunday school students were 11 to 14 years old.

Amazingly one balloon bomb was able to disrupt the Manhattan Project's Hanford site temporarily. Plutonium was being refined for the second nuclear bomb, Fat Man, at this location and was later dropped on Nagasaki. For a final, quirky connection, the B-29 Superfortress, the Enola Gay, which dropped the first atomic bomb, Little Boy, was built by the Glenn L. Martin Company in Omaha, Nebraska.

Culture

At the beginning of electric entertainment, Portland Hoffa (1905-1990) is the perfect complement to Fred Astaire (1899-1987). In the song and dance routine for stardom, these two stars were dancers. Fred Astaire from Omaha, Nebraska, became a national sensation with his freestyle form and charming moves. Portland Hoffa was born in Portland, Oregon, and she started her career as a dancer on Broadway during the 1920s. She eventually became a radio star, setting the mold for the cartoony, high-pitched air head.

Born in the Roaring '20s, Jane Powell pairs with Marlon Brando. Jane Powell from Portland, Oregon (born 1929), tore up the musical world in the 1940s. Some of her bigger hits were "A Date with Judy" (1948) and "Hit the Deck" (1955). As she got older, she starred in *The Love Boat* (1977-1987) and *Growing Pains* (1985-1992). In 1924, Omaha, Nebraska gave us Marlon Brando. Brando was a heavy hitter of 20th century cinema. Starring in movies such as *Guys and Dolls* (1955), *The Godfather* (1972), *Superman* (1978), and cult hit *The Island of Dr. Moreau* (1996).

Two stars who pair up perfectly are Howard Hesseman (1940) and Dick Cavett (1936). Howard Hesseman was from Lebanon, Oregon, and had a seminal role on TV as DJ Johnny Fever on WKRP in Cincinnati. He later became an iconic schoolteacher and *Head of the Class* (1986-1991) as Mr. Moore. Richard Alva Cavett from Gibbon, Nebraska, is class A major television personality. Cavett has truly lived among the stars, having starred in many movies where he usually plays himself. Besides having his own TV show, he starred in *Nightmare on Elm Street 3* (1987), *Beetlejuice* (1988), and *Forrest Gump* (1994).

Two big tough-guy twins include Don Pedro Colley of Klamath Falls, Oregon, and Nick Nolte of Omaha, Nebraska. Colley starred in *Beneath the Planet of the Apes* (1970), *THX 1138* (1971), and *Sugar Hill* (1974). Nick Nolte flew straight into acting and never stopped. Some of his hits include *48 Hrs.* (1982), *Teachers* (1984), *The Prince of Tides* (1991), *Lorenzo's Oil* (1992), *Hulk* (2003), *Noah* (2014), and TV's *Poker Face* (2023).

More recently, two early Gen Xers to slide into America's heart are Ty Burrell (1967) of Grants Pass, Oregon, and Jorge Garcia (1973) of Omaha, Nebraska. Ty Burrell's star has shined bright when he played as Phil Dunphy on ABC's *Modern Family* (2009-2020). Ty Burrell has also starred on Broadway and in movies like *Black Hawk Down* (2001), and *Muppets Most Wanted* (2014). Jorge Garcia became familiar to America on the TV show *Lost* (2004-2010).

Two women who put the boom in boomer are Sally Struthers (1947) and Swoosie Kurtz (1944). Struthers of Portland, Oregon, became a communal member of America's family as the daughter of Archie and Edith Bunker in *All in the Family* (1971-1979) with her role as Gloria Stivic. She has also starred in the *Gilmore Girls* (2000-2007), and more recently starred in *Christmas Harmony* (2018). Swoosie Kurtz of Omaha, Nebraska, is another TV star who had roles in *Carol and Company* (1990), *Pushing Daisies* (2007), and *Mike & Molly* (2010-2016). For movies Swoosie Kurtz starred in *The Positively True Adventures of the Alleged Texas Cheerleader-Murdering Mom* (1993), *Liar Liar* (1997), *Overboard* (2018), and *Call Me Kat* (2021-2023).

Two core Generation X queens are Kaitlin Olson (1975) and Hilary Swank (1974). Kaitlin Olson of Portland, Oregon, has starred in a string of popular movies like *Coyote Ugly* (2000), *Leap Year* (2010), *Vacation* (2015), and *Finding Dory* (2016). Hilary Swank of Lincoln, Nebraska, kicked her way into the American consciousness with *The Next Karate Kid* (1994), *Boys Don't Cry* (1999), and *Freedom Writers* (2007).

Two temporal twin titans who rule the domain of classical counter boomer culture humor are Matt Groening (1954) and Kurt Andersen (1954). Matt Groening of *Portland* is the creator of *The Simpsons*, an animated show that has been ongoing since 1989. It's the longest running prime-time TV show in

U.S. history. Groening also created *Futurama* (since 1999) and *Disenchantment* (2018-2023). Kurt Andersen of Omaha graduated from the exclusive educational fraternity of Harvard and co-founded *Spy Magazine* (1986-1998). *Spy* was a keenly satirical magazine that intelligently lampooned the media and high society. No doubt Andersen's *Spy* influenced Matt Groening.

In the heart of the 1980s, Oregon and Nebraska earned an iconic altar in America. In 1984, a masterpiece of cinema came to pass titled *The Goonies* (1985)—a fictional story that was played out in Astoria, Oregon. It's hard to work with children and even harder to capture lightning in a bottle. In 1984, a Hollywood gem was forged in Oregon. So sacred is this film, a reboot would be sacrilege. *The Goonies* is as cult as it gets. And speaking of cult films, a film about Nebraska children who form a cult came to pass in 1984. *Children of the Corn* (1984) was based on a short story by Stephen King. This movie is set in the fictional town of Gatlin, Nebraska. It is a chilling story that respawned as *Children of the Corn* (2020).

Oregon and Nebraska have banners that mark the transition between the way of our ancestors and ways of our descendants—animal-drawn carts versus vehicles created by a new type of imagination yoked to the austere logic of science. It marks the point of no return for the birth of the new world order, which has been unfolding when transportation was underwritten by math and science rather than by the crack of a whip upon an unintelligent beast. By destiny or mere coincidence, the year 1859 on Oregon's flag marks the end of an old America, where laws and orders were established by the inkwell and the speed of a horse. Nebraska's banner with the year 1867 indicates the start of new industrial, technocratic America, where order and law are supported by the horseless, mechanical chariot and the speed of communication is only limited by the speed of light itself.

six

ALASKA & NEVADA

The Essence of Freemasonry Is Apparent in Their Contours

THE FLAG REVELATION

ALASKA

Two fields of blue, one decorated by a star and the other a field of stars, create a constellation of concord. The single silver star of Nevada matches the eight gold stars of Alaska. It is an iconic match of the classical two most precious metals, silver and gold.

Stars appear on many state flags, but Alaska is the only flag to accurately show their arrangement in the heavens. Further, sage is a sacred plant in Native American traditions. It is used in a manner like incense within the Catholic Church and the various Hindu-Buddheic traditions. Like the sprinkle of Holy Water, the so-called smudging with sage is regarded by Natives as a blessing. According to Native tradition, smudging is a ritual burning of herbs that cleanses and repels evil influence.

The constellation on Alaska's flag is commonly known as the Big Dipper and North Star. But in the framework of the International Astronomical Union (IAU), two constellations are partially present: Ursa Major and Ursa Minor, the Greater Bear and the Lesser Bear, respectively. The stars of the Big Dipper belong to the Greater Bear's bottom half of the bear, while the North Star is the end of the tail of the Lesser Bear.

NEVADA

Coincidentally, the genesis of these flags came about at nearly the same time. Both flags were designed during the Calvin Coolidge administration. Nevada's flag was first designed in 1926. But due to politics, its official adoption was delayed until 1929. Alaska's flag was designed and adopted in 1927.

The story of Alaska's flag is a fairytale come true. Sometimes a higher fate smiles and gives us something to ponder. Is there an intangible force guiding our lives? Is it all a roll of the dice, or are there mysterious forces at work? For a young seventh grader from Chignik, Alaska, he was the chosen one. It is also fitting that Alaska was not yet a state, but an adolescent territory, as was an adolescent Benny Benson. Alaska would not reach adulthood until January 3, 1959. Benny Benson reached adulthood in 1931.

Nevada's flag story was strikingly different. Its design is older by one year, and it was the third "bronze" version. Nevada had two dramatically different versions that were abandoned. There was one final revision in 1989, but it is basically the same flag that was selected in 1926. The small revision was a rearrangement of letters for the word NEVADA. In the 1929 version, the letters E, V, A, D, A were strewn in between the points of the silver star, while the letter

N was just above the upward point of the star, as if pointing north. The strange placement of letters was finally changed when it was discovered that the original 1929 flag committee wanted the word NEVADA to be placed under the star, and not in a circular fashion around the star.

The first Nevada flag looked more like a 19th century Department of Tourism advertisement, which lasted from 1905 to 1915. Then a radically different second version was adopted that featured the state seal surrounded by an arc of silver and gold stars that made the shape of a football; it lasted from 1915 to 1929. Finally in 1929, the fraternal flag of Alaska was set.

But for the record, Nevada's design was put first into the collective consciousness by one year. Did it or could it have an effect on Benny Benson? That my friend, is impossible to determine at this moment. Nevada's final design was by Louis Shellbach—an artist and draftsman for the state highway of Nevada. Other than that, Shellbach (sometimes spelled Shellback) received nothing of the fame to match Benny Benson.

Geography

Alaska dethroned Texas as the largest state in the Union on January 3, 1959. Likewise, Nevada is no pushover. She has always been in the top 10 largest states, currently positioned at seventh. Further, Nevada retains her own undisputed king-size championship belt to lord it over the other states. Of internal states that do not have a coastline or international border, Nevada is the largest. Consequently, as Alaska is king of the hill, Nevada is king within the hill.

Alaska and Nevada contrast like fire and ice, or rather, summer and winter. Both states get the four-season treatment, but parts of Alaska are in perpetual winter, and a certain section of Nevada is always summer. There are comfy cities in both states with malls and parking lots, but each state has a reputation for rugged living. It takes a special kind of inner strength and intelligence to adapt to the more unpopulated regions beyond the city limits.

Traveling through the bush of either state requires special prep and training. Besides the extremes of weather, wildlife can be downright deadly. The bold bears of Alaska can easily make a lunch out of us, just as the snakes and scorpions of Nevada can bring down the fit in a heartbeat. Nonetheless, the natural beauty and wonders of either state are soul stunning. Alaska aspens and pines have a haunting beauty, and a match in Nevada are the bristlecone pine trees. The bristlecone pines of the desert are long lived ancient beings that have borne witness to the opposite end of Buck Rogers and are of the 25th century BC, meaning, some of the trees are as old as the foundations of the pyramids of Giza. Some of these trees were around when the pyramids were being built and long before a single stone was laid in some distant wall in China.

And speaking of pyramids, one of the great natural wonders of the U.S. is in Nevada: Pyramid Lake. As the name indicates, there's a unique landform that is shaped like a pyramid, called Wono by the Natives, which is guarded by an equivalent *"American Sphinx"* known to the local Paiute Indians as Stone Mother. In concert, the American mountain of mountains is found in Alaska. Mount Denali is the highest peak in all of North America at 6.190 km (3.84 miles) above sea level. Mt. Denali, formerly known as Mt. McKinley, changed names in 2015. Nevertheless, there are some who miss the old Mt. McKinley name—mostly a few persons from Ohio and some of McKinley's descendants. Perhaps the humble thing to do is to rename the national park as McKinley National Park?

Another unique aspect of Nevada is she crosses lanes with all the continents of the Old World. Nevada has latitudes parallel to Europe, Africa, and Asia. Thus, southern Nevada is familiar with hot Algerian summers, while northern Nevada knows a chilly winter's night as it is in France. Likewise, Nevada has a similar latitude and climate to Western Asia in countries like Iraq, Iran, and especially Afghanistan.

In a groovy kind of map room alignment, as seen in the film *Raiders of the Lost Ark*—when Indy uses the perfectly aligned staff of Ra to find the location of the secret chamber of the lost ark, Alaska is perfectly aligned on an axis of "Masonic Enchantment." Like Nevada, Alaska is aligned with the three continents, not by latitude, but by longitude. Reason being, Alaska is on the other side of the *trinity zone*. The *trinity zone* is defined as the longitudes where Europe, Asia, and Africa overlap. It is here that Africans, Asians, and Europeans eat, pray, and love at the same time.

The *trinity zone* is located at the area of latitude in the Eastern Hemisphere between the most western point of Asia and the most eastern point of Africa. The most western point of Asia is in Turkey at Cape Baba 24°04' east, while the most eastern point of Africa belongs to Somalia upon the Horn of Africa 51°27' east. Thus, there is 25° of physical-temporal-land unity between Asia, Africa, and Europe.

European countries partially in the *trinity zone* include Russia, Finland, Estonia, Belarus, Ukraine, Romania, Bulgaria, and Greece. African countries in this zone include Egypt, Sudan, East Congo, and South Africa. Asian countries in this area include Yemen, Iran, Saudi Arabia, and Kazakhstan. Most importantly, nations wholly within this area include Israel, Jordan, Lebanon, Syria, Iraq, Azerbaijan, and Kuwait. It just so happens that Alaska is aligned on the other side of the world with the *trinity zone*. Basically, Whittier and Prudhoe Bay, Alaska, are aligned on the opposite meridian of Israel and Jerusalem.

This alignment of Alaska and Nevada with the Old World by latitude and longitude is reflective of a key aspect found in Freemasonry. On a Masonic tracing board, items are positioned in complementary pairs to illuminate secrets and hidden knowledge. Most Masonic tracing boards have a black-and-white checkered floor, which has a similar association with the Taoist yin-yang icon, the black-and-white circle divided by a wave and complementary colored dots. Another symbol of duality often found on Masonic Boards is the sun and moon, usually positioned in the opposite, top corners. Finally, two devices that are universal to nearly all Masonic boards are the measuring level and plumb ruler.

The traditional masonic level looks like an upside-down T and is used to test if something like a table surface is flat. With a perfectly level surface, a marble placed on it would simply lay still and not roll off. The plumb ruler is shaped like a ruler, but it is used to determine if a wall is standing erect. Both the measuring level and the plumb ruler have a string attached to one end and a free hanging metal pointer at the other. As gravity pulls on the heavy metal pointer, also called a plumb, the mason or carpenter can get a reading if his work is level and square. As long as the string is in alignment with the central groove, things can be understood as on the level or plumb. Modern levels no longer use strings, but rather a bubble suspended in a colored liquid gives horizontal and vertical aspects without the need of a string and plumb. Or better yet, modern masons and carpenters use digital tools with lasers and such.

So how does Masonic imagery relate to the longitude and latitude of Alaska and Nevada? Nevada is level with the three continents of the Old World by latitude—like a Masonic level. Concordantly, Alaska is aligned with Asia, Africa, and Europe by longitude—like a Masonic plumb.

As a bonus, there are five nations that have part of their territory at the Nexus. This is where Asia, Africa, and Europe are on the level and plumb with regard to each other; where they equally overlap by both latitude and longitude. When entering this area, one can say that Asia is west of Europe, Africa is north of Europe, Europe is east of Asia, and Europe is south of Africa. This slot-shaped area of the Earth is the Nexus, where the definitions of Easterner, Westerner, and Black and White melt and merge.

In order to find out which nations have territory in the Nexus, an old-fashioned atlas will be handy. Trust me—doing it the old-fashioned way with a book may take more time, but you'll get that exciting map room revelation-like feeling when you draw the lines. You'll also need to know the most northern and southern points of Africa and Europe, respectively, on the continent. The nations that cross into the geographic Nexus—where Asia, Africa, and Europe all see eye to eye and no one can get one over on the other—are at cultural calibration points for civilization, whose histories go way, way back when long, long ago the Earth was in a different realm of the galaxy far, far away.

History

Nevada was a prize of conquest during the Mexican American War (1846-1848), born out of Mexican Alta California. Since Nevada was sparsely populated, there was little fighting within her borders. Thus, Nevada was never on the battlefront of international nations. Even before 1776, none of the colonial powers clashed for its ownership. However, internal conflicts between Native versus Newcomers came to pass when Nevada became American.

The Paiute Wars began just before the U.S. Civil War in 1860. There were two battles at Pyramid Lake in 1860. The Paiute Indians would lose and were confined to reservations. But the Paiute were able to retain control over Pyramid Lake with the Great Stone Mother.

Alaska peacefully became American territory without acrimony between kingdoms and nations. Russia, being strapped for cash, foolishly gave up their claim on Alaska. Initially the American public thought they were bamboozled by the multimillion-dollar deal for an icy wasteland, but before the century closed, Seward's Folly became Seward's Golly. When the Cold War started, Alaska became a priceless territory—and Seward was nearly killed by the team of assassins who killed Lincoln. Imagine if the dagger had done more damage and Alaska had remained in Russian-to-Soviet-to-Russian hands? Mr. Seward purchased Alaska after Lincoln was assassinated.

Two heritage points of concordant caliber are two awesome relays of amazement: the Pony Express and Iditarod. The Pony Express became an iconic part of American heritage on April 1860. But this mail route only lasted for about a year before going out of business on October 1861. During operations, a package could reach from the Atlantic to Pacific coast in less than two weeks. There were nearly 200 stations: five were base stations where riders could sleep, and the others were relay stations where tired horses were exchanged for fresh ones. Relay stations were about five to 25 miles apart, depending on the terrain. In one day, an average rider rode about 75 miles per day.

The eastern terminus of the Pony Express was St. Joseph, Missouri, which is just east next to the Kansas-Nebraska-Missouri tristate area and north of Kansas City. The western terminus was Sacramento, California. In between were the states of Kansas, Nebraska, Colorado, Wyoming, and Utah—but most importantly for this chapter was Nevada.

It was also in Nevada that the Paiute War and Pony Express collided. In early May 1860, the Williams Station was attacked by Paiutes, and a battle with the U.S. Army was fought later that month. But it wasn't the Natives that ended the

Pony Express; rather, the telegraph ended its operations. Nonetheless, the Pony Express is well remembered as an iconic set piece of America's Old West. And no doubt, Nevada was the most perilous part of the journey, especially during the dog days of summer.

It was during the frozen heart of winter that another story of a different sort, also a relay, would enchant the history books—the 1925 serum run to Nome, Alaska. Instead of a relay for mail, this was a life and death relay. In the winter of 1924 to 1925, Nome experienced a diphtheria outbreak. At that time Nome had a population of about 1,500. The town only had one doctor, Dr. Curtis Welch. Unfortunately, the hospital only had expired diphtheria antitoxin. Dr. Welch had ordered more fresh diphtheria antitoxin, but the winter ice closed the port before it could arrive.

After several children died from the disease, an SOS was sent across the nation. Sending the medicine by airplane was not possible, as this was a relatively new technology and flying planes in the depth of Alaska's winter was never done. Consequently, a relay of dog sled teams was put into place.

Twenty mushers and over 150 sled dogs would come to rescue Nome and save countless lives. Dog sled teams faced blizzards, -70 degree temperatures, gale force winds, and the Alaskan wild. Nearly half the mushers were Athabascan Natives. These mushers did not have cell phones or GPS. Radio was around, but it was a relatively new thing. The crisis at Nome, Alaska, was perhaps the first live news action-tragedy that gripped the world, like when the 2018 Thailand soccer team was trapped in a cave, or the 2010 rescue of the Chilean miners. People were informed of the daily progress as to the number of sick and persons who died. The official death toll was five to seven, but Dr. Welch estimated about 100 additional deaths among "the Eskimo camps outside the city."

The 1925 dog sled relay for life began at Nenana, Alaska, on January 27, 1925. A day earlier, 300,000 units of forgotten antitoxin were discovered in Anchorage, and they were quickly sent to Nenana by rail. The 1,085 km (674 miles) journey would normally take more than six weeks to complete, but it was miraculously completed in five and a half days. The trip would cost the lives of several dogs and a few frostbitten fingers. On the final leg, the sled capsized, and

THE FLAG REVELATION

the serum was nearly lost in the snow, but that winter several American legends were born: Balto and Togo.

Balto received the lion's share of glory as the lead dog on the final leg of the journey. Balto was a Siberian Husky who belonged to Leonhard Seppala. Balto was born in Nome in 1919. Seppala was born in Norway (1877). Balto retained his role as Alaska's top dog. So popular was his fame that a statue of Balto in Central Park in Manhattan was dedicated to the canine on December 17, 1925. In 1995, Disney released an animated movie produced by Universal entitled *Balto*, and the titular character was voiced by Kevin Bacon. Unlike Lassie or Rin Tin Tin, Balto was real, and he was able to retire in Cleveland, Ohio. Balto went to heaven, as all dogs do, on π Day, 1933. However, you can see his earthly remains at the Cleveland Museum of Natural History—Balto was mounted by a taxidermist and encased in glass after his death. His remains went on tour back to Alaska twice, in 1998 and 2017, and there is even a movement to bring Balto back home to Alaska permanently.

However, Balto's owner figured the top dog of the ordeal was Togo. Togo was named after the underdog Tōgō Heihachirō of Japan, who is considered the Nelson of the East and who brought the Japanese to victory as commander of the Japanese Imperial Fleet during the Russo-Japanese War (1904-1905). Togo started life as a sickly pup and showed little sign of being a lead sled dog. Togo was the difficult, mischievous, and troublesome bad dog type. Eventually he was given away as a pet at six months old, but Togo smashed through a glass window and ran several miles back to his original home. This was the first sign that Togo was a special type of hyper-curious and clever dog. Togo would later prove his worth as a lead dog of peculiar intelligence, one who knows when to disobey the master for the sake of the master's life.

During the 1925 diphtheria serum run, Togo was the lead dog when Leonhard "Lion Hart" Seppala was the musher for the longest leg of the relay at 91 miles. Togo's leg was perhaps the toughest leg, with up and down ledges, including a peak named Little McKinley Mountain, which rises to 1,200 feet. After the relay, Togo enjoyed fame as well and went on tour across the West Coast, making appearances at department stores and even gained a spot on a Lucky Strike cigarette campaign. Togo was also awarded a gold medal by Roald Amundsen, the first man to the South Pole. Togo was retired in "tropical" Poland Spring, Maine, and like Balto, was called to heaven on December 5, 1929. More recently, Togo's story was retold in a Disney movie *Togo* (2019) that starred William Dafoe as "Lion Hart" Seppala. No doubt, life is like a bag of biscuits; you never know what the master will throw next.

At 674 miles, the 1925 serum run was three times shorter when compared to the 1,900-mile Pony Express of 1860. Nonetheless, both runs left a glittering echo on the American psyche. They are exciting, universal stories that appeal to any nation. The 1860-1861 Pony Express was a domestic interstate American tradition, while the 1925 serum run would enchant international audiences. The Pony Express was an amazing race to connect a nation, coast to coast, while the Serum Run was a heroic race against certain death. Both were herculean endeavors, and demonstrate that ingenuity, resilience, and imagination are essential when times and people are pressed—and best of all, there is no bad guy to hate.

Providentially, the silver star of Nevada and the gold star of Alaska reflect epic moments in mineral wealth: the Comstock Silver Lode of 1859 and the Klondike Gold Rush of 1896. The Comstock Lode is named after Henry Comstock, who was the picture perfect "sanctimonious, illiterate, sassy, loudmouth," with a nickname of "Old Pancake." Mr. Comstock was quite the negative, stereotypically greedy American miner, but with one twist: he was actually Canadian. Henry Comstock was born in Trenton, Ontario, in 1820 and ended his life with his own pistol in 1870. But before Mr. Comstock's untimely exit, no doubt he had many a rip roaring high and low life adventures across the continent. Most importantly, the first American megabucks silver ore discovery would bear his name. It was near Virginia City, Nevada that this event took place, on the eastern slope of Mount Davidson near Lake Tahoe at the obtuse angle/border of California and Nevada.

The Comstock Lode took decades to unload—18 years after the initial rush of 1859, mining of silver ore peaked in 1877. The silver bonanza ended by 1880. Thanks to this mother lode of silver, Nevada became an official state quite rapidly. Nevada was signed in by Lincoln himself on Halloween in 1864. This makes Nevada a boo baby. Ask anyone with a birthday on Halloween, and they'll have six or seven interesting stories to tell; they really are an interesting group of people.

As the Old West was settling down, there was one last mega-city bust and rush for the miners, the Klondike Gold Rush of 1896. Sometimes called the Alaskan Gold Rush or Yukon Gold Rush, it too involved a meeting of Canadians and Americans. When news of the August 1896 gold discovery hit the West Coast, it was the last of a great stampede of roaming miners. The first strike was actually in Canada, in Yukon Territory at Rabbit Creek, which was later renamed Bonanza Creek. The Klondike River is wholly in Canada as a tributary to the Yukon River. Here is the funny concordance, as the Comstock Lode was discovered by a Canadian. Guess what? The Klondike Discovery claim was made by an American—George Washington Carmack from California. However, it was his brother-in-law Keish (Skookum Jim Mason), a Native American from Bennett Lake, Yukon, who was most likely the key master behind the whole operation. Carmack also earned some rather unflattering nicknames, such as "Squaw Man," since he married and socialized with First Nation peoples, aka Native Americans. Carmack married a Tagish Yukon Indian by the name of Kate. "Squaw Man" died literally as a happy fat-cat, with a 10 plus bedroom home at age 61 in Seattle, Washington. He might have gotten a few more years if it wasn't for his obesity and overall lack of good health.

The Klondike Gold Rush was initially centered in Canada, but subsequent strikes all over Alaska fell under the umbrella of the Klondike Rush namesake. The Klondike Gold Rush National Historical Park is found right at the upper nudge of the pot handle of Alaska. Although it was not a gold strike area, it was the staging point for the miners on their way to Dawson's Creek, Yukon, which was the core magnet city of the Klondike Gold Rush.

Eventually, gold rushes wholly within Alaska followed. From 1899 to1909, the Nome Gold Rush turned the capital of the Klondike Gold Rush at Dawson City into a ghost town. Nome's Gold Rush was unique since gold was lying on the beaches. And since beaches were not a part of the lot claim system, anyone could grab the gold where they found it. Instead of collecting seashells, people basically collected golden sand. Nome was literally the Gold Coast of America. The last rush of that era was the Fairbanks Gold Rush (1902-1911), putting Fairbanks on the map.

As technology changed the face of America, the demand for energy changed the contours of Alaska and Nevada. Two monumental civil engineering projects associated with these states are the Hoover Dam and the Alaska Pipeline. The Hoover Dam was a legacy gift from President Hoover, started in the early 1930s but completed during FDR's presidency in 1936. The dam bottled up the Colorado River and created the largest artificial lake in the U.S., Lake Meade. Today it continues to generate clean energy and is a major tourist attraction.

As for Alaska, the Trans-Alaska Pipeline was authorized by President Nixon in 1973, and it was finished in 1977. The pipeline begins within the Arctic Circle on America's North Shore at Prudhoe Bay and terminates at Valdez, Alaska. The feat of the Alaska Pipeline is that it traverses the state across a harsh arctic wilderness. Not only is it an energy lifeline for Alaska, but for the nation.

Coincidentally, both monumental civil engineering projects were spurred under economic stress. The Hoover Dam was passed and built during the Great Depression (domestic issue), while the Oil Crises of 1973 caused by the Yom Kippur War between Israel and Egypt-Syria (international issue), motivated the U.S. to tap Alaska's energy reserves. And go figure, Prudhoe Bay is on the opposite meridian of Jerusalem, Israel/Palestine.

Besides providing energy, Alaska and Nevada are no strangers to the release of thermonuclear radiation. Nevada was first nuked in 1951 during Operation Ranger and subsequently nuked every year until 1992. Thus, from 1951 until 1992 Nevada felt the wrath of over 1,000 atomic age nuclear weapons except for one year in 1959. There are hundreds of craters in Nevada's Nuclear Test Site (NTS), the most famous being at Yucca Flats. Although the government has stopped nuclear testing In Nevada, subcritical nuclear testing continues.

Alaska learned about the joy of nuking oneself in 1971 during the Grommet nuclear testing series at Amchitka Island, Alaska. Amchitka is/was due south of the Soviet Union and was the closest to rival chest-pounding ceremony of the

Cold War. Although Nevada was nuked over a thousand times, the massive underground Alaska nuke at the USSR's doorstep was the "hold my beer" moment for Alaska—it was the single largest underground explosion ever conducted by the U.S. on November 6, 1971. Thus, Alaska holds the record for the biggest under-the-sheets, self-pounding blast across the 50 states.

Speaking of somewhat shameful and controversial practices, Nevada is where the oldest profession is allowed to operate openly. All religions condemn the sale of romantic services, but in a few counties within Nevada, it is regulated commerce like the purchase of tobacco or marijuana. In reality, the exchange of pleasures for cash is present in all major metropolitan cities big and small but usually on the down-low, with some sort of quasi-police regulation. The difference is that Nevada is the only state that allows it to operate safely under the protection of law. As for Alaska's unique freedoms, Alaska was the first state to legally defend a constitutional right to privacy with certain amounts of marijuana in 1975. After some flip flopping, it was not until 2014, when recreational use of this ancient herb was legalized.

Culture

Levi jeans and the parka are fabrics woven into the identity of all things American. First came American jeans, blue-collar work pants with metal rivets. The story of jeans began shortly after the Comstock Silver Rush of 1860. It begins with a Latvian immigrant, Jacob W. Davis, who was a tailor in Virginia City during the 1860s. Due to the population boom of miners, he found plenty of work and somewhere in the run for mineral wealth, he came up with the idea for reinforced copper riveted denim trousers. Apparently, there were weak points in the denim pants that needed a lot of repair, and a novel solution presented itself. So popular were Jacob jeans that he was able to go into business. However, he was not yet a rich man, and he needed major capital to move his business. He teamed up with his dry good's cloth supplier, Levi Strauss, and this dynamic duo put American pants on the map.

Blue jeans eventually became the de facto uniform of people doing work who needed light and durable leg protection. However, jeans leveled up in the 1950s thanks to James Dean and Marlon Brando. Marlon Brando starred in *The Wild One* (1953) where the iconic outlaw biker ideal was cast by Johnny Strabler, played by Brando. Subsequently jeans became charmed as a badass garment. It might have stayed a biker thing if it weren't for James Dean's *Rebel Without a Cause* (1955). James Dean starred as a misunderstood teen dealing with the dark gang-clique mentality of urban teenage life. *Rebel Without a Cause* was a 30-year precursor to suburban teen life pressure as seen in *The Breakfast Club* (1985). Thus, it was during the 1950s that jeans became an iconic symbol of youth counterculture. By the 1980s, marketing departments and sex appeal were added, in part due to the likes of Brooke Shields. Also, the Cold War made them iconic symbols of freedom. Thus, when the Cold War ended there was a mad scramble in Eastern Europe to wear pants that were once the domain of the cowboy, miner, blue-collar roughneck, biker, and cool youth.

Alaska's congruent contribution to the fashion world stems from the parka. This was originally an Inuit thing; a lighter coat made from caribou or seal skin, filled with down, and with a hood attached. You can thank the United States Air Force for bringing this design home, with the military issue snorkel parka. It was developed in the 1950s for use in cold zone operations like Alaska. The first issue snorkel parka was the USAF N-3B, with an attached hood. It was made with sage green DuPont flight silk and padded with a wool blanket.

But the American parka gained a big fashion credit during the Korean War with the military issue fishtail parka. It underwent several modifications, but the M-65 model became an icon of British Mod culture. Mod being short for Modernist, the term represents an iconic counter U.K. youth culture. Mods were precursors to the harder hippy counterculture of the later 1960s and early 1970s. The Mod look went something like this: a scooter, American blue jeans, and the iconic military surplus M-65 parka.

Alaska and Nevada have wide open spaces and clear views of the starry skies, and since the 1950s, tales have abounded about aliens. Nevada is famous for Area 51, a military site where it is rumored that a spaceship crashed and deceased alien bodies were recovered. Since then, it has become the fodder of several thousand books, movies, and TV shows. Alaska's primary alien encounter was a supposed *fourth kind* of interaction.

The first kind is just a sighting, the second kind is actual evidence, as is rumored to happen at Area 51, Nevada. The third kind is actual contact, made famous by Steven Spielberg. According to some residents of Nome, Alaska, from the 1960s to the mid-2000s, people were abducted by aliens and had odd dreamlike memories of a white owl peering in through the windows at night. Area 51 is a real place, but the supposed extra-terrestrial interactions are a different story.

Michelle Johnson (1965) from Anchorage, Alaska, and Mädchen Amick (1970) from Sparks, Nevada, are a pair of queens in Hollywood. Michelle Johnson starred in *Blame It on Rio* (1984), *Gung Ho* (1986), and *Far and Away* (1992). Mädchen was a lead star on the cult series *Twin Peaks* (1989-1991) and *Riverdale* (2017-2023).

Two Gen X minority women who were given head space on the big screen include Irene Bedard (1967) and Rutina Wesley (1978). Irene Bedard of Anchorage, Alaska, is of Inuit heritage. She was the voice of Disney's *Pocahontas* (1995) and became a star in *Smoke Signals* (1998). Rutina Wesley of Las Vegas is African American and is best known as Tara Thornton on HBO's *True Blood* (2008-2014). Rutina also starred on *Queen Sugar* (2016-2022), which aired on the Oprah Winfrey Network (OWN).

Joshua Morrow (1974) of Juneau, Alaska, and Kristoffer Polaha (1977) of Reno, Nevada, are two rugged men that exude Alaska and Nevada man-chismo. Morrow took over the role of Nicholas Newman on *The Young and the Restless* (1994-2023). Polaha has been a Hallmark hunk, appearing in six Hallmark movies and starred in *The Shift* (2023).

Two Gen X majority women to charm America are Annie Parisse (1975) of Anchorage, Alaska, and Charisma Carpenter (1970) of Las Vegas, Nevada. Charisma Carpenter starred as Cordelia Chase in *Buffy the Vampire Slayer* (1997-2002) and *Angel* (1999-2004) and has also starred in *Veronica Mars* (2005-2006). Annie Parisse's hits include *National Treasure* (2004) and recently starred in the movie *Paterno* (2018).

Two reality stars who capture the feels of the states are Ariel and Austin. Ariel Tweto from Unalakleet, Alaska, starred in the Discovery Channel's documentary about the Tweto family airline. The airline operates flights all across Alaska. The show *Flying Wild Alaska* (2011-2012) tracked her progress of getting her pilot's license. Austin Lee "Chumlee" Russell from Henderson, Nevada, was featured on History Channel's *Pawn Stars* (since 2009). Pawn shops are everywhere in America, but Nevada is heads and shoulders above all others with the business of pawning, thanks to the casino biz. Chumlee was initially portrayed as the butt of jokes for his lack of knowledge, but he has emerged as the breakout funny antihero with witty one-liners and comebacks—a fan favorite for his playful charm.

Two television shows that further echo the iconic identities of Alaska and Nevada are *Northern Exposure* (1990-1995) and *Las Vegas* (2003-2008). *Las Vegas* focuses on the earthly delights and dramas of Sin City while *Northern Exposure* created a quirky, original, and spiritual look at the television storyline and was one of the first shows to star Natives as more than just background characters and allowed indigenous perspectives to take center stage in an organic way, without superficial politically correct rancor.

Full fields of blue charged with stars of silver and gold unite these states of wide-open spaces. These simple flags are decorated with a large lode star in each corner, which reflect the harmonious whole of heaven and earth, as it is now known that once upon a time, silver and gold are forged in the furnace of Father Sky from hydrogen in forgotten stars long, long ago, and star systems far, far away. From the sparse and spacious tundra to the barren serenity of the desert, life happens, as it is written in the dance of atoms and code of chemicals—be it the heart of a star or the surface of Mother Earth. Nevada and Alaska's Zen landscapes are able to speak free from the noise and competing clutter of civilization and are further echoed with such similar yet distinct somber state sigils.

seven

IDAHO & MINNESOTA

Everlasting Inner Beauty vs. Fleeting Outer Beauty

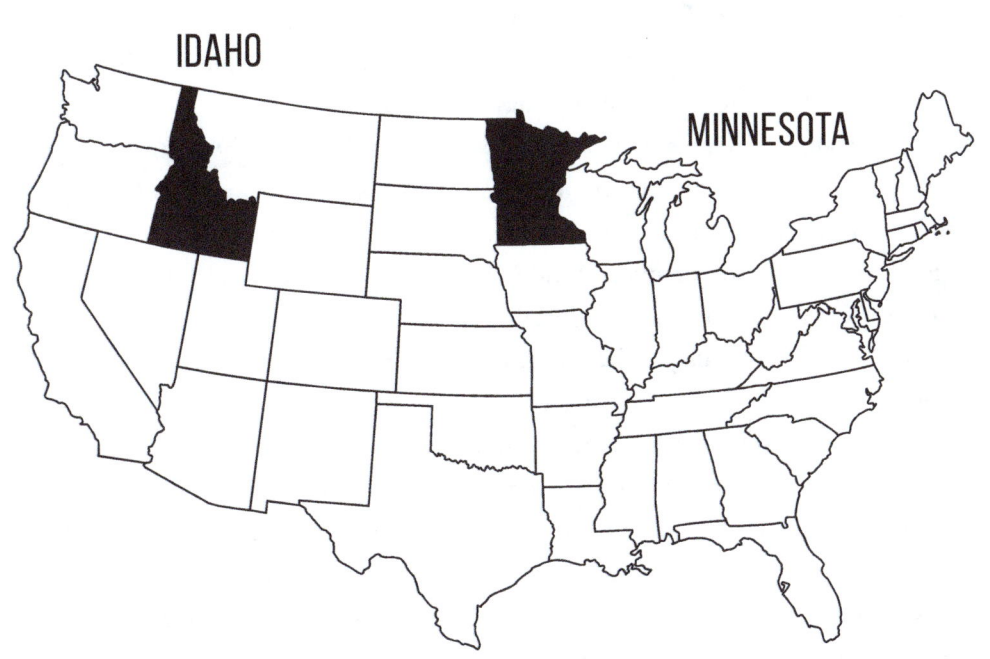

IDAHO

For many, the classical flags of Idaho and Minnesota are a complex beauty, hard on the eyes. *Is it true that beauty is in the eye of the beholder?* Nevertheless, these flags create a perpetual bridge of connectivity outside of time between Idaho and Minnesota, no matter what change may or has come.

The complex designs of the state seals congeal like a fluffy yin and yang wedding cake. As Idaho honors male and female, Minnesota pays homage to the indigenous and immigrant. As men and women unite to share their lives in good times and bad, a perpetual union between locals and move-ins plays out in every community in its own special way.

Idaho is the only flag of the 50 states to feature a co-ed team of supporters. The woman on the left is wearing a white dress with a balance-scale in her left hand and a freedom staff in her right, showing that she embodies the Goddesses of Liberty and Justice. The man is dressed in a brown worker outfit holding tools, a shovel in his left hand and a pickaxe in his right, illustrating the hard-working man who is willing to do back-breaking work. Underneath the woman is a cornucopia of succulent sweet fruit, while at the foot of the man is a horn of plenty with starchy vegetables. For Minnesota, another sharp dichotomy is seen

MINNESOTA

with the immigrant settler from Europe in the foreground plowing the earth with the indigenous person of the New World on horseback.

Natives and women have been present since the birth of the United States. However, their roles in the American Dream provide contrast and clarity to the lofty ideas brought forth by the original Constitution. In a perfect array of numerical synchronicity, the 19th Amendment, which gave women the right to vote, was passed in 1919. It went into effect on August 28, 1920, and women were legally allowed to vote across the nation for the first presidential election in 1920. Native Americans were last in line when voting rights were federally established, regardless of tribal status, across the nation in 1924.

In a fateful bouquet of grace, the state flowers are visible on both flags. Minnesota's lady slipper forms a wreath around the central seal. A red ribbon is interlaced into the seal with two dates and the state motto visible. The date of 1819 refers to the foundation of Fort Snelling, which is located at the conjunction of the Mississippi River and the Minnesota River at Minneapolis-St. Paul. The date of 1893 refers to the first state flag, which previously had a white field with a large red bow at the bottom, and the 19 stars were on the field. The red ribbon that crosses into the central seal has the state motto written in French, "*L'Étoile du Nord*," which means "Star of the North" or "The North Star."

The state flower of Idaho, the wild syringa, is a bit harder to notice. The blossoms of wild white syringa are on the feminine side, behind the uncut wheat, next to the woman's right elbow. Likewise, Idaho's motto is visible on a white ribbon near the top that reads "ESTO PERPETUA," which means "Perpetually and Forever," as it is with men and women to create families and nations.

Idaho's flower, *Philadelphus lewisii*, received its scientific name in honor of Meriwether Lewis since he wrote down the first description in 1806 during his eponymous expedition with Clark. However, this flower has several names: Lewis's mock-orange, Indian arrowwood, or syringa. The name mock-orange is appropriate since the blossoms smell like oranges. Both flowers are native to North America and are protected within their respective states: it's illegal to uproot the lady slipper or mock orange on public lands.

The national motto is apparent when considering the stars upon each flag: Out of One, Many: E Pluribus Unum. Idaho has "One" white star at the bottom of its seal, while Minnesota has the "Many," via the five clusters of yellow stars that make up one large star made from 19 smaller stars. The number 19 refers to Minnesota as the 19th state after the original 13. Coincidentally, if you calibrate Idaho's entry into the newly restored union (after the cessation of slavery) and also count the readmitted states, Idaho is the 19th of the new states born free, after the 13th Amendment. But in the standard way of counting, Minnesota is the 32nd state in the Union, while Idaho is the 43rd state. In order to get, of a nation born-in-bondage 19th state to 19th state of a nation free of slavery state symmetry, one must count Georgia two times. After Georgia was admitted the first time in 1868, several elected Black congressmen of Georgia were kicked out of office. Consequently, Georgia was kicked out of the union, and was readmitted a second time in 1870, after fixing her unfair racial embargo.

By mere luck of the draw, quite literally, both flags were designed by women. Idaho's flag was officially adopted on March 12, 1907, but the state seal was designed in 1890 by Emma Sarah Etine Edwards from California. Emma S. E. Edwards was the daughter of Missouri Governor, John Cummins Edwards.

When Emma S. E. Edwards stopped in Boise, she loved it so much she stayed and became an art teacher. Later, she was invited to submit a design for the state seal of Idaho in a competition organized by the First Legislature of Idaho. Emma's design was selected as the winner, and she received a $100 reward from the governor. She later married James G. Green but did not have any children. Emma Sarah Etine Green died on January 6, 1942. Thus, Idaho's Mrs. Green is the patron saint of American Art Teachers. Minnesota's state flag came into existence when the 1893 Chicago World's Fair took place, and a flag was needed to represent Minnesota. The Women's Auxiliary Board was selected to design a flag through a contest. Over 200 entries were submitted, but the one designed by New York native Amelia Hyde Center was selected.

Amelia Hyde Center's flag was slightly different to the version above. The front was white, and the back was blue; both sides had the same design. The red ribbon flowed from the inner seal like a wreath out upon the field. Center's design was modified in 1957, when the outer ribbon strands were cut and the circular seal was modified, giving it a more masculine look. However, this version makes the outer ring look like a life preserver, and the composite star is harder to detect. The big red bow is still visible at the bottom of the ring, which is sometimes mistaken for a red flower. But two elements of her original contribution were retained: the large composite star and the lady slipper wreath.

Both states also feature scenes down by a river. In Idaho's flag, the inner shield of a river flows down from the mountains, which is balanced with the river by the small waterfall in Minnesota's flag. A forest is barely visible on the lower mountains of Idaho, but one large tree is a standout at the edge of the bluff by the river. In a similar position, a forest is positioned on the right side of the bank of Minnesota, but it has three trees that stand tall above the others.

Within the inner shield of Idaho is a man with a horse plowing the field by the river, which doubly echoes the plowing man in Minnesota. However, the plowing man of Minnesota is doing it by himself in his bare feet, which matches back to the barefoot woman of Idaho.

The story of Betsy Ross as the woman behind the stars of our national banner is the delightful stuff of legends and bestows a hot and deliciously debated honor on one of America's Founding Mothers. However without any doubt, the story and stars at the foundation of Idaho's and Minnesota's state flags trace their genesis to the hands of women.

Geography

You may be familiar with the elementary humdinger, "What did Miss Issippi sip?" The answer is "a Minnie Soda!" This figuratively and literally makes sense, geographically speaking. Reason being, the Mississippi River begins in Minnesota. The headwaters of the Mississippi begin at Lake Itasca in Clearwater County, Minnesota. Thus the Mississippi truly sips from Minnesota, and the opposite southern twin cities of Minneapolis-St. Paul could be New Orleans-St. Bernard.

Consequently, St. Cloud, Minnesota, is hereby matched with St. Rose, Louisiana, as two fleeting and lovely, Zen-inspired objects of heaven and earth, by a rose and a cloud, conjoined by the Father of Waters, should the tears of heaven shed over in Minnesota fall upon the earth, whose somber sadness is destined to sustain the soul of a bittersweet rose of Louisiana.

By the good smile of fate, there is a reprisal for this Minnesota sippy soda joke. It's a joke fashioned in the style of the bear who is fuzzy but that's better described as "fawzy": "Which zone did Ida hoe?" The correct answer is "The airy zone, uh … a waka, waka, waka," as a certain puppet might say. Although Arizona and Idaho are not connected by any sort of river, they are at the north and south end of the Rockies.

Idaho and Minnesota are big states and nearly the same size. By the sweet kiss of synchronicity, both hold a 14th place title. In total area, Idaho is 14th. But if you ignore the surface area of lakes and only focus on land, Minnesota is 14th.

Both states share a border with Canada at the 49th and are completely north of the most southern point in the Canadian mainland. This puts Idaho and Minnesota in the exclusive Chilly Bangers Club (CBC), which puts them in the crosshairs of jokes about hockey and blistering winters. In order to belong in the CBC, a state needs to be completely north of Canada's most southern continental point, Point Pelee. Ontario can take on more heat and always beat these two in a limbo contest, but Idaho and Minnesota can hold their ground in a snowball fight against Canada.

Relative to most of the states, Idaho and Minnesota are considered cold ice box states, but on the global scale, they're smack in the middle as international temperate states. Reason being, the 45th parallel north crosses their states. The 45th is the halfway "50-yard line" in between opposite climatic end zones: the equatorial tropics and freezing north pole. Thus, Idaho and Minnesota get a full-bodied four-season treatment. Due to the wide range of seasons, some animals turn white in the winter—like the long-tailed weasel and the snowshoe hare.

Though states south of Point Pelee of Canada have winters that hit hard every so often, this is not the case for Idaho or Minnesota. This allows for true icy blue winter athletes to rise from these states. Due to differences in terrain, cross-country skiing is king in Minnesota and alpine skiing is the go-to in Idaho. This dichotomy was popularly illustrated with Picabo Street, who was born in Triumph, Idaho. Street was born in 1971 and won the gold in the super giant slalom (super-G) at the 1998 Olympic Games in Nagano, Japan. Super-G skiers reach the bottom of the course via gravity, which can accelerate them through gates at speeds of over 70 mph. In contrast, Minnesota provides the perfect environment for cross-country or Nordic skiing. Speed is not provided by gravity but rather by the skier herself. Born in 1991, Jessie Diggins of St. Paul, Minnesota, won the gold in Korea at the 2018 Pyeongchang Olympics with the team sprint cross-country event.

Two natural wonders that match with sinful names are Hells Canyon, Idaho, and Devil's Kettle, Minnesota. Hells Canyon earns its name because, during the summer, temperatures soar into the 90s and 100s. Devil's Kettle is a strange waterfall where the Brule River splits at a fork. The eastern side falls like a normal waterfall, but the west side empties into a hole where the water seems to disappear. Of the objects thrown into it, none have ever resurfaced.

Waterfalls are numerous in both states, and Shoshone Falls is the perfect match for Minnehaha Falls. Shoshone Falls is a spectacular waterfall that is dubbed the Niagara of the West, making Niagara Falls the Shoshone of the East.

Minnehaha Falls is not the biggest waterfall, but its fame is lasting as it inspired Henry Wadsworth Longfellow to write his epic poem "The Song of Hiawatha." Located in the heart of downtown Minneapolis, Minnehaha Falls is a spectacular sight when it freezes over, yet Longfellow never visited Minneapolis. Both states have a quirky abundance of famous places named after falls. For Idaho, there are Idaho Falls, Twin Falls, Post Falls, and American Falls. In Minnesota, there are International Falls, Thief River Falls, Redwood Falls, and Little Falls.

Further, Idaho and Minnesota have state borders that follow the continental divides. The East-West Continental Divide of the Atlantic and Pacific is on Idaho's eastern border, just south of Montana's nose, the wiggly border south of the nostrils marks the East-West Continental Divide. If you didn't know, the western border of Montana makes the profile of a face. Fatefully, Minnesota is positioned at the North-South Continental Divide. Minnesota has rivers that flow south to the "Gator Gulf of Mexico" and north to the "Polar Bear Hudson Bay." On Minnesota's western border is a tiny nose that sticks into South Dakota. This nose outlines the North-South Continental Divide. The top half of the nose is made up of Lake Traverse in Traverse County, while the bottom half of the nose makes up Big Stone Lake in Big Stone County. Just in between these lakes is where waters flow either toward pelicans or polar bears at Browns Valley, Minnesota—the tip of the nose. Likewise, you can imagine the state of Minnesota looking like the bust of a man with a colonial cap and square beard, facing westward. To a lesser extent, Idaho has a similar profile of a miner with a square beard facing west, with the nose being Washington County, and Montana and Wyoming being big bushy hair.

Both states retain unique keystone titles that connect America. Minnesota is the Keystone State of the Mississippi River. Reason being Minnesota is on the east and west bank of the Mississippi. But most importantly, Minnesota has the cap, since she is home to the headwaters of the Mississippi. When Minnesota became a state in 1858, the Mississippi River became a wholly 100 percent, all-American part of the U.S. since it was no longer a territory or unorganized region anymore. Similarly, when Idaho became a state in 1889, the East and West Coasts were contiguously united instead of being a nation connected by territories. This makes Idaho the coast-to-coast Keystone State. Finally, both have look-alike super-sized cousins in Canada. The look-alike cousin for Minnesota is the province Manitoba, while Idaho's is Yukon.

The interstate that connects Idaho and Minnesota is Interstate 90. It unites Coeur d'Alene, Idaho to Alberta Lea, Minnesota, from the bottom of Idaho's gun barrel to the southern foot of Minnesota. Alberta Lea is at the same latitude of Boise, while Coeur d'Alene matches Red Lake.

Minnesota shares several dozen lakes with Canada, but the primary lake of division along the 49th is Lake of the Woods. Likewise, Idaho also has a small body of water that naturally separates the U.S. and Canada. Just off the northwestern peak of Snowy Top Mountain, Idaho, is the "Pond of the Forest."

A natural balance to the Craters of the Moon National Monument is the Canadian Shield area of Minnesota. The Craters of the Moon is a beautiful otherworldly lava field. But what exactly is the Canadian Shield? This area of land has a thin layer of soil where the hard bedrock is usually exposed. Other states that are a part of the Canadian Shield include Wisconsin, North Dakota, and upstate NY. But nearly half of Minnesota is a part of the "Minnesota Shield." The Canadian Shield has basically shielded Canada and northern Minnesota from human settlement, since agriculture is a challenge due to the general lack of a top layer of soil.

History

Idaho and Minnesota have extra credit associations with the U.K., which were maintained long after the American Revolution ended in 1783. When the treaty of 1818 established the 49th parallel north, Minnesota and the Dakota twins gained the precious southernmost slice of the Hudson Bay Company. When this warmest region of Rupert's Land became a part of Minnesota, Minnesota also inherited all the history that went along with it. Thus, Minnesota has clear memories of the Red River Colony of Assiniboia, which was established in 1811. Not only that, but Minnesota also has an extended connection to Upper Canada via her arrowhead region. This region of Minnesota was a disputed territory between the U.S. and the U.K. from independence in 1776 until 1842.

The arrowhead region of Minnesota was witness to the creation of Upper Canada in 1791, which evolved into Ontario. Minnesota can even remember when Upper Canada (Ontario) and Lower Canada (Quebec) were united in 1841 as the super-sized Province of Canada. What this means is that a small portion of Minnesota was ruled by the three capitals of colonial Canada: Newark, Toronto, and Kingston. So, a little bit of that pre-confederation Canadian magic naturally spilled over into Minnesota.

It wasn't until 1842 that Minnesota was finally cut off from that quirky Canadian magic, when the border was resolved with the Webster-Ashburton Treaty. Perhaps this explains why Minnesota was destined to retain a bit of territory north of the 49th, the area known as the Angle. There is also just a wee bit of Canada in her character. Minnesota and Canada cannot recognize this element themselves, since they're too close to notice, but from the perspective of a southern state, it's quite apparent. If you ever wondered what it would be like if Canada joined the U.S., just visit upper Minnesota. The people are friendly, polite, and keep the cities clean, yet they do not have any qualms about being called "American."

As a small portion of Minnesota was connected to Upper Canada and the Province of Canada, Idaho was completely connected to the British Empire as the Columbia District. Idaho first fell under the shadow of the British Empire in 1790 in the aftermath of the Nootka Convention. With this agreement, Spain conceded that the British had the right to build forts in the Pacific Northwest, and settlements were needed to support a territorial claim. This agreement came about via the Nootka Crisis of 1789 that took place at Vancouver Island's Nootka Sound.

Before this agreement, when the British started to colonize the Pacific Northwest, the Spanish took aim at the British. Spain seized several ships and took the British crews prisoner. The British were outraged, and it nearly led to war. In the end, Spain conceded. Later in 1819, the U.S. claim to Idaho was further reinforced when Spain gave up on the Pacific Northwest and *handed off* her claim to the U.S. So in a weird way, the forts built by the Spanish in British Columbia and Vancouver Island were technically a part of the U.S. claim. However, they are now the forgotten, forlorn, and quirky heritage points of U.S. history. This works for Canada, as well, because the British forts built in Idaho and Minnesota are equally lost chapters of Canadian history.

Consequently, it is possible to back claim U.K. heritage for these states. Since the signing of the 1783 Treaty of Paris, these two states have extended bonus chapters of history with the U.K., since parts were administered by the British Government. Here is a small list of Prime Ministers who were able to impart a little bit of British class, or sass, over Idaho and Minnesota before final settlement in the 1840s.

William Cavendish-Bentinck, 3rd Duke of Portland (1783, 1807-1809)

Cavendish-Bentinck is the first prime minister to officially work with the U.S. as a separate nation. Cavendish-Bentinck was a switch hitter, politically speaking. During his first term in the 18th century, he was a Whig—a liberal of the Enlightenment—and in the 19th century he was a Tory, a patriotic conservative for the empire. Interestingly, Cavendish-Bentinck held every royal rank under a sovereign: duke, marquess, earl, viscount, and baron. In military terms this is like colonel, lieutenant colonel, major, captain, and lieutenant. In modern corporate terms, it's like vice president, regional manager, district manager, and store manager. Also note, in the U.K. earl is equivalent to count, but the word count is not used in England since it can easily be twisted into an insult, making the term earl an early example of politically correct speech. Thus, the purple vampire Muppet who teaches children to count is also an earl.

William Pitt the Younger, Prime Minister of the Arrowhead Region in Minnesota (1783- 1801, 1804-1806)

William Pitt was the son of William Pitt the older. The Pitt family puts a neat beginning and ending—a bookend of sorts as it pertains to U.S. history. William Pitt Sr. (1708-1778) was prime minister during the Stamp Act Crisis in 1765, while William Pitt Jr. (1759-1806) was prime minister when the 13 colonies reinvented themselves with the modern Constitution in 1788. Pitt Jr. welcomed the first president of the United States, George Washington, as an equal. Pitt Sr. was a liberal Whig, but Pitt Jr. was a solid Tory. It was during Pitt Jr.'s term that the modern British flag was born when it "united" as three "kingdoms" with Ireland. Consequently St. Patrick's Cross was added to the flag, which appears as a double recessive red X in four separated sections. St. Patrick's cross, which looks like the state flag of Alabama (as seen on the cover) for Ireland is recessive to the flags of England and Scotland, while St. Andrew's white X cross for Scotland is recessive to England. Only the cross of England, St. George, is unbroken in the modern U.K. flag.

Pitt Jr. attempted to secure Catholic freedom of worship but failed. William Pitt's keen leadership and stability gave the U.K. its proper footing after the confidence- and soul-crushing loss of the American colonies. Finally, the U.K. received a consolation prize for her loss, with the gift of Australia. As it settled that the Yanks had no intention of returning, the Aussies filled the void of heartbreak with a koala bear. The British officially founded New South Wales on January 26, 1788.

Henry Addington, First Viscount Sidmouth: Prime Minister of a Certain Section of the Dakota Twins (1801-1804)

Henry Addington was an old-school Tory who opposed Catholic emancipation. He was also a witness when French Louisiana was added to the United States in 1803. Rumor has it that the Muppet The Count has a sidekick known as Earl Addington who speaks with a Minnesota accent, wears colonial style clothes, and teaches children how to add.

William Grenville, First Baron Grenville: Prime Minister of Northeastern Maine (1806-1807)

Minister of Grenville was in office to oversee the abolition of the slave trade, which was enacted under his leadership in 1807. However, the end of slavery in the U.K. came about in 1833. Grenville was the odd Whig to become prime minister during the Napoleonic Wars. Whigs at this time were suspected to have revolutionary sentiments—namely, equality between men. Tories typically wanted to maintain the establishment and an unequal social hierarchy with a dominance of Anglican Anglo-Saxons of high birth to rule overall. Note, the end of the British slave trade in 1807 and slavery in the U.K. in 1833 happened when a liberal Whig was the prime minister.

Spencer Perceval: Prime Minister of the Minnesota's Red River Region (1809-1812)

Spencer is famous for being the first and only prime minister assassinated in office. Spencer Perceval was shot in the lobby of the House of Commons, the British equivalent of the U.S. House of Representatives, by John Bellingham. Bellingham was a merchant who was distraught that the British government refused to compensate him when he was imprisoned in Russia and singled out the chief executive as the root of his problems. Spencer Perceval was killed on May 11, 1812. One month after Perceval was assassinated, the War of 1812 began on June 18, 1812. Coincidentally, 46 years after his assassination at parliament, Minnesota became a state on May 11, 1858.

Robert Jenkinson, 2nd Earl of Liverpool: Prime Minister of a Nibble of Montana (1812-1827)

Jenkinson faced off with Madison during the last two chapters of the Napoleonic Wars, parts VI and VII. In the U.S., this is known as the War of 1812. During this War of 1812, the U.K. fought in the War of the Sixth and Seventh Coalition against France. The War of 1812 was basically a sideshow to the more pressing battle with Napoleonic France. In total, there were seven episodes of war with Napoleon (one for each day of the week), which is academically known as the Wars of Coalitions that lasted from 1792 to 1815. In the end, the U.S. has largely forgotten the War of 1812, since there are no epic movies or shows about this truly most epic of epic wars. But the fondest memory of the War of 1812 was the creation of the national anthem, "The Star-Spangled Banner."

When the War of 1812 ended, Jenkinson made peace with President Monroe, and the 49th parallel north was chosen as the dividing line in 1818, legally effective in 1819. As a consequence, the warmest, southern slice of the Hudson Bay Company became American while a northwestern cold cut of the Louisiana Purchase became Canadian. However, Minnesota's border was not settled. Her Arrowhead region remained contested and would have to wait another 34 years in limbo as disputed territory until August 9, 1842, but Idaho would have to wait four more years until 1846 when she was finally cut off from her Canadian inheritance when the joint occupation era of the Pacific Northwest ended.

Thus from 1818 until 1842, Idaho and Minnesota were simultaneously under the influence of the U.K. A portion of Minnesota was directly under Canadian influence, while Idaho was a part of British Columbia's history. The difference was that Idaho was legally both U.K. and U.S. territory, while the Arrowhead region of Minnesota was more like a child in a disputed custody battle with two alienated and divorced parents: Ontario and Minnesota. When the border was settled in 1842, Ontario and Minnesota were both losers and winners, since the contested region was divided in the middle.

The biggest losses for Ontario were Duluth and Grand Portage, while the U.S. lost Fort William and the south side of Thunder Bay. Idaho was also a hopeful contender for British Columbia until 1846 when the joint occupation era ended. One historic fort established by the Canadian North West Company includes Kullyspell House.

In a way, the people of Minnesota's Arrowhead and Red River region are the lost tribes of Canada. Perhaps this is part of the reason why the Minnesota accent is sometimes confused as Canadian. To hear good examples, just YouTube the movie *Fargo* (1996) or the Minnesota accent itself.

Every few years a major court case will seize the public's attention along divisive lines. In 1857, *Dred Scott v. Sandford* riled up the nation with the issue of slavery. However, the case also underpinned the nature of American citizenship along racial lines. Dred Scott was born in Virginia and was eventually taken to Missouri. He was then sold to a U.S. Army surgeon, Dr. John Emerson, and taken to Fort Snelling, which was free soil at the time. In 1846, Dred Scott sued for his freedom with abolitionist legal advisors. After an 11-year court battle, Dred Scott's case was finally heard by the Supreme Court in 1857. In a 7-2 decision, the Supreme Justices of the United States concluded that rights given in the U.S. Constitution were for Americans of European descent only. The much less-than-illustrious justices of America concluded that non-Whites, whether enslaved or not, were not entitled to the privileges of the U.S. Constitution, leaving a shameful stain on the robes of the Supreme Court and demonstrating the inherent fallibility of the U.S. justice system. The Supreme Court decided Dred Scott could not sue for his freedom on the account of his ethnic heritage, as he was of African origin. Nonetheless, Dred Scott was freed by manumission on May 26, 1857. Coincidentally, he died the same year Minnesota became a state in 1858.

Idaho also has a court case that highlights the struggle for racial equity. But this case involved a Chinese American doctor in Idaho. Since Idaho was a part of the Pacific zone, Chinese immigration into the state was initially quite high. In 1870, Chinese people made up 30% of Idaho's population. However, those numbers took a big dip when anti-Chinese sentiments took hold across the Pacific states. After the passing of the Chinese Exclusion Act in 1882, the Chinese presence in Idaho all but died out. There were a few Chinese, though, that were able to squeak out an existence. One in particular was C.K. Ah Fong from Guangdong Province, China. Dr. Ah Fong was a pharmacist who graduated from a Chinese medical school in the 1860s and was able to establish a business in Idaho. At his clinic he treated Chinese and Westerners alike. After a fire destroyed his business, he moved to Boise, Idaho, and set up a new clinic in 1892. But in 1899 his medical license was denied renewal on the account that doctors in Idaho were required to have U.S. citizenship and a degree from a recognized college. Dr. Ah Fong sued the Idaho Board of Medical Examiners, and his case made it to the Idaho Supreme Court. Unlike the Dred Scott case, Dr. Ah Fong won and was able to continue practicing medicine in Idaho. Dr. Ah Fong died in 1927.

Idaho proves that, even in times of unjust laws, justice happens, and sometimes lesser courts are superior to the Supreme Court. An extreme minority of Asians who flew under the radar were allowed to become citizens as long as they arrived before the Chinese Exclusion Act in 1882. Although the 14th and 15th Amendments of the Constitution allowed any race to become a citizen, this was effectively rolled back in by the Chinese Exclusion Act of 1882. It wasn't until 1952 that all Asians were effectively allowed to become naturalized American citizens.

THE FLAG REVELATION

Of historical tragedies to visit Idaho and Minnesota there are the Utter-Van Ornum tragedy and Dakota Mass Execution of Sioux warriors. The sad story for Idaho begins with a wagon train of settlers composed of over 40 souls, mostly children, heading west along the Oregon Trail. Apparently, the military escort that joined the party at Fort Hall, Idaho, had an episode of "wagon rage" with one of the pioneers. Consequently, the military escort of 22 dragoons left the wagon train near Twin Falls, Idaho. The assumed unhappy and spiteful departure had grave ramifications for the Utter-Van Ornum Party. It ultimately resulted in one of the most gruesome and deadliest tales along the Oregon Trail.

The environmental pressure of transient pioneers passing by depopulated local game, and by 1860 it would have an adverse effect on local Indians who depended on the plains for their survival. Essentially, wild game on the frontier were their versions of supermarkets, which pioneers raided without any regard to the locals who made their living from these natural stores and aisles of nature for millennia.

On September 9, 1860, the Utter-Van Ornum party was initially harassed by Indians attempting to steal their livestock. Indians attempted to cause a stampede, but the iconic circling of wagons was used to pen and protect the rattled animals, as well as to create a defensive perimeter. No loss of life occurred, and food was even offered to the hostile Indians as a toll. One mile later, the party was attacked again by a force of about 100 Indians—three pioneers died and no doubt many more Indians were killed. The next day they were attacked again on September 10 and were overwhelmed. The pioneers were forced to abandon the wagons and flee on foot.

One party of 27, mostly children, managed to reach the Owyhee River. There they made shelter as they were too weak to continue. Facing starvation, two men were sent out to get help, Goodsel Munson and Christopher Trimble. In mid-September, Goodsel Munson and Chris Trimble ran into three men along the Oregon Trail. The rescue party decided to send Chris Trimble back to the emaciated camp at the Owyhee River with horsemeat. Chris couldn't carry all the meat but was able to make it back to camp. Goodsel Munson, with the three men, continued on the trail and reached the Umatilla Agency on October 2.

In early October, about half the survivors at Camp Starvation left to find help. When they ran into a band of hostile Indians. The adults were killed and four of the Van Ornum children were taken as captive: three girls and one young boy, Reuben Van Ornum. Those who stayed at Camp Starvation continued to die day by day. In mid-October, the survivors were confronted with the crisis of cannibalism. After a short ceremony, the remaining survivors ate the children who had died.

One month and a fortnight would pass after the initial attack on September 9 until a rescue party finally found the remaining survivors at Camp Starvation on October 27. Chris Trimble was later found dead, assumed to have died by his captors. The three Van Ornum girls died in captivity, and Ruben Van Ornum was assimilated into Shoshone culture. He was eight when he was initially captured by the Natives. Reuben was later found in 1862 and custody was granted to his uncle Zachias. But Reuben, by then about age 10, could not re-adapt to White society and was returned to the Shoshone in 1870.

The equally sad chapter in Minnesota was the Dakota War. It erupted in the midst of the War Between the States in 1862, just as Ruben Van Ornum was repossessed by the Whites. The all too familiar pattern visited by states before and after were at the root cause of the Dakota War. Note, the Dakota belong to the Sioux family tree. Indians were forced to live a civilized life as farmers on reservations. They were supposed to be supplemented by the government with food and payments. However, as payments stalled, game populations reduced and severe crop failures on poor soils led to its natural tragic conclusion: war.

Direly needed payments for the Dakota arrived as St. Paul, Minnesota, in August 1862, but it was too late to stop the violence. A hunting party of four Dakota clashed with White settlers, which resulted in the death of five Whites. In this tense atmosphere, a Dakota War council convened, and they chose to continue on the warpath in the hope to drive the European settlers from Minnesota. As the war raged in the summer of 1862, over 350 settlers were killed in Minnesota. As with earlier conflicts between Natives and Newcomers since the Pequot War, the Natives were overpowered by the technologically advanced and more numerous Newcomers. The band of hostile Dakota were defeated on

THE FLAG REVELATION

September 23, 1862, at the Battle of Wood Lake.

The 392 Dakota warriors who surrendered were subsequently put on trial, and 303 warriors were sentenced to death. Lincoln reviewed the decision and reduced the number by basically "moving the decimal place" one place to the left, to 39.

Consequently, Minnesota holds the record for the largest mass execution in the U.S. On December 26, 1862, thirty-eight Dakota were hanged en masse, making it the largest mass execution by a U.S. government at Mankato, Minnesota. Congress then spitefully abolished the eastern Dakota and Winnebago reservations in Minnesota, as their treaties were declared null and void. Dakota Indians, innocent, friendly, and guilty were forced to flee Minnesota, including the Winnebago Tribes who had nothing to do with the conflict.

With the progress of time, the lines between Minnesota Natives and Newcomers would come to a more peaceable accord. In 1886 Congress undid their expulsion and reestablished Dakota lands in Minnesota, and much later the Winnebago (also known as the Ho-Chunk) were able to regain federal recognition of their original homelands in Wisconsin in 1963, a century after they were expelled from Minnesota, when anti-Indian hysteria overtook Minnesota in 1863.

In particular, a leader of mixed heritages arose to become a star state senator of Minnesota, Skip Finn. State Senator Finn was born in Cass Lake, Minnesota, in 1948. His father was a Newcomer of Norwegian heritage, of a branch on the larger Germanic family tree, while his mother was a Native, Ojibwe, also known as Chippewa, of a branch on the larger Algonquin family tree. Skip Finn was the first Native American, albeit an American Métis, to serve in the Minnesota Senate from 1991 until 1996.

However, the success of Skip Finn's legacy is a bittersweet note for Minnesota history. On the positive side, it reflects racial progress between Natives and Newcomers, but Harold Raymond "Skip" Finn was later convicted of fraud and resigned in disgrace. But there's still hope for the Finn family name. His daughter Jamie Becker-Finn (born October 20, 1982) became a member of the Minnesota House of Representatives in 2017. Jamie Becker-Finn not only reflects the dynamic of Native and Newcomer on Minnesota's flag, but she reflects the dynamic of man and woman of Idaho's flag.

Likewise, the first Native American born in Idaho to ever serve in the legislative halls of Idaho was a woman. Jeanne Givens from Plummer, Idaho, was born in 1951 or 1952. Givens was elected to the Idaho House of Representatives in 1985 and served until 1989. Jeanne Givens belonged to the Coeur d'Alene Tribe, which is a part of the greater Salish family tree.

More recently in Idaho a Native American woman was elected to the Idaho House of Representatives from 2014 to 2018. Paulette Jordan has Sinise, Nez Perce, and Yakama-Paulus ancestry. This makes her a mixed descendant of the Salish and Penutian family trees. Mary Kunesh-Pode of Saint Paul, Minnesota, is an American Métis Minnesota state senator and a member of the Standing Rock Sioux Tribe.

Two famously political agents from Idaho and Minnesota who were able to shine a blaring sparkle across America are Sarah Palin and Jesse Ventura. Sarah Palin was born in Sandpoint, Idaho, in 1964 and later became the governor of Alaska from 2006 to 2009. Jesse Ventura was born in Minneapolis, Minnesota, in 1951 and became the governor of Minnesota from 1999 to 2003. Before becoming a well-known media personality, Jesse Ventura served in the Vietnam War and later became a professional wrestler from 1975 until 1986 as The Body Ventura in the WWF/WWE. His charming and original perspective allowed him to smash his way into Hollywood. He is best noted for his roles in *Running Man* (1987) and *Predator* (1987). Governor Ventura is one of the few politicians to speak frankly and is a bit of a counterculture hero in opposition to the Republic and Democratic powers.

Sarah Palin's rise to fame came about in the 2008 presidential election. She was selected as the vice-presidential candidate with Republican presidential hopeful John McCain. With her folksy charm, she enchanted a large segment of America and later became the governor of her adopted state in the far north. Afterward, she became a TV personality with two shows. The first was TLC's *Sarah Palin's Alaska* (2010-2011) and on the Sportsman Channel *Amazing America with Sarah Palin* (2014- 2015). Governor Ventura and Governor Palin are two politicians on opposite sides of the spectrum, yet they share a rogue element as unconventional all-American patriotic superheroes.

Culture

Two women made in the Roaring 20s are the "bad girl" Lana Turner and the "girl next door" Judy Garland. Lana Turner from Wallace, Idaho, was born in 1921 and put the manna in the Lana. After breaking into Hollywood as a pin-up model, she became one of the biggest names in show business. As Hollywood scandals come and go through the ages, the biggest would hit Lana in 1958. Lana Turner entered into a rocky relationship with Johnny Stompanato—a veteran soldier in the underworld and the above-world. Johnny Stompanato fought in the Pacific Theater during WWII and afterward became an enforcer for Mickey Cohen in the Cohen crime family in Los Angeles. However, his physically abusive patterns caught up to him on April 4, 1958, when Lana Turner's daughter from a previous marriage, Cheryl Crane, stabbed him to death in defense of her mother as she was violently attacked. The media circus that followed was the sensational scoop of the decade. Lana's daughter Cheryl Crane was not charged, as her actions were deemed justifiable homicide. This incident actually boosted Lana Turner's career in Hollywood. She starred in *The Adventures of Marco Polo* (1938), *Honky Tonk* (1941), *Madame X* (1966), and *Witches' Brew* (1980).

At the other end of the spectrum is the wholesome Frances Ethel Gumm, better known as Judy Garland. Garland was born in Grand Rapids, Minnesota, in 1922. Garland became an established star for the ages when she played Dorothy Gale in the 1939 version of *The Wizard of Oz*. Yeah, that's right—*The Wizard of Oz* that we all know and love is a reboot. There were versions from 1910 and 1925. It was on the third try in 1939 that they got it right, making the idea of another remake tantamount to sacrilege. Funny how language changes—remakes are what old folks called reboots, no doubt when reboot becomes a tired term, a new word will be uploaded into the public that means the same thing. Also, it was in the 1930s that sound upgraded movies into the 3rd dimension, so a remake was in order. Judy Garland went on to star in a hundred more movies. Like Lana Turner, she had a rocky relationship with her husband Sidney Luft. Sidney Luft was also a tough-guy amateur boxer and bar-room brawler. Like Johnny Stompanato, he was a military man, having served in the Royal Canadian Air Force even though he was born in NYC. Judy Garland was able to sue for divorce on the grounds of mental cruelty and that he was physically violent when drinking. However, her life ended tragically when she died of an overdose of barbiturates in London on June 22, 1969, at age 47.

On the silver screen, Clancy Cooper (1906-1975) of Boise, Idaho, partners with Lew Ayres of Minneapolis, Minnesota (1908-1996). Both their stars have faded from the limelight of entertainment, illustrating the destiny of today's starlets. Nonetheless, their impact on Hollywood is of a similar caliber. Both men starred in over 100 films. Clancy Cooper starred in *The Wild North* (1952) and *Railroaded!* (1947). Cooper's roles closer to the modern era include *Sanford and Son* (1972).

Lew Ayres was another fixture in TV and Hollywood. His best role is perhaps as the German soldier in *All Quiet on the Western Front* (1930). When WWII broke out, Lew Ayres was a rare conscientious objector and served as a combat medic in the Pacific Theater. Ayres worked as co-stars with Jean Harlow in *The Iron Man* (1931) and *The Doorway to Hell* (1930) with James Ganey. He also starred in one of the first movies to combine live action with animation in Disney's *Servants' Entrance* (1934) during a musical dream sequence with Janet Gaynor, the OG of movies like Who Framed Roger Rabbit (1988) and a-ha's video to "Take On Me" (1984). Ayres certainly led a charmed life. The fateful burden of his parents' divorce paved a path to stardom. He moved to Southern California with his single mother and later joined a traveling band in Mexico while playing the banjo. Once in that limelight, he chased it to the end and became one of the big stars of his era. Modern shows that he was able to add his star power to include *Kung Fu* (1972-1945), *The Bionic Woman* (1976-1978), and *Battlestar Galactica* (1978-1979).

A generation later, John and James came from Idaho and Minnesota. John Donavan Cannon, born in 1922, was Chief Detective Peter B. Clifford on the

TV show *McCloud* (1970-1977) opposite Dennis Weaver. A few of the movies he starred in include *Cool Hand Luke* (1967), *Heaven with a Gun* (1969), and *Raise the Titanic* (1980). In the series finale of *The Fugitive* TV series (1963-1967), he was the star witness that cleared Dr. Richard Kimble of guilt. Just as the supreme court of Idaho cleared C.K. Ah Fong's citizenship and license, Minnesota cleared a path for the rise of James Hong from Minneapolis, who was born in 1929. James Hong is a permanent fixture in Hollywood, playing the extra East Asian. One of his first appearances was on *You Bet Your Life with Groucho Marx* (1954). Fong would later star in *The New Adventures of Charlie Chan* (1957-1958), the original *Hawaii Five-O* (1968-1980), and more recently in *The Big Bang Theory* (2007-2019). He also starred in movies like *Airplane!* (1980), *Blade Runner* (1982), *Big Trouble in Little China* (1986), *Balls of Fury* (2007), and *Everything Everywhere All At Once* (2022).

In the spirit of male and female team up of Idaho, we have Kristine and Kevin. Kristine Sutherland of Boise, Idaho, was born in 1955 and starred in *Remington Steele* (1982-1987) and *Buffy the Vampire Slayer* (as Buffy's mom, Joyce Summers) and the movie *Honey, I Shrunk the Kids* (1989). Kevin Sorbo from Mound, Minnesota, was born in 1958 and starred as Hercules in the TV series *Hercules: The Legendary Journeys* (1995-1999).

Two Generation X stars from that '70s generation are Vince Vaughn from Minneapolis, Minnesota (born 1970) and Aaron Paul from Emmett, Idaho (born 1979). Vaughn is a comedic actor who carries a certain chemistry that allows him to break the fourth wall without doing so, as if to read the mind of the audience and say things that need to be said and what everyone is thinking. Vince Vaughn starred in *Wedding Crashers* (2005), *Fred Claus* (2007), and continues to make laughs as in the comedic "Frat Pack." Aaron Paul rose to stardom on *Breaking Bad* (2008-2013). Aaron's character Jesse Pinkman was supposed to be killed off, but the chemistry with the lead, Bryan Cranston, put him in the "break out" category of stars. Hopefully someday we will get to see a Vince Vaughn and Aaron Paul buddy cop movie or something like that.

King jesters who put a smile on America's face from the class of America's bicentennial are Ryan Hamilton and Seann William Scott, both born in 1976.

Ryan Hamilton is the classical stand-up comedian who describes himself as the love child of Jerry and Elaine from the *Seinfeld* TV show, further Ryan Hamilton is a real life "Napoleon Dynamite" since he was born in Ashton, Idaho. Ryan Hamilton's stand-up is a witty G rated, Jerry-Seinfeld-like style. His funny wingman from Cottage Grove, Minnesota, is Seann William Scott. Seann has starred in *Dude, Where's My Car?* (2000), *Road Trip* (2000), *Mr. Woodcock* (2007), and *Ice Age: Collision Course* (2016). No doubt a comedy with Seann William Scott and Ryan Hamilton will put the public in stitches.

Two boomer gals who make 40s matches are Sherry Jackson and Jessica Lange. Sherry Jackson was born in Wendell, Idaho, in 1942. Sherry Jackson grew up as a child star with her breakout role as Terry Williams on *The Danny Thomas Show* (1953-1958). Sherry Jackson was a fixture on TV starring in *Rawhide, Star Trek, The Incredible Hulk, Lost in Space, Starsky and Hutch, Fantasy Island, Charlie's Angels,* and *ChiPs,* variously (1959-1984). Jessica Lange was born in Cloquet, Minnesota, in 1949. Jessica Lange has starred in *Tootsie* (1982), *Rob Roy* (1995), and *Big Fish* (2003). More recently she had a late revival in FX's *American Horror Story* (2011-2018).

Two women from the class of '45 are Ronee and Loni. Ronee Sue Blakley from Nampa, Idaho, is best known for her role in the original *A Nightmare on Elm Street* (1984). Loni Kaye Anderson from Saint Paul, Minnesota, is best known as Jennifer Marlowe on *WKRP in Cincinnati* (1978-1982). Loni was also the voice of Flo in *All Dogs Go to Heaven* (1989).

Two women at the tail end of boomer land are Cheryl Paris (born 1959) and Lea Thompson (born 1961). Cheryl Paris from Burley, Idaho, took the modeling route to become a star. Her movies included *Liberty & Bash* (1989) and *Me, Myself, and I* (1992). Lea Thompson from Rochester, Minnesota, danced her way into Hollywood. She became a superstar with the *Back to the Future* trilogy, playing as Lorraine Maines-McFly. She also starred in *Red Dawn* (1984), *Some Kind of Wonderful* (1987), and *The Beverly Hillbillies* (1993).

Two women born in the heart of the Gen X are Christina Fulton and Winona Ryder, born in 1967 and 1971. Christina Fulton of Boise started out as an elite model. She starred in *The Doors* (1991) and *The Girl with the Hungry Eyes*

(1995). She is a noted famous ex of Nicholas Cage. Winona Ryder, eponymously born in Winona, Minnesota, became the poster girl for Gen X with movies like *Beetlejuice* (1988), *Heathers* (1988), *Edward Scissorhands* (1990), and *Reality Bites* (1994).

Two fraternal sisters in between Gen X and Y are Kimberlee Peterson (born 1980) and Rachael Leigh Cook (born 1979). Kimberlee from Boise has a string of appearances on *Fudge* (1995-1997), *Chicken Soup for the Soul* (1999-2000), and *Secret Cutting* (2000). Rachael Leigh Cook from Minneapolis was launched into the spotlight with the movie *The Baby-Sitters Club* (1995) and has also starred in *Josie and the Pussycats* (2001), *Descent* (2007), and *Nancy Drew* (2007).

A perfect pair of singing fools is Steve Ripley and Bob Dylan. From Boise, Steve Ripley was born in 1950 and was initially the leader of the country rock band The Tractors, whose hits include "Baby Likes to Rock It" and "The Santa Claus Boogie." Funny thing is that Steven Ripley actually teamed up with Bob Dylan as the recording engineer who plays the guitar on "Shot of Love" and went on tour with Dylan on the Shot of Love tour. From the lost Canadian tribal territory of Duluth, Minnesota, we have Bob Dylan, born Robert Allen Zimmerman in 1941. If you didn't know, Bob Dylan is the epitome of American singer-songwriter rock royalty. His hits include "Blowin' in the Wind" (1963) and "The Times They Are A-Changin' " (1964). Dylan was the OG beatnik to lead the rolling waving hippie-counterculture before hippies became a thing.

Two writers minted in 1943 who represent the "lesser half" of the flags they were born under are Marilynne Robinson from Sand Point, Idaho and Jim Northrup from Fond du Lac Indian Reservation, Minnesota. Their identity groups were ignored for the most part until recently. Northrup, an Ojibwe, served in Vietnam and used humor and witty writing to combat PTSD, which he described as "my brain taking a shit." Marilynne is a Phi Beta Kappa member and author of *Housekeeping* (1980) and *Gilead* (2004).

Minnesota and Idaho are states that are similar yet so different. They are no stranger to winter, as ice fishing is a major pastime—more so for Minnesota due to its multitude of lakes. Both are excellent states for hunters and fishermen alike. Consequently, it's necessary that each Minnesota and Idaho outdoorsmen and women put hunting or fishing trips on each other's bucket lists.

Two iconic foods from each state that have become adopted flavors for the world are tater tots and Spam. Put them together and you have a perfect Ida-Minn breakfast. Tater tots are an American invention made from leftover scraps from french fries invented by the Ore-Ida company. Oregon-Idaho Company is too much of a mouthful, so it was chopped down to the first syllables, Ore-Ida. The opposite ending word of the Ore-Ida, would be the Gon-Ho company, Ore-Gon/Ida-Ho. It was in the city of Austin, Minnesota, in 1937 that the world was introduced to Spam—processed canned pork meat that has an extra-long shelf life. During WWII, Spam became an essential element that would help to turn the tide against the Nazi war machine. Nikita Khrushchev wrote in his memoirs, "Without Spam we wouldn't have been able to feed our army." Thus, you can thank a can of Spam for your freedom. Tater tots are a little bit younger, as they were born in 1953 at the height of the Cold War.

Eventually when tater tots became established in Minnesota, it led to the creation of an iconic Minnesota meal, the hotdish, which is something like shepherd's pie. The Minnesota hotdish belongs to the casserole family of dishes. A typical recipe is ground beef mixed with condensed soup and canned or frozen vegetables topped with tater tots.

Two classic American cartoons that forged their way into the hearts of nearly all Americans can trace their roots in Idaho and Minnesota—namely Mickey Mouse and Charlie Brown. Yes, Walt Disney was born in Illinois, but Mickey would have never come to pass it if it wasn't for his wife from Spalding, Idaho. Lillian Disney was born in 1899 and was the youngest of 10 children. Her father died when she was 17. She later worked for Disney Studios as an ink and paint artist, which is when she met Walt. Their knot was actually tied in Idaho at her brother's home on July 13, 1925. When Walt was working on a particular mouse character, he told his wife this figment of his imagination name was going to be named "Mortimer Mouse" during a train trip. But Lillian's intuition spoke up and said it was "too depressing." Mortimer obviously brings up ideas like mortuary, mortician, morgue, and mourning. No doubt few children could rally around a hero named Mortimer. In the end, Walt listened to his wife's good advice and Mortimer Mouse was buried into oblivion in 1928, and with the help of Lillian, Mickey Mouse was born. As the flag of Idaho indicates, when the positive power of woman unites to the predictable power of man, a bountiful and delightful plenty become apparent for all to enjoy. In the wake of this Lillian's and Walt's love was the bounty of several magical kingdoms across the world from China, Tokyo, California, Florida, and France with an endless cast of loveable characters from Fantasia. Thus, if it wasn't for Idaho, who knows how far Disney would have gone.

In matching caliber to the cast of characters from Walt and Lillian's imaginations are the underdog heroes from the mind of Charles Monroe Schulz, born in Minneapolis in 1922. Being of the Greatest Generation, Charles Schulz served in the U.S. Army during WWII. Schulz was a squad leader on a 0.50 caliber machine gun team that saw combat at the tail end of the war. His one war story was quite a real-life Charlie Brown episode. Chuck had one opportunity to kill a Nazi soldier, but a not-so-brown Charlie S. forgot to load the ammo. This just gave the German soldier enough time to surrender willingly before Charlie S.'s mistake could be corrected. Good grief! The psychic burden of killing another person, even a Nazi, would probably have changed Schulz's career path. Eventually, Charles's simple drawings of his childhood dramas and traumas became the fuel to his success that all Americans—strike that—all children and adults of the world could relate to. *Peanuts* was the original diary of a nearly bald wimpy kid, long before 2007.

Finally, two films that unite Idaho and Minnesota with quirky black humor are *Napoleon Dynamite* (2004) and *Fargo* (1996). *Napoleon Dynamite* is a high school comedy that points fun at the often-ridiculous nature of public schools in America. Without humor, the interplay of young egos asserting themselves in high school can make it an unbearably toxic and ugly environment. Likewise, *Fargo* is a cautionary tale on the pressures of adulthood when greed and stupidity collide. In the end, these movies are more than just dark comedies. They are songs of wisdom that demonstrate there are a multitude of unsung heroes in Idaho and Minnesota who bear with grace and humor the burden of bullying and the aftermath of stupid people chasing stupid prizes.

The fierce and ubiquitous dichotomy between men and women is immortalized in the Idaho flag, as it has been since the beginning of time. Likewise, another sharp and dynamic dichotomy, that between the Native and the Newcomer, is enshrined on the original state flag of Minnesota. Is the Newcomer smiling? Perhaps he is squinting with stern resentment? Or maybe he recognizes an old friend? Essentially, it all depends upon the filter and experience of the observer. These sigils have flown in concord for over a century in their shared heavens of North America. Consequently, they have earned the centurion's mark of pride and respect. Only with time and maturity can one appreciate their inner elegance and perceive their profound soul stirring beauty, as conceived not by men, but rather of two women connected now and forever, in that mysterious realm beyond time.

eight

KENTUCKY & DELAWARE

The Blue-Eyed Pauper and Blue-Blooded Prince See Eye to Eye

THE FLAG REVELATION

KENTUCKY

The common element between Kentucky and Delaware's flags is the stance of the supporters. Usually the supporters face forward, but the men of Kentucky and Delaware face each other directly. Delaware employs the typical design, where the supporters hold up the shield in the middle. Kentucky breaks the mold, whereby the shield is missing and the supporters enter a friendly embrace.

But notice the difference in clothing. First, with Delaware, the man on the left is wearing a plain farmer's outfit and carries a hoe, while the man on the right is wearing a fancy hunting outfit with a feather in his cap and carries a long gun. With Kentucky, the man on the left is wearing a frontiersman buckskin outfit, while the man on the left is wearing a wealthy man's business suit. Both states reflect the dynamic of the powerful upper class, and the down-to-earth common folk.

Thomas Jefferson and John Adams debated perpetually about these two classes of society—the powerful elite and the common man. The imprint of this political thought process stems from an Aristotelian view of society: that government is naturally composed of the Patrician and Plebeian classes of society. Patricians were the wealthiest classes of people of ancient Rome that owned

DELAWARE

much of the land and held political power; they are reflected by men on the right dressed to the nines. Plebeians are everyone who is not—basically the commoner. The dynamic of the established powers and the rest of society are reflected by the plainly dressed figures on the left and the elegantly dressed figures on the right of both flags.

In ancient Rome, the Patrician-Plebeian classes were essentially hereditary caste systems. An echo of this structure carries on in the structure of the many modern governments, as most law-making congresses are divided into two teams: Plebeians versus Patricians, or lower and upper houses. In America's case, the Senate is akin to a Patrician Noble House, while the House of Representatives is the Plebeian Commoner House. Even the national congress of the United Kingdom reflects the Patrician-Plebeian arrangement. There is the Upper House of Lords and the Lower House of Commons.

Of the dozen supporters found across the 50 state flags, only Kentucky and Delaware make eye contact with each other. Also, a powder horn can be found on both flags. For Delaware the powder horn hangs off the hip of the gentleman hunter in the green suit on the right, while in Kentucky the powder horn is on the buckskin frontiersman on the left. Likewise, the floral compartment of Kentucky, the Golden Rod, bears a slight resemblance to the floral floor that the Delaware men are standing on. However, Delaware's floral leaf design points toward the center, while Kentucky's Goldenrod blooms outward like crossed olive leaves.

Upon Delaware's shield in the upper part, two sacred plants can be found along with an ear of corn and a sheaf of wheat. Wheat is a sacrament for many of the old world, just as corn is considered a divine gift by indigenous peoples from Canada to Chile. The goldenrod is also another plant of a spiritual context since it is associated with healing. The official scientific name is *Solidago gigantea*. In Latin, *Solidago* describes an herb that heals wounds.

Kentucky was among the most bitterly divided states during the Civil War. Like Delaware, Kentucky is classified as a border state. However, the magnitude of Kentucky's division was so intense that the Civil War can be framed as a war between the counties rather than a war between the states. On the other hand, Delaware was at the polar opposite of border states. Although Delaware was a slave state, she sent the least number of men to fight for the Confederacy from a border state, and relatively speaking, received a grazing wound compared to her sister state of Kentucky. Of the border states, Kentucky sent the most men to fight for the North. But the most significant illustration of Kentucky's deep division was the fact that the executives of the Union and Confederacy were born in Kentucky.

Abraham Lincoln was born in a county next to free soil to the north, while Jefferson Davis was born in southern Christian County on the border of Tennessee. When Lincoln was born in 1809, his birthplace was within Hardin County which shares a border with Indiana. But in 1843, the south eastern region of Hardin County, where Lincoln was born, separated to become LaRue County. Likewise, Jefferson Davis was originally born in Christian County on June 3, 1808. But as borders were redrawn in 1820, Davis's birthplace changed to Todd County, no longer of Christian.

Of a hidden yin and yang dynamic, when Kentucky was in utero within Mother Virginia—Jefferson Davis's birthplace, from 1780 until 1792, was a part of Lincoln County, while Abraham Lincoln's birthplace from 1780 until 1784, was a part of Jefferson County. In other words, Jefferson Davis was born in a land, once upon a time known as Lincoln, while Abraham Lincoln was born in a land formerly known as Jefferson.

In the aftermath of such horrific civil war, it's fitting that the central Civil War state is represented by an herb with mysterious healing powers, the goldenrod. Herbalists know that this plant provides medicine that cures ailments such as kidney problems, fungal infections, and reduces inflammation. The goldenrod truly is a wholesome plant that has more antioxidants than green tea. Its Latin name means "to make one whole again," due to its healing properties.

Also note, Kentucky's flag conveys the primary value of healing, rather than peace. Crossed olive branches would have worked, but instead, a healing herb with two men embracing enshrines the theme of recovery as paramount, which is further underscored by Kentucky's motto "United We Stand, Divided We Fall."

As Kentucky's flag implicitly makes reference to the U.S. Civil War, Delaware's flag explicitly refers to the American Revolution. The motto is seen on a white ribbon along the compartment that reads, "Liberty and Independence," which was declared on July 4, 1776. However, the date underneath is not aligned to Independence Day; instead the date December 7, 1787, refers to Delaware's ratification of the U.S. Constitution. This 1787 date is akin to America's Graduation Day. Like most high school seniors, it would take the U.S. 12 years of hard challenges and mistakes to mature into the formal government it is today. And Delaware was the first state to do so on December 7th, eleven years after the political bonds to the United Kingdom were broken, and six months before George Washington became the first President.

Delaware takes special pride as the first state to affirm and ratify the rules and regulations that affect our daily lives: the core programming of the American matrix, the U.S. Constitution of 1787. Before an idea becomes something, it is first a nothing. On the journey from nothing to something it must duly face the fury of broken dreams, since so many lost some things often become nothing. An early something will be hazed, judged, and perhaps discarded. But if a rare and special something passes these tests, the something small may start its perilous journey to become something big. Every hero's journey must face the doubting Tammies and Thomases. This is good, as it brings clarity and tests the hero if he or she really wants this something and is strong enough to see out its final conclusion.

But for the American Dream, Delaware was first to fall in and give the first feather of faith for a fledgling nation. Delaware was the first to become a believer. In hindsight, all heroes remember in fondness those first supporters, those early fans who showed up at the beginning. Delaware's flag is not necessarily a call to brag and boast. But rather, it honors that positive voice at the beginning, the quickening. It's a voice that echoes the first calling that should be cherished. Dangerous it is to be first, as the first to stick one's neck out is potentially the first to lose their head. Just as the first faithful who believe in a dream before its fulfillment can surely be trusted, Delaware enshrines that initial burst of trust. In other words, Delaware's flag seems to say, "Look, I was first to believe in you. I knew you before you were famous, and I always knew then that you could do it."

Geography

The shape of Kentucky and Delaware nominally looks like footwear. If you rotate Delaware counterclockwise 45 degrees, it looks like an elf shoe. Kentucky does not require rotation, but only to recognize that it looks like a bedroom slipper. You just have to imagine Indiana as the lower leg. Warning! After you look at the map of America, you won't be able to un-see this. Indiana's Wabash River makes the perfect outline of a back heel. Hey, if the shoe fits. Kentucky is Delaware's matching patriotic shoe, in a weird sort of way.

Kentucky and Delaware are in the all-American belt. This is the region of the U.S. that is completely south of Canada and completely north of Mexico. They share no latitudes with Canada and Mexico. Currently there are 13 states in this category, whose summer and winters are justifiably nothing like Canada or Mexico.

Kentucky is famous for its Land Between the Lakes National Recreation Area.

Two lakes were made out of the Tennessee and Cumberland Rivers when dams were built at their convergence point during the 1960s. Lake Kentucky was born out of the Tennessee River, while Lake Barkley was born out of the Cumberland River. A matching nickname for Delaware is the "Barnyard Between the Bays." The two bays associated with Delaware are the Chesapeake Bay and Delaware Bay. Delaware also has a canal that connects the two bays, the Chesapeake and Delaware Canal. The canal project to connect the bays started in the early 1800s and was completed in 1829. Unlike the Land Between the Lakes Canal, the Barnyard Between the Bays canal is much longer. Delaware's Between the Bays Canal is 14 miles long while Kentucky's Between the Lakes Canal is only one and three quarters of a mile long. It should also be said that Delaware's Bay connecting canal is akin to Delaware's own local cultural Mason-Dixon Line, where Delaware takes on a southern orientation. North of the Bay Canal, life has that stressful "rush to the red light" pace, while south of the Bay Canal, it is known as Lower Slower Delaware.

On the matters of equal latitude, the northern top of Kentucky's slipper is on par with the southern back heel of Delaware. In other words, 22 counties in Kentucky can see eye to eye with Delaware along matching lines of latitude within the *Delatucky Belt*. The 'eye to eye' counties of Kentucky include Oldham, Henry, Owen, Scott, Harrison, Nicholas, Fleming, Lewis, Carter, Boyd, Trimble, Carroll, Gallatin, Kenton, Campbell, Bracken, Mason, Greenup, Grant, Pendleton, Robertson, and most importantly, Boone County. As for Delaware, Sussex and Kent Counties have a matching east to west gaze with Kentucky.

History

Kentucky and Delaware are the union of the Bluegrass state with the Blue Hen state. Kentucky is also known for its well-to-do, blue-blooded Americans that have connections to the founding fathers and relatives who own buildings and blocks. And speaking out of the blue, Delaware is home to the largest population of blue-blooded organisms: the horseshoe crab. Horseshoe crabs, *Limulidae leach*, are an ancient species that bleed blue. Their blood has a light sky-blue blood coloration. Blood is typically colored red due to the element of iron in the protein hemoglobin, but horseshoe crabs use copper instead, which gives it its blue hue. A small cottage industry has arisen to harmlessly milk these ancient creatures of their royal blue blood.

Of icons to represent America, perhaps the most renowned is the log cabin. It appears on state seals and is a symbol of the U.S., in the league of apple pie and the bald eagle. But how did log cabins become intimately associated with Kentucky? And why Kentucky instead of Tennessee, Ohio, or Mississippi? These other states certainly have plenty of log cabins. Part of the reason that Kentucky steals the limelight is that she was the first western frontier state to receive the bounty of settlers on the frontier after the American Revolution. When settlers poured through the Cumberland Gap that spilled into Kentucky, making log cabins was a relatively quick and easy way to make a sturdy home. Kentucky had plenty of woodlands at the time, and if you had the right tools and know-how, building a house with your bare hands would only take about a month. But long before the log cabin became a Kentucky icon, it was providentially first established in Delaware. In fact, it happened before Delaware knew she was Delaware.

The first Old World nation to settle Delaware was Sweden, who called the area destined to become Delaware, New Sweden. The Swedish can claim first settlement in Pennsylvania, too. During the Swedish chapter of Delaware and Pennsylvania, Sweden held sway over Finland in a different kind of United Kingdom of the far north. The robust forest Finns were already handy frontiersmen who were keenly selected by the Swedes to settle the Delaware Valley. Thus, Sweden via the Finnish brought over log cabin technologies to America. When the British eventually took over the Delaware Valley in 1664, they allowed the Swedes and Finns to stay, and the log cabin subsequently became an American icon.

Caesar Rodney is the first hero of the first state. When the Delaware delegation was voting for independence, their vote was tied one to one. Delaware's representative born in Pennsylvania was for independence, Thomas McKean, while the other Delaware rep born in Maryland, George Read, who voted to stay in the Kingdom. Of charming history, it was up to the Delaware-born representative to decide the final vote. In order to break the deadlock, Caesar Rodney rode 70 miles through an overnight thunderstorm on July 1, 1776. Rodney didn't even have time to remove his spurs when the voting started. Since then, the ride of the American Caesar at midnight became a hallowed point for Delaware's history that often garnishes every state heritage site in Delaware. Kentucky too is no stranger to speedy horses. The nation's premier horse race is known as the Kentucky Derby. It was first held at Churchill Downs in Louisville, Kentucky, on May 17, 1875. The race lasts less than three minutes, but it is all the hype and partying that takes the cake.

Perhaps Delaware can host a street horse race to match the Kentucky Derby? Instead of fast sprinting horses, there's a 25-mile road track, set across the back roads and beaches of Delaware. It'd be a Tour de Delaware, held the day before the Kentucky Derby in honor of Caesar Rodney's midnight run. Thus, the Kentucky Derby is akin to the ultimate NASCAR horse race in America, while a could be *The Rodney Run* of Delaware would be the equivalent pony-cross sport.

Two ultimate forefathers connected to the national drama are Daniel Boone and Kit Carson. Daniel Boone was not born in Delaware exactly. He was born in what is now known as Reading, Pennsylvania—part of the Delaware Valley. The entire city of Reading is connected to the Delaware River watershed and is Boone's homestead.

Similarly, much of Daniel Boone's hunting adventures with the west and his iconic crossing into Kentucky all happened when Delaware was a part of Pennsylvania, or rather, when Pennsylvania was a part of Delaware. Delaware is the older state after all, settled long before Pennsylvania. In fact, the colonials who first settled Pennsylvania came out of Delaware. Thus, it is more fit to say that Daniel Boone was born in the northern half of Delaware that became Pennsylvania.

Daniel Boone learned much from playing with his Indian neighbors in the Delaware Valley, which gave him an invaluable education on sporting after the local fauna. After his fame was established, no doubt several extra layers of yarn were added to his story. In the end, Boone became the iconic frontiersman born at the birth of a nation. In complement to Boone, Kentucky gave America her second iconic frontiersman who saw to the completion of the American mainland from coast to coast in Kit Carson. In a similar manner, as tall tales about Kit Carson were retold, they would get taller and taller each time. As Boone is associated with the opening of the colonial frontier, Carson is similarly so with the western frontier.

Both men would have extensive relations with Native Americans. They ran the entire range of good, bad, and ugly. They were Indian fighters as much as they were Indian lovers. There were many men like Boone and Carson, but the difference is the halo of fame squarely landed on the Delaware Valley via Boone and Kentucky Valley via Carson. These men wore many hats and were real-life action heroes, lauded in their generations. Christopher "Kit" Carson was born in Richmond, Kentucky, which is a major city in the valley of the Kentucky River.

Daniel Boone is a part of generation one of American folk heroes at the beginning of America's birthday. Since Boone was born on November 2, 1734, he landed on prime temporal real estate. He was 41 years old for America's birthday. Boone's adventures would play out in the original backyard of America long before the Louisiana Purchase. In proper continuation, Kit Carson was born for the next chapter of American history on Christmas Eve, 1809. Kit Carson's adventures played out across the West Coast. Their lives were dramatic, star-struck, quasi fairytales like the fictional Forrest Gump as played by Tom Hanks in 1994. Kit and Boone were men of low birth and would participate in America's destiny manifesting before their very own eyes and by the choices they made. They rubbed elbows with all sorts of people, including other famous persons and would even meet the president.

Mountain men and soldiers were a dime dozen back then, but something extraordinary paved a path for Boone and Carson. Boone's seminal action hero story occurred in the midst of the American Revolution. On July 14, 1776, his daughter Jemima and two other girls were kidnapped near Boonesborough, Virginia (not yet the state of Kentucky until 1792). Boone was able to gather up a rescue party, and 48 hours later they tracked down the hostile war party and rescued the damsels in distress. Boone's daring rescue inspired the novel *The Last of the Mohicans* in 1826, and movies to this day continue to echo this event—including *The Last of the Mohicans* movie in 1992, starring Daniel Day-Lewis. Other movies that take a note from Boone include *Commando* (1985) and every other Liam Neeson film since *Taken* (2008).

Kit Carson had a similar story that put the nation in a fervor over a daring rescue: the attempted rescue of Mrs. Ann White in late October 1849. The White wagon train party was heading to Santa Fe, New Mexico, from Independence, Missouri. But when the White party made the fateful decision to separate from the main party, drama ensued. Eventually, the party was attacked by a band of hostile Apache. The entire White party was killed except for Mrs. Ann White, her baby, and her Black servant. A short while later, a group of Mexicans found the wreckage and dead bodies but were themselves attacked by the militant Indians. Some of the Mexicans were killed, but most were able to get away. Eventually word reached the nearby U.S. Army post at Taos, New Mexico. Kit Carson joined the rescue party for the unaccounted three: Mrs. White, her baby, and her servant. When Carson found the militant party, he was gung-ho on attacking, but his idea was overruled since the hostiles signaled to a talk. The bandits used the white flag as a stall tactic to delay and get away. All the militant Apache managed to get away except for one. Kit Carson himself then found the still-warm body of Mrs. White, which was recently pierced in the chest by an arrow. Mere minutes earlier, she was alive. Kit Carson was confident if they'd initially attacked instead of holding out to talk, Mrs. Ann White could have been rescued alive. The extra burn was that Mrs. White had a copy of the dime novel *Kit Carson: Prince of the Gold Hunters* (1849), a fictional story where Kit saves a beautiful woman from a band of hostile Indians. However, life is rarely like exciting fiction, and tragedies often win out to happy endings. Mrs. White's baby and servant were never recovered and are assumed to have been killed.

Both Daniel Boone and Kit Carson are known for being trailblazers. Daniel Boone was not the first White man in Kentucky. However, in 1775 Boone worked for a Transylvania Company to literally blaze a trail through the Cumberland Gap. This is a low point in the Appalachian Mountains near the tippy tip of Virginia and Kentucky. This makes Daniel Boone a patron saint for the 50 state DOTs (Department of Transportation), which in Boone's case would be *FDOT*, as in *Frontier Department of Transportation.*

Starting on March 10, 1775, Boone, with a party of at least 30 lumberjacks, cut a trail from Kingsport, Tennessee, to the forests of Kentucky headwaters of the Kentucky River. However, when they were about 15 miles from their destination, they were attacked by hostile Indians who were upset that colonists were encroaching on their hunting grounds. A few road construction workers were killed, but Boone got away. Kit Carson also helped pave a path for the Oregon Trail. When Kit bumped into John Fremont on a steamboat on the Missouri River, Kit was able to convince his way on to John Fremont's team of the Corps of Topographical Engineers.

John Fremont was on his way to publishing maps on the Oregon Trail for the public. In 1842, Kit Carson became a lauded pathfinder for Fremont, who took him to the lauded point of South Pass. In a way, South Pass is the Cumberland Gap of the Oregon Trail. South Pass is a lower valley where one crosses into the watersheds between the Atlantic to the Pacific. The following year in 1843, Kit Carson was hired again to take the Fremont Party to the Columbia River in Oregon. The Oregon Trail was already known before Kit Carson led Fremont, but the information that Carson helped provide helped procure government documents and spurred traffic along the Oregon Trail, since a new and improved government-issued map was created.

The third hat of importance for both men was their patriotic war record. Boone's first war effort was alongside a yet to be famous George Washington at the Battle of Monongahela at the start of the last French and Indian War (1754-1763). Although the British and English colonies were victorious overall, the Battle at Monongahela was a disaster. Yet George Washington was able to prove his worth as a gallant commander under fire. The second war that drafted Boone was Dunmore's War in 1774. Before the official outbreak in 1774, Boone led several families into Kentucky. On October 9, 1773, his oldest son James and several others were captured when they went off to get supplies. However, there would be no rescue as they were tortured and killed. The last war that served to underscore Daniel Boone's role in shaping the American nation was the American Revolution. Boone fought on the western frontier, mostly against bands of British-supported Indian war parties.

Kit Carson's war record is just as gleaming. Kit, like Boone, had a knack for fighting on the winning side. Kit Carson helped park California in the American orbit during the Bear Flag Revolt. Kit Carson later fought the Mexicans in Southern California, helping the U.S. finish its conquest of the Golden State. And during the Civil War, Kit Carson helped repel the Confederates in New Mexico Territory. But Carson and Boone are best known as Indian fighters.

They were also Indian lovers. Two Indians connected to Carson and Boone are Singing Grass and Chief Blackfish. Singing Grass was Kit Carson's first wife of the Arapaho Tribe. She gave Carson his first daughter, Adaline. But Singing Grass died after she gave birth to his second daughter, as did the baby soon afterward. Daniel Boone was captured by Chief Blackfish's warriors in early February 1778 and was soon adopted into Blackfish's family, in the then standard, prisoner-adoption practice. Boone passed through the gauntlet and his skills as a hunter impressed all in the tribe. Daniel Boone was given the Shawnee name of Big Turtle. But this primitive compulsory "study abroad" program only lasted five months, or about one semester. When Boone learned that his adopted family was going to attack Boonesborough, Boone quit the study abroad program and made his escape to warn his White family. Boone traversed 160 miles in five days—first on horseback but after it gave out, he finished on foot. Even though Boone provided critical intelligence, arguably saving many lives if not the entire village, Boone was not wholly welcomed as a hero upon his return. Big Turtle was suspect, akin to a Manchurian Candidate, or rather as a Shawnee Candidate.

After Boonesborough (*Big Turtleborough*) fended off the impending attack as forewarned by Boone, Boone was put on trial. In Star Trek terms, Boone was in a situation similar to *Star Trek IV: The Voyage Home* (1984), when Kirk returns home to save the day but breaks several laws in the process and oddly returns home in an enemy warship. But Boone's life was not a work of fiction, and he was able to defend himself from a court-martial.

Kit Carson also has an enchanting story of running the distance to save the day. It was during the Mexican American War that the Battle of San Pasqual occurred, which is near San Diego. General Kearny's forces were outnumbered by a superior Mexican force. They were on their way to San Diego to meet up with U.S. forces there but were pinned down. Under the cover of night Kit Carson, Edward F. Beale, and an Indian scout were sent out to gather reinforcements from San Diego. They snuck past the sentries barefoot to not make any noise, but they ended up losing their shoes. Thus, they had to run 25 miles over rocks and prickly pears, and another 10,000 Lego-like hazards of Southern California. Their efforts were successful. A cavalry force of about 200 U.S. mounted soldiers came to lay siege to Kearny's forces. It was victories like this one that helped make that California Dream real.

From the lens of the early 1900s, they were regarded as national treasures whose daring tales were retold with extra layers of plaster and putty in comics and dime novels. They were the Indiana Joneses and Han Solos of America's middle passage. In the 1950s, both were surefire heroes of Disney's whimsical and less-than-factual Westerns. But as the nation matured, we can recognize that they were fully rounded men, far from perfect and with fault lines. Yet they led quite interesting, and at times inspiring, lives. Their generations (Generation A for Boone of the Delaware River Valley and Generation B for Carson of the Kentucky River Valley) did not have the cultural sophistication, nor was social science a thing, let alone science. Nevertheless, there was something enchanting about both men who filled the role of inspiring heroes for the nation.

Kentucky and Delaware were the last states to officially close the book on slavery by action of the 13th Amendment. The southern states that officially formed the Confederacy forfeited their right of slavery through the legal action of the Emancipation Proclamation in the midst of the war. The other slave states that remained loyal ended slavery by their own accord through the action of their state governments. Consequently, Kentucky and Delaware closed and sealed the door shut on this ancient relationship, explicitly permitted by several divine ordinances of one man's right to own another man's wife and children on

December 6, 1865.

In the following century, Delaware and Kentucky were again border states during the Civil Rights Era, as they were required to desegregate their public schools in the wake of *Brown v. Board of Education*. Less of a spectacle than it was in the Deep South, the segregated age of Delaware and Kentucky came to an end during the 1960s. The landmark case of *Brown v. Board of Education 1954* was a class action lawsuit that involved several state's cases, including one case from Delaware, *Gebhardt v. Belton 1952*. Delaware may appear like a northern state to most, but believe it or not, Delaware has as a strong, yet soft, swath of Southern DNA in her genetic makeup.

Another historical harmonic is that Delaware is the first of the first 13 states, while Kentucky is the second of the second round of 13 states.

The majority of educationally approved history books list Kentucky as a border state during the U.S. Civil War. However, from the view of the Confederate government, Kentucky was the 13th state to join the Confederacy on December 10, 1861. It is noted that the central star on the "modern" Confederate flag represents Kentucky. Confederate Kentucky selected Bowling Green as the capital, in opposition to Union Kentucky that maintained the capital at Frankfort—except for an interlude when Confederate forces overran it. Confederates were able to occupy the state capital of Kentucky for a short while, but when they were in the process of holding an inauguration ceremony for the unelected pro-Southern government of Kentucky, they were attacked mid-ceremony and had to stop the celebration. They were forced to retreat southward into Tennessee.

Even though Delaware was a border state, she never formed a breakaway pro-Southern government and never got a star of representation on the Confederate flag. However, during the American Revolution, southern Delaware was home to a counter-rebellion Loyalist uprising at Ellendale, Delaware. As the revolutionary war dragged on, a small fraction of disgruntled Delaware residents created their own paramilitary Loyalist force without British authorization. It was known as the Black Camp Loyalist Rebellion of 1780. However, the Black Camp counter revolutionary Loyalists—who had their capital in Ellendale, Delaware—were quickly put down. Nonetheless Bowling Green, Kentucky, and

Ellendale, Delaware, share a heritage of having unelected, unrecognized "rump factions" lost between the pages of official history.

Fort Knox and Dover Air Force Base are two relatively famous military bases. Fort Knox became famous for its impregnable vault that secures the nation's gold bullion. So secure is Fort Knox's vault that during WWII other important historical relics were temporarily stored there—the U.S. Constitution and the Gettysburg Address to name a few. Dover Air Force Base perennially breaks into the news cycle due it being the largest military mortuary operated by the Department of Defense. Dover became the leading mortuary hub during the Vietnam War when over 20,000 recently departed servicemen returned to the United States. On rare occasions the remains of civilians are allowed to pass through Dover's honored mortuary. Persons of this sort included the remains of the Peoples Temple mass suicide, as led by Jim Jones, and the space shuttle Challenger disaster in 1986. With the more recent War on Terror, many more American heroes, male and female, have passed though Dover since 2001. Fort Knox and Dover Air Force Base are more than extraordinary military centers; they are sacred trusts given to Delaware and Kentucky.

Culture

France has champagne, Scotland has scotch, Japan has sake, and America has bourbon. Bourbon whisky is a specially designed spirit made from at least 51% fermented corn that is aged in a charred oak barrel. So respected a spirit, Kentucky has a bourbon heritage trail, where nationally recognized distilleries present the public with taste tours. Famous Kentucky brand bourbons include Jim Beam, Maker's Mark, Wild Turkey, Woodford Reserve, and Four Roses. Delaware has entered the conversation with its own cottage industry of flavorful crafted beer with Dogfish Head Craft Brewery. The company is known for brewing unique beer concoctions. Their first successful flavor of the week was Midas Touch, a brew with a touch of honey and floral elements. Since then, this small company has cracked into the beer market that is dominated by big box brewers and was recently acquired by the Boston Beer Company, which produces Sam Adams.

Coincidentally, chickens are honored cuisines in Kentucky and Delaware. The world-famous Kentucky Fried Chicken is an international behemoth, but fried chicken in the Kentucky style is an American flavor to savor. For Delaware, chicken and waffles is an honored tradition that can be eaten anytime of the day. Chicken is usually fried, but it comes with special Delaware seasonings and a side dish of peaches and cream. And yes, they add syrup and butter for the waffles. This peculiar combo of chicken and waffles stems from the German immigrants, often confusingly known as the Pennsylvania Dutch. Many times over the term Dutch (of the Netherlands) was often confused with Deutsch (of the many petty German states); reason being Germany did not exist as a 'name for a nation' when the first waves of 'Germans/Deutsch' immigrated to America.

A pair of kings are Johnny Depp (1963) of Owensboro, Kentucky and David Sheridan (1969) of Newark, Delaware. Both men became heartthrobs early in their careers. First, Johnny Depp became a teenage star in the latter '80s with *21 Jump Street* (1987-1991), while Dave Sheridan became a star on MTV's *Buzzkill* (1996) and starred in *Scary Movie* (2000) and *Fifty Shades of Black* (2016).

A pair of queens from Kentucky and Delaware are Melissa McBride (1965) from Lexington and Elisabeth Shue (1963) from Wilmington. Melissa McBride has recently become a star on *The Walking Dead* (2010-2022) as Carol Pelletier, while Elisabeth Shue starred as Julie Finlay on *CSI: Crime Scene Investigation* (2000-2015). Previously, Shue was a youth Hollywood hitter with films like *The Karate Kid* (1984), *Cocktail* (1988), and *Back to the Future II and III* (1989/1990), and more recently in *Battle of the Sexes* (2017). McBride's rise to stardom was a little later with modest parts across TV and Hollywood, but in 2010 she became a zombie fighter extraordinaire.

George Clooney (1961) of Lexington, Kentucky pairs nicely with Doug Hutchison (1960) from Dover, Delaware. They both gained a rather intense undercurrent of fame due to their romantic affairs. Clooney has a little black book that is perhaps many times bigger than Fonzie's. Clooney has often scored roles as the hero, starting as a doctor in the medical drama *ER* (1994-1999). He has since become the leading man in nearly all his movies. On the other hand,

THE FLAG REVELATION

Doug Hutchison is most often the antagonist, in villain lane.

Two loveable, all-around fun guys from Kentucky are Jim and Judge: Jim Varney (1949-2000) from Lexington and Judge Reinhold (1957) from Wilmington. Jim Varney captures that silly hillbilly with his character Ernest—the hairbrained, good-hearted, wacky southern uncle. Judge Reinhold became a bathroom-household name with *Fast Times at Ridgemont High* (1982). Coincidentally, both men would star in fish out of water movies that framed the fame of Beverly Hills, California. First Reinhold would star in *Beverly Hills Cop I, II, and III* (1984-1994), while Varney starred in the *Beverly Hillbillies* (1993) movie. Another pair of Gen X stars are Ryan Phillippe from New Castle, Delaware, born in 1974, and Boyd Holbrook from Prestonsburg, Kentucky, born in 1981.

Two super starlets of the millennial sort include Jennifer Lawrence (1990) and Aubrey Plaza (1984). Their stars flared up in the 2010s: Plaza of Wilmington became a star on *Parks and Recreation* (2009-2015), while Jenny of Indian Hills, Kentucky, became a blockbuster star in deadly games about being hungry. Their stars have only started to shine, and they will no doubt continue to blast their photons into the public eye. Louisville and Wilmington pair up again with Sean Young (1959) and Valerie Bertinelli (1960). Sean Young was the 1980s action attraction in *Stripes* (1981), *Blade Runner* (1982), *Dune* (1984), and *Wall Street* (1987). Valerie Bertinelli was of the minority of childhood actresses to keep a lid on it. She starred in *On Day at a Time* (1975-1984), *Touched by An Angel* (2001-2003), and *Hot in Cleveland* (2010-2015).

Rebecca Gayheart (1971) and Teri Polo (1969) are Gen X sweets. Gayheart from Hazard, Kentucky, was a guest star on *Ugly Betty* (2007) and has starred in *Jawbreaker* (1999) and *Once Upon a Time in Hollywood* (2019). Teri Polo from Dover, Delaware, became familiar to the public with the movie *Meet the Parents* (2000), the first in the Focker's Saga.

Delaware and Kentucky are truly states of the all-American belt, with a full range of personalities from the country bumpkin to the city slicker, and, for those who want the best of both worlds, the "Suburban Herman." As Delaware was middle ground as witness to the War Between the Colonies on the international stage of nations, as was Kentucky on the domestic and private theater of a War Between the Counties. Delaware and Kentucky are a happy and unexpected marriage of the first on the frontier and first of the Constitution. Coincidentally, their flags demonstrate the power and grace of making eye contact, where the windows of the soul can come to concord, regardless of one's caste or creed.

nine

SOUTH DAKOTA & OKLAHOMA

The Sacred Center of America Is Sheltered in This Harbor

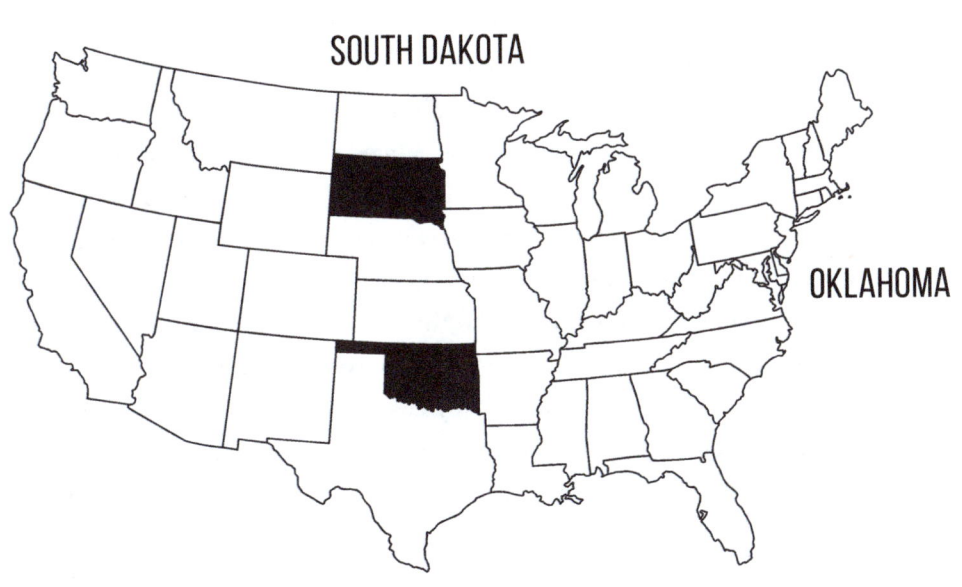

SOUTH DAKOTA

Similar hues unite the states of the Great Plains, where the sunny blues skies often welcome the day and concordantly end it with broad stunning sunsets. South Dakota's flag features the state seal resting on a sun with 24 short triangular rays. Oklahoma's flag features a circular shield of Sioux heritage. Oklahoma also features a stellar design, with the brown crosses painted on the shield representing stars in Native American tradition. South Dakota's name is written on top of the sea on the circular seal, while Oklahoma's name is written underneath the central shield in white along a straight path.

The peace pipe of Oklahoma aligns with the towering chimney of South Dakota. The peace pipe is more than just a mere means of nicotine insertion. Peace pipes are sacred vessels in the manner of holy chalices used on Sunday communion. Smoking the peace pipe is essentially a Native American sacrament. This medicine allows one to connect directly to the spirit realm of Mother Earth, but in the Western mind, it is simply regarded as a micro-narcotic.

Tobacco has a meditative effect on the mind, which creates an invisible bubble for increased calm and clarity. This explains why when heavy smokers get stressed, they need a cigarette to assess and or to get through trying situations.

OKLAHOMA

Smoking is also a positive catalyst for social mediation, which can work wonders with people who suffer from social anxiety. Basically, tobacco is a great way to make new friends and build relationships with strangers and coworkers, under a Zen, chillax, mostly sober mindset. Thus, tobacco is the key substance that empowers the spirit of a peace pipe. Unlike most other drugs, it can enhance one's work ethic and productivity, but it is highly addictive.

Like any drug, tobacco has a downside. There are numerous health hazards that include lung and cardiovascular disease, bad breath, and a stink that tags along long after a smoking session has passed. Worst of all, when a smoker becomes chemically dependent on tobacco, the withdrawal symptoms are horrible. A nicotine junkie going clean will become irritable, short-tempered, subject to rash mood swings, and sometimes a psychosomatic sickness may arise.

The balance to the smoking pipe on Oklahoma's flag is the tall smokestack on South Dakota's flag. The smokestack represents the amazing ingenuity of the Newcomer. As a counter to ingesting the smoke to connect with Mother Earth, the Western mind has constructed a larger than man, man-made pipe in order to manipulate Mother Earth herself. In a way, the smokestack is a magical device that allows one to shrink in size to climb inside a smoking pipe.

When put to proper use, industrial technologies allow civilizations to extract a manifold increase of riches and work. The scientific-industrial process can be highly profitable, allowing one man to feed ten thousand. But like smoking, there are negative consequences that tag along. Labor issues, harmful pollution, criminal activity, and economic jealousies arise when great wealth is concentrated in the hands of a hyper-minority.

The peace pipe and smokestack are two technologies that extract a certain experience from Mother Earth. The peace pipe is considered sacred, while the smokestack is considered mundane. Nonetheless, there is a mundane element to smoking, and there is something of a sacred nature to a billowing smokestack.

Another element of concord between South Dakota and Oklahoma are the eagle feathers and the cattle in the field. Eagle feathers have long been considered sacred to all Indian tribes. Typically, only chiefs of a certain rank and stature were allowed to adorn their hair with these heavenly tokens. Although eagles are not considered divine by the West, the bald eagle has become the national bird that retains a dignified reverence. As for ordinary people, to own an eagle feather is a federal offense that can result in a stiff fine and jail time. The element of South Dakota that matches in divine proportion are the cattle in the pastures of South Dakota. Although not considered sacred by most Americans, it was a different group of Newcomers to America—those from majority Hindu nations like India and Nepal—who view this animal with sacred significance.

Since 2020, the inclusion of the Old and New World Indians as fully empowered Americans underscores the alignment of the sacred eagle feathers of Oklahoma to the sacred cattle of South Dakota. Although not sacred to all, the eagle and cow have been sacred spirits within Indian culture for millennia—long before the rise of the Roman, Mughal, Aztec, and British Empires. Within the Judeo-Christian and Islamic teachings, the idea of a sacred cow is abhorrent. However, when properly considered in the Hindu-Buddheic and Jain teachings, the idea of a sacred cow is in regard to a deep respect of life and the gifts that they bear, rather than as a mere cash cow or idol to be worshiped.

Geography

South Dakota and Oklahoma are hinterland set in the middle, equidistant from the West and East Coasts. Further, they are nearly at opposite distances from the domestic cultural divide between the north and the south of a would-be extended Mason-Dixon Line at 39°43' north. This gives Oklahoma a southern tilt with sweltering summers, while South Dakota has a northern tilt with soul-chilling winters and is cut by the international monkey in the middle line of 45° north.

As for their historical territory, they are international opposites to Mexico and Canada. The northeastern end of South Dakota has a centuries-long stint of Canadian history, while a western nibble of Oklahoma waddled her toes into Mexican history. Basically, a fraction of South Dakota was a part of the Hudson Bay Company from 1670 until 1818, while the panhandle of Oklahoma was a part of Mexico from 1821 until 1848. However, most of their territory is tied to the Louisiana Purchase.

During their primary school years of learning about the American way, they were classmates in the District of Louisiana from 1804 until 1812. They were also a part of Missouri Territory from 1812 until 1821. In 1821, they went their separate ways. This makes South Dakota and Oklahoma long-lost elementary school friends who can reminisce about the good old days when their teacher—a saintly Mrs. Louis, taught them the ropes about America. Saint Louis in Missouri was in charge of what was to become South Dakota and Oklahoma for 16 years from 1805 to 1821. However, they shared a secret fort in the woods, because a small part of their area was classified as "unorganized territory" which lasted until 1854.

Essentially, South Dakota and Oklahoma parted ways as official classmates in 1821, but they would follow a semi-parallel path. Two centuries later, in 2020, both states would retain a strong fiber of the Native American spirit. Most states would expel and repress the spirit of Native America, but South Dakota and Oklahoma became the refuge where many Native languages, cultures, and traditions would thrive. The vast majority of states have a Native population of less than half a percent. However, South Dakota and Oklahoma are standouts who both have a healthy and unignorable 10% of the state residents of established pre-Columbian heritage. If you include some factor of Latin Americans with Indian heritage, the number is even higher.

Oklahoma is famous for its instantly recognizable panhandle, which balances with the secret panel of South Dakota. At first glance South Dakota looks like a commonplace semi-rectangular state. But upon close inspection along the western border, you can detect a little kink. This discrepancy is due to a time rift and a literally half-assed effort in setting the border. In 1877, the first survey started from the south at the tristate corner of Nebraska, Wyoming, and Colorado. The 1877 survey team called it quits when they reached Montana. Eight years later, in 1885, another survey team was sent from the northern border area of North Dakota and Montana.

When the second team reached the southern border of Montana, it was off by nearly a mile—4,600 feet west of the 104th western meridian. Instead of redoing the survey they just cut corners. Depending on how one looks at it, South Dakota either lost a mile or gained a mile along its western border. It's impossible to notice on most maps, but if you zoom in on Google Earth, you'll see it. Rumor has it there are two secret switches at Mount Rushmore—one is an obvious panhandle lever that makes lasers shoot out of Lincoln's eyes, while a secret panel will make a missile shoot out of Teddy Roosevelt's mouth.

History

South Dakota and Oklahoma have a conspicuous Native American character. Initially, these areas were to remain wholly as Indian lands, however the unquenchable desire for land and wealth would leave a trail of broken promises. The Natives of South Dakota and Oklahoma bear witness to the insatiable greed of gold, which can make a monster of men. Before the gold rushes of the 99ers to Alaska, the 49ers to California, and the 76ers of the Black Hills, there was the original gold rush: the 29ers of Georgia. This earliest gold rush within the original 13 colonies set the pace for the cruel and unusual treatment of Native Americans for the next century.

Gold was discovered in northern Appalachia regions of Georgia around 1828. However, many of the gold deposits were on Cherokee Lands. As miners flocked to this area, tensions naturally arose. Besides gold, settlers coveted the vast virgin lands held by the civilized Muskogee family tree. Two years later, Andrew Jackson was delighted to sign, with strong popular support, the Indian Removal Act on May 28, 1830, which resulted in the tragic Trail of Tears. The forced population transfer to shove Indians from their homelands in Georgia, Alabama, and Mississippi toward Oklahoma for the want of wealth left a permanent stain on the fabric of American history.

The coveted lands of the tribes specifically targeted for expulsion were all of the Muskogee, which included the Choctaw, Chickasaw, Creek, Seminole, and Cherokee. Even though these five nations were "civilized" by Western metrics—they adopted Western cultural practices such as private property, farming, religion, and trading—they were still regarded as savages. The consequent ethnic cleansing of Indians from the southeastern region of the U.S. led to an estimated minimum of 6,000 lives lost. Some figures put this number a little lower while others much higher. Once in Oklahoma, the five civilized tribes were promised to be left alone. This promise, like many before, was later broken.

Perhaps if the five civilized tribes were to have kept their homelands in Mississippi, Alabama, and Georgia, cotton cultivation would have died out much earlier. Just maybe, on that forlorn timeline, President Jackson would never have forced the five civilized tribes to move to Oklahoma; consequently, Sherman's soul-crushing March to the Sea would have never taken place.

In South Dakota, another discovery of gold led to an equally soul shattering chapter in American history. Much of this violence can be traced back to the famous Civil War hero and Indian fighter, George Armstrong Custer. In 1874, Lieutenant Colonel Custer led an expedition into the Black Hills of South Dakota, which led to the discovery of gold. Consequently, the scent of gold attracted hordes of surly and shrewd miners. The experience gleaned for the 29ers and 49ers turned many miners into seasoned roughnecks who were prepared to shoot first and ask questions later. Unfortunately, the new centennial 76ers of South Dakota were de facto illegal immigrants encroaching on the promised land of the Sioux Indians of South Dakota. President Grant initially sided with the Sioux Nations and made a feeble attempt to keep miners out but failed miserably. It should be noted that no person then, now, or ever, could have possibly stemmed that tidal wave of avarice.

In 1868, the western half of South Dakota made up the Great Sioux Reservation; it was an equivalent "Oklahoma of the North" for the Sioux, as was Oklahoma for the Muskogee family from the southeast. The refusal of the Sioux to sell their promised land to the U.S. government ultimately led to the Great Sioux War. This war led to Custer's death at the Battle of Little Bighorn on the eve of America's centennial in late June 1876. It was an equally bitter pill that rained on America's 100th birthday.

South Dakota and Oklahoma have served as protective harbors for Native Americans, but they differ as to their indigenous diversity. The Indians of South Dakota all nominally come from the one family tree, the Sioux, while the Indians of Oklahoma are from a diverse forest of family lines from the four corners of America.

The first family tree transplanted to Oklahoma was the Muskogee. The secondary family tree, which is also the one with the most branches, is the Algonquin. These include the Lenape, Kickapoo, Cheyenne, Arapaho, Shawnee, Miami, Potawatomi, Sac and Fox, and Wyandot (Huron). Another family tree from the northeast are the Iroquois represented by the Seneca, Cayuga, and Cherokee.

The family trees that came from the west, a single Aztecan tree is represented by the Comanche. From the northwest, two family trees made a home in Oklahoma—the Athabasca tree famously represented by Apache and the lesser-known Penutian tree, the Modoc Nation.

Finally, three native trees stem from Oklahoma herself. The Tanoan tree is singly represented by the Tanoan, a language isolate. And finally, perhaps the most well-known native tree, as made famous by *Dances with Wolves*, the Sioux family tree has several branches of the Osage, Quapaw, Kansa, Kickapoo, Oto, Ottawa, and Ponca.

Fatefully, the Sioux have connections to both South Dakota and Oklahoma, who also have branches in Canada where their generic modern politically correct exonym of "Native American" switches to "First Nation." But note, the Sioux family tree has many languages that are not mutually intelligible, as it is with other branches of a family tree—be it red, white, black, yellow, and brown.

Uniquely, the Caddoan branches of the Wichita, Kichai, and Caddo are native to Oklahoma; and the native Caddoan of South Dakota are the Arikara and Pawnee. However, as of this writing, the Arikara were confined to a reservation in North Dakota while the Pawnee were pushed into Oklahoma. Interestingly, the Caddoan family tree is only found in the United States since this tree does not have any roots in Mexico or Canada. Note, the city of Nacogdoches in East Texas is blessed with a name based on the Caddoan family tree.

It is also a major synchronicity that the Great Iroquois family tree, hereby represented by the Great Sycamore, was given the spotlight for the final curtain call of the Confederacy, on both sides. When General Lee surrendered to General Grant at Appomattox Court House on April 9, 1865, a Seneca Indian was a part of the Union delegation: Ely Parker. General Parker, who was born in New York, was mostly responsible for drafting the surrender documents for General Robert E. Lee. Apparently, before the war Ely Parker was a friend of General Grant and came to his aid in a bar fight, when they were nobodies. Thus it can be assumed that Grant was able to counter any racial opposition towards Ely Parker—due to loyalty earned. Concordantly, with another branch of the Iroquois/Sycamore family tree of the Cherokee branch, General Stand Waite was the last Confederate general to surrender to a Union force on June 23, 1865, at Doaksville, Oklahoma.

As the unceasing growth of the modern world continued, they became evermore covetous of the promised virgin lands of South Dakota and Oklahoma. As the 1890s approached, the modern world could no longer hold back their vampiric thirst for land and proceeded to subsume the unused lots of the virgin prairie simultaneously in South Dakota and Oklahoma.

In the spring of 1889, President Grover Cleveland signed the Indian Appropriations Act that officially opened unassigned lands to White settlers via the Homestead Act. The Sioux Reservations in South Dakota were cut in half, while in Oklahoma, a controlled expansion for more White American *Lebensraum* commenced, 48 hours after the birth of the infamous *Fuhr* in Austria.

Nonetheless, the land run became a beloved and romantic moment in history when 50,000 people at several starting gates around Oklahoma were set to claim unassigned Indian lands. It was the first reality game show that had real contestants vying for real estate prizes broadcast via the original Internet through Morse code. It was an Earth Day, April 22, 1889, on a bright and clear sunny day, that the ultimate frontier race of the frontier races began at noon. Depending on the particular gate, the iconic land race began with a military officer firing his pistol, a trumpeter, or the boom of a cannon. No matter the signal device, it was an awesome spectacle and stampede of over 50,000 settlers who rode horses, carriages, and wagons. The following year, 1890, Oklahoma Territory was created.

But just as Oklahoma Territory came into existence, the last sad chapter of violence left its mark at Wounded Knee in South Dakota. The massacre at Wounded Knee was the last spasm of major violence between White skins and Indians. It marked the end of the Old West.

Wounded Knee in 1890 and the Trail of Tears in 1830 are at the beginning and ending of lamentations shared between Native Americans of Oklahoma and South Dakota. The arrival of Europeans upon the shores of the Americas was as much a blessing as it was a curse. For millennia, the nations of America lived in a lucid dreamscape of oral tradition where a previous 10,000 chiefs and princesses sang a song of life from Point Barrow, Alaska, to the Tierra del Fuego, Chile. They would live and make war and peace in a primitive yet deeply connected way to the Earth. And who can recall the countless nations lost by war and assimilation before the awakening of hemispheres in 1492?

In the clash of cultures between Europeans and indigenous peoples of America, two stars of hope who were able to shine through the darkness were Jim Thorpe and Bill Mills.

Thorpe, an American hero for the ages, came from the heart of Oklahoma and was born in 1887. Just as Oklahoma is a fused state of Red and White identities, Jim Thorpe is of mixed Native and Newcomer heritages, as the ultimate

American Métis. Jim Thorpe's father was mixed Irish and Sac and Fox, while his mother was mixed French and Potawatomi. Both the Potawatomi and Sac and Fox are branches of the Algonquin family tree, hereby represented by the great North American oak.

Thorpe became the first Native American to win a gold medal at the 1912 Summer Olympics in Stockholm, Sweden. He won two golds, one in the decathlon and the other in the pentathlon. The pentathlon consisted of five trials: long jump, javelin throw, discus throw, and running 200 meters and 1500 meters. The decathlon consisted of the long jump, shot put, high jump, discus, pole vault, javelin, 110-meter hurdles, 100-meter run, 400-meter run, and 1500-meter run. But Thorpe's Olympic glory was truncated by controversy. Thorpe was stripped of his Olympic medals since it was found out he was a paid professional athlete in minor league baseball—even if they were crappy wages. It was 30 years after his death in 1953 that the International Olympic Committee finally reinstated his medals during a special ceremony on January 18, 1983.

Besides winning gold at the Olympics, Jim Thorpe was able to play professional baseball and football during its golden age. Thorpe played as an outfielder for the New York Giants, Cincinnati Reds, and Boston Braves from 1913 to 1919. He also played professional football as a running back, and Jim Thorpe was elected the first president of the NFL on September 17, 1920, which was then called the American Professional Football Association (APFA).

Like a modern superstar athlete, Jim Thorpe was also able to break into Hollywood. He played an extra and odd Indian in Westerns. But as Thorpe made a bundle, he spent a bundle, and by 1950 he was broke. He died at the age of 65 as a faded star, only to be later memorialized after his death.

Mills, a fellow athletic icon, was born in Pine Ridge, South Dakota in 1938, and is a member of the Oglala Lakota Tribe of the Great Sioux family tree. After college, Bill Mills entered the U.S. Marine Corps Reserve. In 1964, he was able to compete in the Tokyo Olympics and won the gold medal as a dark horse athlete in the 10,000-meter race. Bill Mills's victory was a part of a greater healing moment as this Olympics signaled the return of Japan to the global community since it took place 20 years after World War II. In 1964 the world had turned a corner, and love gave birth to something better. As an element of pride returned to Japan, it too fell upon Native Americans, and the United States, as well.

Two Native Americans who were able to gain high seats among the storytelling sermons of Hollywood are Russell Means and Wes Studi. Russell Means was born on the Pine Ridge Indian Reservation in South Dakota in 1939, and Wes Studi was born in Nofire Hollow, Oklahoma, in 1947. Their stars were written to cross in 1992 in the film *Last of the Mohicans* directed by Michael Mann. Russell Means starred as Chingachgook of the Mohican Tribe (Algonquin family), who has a son named Uncas and an adopted White son, "Hawkeye"— played by Daniel Day-Lewis. Wes Studi played the antagonist Magua, a Huron Indian chief (Algonquin family) who was on a mission to seek revenge upon the British Colonel Edmund Munro. In the climactic battle scene, Chingachgook and Magua square off in a semi-sacred scene that captures the gravity and tensions between Natives as incited by Newcomers. Russell Means also starred in Disney's animated movie *Pocahontas* (1995) and *Pocahontas II: Journey to a New World* (1998) as Chief Powhatan. Wes Studi also starred in *Dances with Wolves* (1990) and in *Street Fighter* (1994) as Sagat, and more recently as in James Cameron's *Avatar* (2009) as Eytukan.

As Indians from the Old World continue to further mingle with Indians of the New World, new words are currently jostling for supremacy to sort out this confusion. But from a providential perspective of the third eye, this is no accident. Old World Indians, like New World Indians, were oppressed by English-speaking peoples within their native lands. However, Indians of the Old had immunity to the various diseases that decimated the Indians of the new. They also had their own written language, which allowed for the protection and preservation of their religion and culture.

Fatefully, a Native and Newcomer Indian were elected to the office of vice presidency. The 31st Vice President, Charles Curtis, was of Native American heritage. Three of his great grandparents were of the Kaw, Osage, and Potawatomi Tribes; and they belong to the Sioux and Algonquin family trees. Concordantly for India, the 49th vice president has direct ancestry to the subcontinent, South Asia. Kamala Harris's mother, Shyamala Gopalan, is from Madras, Tamil

Nadu in modern-day India. She worked as a successful molecular biologist in cancer research in the U.S., where she gave birth to Kamala Harris on October 20, 1964.

The literally paramount attraction in South Dakota is Mount Rushmore. It features the super-sized busts of four American presidents. Two are of the first class of founding fathers, Washington and Jefferson. Like yin and yang, they evolved into political opposites. Washington of the Federalist party fought for a strong central government where elites held more power over the commoners. However, Jefferson was of the party for the Republic, who advocated for a weaker government and more power for the masses.

Additionally, Lincoln and Teddy Roosevelt represent the middle passage of America from 1860 until 1912, when the map of America was ripped apart and pasted back together during their tenure. Lincoln reattached the Southern states to the U.S., leaving a scar along northwestern Virginia, while Teddy sewed up the modern map of the U.S. with the creation of Oklahoma in 1907.

The equivalent item to balance South Dakota's Mount Rushmore is Oklahoma's National Cowboy & Western Heritage Museum in Oklahoma City. It is here that lauded halls are dedicated to pioneers and the rough riding men and women who settled the wild frontier. As the presidents of Mount Rushmore are the highest of leaders, the story of America also belongs to the frontiersman who blazed trails and settled the west. The cowboy is an iconic spirit of America. Mount Rushmore and the National Cowboy & Western Heritage Museum honor the two ends of society that laid the foundation of America, the leaders and its people.

As an equivalent honor for America's Native heritage, the monumental mountain sculpture of Crazy Horse is concordantly balanced with the First Americans Museum in Oklahoma City. The Crazy Horse monument is still under construction in South Dakota and set to become America's largest statue carved from a mountain, bigger than Mount Rushmore. The First Americans Museum was completed in 2021 and serves to educate and honor the Indians of Oklahoma. Thus, South Dakota and Oklahoma honor the iconic heritage of cowboys and Indians in a parallel manner.

THE FLAG REVELATION

A pair of aces who found a path into the invisible micro-cosmos and previously non-visible macro-cosmos are Ernest Orlando Lawrence and Karl Guthe Jansky. Ernest Lawrence was born in Canton, South Dakota, in 1901 and won the Nobel Prize in Physics for his invention of the cyclotron. The cyclotron opened the door to the fourth dimension, where several new elements were discovered. His work gives him the title as the first Ant Man of America—he was able to measure and observe the microscopic universe at the atomic level. Lawrence's work also allowed for the building of nuclear technologies, as science was able to refine uranium into its powerful form. In honor of Lawrence's efforts, element 103 was named after him: Lawrencium, Lr. Lr is in the scandium group of elements, which is named after Scandinavia. Coincidentally, Lawrence is of Norwegian heritage.

Karl Guthe Jansky, however, was born of Czech immigrants in Norman, Oklahoma, in 1905. Jansky's achievements were in the opposite direction, since he is considered the founding father of radio astronomy. Karl G. Jansky was also a physicist but became a radio engineer with Bell Telephone Laboratories. In 1931, Jansky discovered that radio waves were being emitted from outer space and built himself the world's first radio telescope. Jansky's findings were published on May 5, 1933, in the *New York Times*. He later became an advocate of radio astronomy but was given the cold shoulder by Bell Labs who didn't want to pay for such skylarking, and traditional optical light astronomers couldn't wrap their head around the "wacky" idea of radio astronomy. Eventually time would vindicate Jansky's work with cosmic radio waves. One of the craters of the moon was named after Jansky as well as asteroid 1932 Jansky. More recently, the iconic radio telescope array that appeared in the movie *Contact* (1997) was renamed in 2012 as the Karl G. Jansky Very Large Array. Thus, a man from Oklahoma discovered a new layer of reality among the heavens, Karl G. Jansky, with his radio telescope, while a man from North Dakota, Earnest O. Lawrence, dug deeply into the smallest realms of earth with a cyclotron.

Thus, if Ernest Lawrence is the first American Ant Man, who discovered new realities in the smallest of quantum universes, then Jansky was the first of the Green Lantern Corps, because he was able to discover and soar across new galactic realms with the power of his mind, by first imagining it and then making it real.

Culture

Stars come and go. In the big picture they shine and have their day in the public sun, but no matter how big, all stars from heaven and Earth are destined to fade. Nevertheless, entertainers create bonds of affection across the Americas, gluing together a national family and making collective memories for the national scrapbook. But only a select few are able to string and sew a golden thread of community between all sorts in the public, beyond their caste and class. From the first generation of movies, two golden stars came from South Dakota and Oklahoma: Charles "Chic" Sale and Will Rogers. Charles Sale of Huron, Dakota Territory (1885-1936) worked his way up from Vaudeville to the big screen. William Rogers of Oologah, Indian Territory (1879-1935) also learned the ropes of Vaudeville. Rogers for a while had the nation eating from his hand and has since become legend.

Charles Sale was part of the first generation to partake in talking movies and sparkled as the witty old timer who could remember the details of the Old West. Will Rogers also exuded an old-school folksy charm that poked fun at all parts of America. He kept a humble profile but was still able to talk big. What made Will Rogers stick out from his generation was a folksy wit and an all-encompassing love for all the hues of humanity. In the wake of his life, it inspired the nation to do better; The Will Rogers Institute was born, which has contributed to pioneering medical research.

Two women from the golden age of entertainment are Dorothy Provine (1935) and Rue McClanahan (1934). Dorothy Provine from Deadwood, South Dakota starred in classic movies like *It's a Mad, Mad, Mad, Mad World* (1963), *That Darn Cat!* (1965), and *Never a Dull Moment* (1968). Rue McClanahan from Healdton, Oklahoma, starred in *Mama's Family* (1983-1990), *Starship Troopers* (1997) and was the iconic Blanche Devereaux on *The Golden Girls* (1985-1992). McClanahan's reputation as the eager beaver began when she played the role of a swinging couple who ran into the Bunkers on *All in the Family* in 1972. Both spectacular stars exited stage left on the same boat in 2010.

Two heavy duty news anchors from South Dakota and Oklahoma who set it square with the American public are Tom Brokaw from Webster, South Dakota, and Judy Woodruff from Tulsa, Oklahoma.

On the lighter side of news and public talk, two sparkling sharpshooters born in 1950 are Mary and McGraw: Mary Hart of Madison, South Dakota, and Dr. Phil McGraw of Vinita, Oklahoma. Mary Hart was the host on the syndicated gossip news show on *Entertainment Tonight* from (1982-2011) that focused on heart matters of the rich and famous. Hart's voice encapsulates the essence of the broadcast speech via a hyper-confident, direct, full frontal, booming, quasi-hypnotic, and paradoxically artificial-yet-authentic broadcast cadence. On the other hand, Dr. Phil does not speak with that compulsory broadcast booming style. Instead, McGraw was able to keep his folksy southern accent and take deep dives on issues about the human heart for regular folks while making valiant attempts to remedy each situation.

Two boomers who are also the "Best of American Burgs" to impact several generations at once are Michael Steinberg (born 1959) and Steven Hillenburg (born 1961). Michael Steinberg of Rapid City, South Dakota, produced *There is Something About Mary* (1998) and *Hell Ride* (2008). Steven Hillenburg created a none too famous transgenerational animated superstar that appeals to adults and children alike with wacky and insightful humor—*SpongeBob SquarePants*, airing in 1999. Two comedic kings of the Generation X sort are Timmy Williams from Watertown, South Dakota (1981), who starred in *The Whitest Kids U'Know* and Bill Hader of Oklahoma (1978), who launched to stardom on *Saturday Night Live*.

Two storytellers who match like ketchup and mustard are Ron Howard and Christopher Cain. Blond-haired film director Christopher Cain from Sioux Falls, South Dakota, was born in 1943 and has directed many hit movies including *The Stone Boy* (1984), *Young Guns* (1988), *The Next Karate Kid* (1994), and *Gone Fishin'* (1997). A cinematic wonder to match from Duncan, Oklahoma, and born in 1954 is the red-headed Ron Howard. He has enchanted audiences across America and the world with the films *Cocoon* (1985), *Backdraft* (1991), *The Da Vinci Code* (2006), and *Solo: A Star Wars Story* (2018). Ron Howard also directed *Far and Away* in 1992, which tells a lovely story of the 1889 land rush in Oklahoma of the Boomers and Sooners.

A quirky fun fact that further sews a line between South Dakota and Oklahoma is made with January Jones (1978) and James Paul Marsden (1973), since both stars starred as *Amazing X-Men* with superhuman mutant powers. James Marsden from Stillwater, Oklahoma, set the mold as Scott Summers, better known as Cyclops, who has the ability to blast a powerful stream of energy from his eyes and must wear a red visor to keep himself from harming others and to control his ability. January Jones from Sioux Falls, South Dakota, starred as Emma Frost who has extremely powerful telepathy.

A pair of classy jokers from the cartoon world set the mold for animated stars of Donald Duck and Space Ghost. Donald Duck's distinct voice was born from the imagination of an Oklahoman—Clarence Nash of Watonga. Space Ghost was voiced by Gary Owens from Mitchell, South Dakota. Their voices are at opposite ends of the spectrum in the cartoon universe.

The king and queen of blonde and blond America are Cheryl Ladd and Brad Pitt. They are the superstar poster children for the beautiful, larger-than-life, flaxen-haired American. Cheryl Ladd of Huron, South Dakota, became an American star when she replaced Farrah Fawcett in 1977 as the blonde in the original TV series of *Charlie's Angels* (1976-1981). Other credits include *Millennium* (1989), *Poison Ivy* (1992), and *Santa Paws 2: The Santa Pups* (2012). Brad Pitt from Shawnee, Oklahoma, is at the top of his class of celebrity stars and will continue garner the lodestar of the public's attention, and the excellence of his resume of work is beyond counting.

Another king and queen of the non-blond bunch are Michael Spears (1977) and Olivia Munn (1980). Michael Spears from Chamberlain, South Dakota, broke into the big screen as Otter in *Dances with Wolves* (1990). Michael Spears also starred in *Into the West* (2005), *Winter in the Blood* (2013), and *Z Nation* (2018). Munn from Oklahoma City starred in *X-Men: Apocalypse* (2016) as Psylocke, *Iron Man 2* (2010), and in *The Predator* (2018) as the action hero biologist.

Two queens of clubs who killed it on the big screen are Amy Hill (1953) and Alfre Woodard (1952). Amy Hill from Deadwood, South Dakota, starred in *Lilo & Stitch* (2002) and *Magnum P.I.* (2018-2023). Alfre Woodard is from Tulsa, Oklahoma, and has had a rocking career all across Hollywood. She starred as Lily (from Chapter 3) in *Star Trek: First Contact* (1996), *Crooklyn* (1994), *12 Years a Slave* (2013), *Luke Cage* (2016-2018), and *Memphis Beat* (2010-2011).

Another pair of Native kings are Floyd Red Crow Westerman was born in 1936, and Will Sampson, born in 1933. Will Sampson of Okmulgee, Oklahoma, became an iconic star for his role as the silent Chief in *One Who Flew Over the Cuckoo's Nest* (1975). Floyd Westerman of the Lake Traverse Indian Reservation in South Dakota gained national fame in the film *Dances with Wolves* (1990) with the role of Ten Bears who also gave a closing speech, explaining to John Dunbar (Kevin Costner) that he need not worry about the White men, since Dunbar was now dead and was reborn a Sioux with the name *Dances with Wolves*.

Lighter shades of blue connect Oklahoma with South Dakota, distinguishing this very special pair from the vast armada of navy blue. Their connection is further reinforced as the fundamental fibers of the American spirit found refuge in their domain. Oklahoma and South Dakota are where the Great Spirit was given quarter in the sacred and ancient ceremony of smoke and fire, where the singing grass of the prairie is permitted to sing its photosynthetic psalms to Father Sky, by the hands and heart of the first nations to make a hearth in this hemisphere. It is where the ancient memory of yesteryear is permitted to beat in harmony with the hallowed drum of life, some 12,000-fold times 10,001 moons before the birth of Remus and Romulus, under the auspices of a howling she-wolf. As the Native Americans from the four corners call Oklahoma and South Dakota home, so too would the Newcomers from the four corners of the Elder World, beyond the shores of America. All have been chosen by the Great Spirit to meet the burdens and blessings of living on Mother Earth under the pipe of peace, below the glorious yellow Sun.

ten

UTAH & LOUISIANA

Prayers of Different Feathers Bring Faith to the Few and Many

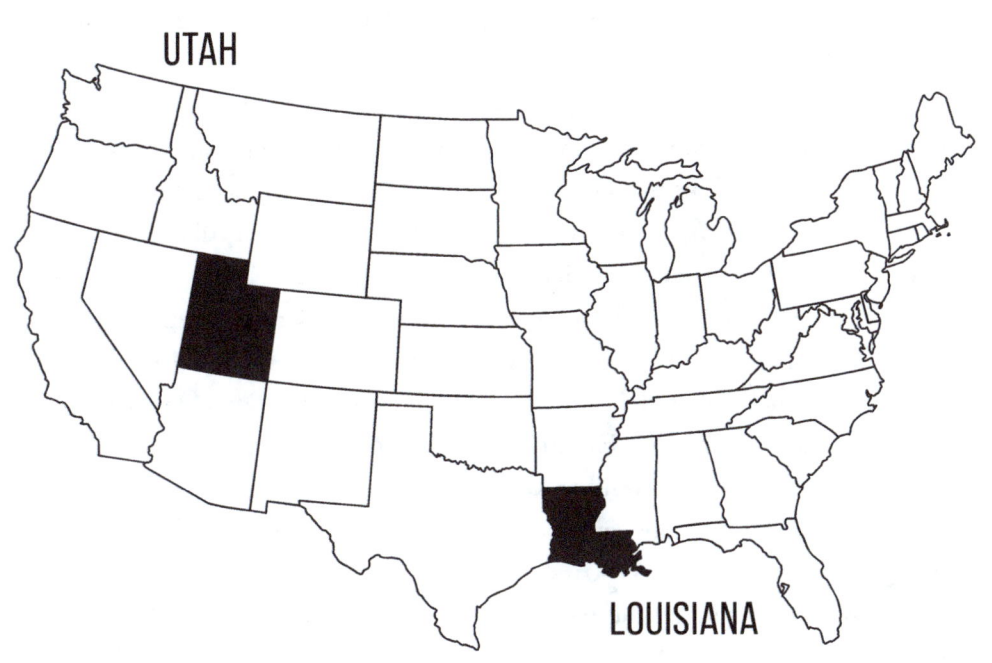

THE FLAG REVELATION

UTAH

Blue backgrounds contrast with a central white logo on Utah and Louisiana's flags. In Utah, an eagle with a white feathered head is visible at the crest. For Louisiana, a white pelican on a bird's nest mimics the bald eagle of Utah.

Many humans erroneously conclude that we are the only species with the capacity to build a home. However, the birds and bees have proven otherwise. How do insects and birds know how to construct such domiciles? It seems a mysterious non-human intelligence is at work. One can call it instinct, but what exactly is instinct, if not a mysterious type of intelligence?

The beehive featured on Utah's flag is a classical ancient beekeeper design. Beehives do not naturally look like that, like a Winne the Pooh hive. Most modern beekeeper beehives look like boxes or miniature condos. Somehow the general conception of a beehive has blended with the structure of a hornet's nest. In the wild, most beehives tend to look more like quirky modern architecture. Regardless of a hive's shape, at the core of all beehives is a repeating, precise, hexagonal structure, the honeycomb.

The honeybee may be the most famous organism with an established behavior for self-sacrifice. After a honeybee delivers its sting, it dies. As for the

LOUISIANA

pelican, its style of self-sacrifice is known as vulning. Looking closely at the flag of Louisiana, there are three droplets of blood visible on the mother's chest. This is because it was assumed that the mother pelican injured herself to draw blood in order to feed the hungry chicks.

It is a known fact that honeybees will surrender their lives for their mother, but it's fiction that mother pelicans vuln themselves for the livelihood of their children. The notion of pelican self-injury has origins in the Middle Ages and was amplified by the Catholic Church.

When the parent bird, male or female, mashes up the meal in their pouch, it can sometimes be seen pressing the beak and bottom mouth bag against their breasts. While mashing, guts and blood would sometimes spill out of the pouch while it is being tenderized, giving the impression that vulning is occurring. Pelicans sometimes form holes in the bottom pouch where blood and guts can spill out. From a distance, it would look as if the bird had cut open its own breast. In heraldic terms this became known as "Pelican in Her Piety."

It was Dominican friar Thomas Aquinas who wrote a Eucharist hymn that was adopted by Pope Urban IV in 1265 that underscored the symbolism of the pelican with Christianity. Aquinas had tremendous clout across Western Europe and is recognized as a Doctor of the Church, whence all of Germany, the entire Netherlands, the British Isles, and Scandinavia were in communion with the Church of Rome. Thomas's poetic hymn "Adoro te Devote" has a stanza that says, "Pie Pelicane, Jesu Domine; Me immundum munda tuo Sanguine," which translates to "Pious Pelican, Divine Jesus; clean the unclean with Your Blood."

While the pelican remains a potent symbol in the Catholic Church, the beehive is a prominent symbol for the Mormon Church. The Mormon leader Brigham Young (1801-1877) originally wanted to name Utah the state of Deseret; at the time, the proposed state of Deseret encompassed much more area than present-day Utah does. According to the Book of Mormon (Ether 2:3), "deseret" is a Jaredite word for "honeybee."

Coincidentally, these flags are redesigns from the 21st century. In 2010, the flag of Louisiana underwent a major rework. Then in 2011, Utah's flag also underwent a major modification. The 2010 Louisiana modification stems from the efforts of an eighth grader at Vandebilt Catholic High School in Houma, Louisiana. In 2006, a 14-year-old Joseph Louviere wrote to his local state representative Damon Baldone, who raised an issue about the missing blood spots on the pelican. But note, the shedding of blood officially represents the willingness of Louisiana to sacrifice itself for the people of the state, rather than the symbolism employed by the Catholic Church. If the state explicitly made reference to a Catholic concept, it could cause controversy, as a separation of church and state issue. Also, the 2006 pelican had a makeover. It was redesigned to look less like a comic strip drawing and more like a realistic pelican in 2010, partially due to advanced printing technologies.

This version of the Utah state flag with a white shield that does not obscure the date of 1847 was changed due to the efforts of a vexillologist, John M. Hartvigsen. In the 1980s Hartvigsen reported that the error began in 1922, due to a printing mistake. But it was not until 2010 that he was able to get state legislative support to fix Utah's flag as it was intended, which took place at nearly the same time when the three droplets of blood on Louisiana's flag were reinstated in 2010. Fatefully, Hartvigsen is a member of the LDS church, as

Joseph Louviere is Catholic.

Louisiana had several state flag versions starting in 1861; likewise, the pelican design for Utah has several versions. The first version for Louisiana was simply a white outline of the seal on blue from 1861 to 1912. Coincidentally, the first three versions of the Utah flag employed a white outline of the seal on blue from 1903 to 1913. After WWI, both flags became colored.

The most recent 2011 modification of Utah's flag was also made for corrective purposes. In 1922, the year "1847" (when the first settlement by the Mormon pioneers was made in "Mexican Utah") was placed outside; at the bottom of the shield, it was partially covered by the shield itself. This design made the flag look just a bit off. In fact, this error was made by the flag manufacturer. But nobody spoke up—either they were too polite or didn't notice or care enough to make a change. Nevertheless, this error stuck for the next 89 years. Finally in 2011, the position for the year "1847" was properly placed within the shield and below the beehive, as it was originally intended. Also the shield's background was made white, adding pop and contrast to the shield instead of being a boring blue on blue.

Geography

As geographic partners, Utah and Louisiana are contrasted to the extreme. They are opposites like a washing machine and dryer. Louisiana, the washing machine, is a part of the Deep South, and she is totally at Afro-centric latitudes. Utah, the dryer, is a western state that has an upper south orientation, and she is the last state to have a Virginia tilt. Also note Utah looks like a dryer, while Louisiana somewhat looks like an antique, hand cranked washing machine.

And by the luck of the draw or perhaps the footprint of destiny, Louisiana is perfectly parallel to Israel, north to south. To get a sense of the size of Israel compared to the U.S., just look at Louisiana but imagine it being only a third the thickness, east to west. The north end of Louisiana is parallel to the Golan Heights, while the Mississippi Delta at Bohemia, Louisiana, matches latitudes to the southern Israeli port of Eilat at the Red Sea. Of course, the climate is radically different due to differences in rainfall. Instead, Utah in the summer is a fine fit for the Holy Land's weather.

As for Utah's comparison to the Old World, she is parallel to Italy, starting from the north at Rome and heading south to Syracuse on the isle of Sicily. Another coincidence is the famous journey of St. Paul from Jerusalem to Rome, which covers nearly the equivalent distance from New Orleans to Salt Lake City. Likewise, St. Peter is considered the first Pope by establishing the church of Rome and had a life's journey whose birthplace and resting place mirrors this distance. In this case, New Orleans is on par with Jerusalem, while Salt Lake City can play the part of Rome. The Great Salt Lake of Utah is famously the largest lake in the U.S., with the nickname, "America's Dead Sea," while the proverbial Mississippi is the equivalent "Egyptian Nile" of North America. During the summer, the delta of the Mississippi is a perfect match for the delta of the Nile with cranes, weeds, willows, and crocodilians.

Utah and Louisiana are lands of stark contrast between the delta and the desert. They both have thriving mega-cities and suburbs, but there are parts yonder, where the average man should be wary to travel unless he is led by a local. The swampy bayou of Louisiana and dry valleys of Utah are where local folk become guardians of the keep, who have the duty to look after out-of-towners who might trespass into the unforgiving lands of the deep desert or winding streams of the swamp. Utah captures the dry poetry of the mineral kingdom that speaks through its hypnotic, Zen-inducing rock formations, while Louisiana dishes out a saturated vivacious poetry of the plant kingdom with its lush, full-bodied bayou.

As Louisiana is famous for hosting the king of American reptiles, the alligator, Utah is home to the jester of lizards, the Gila monster, which has a body coloration worthy of the royal jester at the queen's court. The Gila monster is not quite a monster, but its fearsome name stems from its venomous bite, which is reported to feel like hot lava flowing through one's arms. Gila monsters or "harlequin lizards" are the only venomous lizard native to the United States. However, the Gila monster's bite is not as deadly as a rattlesnake bite, but an alligator bite can easily end a life.

Finally, the expansive salt flats are a unique geographic match to the vast bayous of Louisiana. With these special geographic zones, unique vehicles have arisen for these unconventional environs. The swamp buggy and air boats are no stranger to Louisiana, as the speeding salt flat demons' cars and dune buggies make tracks across the sparse interiors of Utah.

Louisiana and Utah are the special teams unit that the rest of America can rely on in places high and dry or wet and muddy. When they work together, they guard each other's weak spots and can form a defensive force field that can fend off the ferocious temper tantrums of mother nature during any season—be it winter, spring, summer, or fall.

History

Utah and Louisiana are outstanding states of their respective regions due to their unique signature cultures. For Louisiana, French Cajun culture distinguishes her from her southern cousins, while the Mormons of Utah are a change up from the norm of the Pacific Pack. Beyond the French elements of Louisiana, much of Louisiana beats a bright red southern hue. This is similar to the tightly knit Mormon community, where the great swath of Utah is tilted with a crunchy granola, chill-lax West Coast vibe, as it is in California and Colorado. As a reminder, the recipe for Utah calls for one cup of Colorado and Arizona, one and one quarter cup of Nevada, a half cup of Idaho and Wyoming, and lastly one drop of New Mexico. The recipe for Louisiana calls for one cup of Texas and Mississippi, stirred with a half cup of Arkansas kickers, making a unique southern-style cake with a delightfully sweet, French toasted aroma.

Providentially, the French, or rather Cajun, element of Louisiana and the Mormon element of Utah share a partially parallel concourse, as they bore witness to true-blue biblical Exoduses in the New World. Starting with Louisiana, this North American Exodus took place in America B.C., "Before the Constitution." As a consequence, this story is hardly touched upon in the history books of America. But a century before the War of 1812, or rather, the Proverbial War of 1712, a seismic shift in the population of Canada would take place in Acadia, which is now known as Nova Scotia, New Brunswick, Prince Edward Island, and the eastern region of Maine.

In Europe, the *Proverbial War of 1712* is known as the War of Spanish Succession, but the conventional view by U.S. historians labels it as Queen Anne's War (1702-1713) or alternatively as a "French and Indian War." It was during this War, the *Pre-Centennial War of 1812*, that the French-Acadian peninsula was conquered by the British. Acadia is essentially the Virginia of New France, since it was the oldest permanent colony founded in 1604. All during its rule as a French colony, it was a thorn in the side of Massachusetts. French-Acadian ships would harass New England and incite the Wabanaki Confederacy to raid English settlements along the frontier. As British power grew in Nova Scotia/Acadia in 1712, they sought to consolidate their power over the majority of the French-Acadian population. It was an uneasy relationship as French-Acadians hoped for liberation with the help of Quebec or France. But when war broke out again during the Seven Years War (1756-1763), the final "French and Indian War," the U.K. finally conquered New France. And a final solution was chosen—to expel the French from Acadia. And this war was ignited by George Washing by what was to become Pittsburgh in 1754.

From 1755 to 1764, Acadia was depopulated of its French population by orders of the British government. Over 10,000 Acadians were uprooted from their homes and were forced to move elsewhere. Some returned to France while others were deported to other regions of colonial France. A sizable portion did find refuge in New Orleans, which had recently been transferred to Spain at the time. As a consequence of this diaspora enforced by the "Supreme Christian Pharaoh" of the British Isles—King George II—the spirit of Louisiana became a second home of Acadia, whose name was transmuted into Cajun.

As for the biblical-like Exodus with Utah, this came about during America A.D., "After the Declaration" of Independence. Consequently, it's better remembered. As the Mormon church established a vibrant and radical new congregation, it was harshly persecuted. In 1838, the Mormons living in Missouri were expelled during the first Mormon War. The Missouri Governor Lilburn Boggs issued Missouri Executive Order 44 on October 27, 1838, which expelled Mormons from Missouri. The Mormons fled to Illinois. But once again, conflict arose again at Nauvoo, Illinois, which ultimately led to the death of the founder, Joseph Smith. After this sorest of losses, the community resolved to move far, far away, and they chose the area around the remote Great Salt Lake region as their promise land. They were led by Brigham Young, who acted as a proverbial Moses who led their Exodus out of the United States into Mexico. Unlike Moses, Brigham Young was allowed to see and settle in the promised land that became Utah. The first Mormon wagon train left for the frontiers beyond America on April 5, 1847, and the first company reached the Mexican Salt Lake Valley three months later on July 24, 1847.

The date of July 24 has now become the Mormon holiday known as Pioneer Day. It is celebrated in a similar fashion to the 4th of July, but with rodeos and wagon train parades. Pioneer Day is an official state holiday in Utah and observed in states near the Salt Lake. As for Acadians who fled to Louisiana starting with the British take over in 1713, the state of Louisiana recently introduced a new state holiday known as Acadian Day, which falls on the Friday after Thanksgiving on Black Friday. But in Canada, Acadian Day falls on August 15. Louisiana's Acadian Day is still in its early phases of development and will no doubt take on some of the characteristics of Acadian Day as it is celebrated in Canada. But as Mormons established their community along the northern frontier of Mexico, they would ironically return to America without moving. Mexico surrendered the chosen Promise Land to the United States a year later in 1848. This gives the Mormon community a semi-first nations people status, as they were in Utah before the U.S. conquered it; likewise, the Acadians were in Louisiana before the purchase of 1803.

From a certain point of view, the flags of Utah and Louisiana are reflective of the two distinct and well-organized branches of Christianity. Utah has a flag reflective of Mormonism, while Louisiana has a flag reflective of the Roman Catholic Church.

A major difference between Protestants and Catholics is an alteration of the Bible. Protestant Bibles are lighter reads, because seven books from the Old Testament were deleted after Martin Luther posted his 95 theses in 1517. The books of Esther and Daniel also underwent sharp revisions during the 16th century. The reworking of the Bible is just one of the many theological issues that had bitterly divided Western Europe for 500 years, nominally into a northwestern Protestant half and southwestern Catholic half.

Similarly, the Mormon community of Utah can be seen as a further break from the Protestant tradition. If one can imagine, American Christianity is like a hamburger. The meat of American Christianity is made up of mostly Protestant denominations. The bun at the bottom would then represent the Catholic Church since the Protestant branches have roots to the Catholic Church. Finally, the bun on top would be the Mormon church. As the Protestant community sprung forth from Roman Catholic tradition, so would the Mormon community, at least initially, spring forth from the Protestant community. Also note, Joseph Smith was reared in the Presbyterian (Protestant) tradition by his mother, Lucy Smith, just as Martin Luther grew up in the Catholic tradition. However, it is important to note that the point of unity between Catholics, Protestants, and Mormons remains as whole via the documents of the New Testament.

Further, the initial Christian community sprung up from within the Jewish community. Thus, the proverbial dish of the "Wholly All-American Burger" sits on the finest of fine pottery work from Israel. Likewise, the extra toppings like lettuce, tomato, onions, pickles, and special sauce can represent the other religions of America: Buddhism, Native American religions, Hinduism, Islam, and other unique religions. And just to be wholly inclusive, perhaps Americans of a non-faith path can serve as the serviette? Finally, to misquote Jimmy Buffett, this is "Truly a Cheeseburger of Paradise." And which team gets to claim the cheese? It's made up of Americans who regard love as the foremost and highest aspect and attribute of the divine.

Two other faiths far off the beaten path in that special sauce have found a certain and special flock in Utah and Louisiana are connected via the mummy and magic. In Utah the American mummy arose with the work of Claude Rex Nowell, who founded the Summum—a philosophical and religious organization that practices modern mummification. Claude Nowell was born in Salt Lake City in 1944, and after an encounter in 1975 with what he called, "highly intelligent beings," he was driven to form Summum and change his name to Summum Bonum Amon Ra. However, he's best known as Corky Ra in the press. Corky Ra became the first person to undergo the Summum mummification process in 2008, when his body was encased in a bronze mummiform casket covered in gold that rests in the group's pyramid. This new religion has seven aphorisms. The 4th Summum Aphorism states that everything is manifested as dichotomy. As for Louisiana, the High Priest Oswan Chamani and Priestess Miriam Chamani founded the New Orleans Voodoo Spiritual Temple in 1990. Just as Summum is based upon ancient African traditions of the Nile, so too is the Voodoo Spiritual Temple a congregation religion that is based upon the animistic traditions from Africa. The Voodoo Temple has a troupe of sacred drummers called the Krewe of Nutria. Voodoo operates in a similar tone to the traditional native American religions, whereby ritual and communion with spirits is conveyed with ceremonial fashions via song and dance.

On the more surreal and somewhat spine-tingling end, Utah and Louisiana are home to two famous UFO and vampire stories. The Skinwalker Ranch in Uintah County, Utah, is the site of the most paranormal activity ever studied by science and mystics alike. People have reported seeing UFOs, malevolent orbs, bigfoot-like creatures, and other poltergeist-like activity. Several TV shows and documentaries were made about the Skinwalker Ranch, but a feature Hollywood film is yet to be made. In Louisiana, several high-profile vampire movies were made about the community around New Orleans, notably *Interview with the Vampire* (1994), which starred Brad Pitt and Tom Cruise. Since there is a legendary vampire community connected to New Orleans, it has become something of a tourist trap—yet there are dedicated members of the community who take the stories of the vampire quite seriously.

Two famous writers from Utah and Louisiana of the boomer generation who have extensively explored these paranormal and spiritual aspects with a positive interpretation are Esther Hicks from Coalville, Utah (born in 1948), and Anne Rice from New Orleans, who was born in 1941. Anne Rice was the author of *Interview With the Vampire*, written in 1976. Anne Rice has written in several voices from gothic fiction, erotic literature, and even hard core devout Christian stories. She was reared Catholic but retains her own unique view on the matters of the divine. Anne Rice passed into the great unknown on December 11, 2021. Esther Hicks, on the other hand, is a guru in the New Thought community who has written several books about the law of attraction, as promoted in the film *The Secret* (2006). Esther Hicks states that her understanding about the law of attraction came from "a group consciousness from the non-physical dimension" called Abraham, which allows her to tap into "infinite intelligence." Esther Hicks has co-written several self-help books with her late husband Jerry Hicks.

The making of the American nation was immortalized with the completion of the transcontinental railroad that was built with over 21 million swings of the hammer. Two teams worked in tandem, one from the East and the other from the West, determined to meet up at Promontory Summit, Utah, on May 10, 1869, with a celebrated golden spike ceremony. The Eastern team built a track from Sacramento, California, and much of the labor force was composed of Easterners from China. The Western team started out in Council Bluffs, Iowa, and was composed of Westerners from Europe. This science-age technology form of transport cut journey time down from six months to six weeks, and at a fraction of the cost. It was an amazing technological worldwide wonder of its time that was honored and echoed in the same manner when the first man walked on the moon in 1969. The nation and the world were awestruck by this first of miraculous technological wonders of the world in 1869. If things repeat themselves, perhaps in 2069 another technological wonder from the U.S. will amaze the world. Also note, in 1869 the periodic nature of the table of elements was discovered by Mendeleev, as well.

As Utah was witness to the making of a modern nation from the union of the east and the west, Louisiana bore witness to the making of a nation from the north to the south. However, this operation called upon the genus of military engineers rather than civilian engineers. The United States was on the verge of falling apart during the 1860s. But before the nation could go forward, the Union needed to take control of the Mississippi River. Two military teams in tandem—one from the north end and another from the southern end. The southern team was led by David Farragut, who was able to make some headway by capturing New Orleans. However, the southern advance was bottled up at Port Hudson, Louisiana. The northern team was led by Ulysses S. Grant. His task was to wrestle the citadel of Vicksburg from Confederate hands. A critical key to winning the Civil War, according to Lincoln, was to take control of the Mississippi River. Until that was done, the South was virtually invincible. Precious livestock, supplies, and manpower from Texas, Arkansas, and Louisiana could easily shuttle across the Mississippi to support the war effort in Virginia or Georgia and vice versa. The region of the Mississippi River between Vicksburg and Port Hudson was the corpus callosum of the Confederacy. The corpus callosum is an anatomical structure that connects the left and right hemispheres of the brain in a man, woman, dog, cat, or mouse. No doubt if the Union was unable to sever this link, it would have led to the liberation of the Confederacy.

After the fall of Vicksburg, the last link between the two halves of the Confederacy was severed at Port Hudson, Louisiana. Previously, the defenders of Port Hudson were able to repulse the massive armies of the Union. However, when they got word Vicksburg fell, the writing was on the wall. On July 9, 1863, the longest siege in American history—which lasted 48 days—ended when the last "golden cannonball" was fired for control of the Mississippi River.

The yin and yang aspect of Promontory Summit, Utah, and Port Hudson, Louisiana, is that the completion of the transcontinental railroad was done as a constructive process from the western and eastern halves of the continent, while control over the Mississippi River was affected by a destructive process coming from the north and the south.

Although the railroad is considered a cultural touchstone success for America, it heralded the destruction for the way of life for the Plains Indians. Likewise, the fall of Port Hudson was the harbinger of things to come for the Confederacy. Thus, Promontory Summit and Port Hudson were the last stops in Utah and Louisiana that connected the nation from opposite cardinal directions and were gargantuan feats completed with the greatest costs of time, money, and life. A benefit for the modern United States, but at a dear loss for the Confederacy and Plains Indians.

Culture

Let us begin with two Gen X erroneous doppelgangers Jaime Bergman from Salt Lake City and Reese Witherspoon from New Orleans. Jamie Bergman (born 1975) earned her path to fame via the modeling route. Afterward, she was able to open the drawbridge into Hollywood and star in movies like *Any Given Sunday* (1999) and *Son of the Beach* (2000-2002). Reese Witherspoon (born 1976) was able to break into movie-town with the film *The Man in the Moon* (1991). Reese Witherspoon then boosted herself into the big leagues with movies like *Little Nicky* (2000), *Legally Blonde* (2001), and *Sweet Home Alabama* (2002). No doubt a sister drama or sci-fi movie with Bergman and Witherspoon would be the cat's meow.

Two super mega stars that form a binary boomer star system with a front row spot in the private memory of every American demographic are Roseanne Barr (born 1952) from Salt Lake City and Ellen DeGeneres from Metairie, Louisiana (born 1958). Both women cut their initial cloth on stand-up comedy in the 1980s. They used their nationally approved visa from "Chuckle-stan" to punch a funny hole on American TV. Roseanne starred in the eponymous blue-collar *Roseanne* TV family about a semi-dysfunctional family in middle America, while Ellen DeGeneres became daytime TV talk show royalty. Sadly, both their careers were torpedoed by their own over-the-top personalities. Roseanne Barr was ejected from her reboot of the *Roseanne* TV show in 2018 due to an off-the-cuff tweet. Ellen lost her show due to accusations of a toxic workplace behind the scenes on her daytime TV show. Nevertheless, both women left a trail of happy and silly notes that were able to tickle the funny bone of America for the maximum range of generations to become familiar with.

Chrissy Teigen from Delta, Utah (born 1985), is wingwoman to Danneel Ackles from Lafayette, Louisiana (born 1979). Chrissy Teigen popped onto the public radar with *Deal or No Deal* as a briefcase model in 2007 and has since become a core TV and social media personality. Danneel Ackles starred in *Ten Inch Hero* (2007) and *Harold & Kumar Escape from Guantanamo Bay* (2008).

Two beauts from the classical black-and-white era are Donna Douglas from Pride, Louisiana (born 1932), and Pat Priest from Bountiful, Utah (born 1936).

Donna Douglas is best known as the original May Clampett from *The Beverly Hillbillies* (1962-1971), while Pat Priest is best known as the second Marilyn Munster from the TV show *The Munsters* (1964-1966), replacing Beverley Owen, who left after only 13 episodes. Donna died in 2015, but Pat Priest is still kicking.

A pair of pistols from the Old West are Butch Cassidy from Beaver, Utah (born 1866), and George Scarborough from Natchitoches Parish, Louisiana (born 1859). Butch Cassidy is one of the few Old West legends to transcend popularity due to a modern era sleeper, which is now a culturally significant hit, of *Butch Cassidy and the Sundance Kid* (1969). The movie is based upon the real-life exploits of Butch's life as an outlaw, which ended in South A—snap that, you should just see the movie yourself. The movie was something that old-school conservative boomers and hippies could both get behind for various reasons. Cassidy's fraternal gun-toting partner in crime from Louisiana, George Scarborough, is another Wild West legend. He lived the true black-and-blue life of the cowboy, lawman, and outlaw. Deputy Scarborough was the calculating, quick to draw, lead lawman who was willing to play dirty to catch his prey or get even. It should be noted that the Wild West was so wild by many factors. The lack of lawmen was one reason, and the frontier was not completely settled, but a significant catalyst that added that extra level of crazy was a grand multitude of disgruntled Civil War veterans, from both the South and North, who were no strangers to putting their fellow man six feet under. Taking that, with PTSD on the harshest and goriest of levels, gangs of drop out vets-to-outlaws bent on getting their own or taking their rage out on the system, fueled the flames of the Wild West to that extra level, especially during the 1870s and 1880s. George Scarborough ended his life in a shootout in Arizona in 1900.

As the computer advances, the two ends of the binary multiverse are apparent with Utah and Louisiana. Nolan Kay Bushnell from Clearfield, Utah (born 1943) was part of the first generation to lead the home video game industry with Atari. Bushnell's electrically coded wingman is Jeffrey Vitter. Vitter, born in 1955, is a member of the first generation of computer scientists who helped design mathematical analysis of algorithms that deal with big data and evaluate data science. Vitter has coded contributions to data compression, image compressing, arithmetic coding, randomized algorithms, and machine learning. Bushnell helped launch the first mass market of home video game consoles into the stratosphere in the 1970s. Although there were other earlier, more primitive home consoles that played Pong and a few crappy consoles not worth mentioning, Atari was in a league of its own and became the first established brand like the NFL or Netflix. But unlike with the NFL or Netflix, participants played an active role in controlling the ongoing drama-game play on the TV screen rather than watching as passive spectators—unless one believes in woo or astral-projection, as apparently many men do when the magic of alcohol gives them psychic abilities to affect the outcome of a televised contest. The original Atari home computer gaming console came with one button and a handle called the joystick. One key to Atari's success was having one good game on par with arcade parlors of the 1970s, which was Space Invaders—the first video game shooter to take the world by storm. Two of the best games on the Atari console that hold water today are Adventure (1980) and H.E.R.O. (1984). If we are lucky, several 1980s action hero, punch the air, style movies based upon Atari classics are in the future, with a little help from AI?

Two singers from the delta and desert are Amie Comeaux and Jewel Kilcher (born 1974). Amie Comeaux from Brusly, Louisiana (born 1976), became a 1990s hit wonder with her songs "Who's She to You" and released two posthumous albums *A Very Special Angel* (1998) and *Memories Left Behind* (2007). Sadly, Amie Comeaux died in a car crash due to a heavy rainstorm that caused her car to hydroplane and smash into a tree. Jewel Kilcher was born in Payson, Utah, but her star ignited after she moved to Alaska. She is known simply as Jewel and is another classic 1990s singer whose hits include "Who Will Save Your Soul," "You Were Meant for Me," and "Foolish Games."

Movies play to all kinds of audiences and two outspoken Christian filmmakers who were able to place those themes center stage for their flock and beyond are Thomas and Tyler. Thomas C. Christensen, better known as T. C. Christensen from Salt Lake City, is known for films about the Church of Latter-day Saints like *Joseph Smith: The Prophet of the Restoration* (2011), *17 Mir-*

acles (2011), and *Ephraim's Rescue* (2013). Tyler Perry from New Orleans has made a library of movies since 2002, starting with *Madea's Family Reunion* with a focus on the Black community and is best known for playing the ruthless Madea, a self-confident, no-nonsense, elderly Black woman who knows how to dish out the good, the bad, and the funny.

A quirky sports connection is the story of the Utah Jazz. Utah is hardly the state that is considered a mecca for jazz, the so-called "devil's music" of the 1920s and 1930s according to proper upright Christians of the time. The Utah Jazz started out in New Orleans and moved to Salt Lake City in 1979. Perhaps someday a sports franchise that starts in Utah will move to New Orleans?

Ned Miller and Fats Domino are two classic American minstrels who make a harmonious whole of ebony and ivory. Ned Miller from Rains, Utah (born 1925), was a singer who implicitly demonstrated the Virginia tilt aspect of Utah with country music. Ned Miller's hits include "From Jack to King" and "Invisible Tears." Miller's wingman from the Big Easy is Fats Domino from New Orleans (born 1928), who was a pioneer of rock and roll. Domino's hits include "The Fat Man" (1949), "Lawdy Miss Clawdy" (1952), and "Ain't That a Shame" (1955). Thus, if New Orleans is the Big Easy, this makes Salt Lake City, Le Petit Challenge.

Louisiana and Utah are like birds of similar but different feathers, like the pelican and seagull. The seagull is a spiritual icon with Mormonism, and the main Mormon Tabernacle at Salt Lake City is decorated with a seagull due to the providential arrival of a flock of seagulls. The first crops of the year were being destroyed by insects, putting the colony in peril, but then a flock of hungry seagulls appeared and proceeded to devour the insects, saving the colony from starvation. This event is interpreted as divine Providence and is dubbed the Miracle of the Gulls by the Latter-day Saints.

In congruence, the Catholic community within Louisiana can be dubbed the Former-Day Saints. The reason being, as the latter comes later, from a Protestant point of view, while the Former came earlier, as the Catholic Church arose before Protestantism.

Nevertheless, Louisiana and Utah maintain a traditional tilt in politics toward conservative family values, which are deeply rooted in that old-fashioned religion of the most holy of holy books, regardless of the version or edition. Thus, the flags of Louisiana and Utah are a proverbial line up of the Church of Latter-day Saints with the Church of Former-day Saints, when taken from a Middle-day Saints Protestant perspective. Also, note both states are packed with several hundred churches and saints founded somewhere in the middle, neither of the former nor latter, and with just a few that are quite beyond. Amen.

eleven

SOUTH CAROLINA & REVERSE OREGON

A Tale of Two States and/or Two Dreams of Janus

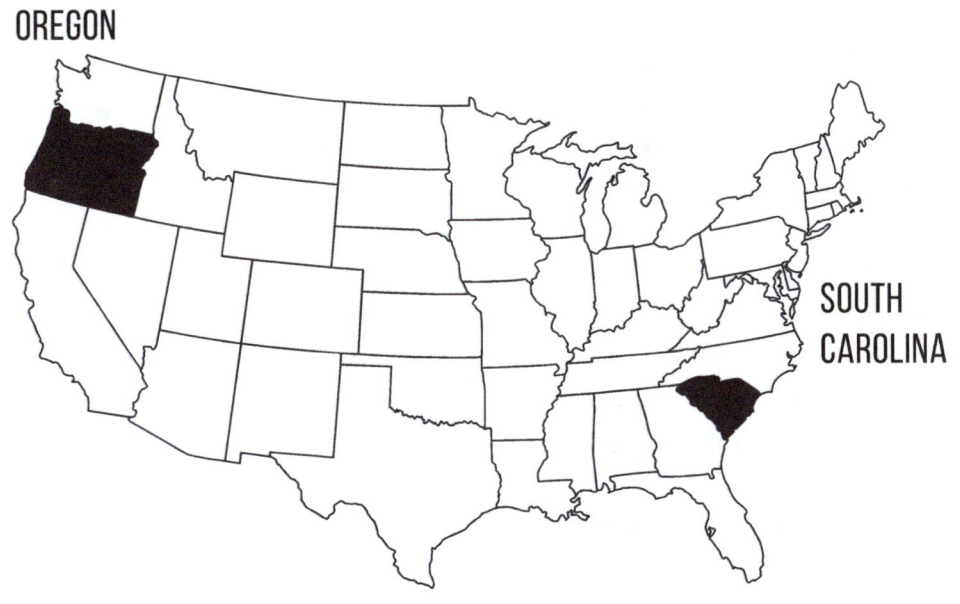

THE FLAG REVELATION

SOUTH CAROLINA

The flag of South Carolina is partnered with the backside of Oregon. It is a peculiar relationship, but South Carolina retains a special place in American history that deserves a unique partner. Dark blue fields pair concordantly with central silhouettes. Harmoniously, two items are visible on both: South Carolina features a crescent in the shape of a moon and palmetto, while Oregon has a beaver and a log.

A critical linking point between South Carolina and Oregon is their Janus-faced heritage. Janus is an ancient two-faced Roman God associated with times of transition—at the beginning of the end, or rather the ending of a beginning. Charles Dickens captures the essence of Janus double speak via the "best of times, worst of times" intro passage in *The Tale of Two Cities*, written in 1859. It just so happens that Oregon has a Janus-faced flag, and, coincidentally, the year 1859 is on the front.

Every so often, one's path is set upon two possible destinies—be it a new job, new lover, new dress, new car, a new whatever, and Janus is associated with bi-dimensionality of a profound fork in the road that can tear one's soul in two.

Even today South Carolina retains two loving faces. One face cherishes her

OREGON REVERSE

Southern heritage, while the other embraces her identity as a core element in the U.S. Arguably, South Carolina also has the most intensely Janus view of the federal flag; it is as much a source of pain as it is a point of pride, as it is can be for the White communities of the South and Black communities across the nation.

The state flag of South Carolina conveys power and serenity at the same time. The crescent unwittingly connects South Carolina to the Islamic world. The crescent is iconic of Islam, in a similar vein as the cross is for Christianity. The crescent appears on the flags of many Islamic nations, like the flags of Algeria and Tunisia, which are coincidentally at the same latitudes as South Carolina. As per chance, a large swath of Muslims from Africa were fated to call South Carolina home. However, their connection to the Koran was effectively circumcised when they were purchased by European Christian slavers—often sold by African Islamic slave traders. During the slave trade, much of West Africa was, and still is, oriented toward Islam.

As for the history of America, South Carolina's initial secession marked the passing of an Old America, conceived in 1776. Fatefully, Oregon was the last state to bear witness to the Virgin Union before the Civil War. It was a time when the balance of loyalty between the nation and the individual states was more pronounced. It was time before any state would make war upon another state. It was a time when a man had the wicked freedom and right to own another man. The power of the federal government was meager compared to what would become afterward. The debate between states' rights and the rights of the federal government was to be fully tested a year after Oregon became the 33rd state. At the lead of that test was South Carolina.

On Christmas Eve 1860, South Carolina would cut down America's formerly perfect cherry tree. When America's formerly intact cherry tree fell, rivers of blood would flow across the nation. Indeed, it can be uncomfortable to talk about the Civil War, especially when the two sides that engendered the Union and Confederacy are present. Some Americans will fly off the handle as a gush of emotions overtakes their ability to stay centered. Yet some have the maturity and peace of mind to see the issue from all sides. The same volatile and touchy feelings naturally arise when speaking of conception and the loss of virginity.

Besides being the final state to bear witness to the Virgin Union, Oregon's political heritage is also Janus-faced, but in a different way. Oregon had a bi-national period when she remerged with "Canada" from 1818 until 1846. This is known as the joint occupation period when the U.K. and U.S. jointly ruled over Oregon Territory. Before the regions of Oregon Territory made up their mind on whether to become Canadian or American, there was talk that this region should go their own way as a new nation—neither American nor Canadian. In a way, Oregon was gender fluid, politically speaking, for 28 years.

Just as the beaver is an honored symbol for Oregon, it is a patriotic icon for Canada. As the U.S. has the buffalo nickel, Canada has the beaver shilling (a shilling is basically a nickel). The Canadian government officially recognized the beaver as a symbol of the sovereignty of Canada on March 24, 1975. As Oregon shares a special 28-year joint history period with Canada, her backside beaver unwittingly echoes Oregon's connection to Canada—or rather, by serendipity demonstrates Canada's connection to Oregon. On the subject of fraternal flag partners, the reverse of Oregon makes a harmonious whole with South Carolina.

So what does the beaver and the moon of South Carolina have in common?

For one thing, they both control waterways, in radically different manners. The moon is the key player in controlling the tides. There are other factors, such as the sun and rotation of the Earth. But it is the interplay of these gravitational forces, whereby the moon is given most credit. If we didn't have a moon, we'd always have a high tide at noon and then again at midnight. Obviously, beavers don't have such cosmic powers like the moon—instead their power is earthly, yet can have just as strong an impact on their local community. Instead of an intertidal zone, the damming of rivers by the beaver can impact the ecology of a forest with flooded pond zones. In scientific circles, the beaver is an ecosystem engineer and keystone species, due to their impact on landscape and effect on biodiversity of wherever they live. Of the positive impacts, beavers on the land keep the soil healthy and intact.

Note that beavers don't just live in Canada—their natural habitat is in every U.S. state except for Hawaii, and they even range in Mexico. The beaver truly is a North American animal. However, the palmetto is a southern thing. They grow mostly in the Deep South, as freezing conditions kill them off.

Another interesting parallel is that the palmetto is edible, and beavers can eat wooden logs. The palmetto is scientifically known as the *Sabal palmetto*. But for country living folks of the Deep South, it is also known as swamp cabbage. Native Americans long knew that the soft heart of the palmetto made a delightful meal. When properly prepared, the soft trunk of the palmetto tastes like cabbage, ergo swamp cabbage. As for beavers eating wood, the part of trees that they enjoy eating is the bark just under the dead surface and the soft woody trunk known as the cambium. In truth beavers don't eat hard wood, just the spongy parts of the bark. As beavers eat a part of the outer trunk of a tree, humans can eat the heart of a palm tree on South Carolina's flag.

Geography

Oregon and South Carolina pair up like champion superlatives that run the entire spectrum of weather from the Pacific Northwest to the Atlantic Southeast. It is a union of the sunny south with the cool, rainy north. Oregon is the first of the Pacific Northwest as South Carolina is the first of the Deep South.

Since these states make the only coast-to-coast pair, it's appropriate to give them relative bearings. Typically, LA and NY are the key reps for the West and East Coasts. Now with the added layer of fraternal flag twins; Portland, Oregon, and Charleston, South Carolina, finishes the east-west-north-south crisscross of coastal corners. When you overlay lines of these iconic four corners from LA-to-NYC with PO-to-CSC, an X marks the spot over the heart of America in Kansas.

South Carolina also marks the transition to Mexican latitudes. This means that the northern part of South Carolina is in the All-American Belt, but her southern half has territory south of Mexico's most northern point. Charleston Harbor is the last harbor whose entrance is completely north of Mexico. Thus, Charleston County is on the cusp, as are Hampton, Jasper, and Beaufort. When riding on I-95, the city of Yemassee in Hampton County has the proper claim of "South of the Border." Thus everything in between, from Follow Beach to Hilton Head, is also south of the border. Basically, the southern tip of South Carolina is at the latitude of Tijuana, Mexico. Likewise, Myrtle Beach is equal to Los Angeles's Long Beach. Also, the northern border of South Carolina is parallel to Bakersfield, California.

As for Oregon, its southern state border is roughly the same as the northern line of Connecticut/Rhode Island with Massachusetts at 42° north. Portland is also on par with New York's northern border with Canada along the 45th. The equivalent "Goonie Country" of Astoria crosses at Houlton, Maine. But a better coastal example of "Goonie Country" in latitude is "Anne of Green Gables Country" on Canada's Prince Edward Island near Charlottetown. Oregon is totally north of Canada's most southern point, Point Pelee in Ontario. This puts Oregon in the snowy CBC (Cool Brewers Club). There are over a dozen states that are completely north of Canada's most southern point, meaning Canada will always beat them in a limbo contest but not a snowball fight.

South Carolina is completely south of Europe and on par with Africa. Oregon is also completely north of Africa, on par with Europe. South Carolina became a part of the exclusive southern six-pack of states that formed the original core of the Confederacy on February 8, 1861, along with Mississippi, Florida, Alabama, Georgia, and Louisiana. Thus, from a particular southern point of view, the southern six-pack was never ruled by the first democratically elected Republican president, Abraham Lincoln.

Coincidentally, Oregon Territory has a unique six-pack formula of her own. There are five U.S. states and one Canadian province that make up the Oregon Territory six-pack, meaning that some part of the modern state can trace territorial heritage back to the joint U.S./U.K. occupation period from 1818 to 1846. The Oregon Territory six-pack flavors include Oregon, Washington State, Idaho, Wyoming, Montana and one special collector's edition can for British Columbia.

Both of these six packs have unique influences distinct from the rest of the United States. For the Carolina six-pack, they were all a part of the provisional election of Jefferson Davis and creation of the Confederate Constitution. Texas would have been a part of the group, but Sam Houston refused to swear allegiance to the Confederacy. Thus, Texas was delayed and missed out on the inauguration and official writing of the first provisional Confederate Constitution. Additionally, if Texas would have joined that first shindig with Jefferson Davis, the whole six-pack paragraph would fall apart. Unlike the Deep Southern six, Texas has a northern tip parallel to Europe, and this is why Texans are able to make that click-ka-dee-clack "gotcha" sound, when a wise and wily Texan puts somebody in their place.

County names that can be found in either state are Union and Marion. Charleston is also the name of cities on opposite coastlines. South Carolina's Charleston is far more famous, while Oregon's Charleston is a happy little hamlet.

History

The first document to establish European ownership over South Carolina and Oregon was issued by the Spanish Pope Alexander VI on May 3, 1493. This Papal Bull, or rather *The 1493 Pope's Bulletin of May 3—Eximiae devotionis*—was largely ignored by the Protestants as they started to break away from the Catholic Church soon after the awakening of hemispheres in 1521.

The Spanish had a tenuous hold on both colonial Oregon Country and colonial South Carolina, but the British were able to subvert Spanish authority. Two failed Spanish colonies were the 1526 San Miguel De Gualdape for South Carolina and the 1789 Santa Cruz de Nuca colony for Oregon Territory.

Long before 1619, Plymouth Rock, Jamestown, and Roanoke, and three generations before the foundation of St. Augustine in Florida, there was the original colony of colonies first planted in South Carolina—San Miguel de Gualdape. Five years after Ferdinand Magellan circumnavigated the world in 1521, a colony was attempted in what was destined to become South Carolina with over 500 persons that included White, Blacks, and Natives. Eventually hunger, indigenous hostiles, and the planting of the colony before the start of winter took their toll, and it was abandoned. But one of the first slave uprisings took place at this colony. The exact location of the colony proper is not known, but the initial location is known. It was located near the mouth of Winyah Bay in Georgetown County, South Carolina. After a month in South Carolina, the Spanish moved to a disputed location, perhaps in Georgia or Virginia. However, when the British established the colony of Carolina in 1663, Spanish power was waning, and they lost the will to remove the latter-day colonial powers in the Americas.

In 1789 the Spanish had control along the North Pacific, but they did little to develop the area, so the Russian and British Empires took advantage. The Russians were able to colonize Alaska, while the British established trading routes in Oregon Territory. In a mad, mad, mad, mad scramble to reassert their claim over the entire Pacific Northwest, the Spanish planted their first European colony in Oregon Territory at Santa Cruz de Nuca on Vancouver Island. In defense of this first colony, Fort San Miguel was built. Interestingly, this first Spanish fort of the North Pacific was built with Chinese laborers. The Spanish then asserted their dominance in the area by seizing several British trading ships in the area. This action led to the Nootka Crisis, which nearly brought England and Spain to the brink of war. But it was too little, too late for the Spanish.

The British were strong enough to hold their ground. Rather than go to war over territory, the Spanish made concessions to Russians and British claims, made legally effective by the Nootka Conventions. By 1795, the Spanish colony on Vancouver Island was abandoned. However, the Spanish left footprints all across the Pacific Northwest with names of places like Valdez, Alaska, and the San Juan Islands snuggled between British Columbia and Washington, BC.

Captain Gray reached the Pacific Northwest in summer of 1788 and was the first documented American to enter Tillamook Bay, Oregon. Gray coincidentally bore witness to the Nootka Crisis—when the Spanish military detained several British ships for trespassing in 1789—when it unfolded. Besides establishing America's claim to Oregon Territory, Captain Gray commanded the first American voyage around the world with the *Columbia Rediviva*, a three year voyage from 1787 to 1790 on a westerly course from Boston. Captain Gray was also first to sail a ship into the Columbia River, ergo the "unnamed" river received its Newcomer name as the Columbia. In the wake of this exploration, British Columbia also got its namesake as British Columbia. Consequently, Captain Robert Gray is best remembered for setting anchor on America's claim to Oregon Territory. It is a small synchronicity that his imprint on Oregon is equally matched to his final destiny in South Carolina. And note, the capital of South Carolina is Columbia. Captain Gray passed away at Charleston, South Carolina, in 1806.

In 1819 the Spanish gave up on their dreams for Oregon Territory. However, they didn't let their dream totally die out, in a way they handed off their claims to the U.S. with the Adams-Onís Treaty of 1819. Unlike the 1803 Louisiana Purchase when no other colonial empire stood in the way, the "Two for One: Florida and Oregon Territory Going Out of Business Purchase" from Spain gave the U.S. another powerful position in the rat race for Oregon, against British and Russian interests. Bottom line is that the mad, mad, mad, mad Spanish scramble for the Pacific Northwest was ultimately beneficial for the United States, which added fuel to the flame of the Manifest Destiny for a nation from sea to shining sea.

The initial west coast of America included Oregon, Washington State, Vancouver Island, and British Columbia. Up to 1846, the U.S. didn't know how much of the initial west coast would permanently become American. However, it was pretty certain that the lands that would become Oregon were ground zero for America's west coast.

You may have noticed when speaking of Oregon's connection to Canada, the books switch back and forth with the U.K. Obviously, Canada and the U.K. are completely different nations, but before 1867, Canada was the loyal American colony, or British North America. And before 1965, the official flag of Canada was the British flag. Further, the War of 1812 is considered an important part of Canadian history. Thus, the battles that took place are viewed as sore losses or patriotic victories by Canada. It can get weird juggling the viewpoints of the U.K., Canada, and U.S. before 1867—the year Canada was constitutionally established. Nonetheless, this chapter shall attempt.

The last official Prime Minister who ruled over the original 13 colonies that included South Carolina, was Frederick North. But for the Oregon six-pack it was Sir Robert Peel. Reason being, nine British Prime Ministers returned as administrators in a condominium with the U.S. concerning Oregon Territory/Columbia District, from 1818 to 1846, for a quirky bi-national period. This was not the only time two nations merged as one for a little while. In the South Pacific the U.K. and France had joint condominium with The New Hebrides from 1906 to 1980, which is now the nation of Vanuatu.

Under the 1819 agreement, Oregon was under the rule of British Prime Ministers Robert Jenkinson to Robert Peel; and this matches concurrently with the time frame between U.S. presidents, James Monroe to James Polk. Due to the peculiar nature of this bi-national "politically hermaphroditic" Janus-faced phase, it can be branded as the Jimmy-Jim-Robby-Rob period, since the first names of the beginning and ending executive heads of state of the U.K. and U.S. were the same, respective to their start to finish. A wonderful Janus thematic, indeed, which is rooted to the synchronicity of executive heads, echoing to this unique period of Oregon.

In total, Oregon Territory had seven British Prime Ministers partially administer Oregon Territory during this phase.

The Jimmy-Jim-Robby-Rob Era
1818-1846
A Reunion with the U.K.
In loving memory of the forlorn British-American
Territorial District of the U.K.S.A.
United Kingdom States of America

ROBERT JENKINSON – Prime Minister (1819-1827) of Oregon Territory

The most important prime minister of the Jimmy-Jim-Robby-Rob Era was Robert Jenkinson, 2nd Earl of Liverpool (1770-1828). It was during the Jenkinson administration that the War of 1812 would rage. Yet when peace came, Robby Jenkinson was able to kick off the first joint administrator phase over Oregon Territory with his "enemy mine" administrator, Jimmy Monroe. Mr. Jenkinson, Robby technically, ruled over Oregon from 1818 until April 9, 1827.

GEORGE CANNING – Prime Minister (1827-1827) of the Region that Became Washington State

The next prime minister was Minister George Canning. Mr. Canning's term only lasted four months, from April 12 to August 8, 1827. Canning was a war hero and Tory who directed the seizure of the Danish fleet in 1807 during the Napoleonic Wars. Canning also helped secure the rebelling Spanish colonies independence from colonial Spain. As Spain helped liberate the United States from the United Kingdom, Great Britain was naturally inclined to return the favor.

FREDERICK JOHN ROBINSON – Prime Minister (1827-1828) over a Western Portion of What Became Wyoming

Frederick John Robinson, 1st Earl of Ripon (1782-1859) was a middle grounder, in the purple, between a Patriotic Tory and Liberal Whig, who dared to support Catholic empowerment and the abolition of slavery.

ARTHUR WELLESLEY – Prime Minister (1828-1830, 1834) over What Became Idaho

Perhaps the most famous British prime minister to hold sway over Oregon Territory was Artie Wellesley, better known as the 1st Duke of Wellington. Wellesley's first term lasted from January 22, 1828, until November 16, 1830. The Duke of Wellington is best known for leading the coalition that defeated Napoleon at the Battle of Waterloo in 1815. Being a right-wing Tory of his time, he was supremely confident that building a British empire in the heart of Asia was the right thing to do. A distinct difference from the Tory line, Arthur Wellesley also allowed for the passage of the Catholic Relief Act of 1829, whereby Catholics were allowed to take office in Parliament, otherwise known as British Congress.

CHARLES GREY – Prime Minister (1830-1834) of What Became the Western Face of Montana

Charles Grey, 2nd Earl of Grey, was a liberal Whig. In Grey's first term, he ruled Britannia and Oregon from November 22, 1830, until July 9, 1834. During Grey's watch, the government officially abolished slavery with the Slavery Abolition Act of 1833.

And if you're wondering about Earl Grey tea, the choice tea does indeed get its namesake from Mr. Grey. It was his particular blend that later became the savored flavor of tea that was favored by Captain Jean-Luc Picard, played by Patrick Stewart in *Star Trek the Next Generation* (1987-1994). Patrick Stewart (born 1940) is also known for his iconic role as Professor X in the *X-Men* original movies. Thus, Earl Grey tea should be the official drink of Oregon, instead of milk. Why!? Because over 20 states already assign milk as their state beverage. And when drinking Earl Grey, remember to give three cheers: "Cheers to the U.K., cheers to Canada, and lastly, cheers to the USA for the end of slavery."

WILLIAM LAMB, Lord Melbourne – Prime Minister (1834, 1835-1841) of What Became the San Juan Islands

William Lamb, 2nd Viscount of Melbourne, was the last Prime Minister dismissed by a British Monarch, King William IV in 1834. However, the 2nd Viscount of Melbourne was rehired by Queen Victoria in order to tutor her on British politics as MP from 1835 to 1841, over Oregon Territory. Thus, the Viscount of Melbourne was able to pull the "Cleveland Shuffle" or "Napoleon Two-Step." President Cleveland is famous for having two non-consecutive terms in office, and if you don't know about Napoleon, too bad.

ROBERT PEEL – Prime Minister (1834-1835, 1841-1846) over What Is Now the Currently Disputed Juan de Fuca Strait Between Canada and the USA

Finally, the last prime minister with the capacity to send a wee bit of TLC in the affairs of Oregon Territory was Sir Robert Peel. Peel is considered the key founder of the modern British Conservative Party, when in 1834 Peel issued the Tamworth Manifesto. The effect was that the Tory Party metamorphosed into the modern British Conservative Party.

Coincidentally, and eventually, the British Conservative Party gave the U.K. its first American-born prime minister, Boris Johnson. On July 24, 2019, Alexander Boris De Pfeffel Johnson became the head of the United Kingdom. Johnson was born in Manhattan on June 19, 1964. By synchronicity, Johnson became head of the U.K. on the 200th anniversary of the joint U.S-U.K. occupation period of Oregon Territory, while his "American twin," another New Yorker, was the president of the United States.

Mr. A. B. Pfeffel J. was born in Manhattan, while Mr. D. J. T. "Covfefe" was born in Queens, and both executives, born in June, were made fun of for their wispy blond hair. From July 2019, upon the entirety of 2020, until January 2021 two NYC born gentlemen under the sign of Gemini, with wispy blonde hair were in charge of the U.K. & U.S., two centuries after the joint rule of the *United Kingdom States of America*.

As for the British monarchs who were able to reign over part of the U.S. during the condominium period of The Columbia District/Oregon Territory, they are:

His Majesty King George IV (1820-1830)
His Majesty King William IV (1830-1837)
Her Majesty Queen Victoria (1837-1846)

THE FLAG REVELATION

And, finally a "special memba'berry" cameo,
return guest appearance by the so beloved
[{(In Time)}]
His Majesty King George III (1818-1820)

As South Carolina and 12 other colonies along the Atlantic were under the rule of King George III, so too, at a different phase, were Oregon and five other states of the Pacific. South Carolina was present to witness King George's arrival on planet Earth on June 4, 1738, and honor his ascendency to the throne on October 25, 1760. Likewise, Oregon was a proverbial half-breed colony subject of the United Kingdom upon his latter half. Concordantly, Oregon would witness King George III's final ascent into the heavens when he exited stage left on January 29, 1820.

Just as the United States had two rival capitals during the Civil War from February 1861 until March 1865, Oregon Territory had two capitals from 1819 until 1846—the American one being at Oregon City near Portland, while the British/Canadian administrative center was at Fort Vancouver, in modern Washington, BC (BC indicates Washington State "By Canada" as opposed to Washington, DC).

As Oregon City was the American terminus of the Oregon Trail, Fort Vancouver (in Washington State) was the terminus of the Canadian York Factory Express. The two rival anchor cities were also separated by just 10 miles. You can think of the York Factory Express as an equivalent *"Canadian Oregon Trail."* Consequently, from the Canadian perspective, the American Oregon Trail can be dubbed the *"Independence Factory Express."* Reason being, the American Oregon Trail started at Independence, Missouri, and the Canadian Oregon Trail started at York Factory, Manitoba. Note, though, that the York Factory Express never bore witness to wagon trains of Canadian settlers. It was mostly used by the Hudson Bay Company and other voyagers to send goods back and forth.

The original west coast of Canada and America was one and the same in Oregon Territory from 1818 to 1846. Just as the Pacific Northwest has a blurred bifurcated history, so too does the Atlantic Southeast from 1860 to 1865. The big difference is that Oregon's Janus-faced era was not as deadly, yet lasted much longer, while South Carolina's Janus-faced era was extremely deadly and much shorter—a difference of five years versus 28 years.

Coincidentally, two key forts exchanged hands during the War between the North and South of 1861, and South and North of 1812. During the War of 1812, a fort in Oregon fell into British hands, Fort Astoria. Since Fort Astoria was isolated and had little protection, it was acquired easily by a semi-hostile economic takeover by the North West Company. No shots were fired nor lives lost, but pressure and winds of the War Between the Anglophone States reached Oregon in 1813. Five months later, the *HMS Racoon* arrived in the fall of 1813 with instructions to conquer Fort Astoria, but it had already been peacefully drafted into the empire. The captain of His Majesty's Ship (HMS) *Racoon*, William Black, formally claimed Fort Astoria and renamed it Fort George in honor of the most despised king of the 13 colonies, King George III, in December 1813.

Eventually the War of 1812 ended with no change of territory in 1815. In 1817, the *USS Ontario* was sent to repossess Fort George and reassert its maiden name, Fort Astoria. The *USS Ontario* (a perfect name for this mission, since it implies Canadian power, yet was a U.S. naval Vessel) simply conducted a short flag ceremony reclaiming Fort George as Fort Astoria but allowed the North West Company to retain control. It wasn't until 1846, under President Jimmy Polk and Prime Minister Robby Peel, that Fort George was truly restored back in American hands as Fort Astoria, and the rest of history was *Goonies*. But sadly, none of the *Goonies* cast is Canadian, yet they could easily pass as Canadian.

The complementary contested fort for South Carolina was Fort Sumter, however there was never a name change. When it exchanged hands from the North to the South, it was a much more politically charged event. Historians mark it as the beginning of the military phase of war that started on April 12, 1861. Eventually, Fort Sumter was returned to Union control by the war's end and reincorporated into South Carolina as a National Historical Park.

The two great patriarchs who had a heavy hand in shaping the destiny of Oregon Territory and South Carolina are John B. McLoughlin and John C.

Calhoun. Although these Johns would never cross paths, their political impact cannot be overstated. Their leadership moved proverbial mountains in shaping America's destiny, notably South Carolina and Oregon.

John C. Calhoun was born on March 18, 1782, in Abbeville, South Carolina, and died on March 31, 1850, in Washington, DC. John B. McLoughlin was born on October 19, 1784, in Rivière-du-Loup, Quebec, and died on September 3, 1857, at Oregon City. Both men had a similar phenotype—they were tall and white-haired with hallowed eyes of a would-be tenured professor at Hogwarts School of Witchcraft and Wizardry. For the record, Calhoun is a perfect fit for House Slytherin, the snake, while McLoughlin is a congenial fit for Gryffindor, the lion.

They were nearly of the same ethnic stock, as well. Being Scotch Irish naturally pitted them against the powerful English-Anglican families of Charleston and Canada. John McLoughlin also has an element of French Canadian added to his heritage. Both Calhoun and McLoughlin can trace part of their names to County Donegal, which is part of the modern Republic of Ireland. This is the one county of Ireland that is further north than Northern Ireland.

Both men had a gifted intelligence that manifested in different ways. John McLoughlin went the route of the doctor while John Calhoun became a lawyer. John McLoughlin earned his medical stripes on the frontier at Fort William—now called Grand Portage in Ontario. Besides healing the sick, he became familiar with several Native American languages. As his talent shined, he became a partner of the North West Company. John Calhoun had his mind molded by Yale College and later attended Litchfield Law School in Connecticut.

When the War of 1812 broke out, John Calhoun was a representative for South Carolina and became the firebrand leader of the War Hawks. John McLoughlin also became familiar to the bitter pill of war when he was indicted with the massacre at the *Battle of Seven Oaks*, where a civil war of Canadian corporations took place when the "half-breed" Native-European mixed Métis of the North West Company soundly defeated the Whites of the Hudson Bay Company. But after clearing his name from the British authorities, the newly forcibly united Hudson Bay Company (united with the North West Company) chose him to become Chief Factor for the Columbia Department by the British. John McLoughlin moved British headquarters from Fort George (British-occupied Fort Astoria) to Fort Vancouver, which is now a part of modern Washington, BC. It was here that he regulated trade with Mexico, Russian, Hawaii, and the United States.

After the War of 1812, John Calhoun became the paramount spokesman for the American South. Although a War Hawk with Britain, he was a peacenik when it came to war with Mexico. John Calhoun's anti-war stance was that it would undo the balance of power between the Northern free-soil states and the Southern slave states. As his pro-Southern and pro-slavery view evolved, it laid the foundation for the ideas of the Confederacy. Calhoun was the chief supporter of states' rights of nullification, whereby a state could ignore federal laws that were deemed unconstitutional by the state.

Had South Carolina dug her heels into nullification rather than secession, would there have been a Civil War? God only knows, but Calhoun's lasting legacy to the South was his go-for-broke defense of slavery. He took the view that the institution was not a necessary evil, but rather a systemic good that provided the best quality of life for African Americans.

Through today's lens, John Calhoun was squarely on the wrong side of history. Nonetheless, Calhoun provides a crystal clear view of 19th century political thought. Is it fair to judge the past? How might the people of 3030 judge the society of 2020? Without a doubt, our modern culture will be viewed as backward and savage.

As a modern comparison, factory farming provides a semi-suitable equivalent. This scientifically engineered, economically maximized, and profit driven farming practice has spread across the nation. However, this type of farming is predicated on inhumane suffering. No dog or cat lover would subject his or her pet to the death camp like confinement of factory farming, and would gladly fine, incarcerate, or perhaps remove any such person from society who treated pets in such a manner.

One could easily apply John Calhoun's arguments from slavery to factory farming. In a Calhounian perspective, humans are the would-be master of the plantation. No doubt Calhoun would argue in favor of factory farming because animals get quality medical treatment and plenty of food. He may conclude the quality of life is better at a factory farm, because in the wild they would be subject to constant hunger, parasites, disease, and sudden attacks by predators.

Another parallel between factory farming of today and the institution of slavery in 1818 is that both systems depend on a great deal of suffering for the want of ridiculous wealth. Lastly, the right to subjugate animals to mankind's will is supported by scripture.

Although slavery and factory farming are two very different institutions, parallels can be drawn. It is only presented here to give the reader a glimpse into how political issues challenged America before the outbreak of the Civil War. No doubt many would consider it an egregious sin to compare factory farming to slavery, but it is used here as a demonstration to show the complexities of how cruel institutions are entrenched—at the time, slavery was considered a "gray/grey issue" or "not my problem." Just as many Americans of 1818 had nothing to do or see about slavery, so it is today with factory farming. The war to end factory farming is unlikely to form on ours or our grandchildren's horizon, if at all, ever.

Calhoun was a brilliant man with a myopic vision. His heart was ruled by the cold logic of mind, beset by tradition. He was dead a decade before the start of the Civil War, but his ideas lived on to embody the spirit of the Confederacy. Calhoun was a man of his environment. In retrospect some will consider him a traitor to American values, yet he was loyal to the ancient and established values set forth by his cultural conditioning.

Likewise, John B. McLoughlin is considered a traitor to the South, as seen from Canada. As chief factor of the Hudson Bay Company, John B. McLoughlin is akin to being a chief executive officer (CEO)-governor of Oregon Territory. It is proper to say that John McLoughlin wielded incredible power over the Columbia District. He was at times wary of the influx of American pioneers, and he was ordered by the HBC not to help them. For whatever reason, perhaps a love of American equity versus British elitism, he ignored those orders and provided crucial support to the Americans flowing into Oregon Territory. He also owned the proverbial "essentials gift shop" at the end of the Oregon Trail at Oregon City. It didn't help that the Hudson Bay Company initially discouraged Canadian settlement of Oregon Territory, as profit lines from trapping and fur trading put colonial settlement in fourth place. In the end, the "Traitor of the Columbia District," or rather the "Father of Oregon," became an U.S. citizen in 1851—eight years before Oregon became a state.

The North often points the finger at the South for its heritage of institutional racism; however, when Oregon is considered, the South can finally point the finger right back at the North. When Oregon became a state in 1859, it was the only state to enter the Union with a Black exclusionary law. In order to keep the peace between races, Oregon made a shortsighted decision to exclude Blacks from settlement as a final solution.

The provisional government of Oregon voted to exclude Black settlers from Oregon's borders. The law authorized Oregon's officials to whip any Black settler in the territory a maximum of 39 times for every six months they remained. Although Oregon entered as a free-soil state in 1859, early Oregon was basically a White supremacist state at its roots. The first Oregon territorial law to exclude Blacks upon penalty of the whip was passed in 1844.

The ramifications of Oregon's anti-Black laws resulted in the first settlement on Puget Sound in Washington State. A Black settler by the name of George Washington Bush (1779-1863) became the proverbial Black forefather of the Pacific Northwest. Like Daniel Boone, Bush was a skilled frontiersman who was born in the northern part of Delaware that became Pennsylvania, and in his youth would traverse the wild frontier and even found work with the Hudson Bay Company. When Bush became a grown family man in 1844, he embarked to the West Coast upon the Oregon Trail with five other families, as the Bush-Simmons party. Upon hearing about Oregon's anti-Black policies, they were forced to cut a trail north toward Washington Territory.

Besides having anti-Black laws, Oregon was at the head of the class with anti-Asian laws. The original Constitution not only barred Blacks from living in Oregon; "Chinamen" were excluded as well. In 1862 Oregon, all Black, Chinese, Hawaiian, Métis, and mixed-race people were forced to pay a race tax of

$5, which is about $152 in today's dollars. The penalty for not paying those taxes was two weeks of hard labor for the Department of Transportation. Although the 14th Amendment of the U.S. Constitution guaranteed citizenship regardless of ethnicity, Oregon did a two-step sneak back. Oregon first ratified the 14th Amendment in 1866 but later rescinded it in 1868. It wasn't until 1973 that Oregon finally relented and re-ratified the 14th Amendment, which would, under state law, legally allow Black, Métis, Hawaiian, Asian, Native American, and mixed-race people to legally own land, vote, and become enfranchised citizens of Oregon. Just as South Carolina had to re-ratify U.S. law, so too would Oregon, but at a different magnitude. Although much diminished compared to Jim Crow, Oregon indeed had her own form of racism, albeit with a lighter touch. An appropriate name for this era is Rob Crow, which is in reference to the Robert Jenkinson and Robert Peel Era, and the fact that people with a high melanin aspect along the West Coast were robbed of their rights granted by the 14th Amendment.

In the aftermath of the U.S. Civil War, the 14th and 15th Amendments extended citizenship to all races. However, this liberal policy was effectively rolled back by 1881. The big win of the Civil War was that slavery ended; however, civil rights for non-Whites would have to wait.

The Jim Crow era can be defined as starting when the Democratic Party gained control over the last of the readmitted states on April 11, 1877, which just happens to be South Carolina. However, the start of Rob Crow (Asian American suppression) started with the Chinese Exclusion Act of 1882 and ended when Oregon re-ratified the 14th Amendment in 1973. Also note that Rob Crow affected states along the Pacific coast, as Jim Crow affected the southern coast. It was mostly due to Rob Crow that the American Chinatown became a separate and conspicuous element of major metropolitan cities across the U.S. Since Chinese Americans were not allowed to properly own land, they were forced to live in segregated neighborhoods, so as to afford them basic protections and support.

Shortly after 1881, hordes of anti-Asian mobs across the Pacific became especially violent during the winter of hate in 1885 and the summer of segregation in 1886. Chinese in the countryside were ethnically cleansed and given limited opportunities in the cities. They were allowed to stay in Chinatown to do menial jobs like laundry and helping with commercial shipping needs related to China. The worst anti-Chinese event in Oregon took place at the Hells Canyon Massacre on May 27, 1887. Over 30 Chinese American miners, who did not get the memo that they were not welcome in Oregon, had their gold stolen and lives lost in Wallowa County, Oregon.

Although Jim Crow and Rob Crow left a tragic footnote on Oregon and South Carolina, a squadron of African and Asian Americans were able to blaze a trail built upon the original inspiring promise of America. The Tuskegee African Airmen served with pride and passion during WWII. Although segregated from Whites, their unrequited love for America demonstrated the best elements of character, which makes us human. These Black airmen came from all across America. Two of note were from the Palmetto State: Paul Adams (1920-2013) of Greenville, South Carolina, and Robert Friend (1920-2019) from Columbia, South Carolina.

Paul Adams earned the Congressional Bronze Medal for his service in WWII. After the war he went on to become a teacher in Lincoln, Nebraska, and served as the President of the NAACP of the Lincoln Chapter. In 2008, an elementary school took his name to become Paul Adams Elementary School, and he was alive to witness this event. After WWII, Robert Friend continued his work in the Army Air Service and was witness to its birth as a father for the U.S. Air Force in the summer of 1947, serving in the Korean and Vietnam Wars.

In concord, a select brave and few Chinese Americans from Oregon doubled down on their one-sided, unreciprocated love of America. Of particular note are Arthur Chin and Hazel Ying Lee. Arthur Chin was born in Portland, Oregon, in 1913. He earned the Distinguished Fly Cross and Air Medal and is recognized as the first American Ace of WWII. In order to become a pilot ace, five enemy planes need to be shot down.

Hazel Ying Lee was born on August 24, 1912, in Portland, Oregon. She led an exciting life and immersed herself into American culture, despite the systematic anti-Asian climate. However, the bombing of Pearl Harbor was a boon that paved a path for her citizenship in 1943. Consequently, she was able to join the Women Airforce Service Pilots (WASP) program, where she shined. Hazel Ying Lee had two infamous close calls with death. The first being when she fell out of an airplane when her pilot instructor made a loop. She was able to land safely after deploying her parachute. The second close encounter happened when she made an emergency landing in Kansas. The farmer assumed she was Japanese and chased after her, shouting to the neighbors that the "Japanese had invaded Kansas." After dodging the farmer's pitchfork, she was able to convince him she was not a Japanese invader. The final incident was her last, when her P-63 King Cobra collided with another P-63 at Fargo, North Dakota. She was pulled from the wreckage with severe burns and died two days later on November 25, 1944. The error was not hers but the control tower's. Sadly, her brother, Victor Lee, died at nearly the same time with the U.S. Tank Corps serving in France. When their bodies were returned home to Oregon, the cemetery refused burial on the account it was a "Whites only" section. After a lengthy battle, the cemetery relented, and they were buried at a formerly White only section of the River View Cemetery, overlooking the Willamette River.

Remembering the misdeeds of the past and indulging the passions of finger pointing can be trying to one's soul, but the silver lining is the profound lessons they provide. Oregon and South Carolina share the burden and blessings of a multi-racial society—neither better nor worse than the other. Alas, all nations have a sordid history of oppression, and the scars of tribal infighting are ubiquitous from Rwanda to Auschwitz, and upon the killing fields of Cambodia. Collective guilt and collective blaming hardly help. With time, the stings of past sins are eventually understood and can tap a multitude of secret blessings that illuminate the proper way forward, as these tragic mistakes ultimately reveal the firmament of wisdom.

Culture

A plain murmur fills an auditorium. Puffy hair with neon pink headbands can be seen among the sea of students eagerly anticipating for the weekend to start.

SOUTH CAROLINA & REVERSE OREGON

Suddenly, the lights dim. The chatting of students continues, but it is noticeably lower. The red curtain opens to a dark stage. On the backstage wall, a neon red light appears like a laser making a straight line, but when it reaches the center, it makes a red circle and continues across. A second neon light of orange appears underneath. Finally in the center of the circle, a letter K slowly blinks on. At that moment, the crowd was dead silent. A perplexing wonder fills the audience as to what is going on. Seconds after the silence, there's a shearing sound that gets louder and louder, until a thunderous spark and flash of lights strobe across the stage and a box drops to the floor, squarely positioned in front of the glowing circled K. A soft rock guitar solo starts, and the auditorium is filled with youthful hooting and applause.

When the booth opens up with a cloud of smoke and a 17-year-old Keanu Reeves emerges holding a South Carolina flag while a 17-year-old Alex Winter holds a one-sided beaver Oregon flag, they begin to explain the idea of fraternal flag partners. Keanu and Alex follow all the talking points covered in this chapter with a collage of video and music, underscored with a rocking soundtrack. As they breach each topic, the heroes of history highlighted from either state, those legends appear in pairs from the booth or cloud of smoke and share a comical anecdote. After all the historical figures are seated, Keanu tells the student body and teachers that popular cultural icons from the fraternal flag states are going to begin the talent show portion of their presentation.

A wooden welcome wagon rises from the floor, and wearing white sparkly sequin dresses are two stunningly beautiful women sitting cross-legged: Delilah Rene and Vanna White. Delilah grabs the Oregon backside flag and explains that she is one of the most popular and renowned syndicated radio personalities. She often discusses issues of the human heart and makes on-air dedications for persons with sore hearts. Vanna White then takes the South Carolina flag and begins her presentation with a video of herself as a contestant on the *Price Is Right* on June 20, 1980. Although she did not make it to the showcase showdown, let alone on stage, she explains that she has surpassed any potential winnings when the wheel of fortune turned in her favor. Eventually, she became the iconic game show co-host for the *Wheel of Fortune* starting in 1982. Delilah and Vanna give two big smiles and plant the flags on the floor while waving and disappear when a glitter bomb explodes.

As the flags begin to fall to the floor, two men catch the flags. The two men who catch the flags are two chuckle busters who can jab the funny with harsh hooks and uppercuts: Andy Andrist and Chris Rock. Rock and Andrist are temporal twins born in 1965. Andy J. Andrist is from Oregon and makes jokes at a UFC fight club-triple black belt level—meaning, thin-skinned persons should avoid his humor at all costs. Andrist was a writer for the *Man Show* (1999-2014) on Comedy Central. Chris Rock is from Andrews, South Carolina, and is a southern cornerstone of comedy of *SNL* origins. Rock has appeared in numerous films such as *Top Five* (2014), *Head of State* (2003) and *Osmosis Jones* (2001). If the two should ever meet, it would be a gut-busting nuclear funny-bomb the likes of which no one has seen before. After telling several jokes that make the audience stomp the floor with a thunderous roar, they disappear in a patch of laser smoke.

Then a video montage of River Phoenix and Chadwick Boseman is given. River Phoenix was born on August 23, 1970, and was a star-powered actor during his childhood. His paramount role was in *Stand By Me* (1986), where he was the effective leader of an outcast group of friends. However, he passed away on Halloween 1993 due to a cocaine-fueled mix-drug overdose. Chadwick Boseman was born November 29, 1976, in Anderson, South Carolina. Boseman's career started soon after River Phoenix died in 1993 as the playwright for a college play. Chadwick Boseman's seminal role was when he cast the die for *Black Panther* in 2018. However, Chadwick was ravaged by colon cancer and died on August 28, 2020.

Another team appears from the phone booth, Austin O'Brien and Aziz Ansari. Austin O'Brien was born in Eugene, Oregon, in 1981 and is best known as the kid hero lead in *The Lawnmower Man* (1992) and *Last Action Hero* (1993) alongside Arnold Schwarzenegger. Aziz Ansari from Columbia, South Carolina, was born in 1983, and became a star on *Parks and Recreation* (2009-2015). He is also a stand-up comedian.

Two boomer town queens who enchanted America float down from the ceiling with wings: Margaux Hemingway and Andie MacDowell. Margaux Hemingway was born in Portland, Oregon, in 1954. Margaux and Andie started their careers as models, both making a splash in *Vogue*. Margaux Hemingway starred in the films *Lipstick* (1976), *Inner Sanctum* (1991), and *Dangerous Cargo* (1996). Andie MacDowell was born in Gaffney, South Carolina, in 1958. After her modeling career, she was able to star in a string popular hits with *Groundhog Day* (1993), *Multiplicity* (1996), and *Magic Mike XXL* (2015). They remain on stage and two other women come from the phone booth, but there is '60s music grooving in the background. When Margaux and Andie sit, from the heart of the '60s we get Rebecca Schaeffer and Viola Davis. Rebecca Schaeffer was born in Eugene, Oregon, in 1967. She started as a teen model and went on to become a star in '80s TV shows like *Amazing Stories* (1985-1987) and *My Sister Sam* (1986-1988). Viola Davis was born in St. Matthews, South Carolina, in 1965. Davis has starred in *Madea Goes to Jail* (2009), *Eat Pray Love* (2010), and *The Suicide Squad* (2016).

After a short montage of their movies, there is another explosion on stage and two huge dudes each carrying the flags step on the stage, and they are welcomed by a loud booming jocular hooting. It is Big Show and Tucker Knight. Levi Rolla Cooper, aka Tucker, is a six-foot-two inch, 320-pound man from Clackamas, Oregon. Tucker is Oregon's answer and counterbalance to Paul Donald Wight II of Aiken, South Carolina. Paul, aka Big Show, stands at seven feet and 383 pounds, and is the king of the wrestling ring. They are men of massive means who echo the big and jolly spirit of America. After demonstrating several wrestling moves, they exit as flames blast on stage in spectacular WWE fashion.

Then two professionally dressed people in black suits walk from the booth, Frances Moore Lappé and Jesse Louis Jackson, and proceed to list their accomplishments. Frances M. Lappé was born in Pendleton, Oregon, in 1944 and has dedicated her life to addressing poverty, hunger, and environmental issues. Lappé has advocated against greed and for social programs to help the less fortunate. Frances's seminal book was a *Diet for a Small Planet* (1971) and studied the impact of meat production as the culprit of food scarcity. She is a pioneer in taking a public stance against factory farming. Jesse Jackson was born in Greenville, South Carolina, in 1941. Jesse Jackson begins to describe how on Christmas 1971 he helped organize the People United to Save Humanity (PUSH) organization. This organization serves to push social justice programs into corporate and government action. In 1984 when Jesse Jackson ran for president, PUSH expanded to include "The Rainbow Coalition," which sought to include other outsider groups like gays, lesbians, Asians, Muslims, Native Americans, the poor, unemployed, single moms, and basically any other group ignored by Reagan republicans. As Jesse Jackson ends his speech, his spotlight begins to change into the spectrum of the rainbow, followed by ooh, aahs, and applause.

And for the grand finale, Alex announces that we will be enjoying the sounds from the early days of rock and roll, when the rock began to overpower the roll to become solid rock. The Kingsmen walk on stage with guitars strapped and instruments in hands. Before they start playing, James Brown does a backflip from the booth and lands in a leg split, and the band begins to play "Louie," with Brown in the lead. They also play a few other hits from their era.

Keanu explains that The Kingsmen set the stage as the iconic garage band of all rock garage bands. All subsequent rockers and genres of music can trace some lineage to The Kingsmen with the seminal hit "Louie" in 1963. This song sounded the death knell to structured dancing like the jitterbug and foxtrot that went extinct at dance clubs, in favor of the free-flowing, wiggle-waggle, freestyle dancing seen in modern dance clubs. Keanu explains that The Kingsmen is an influential band where surf, grunge, and alternative rock get their roots. Alex then explains how James Brown's passionate performances and unique combinations of dancing set him in his own personal league of musicians. Keanu further explains that James Brown was the Chuck Yeager who broke the rhythm and dance barrier that no man has yet to cross, and also adds that James Brown "walked on the moon" long before Michael Jackson, and James Brown immediately obliges. Alex also tells of The Kingsmen and James Brown previous unfair troubles with the law. The FBI ran a totally bogus investigation into whether "Louie" was a pornographic song that was like a totally ridiculous waste of time and money.

At the end, all the previously mentioned figures from history appear for a final roll call and they take a bow and somehow, all mysteriously fit back into the red and silver booth, encased in glass and metal. As the booth begins to shake and sparkle, it glows eerie blue and white, then disappears into the floor with a crackling thunder as when it entered. In the fading mist, a neon circle K fades to black.

The student body goes wild. Just then, a holographic image of a 40-year-old George Carlin in the spotlight appears, dressed in a 1970s space age funky, shiny purple outfit with black polka dots, and mirrored 1980s sunglasses. After the cheering and hooting dies down, Carlin says, "Ladies and germs, thank you for your attention. The following show has been pre-recorded, post-recorded, uploaded, side-loaded, and over-loaded to the orbiting, quantum, entangled, nonspecific, gender-less cloud, for all temporal chrono-legionaries to appreciate. We hope you enjoyed the show and please feel free to reread or listen to any other chapter with this… [he takes off his sunglasses and his voice drops an octave] Keanu … Neo … Reeves and Mr. … Alex … Argh …Winter filter. [His voice is back to normal.] Remember folks… no corporation, disembodied entity, religious institution, tunneling AI, machine elf, or government can copyright your inner mind. Thus, as you read a book, you have all the freedom in the known universe to let your imaginations run wild … like stallions."

[The students hoot and stomp their feet in the auditorium.]

"And remember, boys and girls, happy endings do happen, history is cool, so stay in school. And… do not take life too seriously. Plus, breaking the rules every once in a while is a good thing! If all else fails, music is a wonderful outlet that can cleanse the soul from the mountains of bullshit hurled your way. But most importantly [he puts his sunglasses back on], everyone, please, together, repeat after me [the entire audience chimes in as Carlin lifts his arms]: 'MY COMPADRES, BE EXCELLENT TO EACH OTHER AND PARTY ON!!!' "

His image then zaps out with a slow-motion flash of neon purple lights, with fast flowing neon green and yellow sparkles.

The Kingsmen and James Brown recording set becomes one of the all-time most sought after, censored, and disputed bootlegs of all time.

PART II

BALANCE BETWEEN A DARK AND LIGHT FORCE

twelve

NORTH DAKOTA & ILLINOIS

A Union of Heaven and Earth

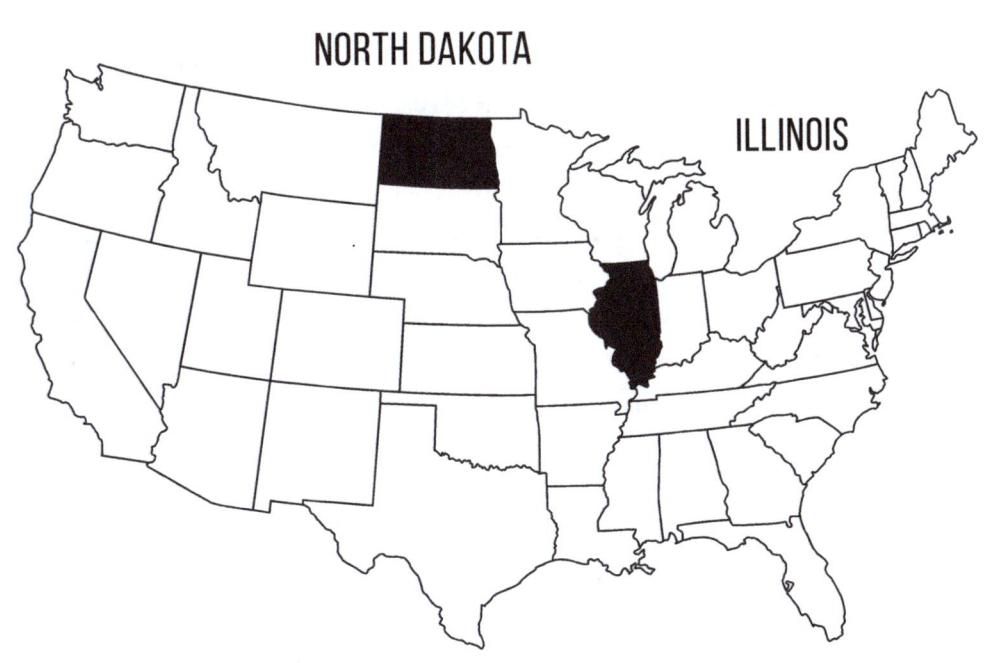

NORTH DAKOTA

North Dakota and Illinois's flags give center stage to the North American bald eagle. The bald eagle appears on several state flags, but not at the primary focal point.

North Dakota and Illinois create a contrasted harmony like night and day, as it is with Indiana and Rhode Island, and Massachusetts and Virginia.

A red ribbon is present in the beaks of both eagles. The U.S. shield is also present on both flags, but ever so slightly different. For North Dakota, it's on the eagle's torso, while in Illinois it is on the ground resting against a rock. If you look closely, the stars are missing on North Dakota's shield. Instead, they are placed above the eagle's head with a seven-pointed, crown-like aurora. Below the crown aurora are two rows of stars. Illinois also has a stellar aurora. But it is less defined and only composed of one star: the sun. Just below the eagle's tail feathers is the sun at the horizon. It is sunrise, since Illinois has an east coast with regard to the Great Lakes.

Another common element is the olive branch. Illinois has 13 leaves but no fruit. North Dakota also has 13 leaves yet has ripe fruit. Both states have their names below the bald eagle. Illinois's name is written in all caps—blue with a Roman Times font. North Dakota's name is written in bold white upon a red

ILLINOIS

background framed with yellow curly, twirls, and whirls.

And for an ultimate dichotomy between war and peace, the flag of North Dakota is akin to a war banner, while the flag of Illinois is a sigil for peace. The flag of North Dakota resembles the flags of countless military regimental banners. Regiments are usually commanded by a colonel, the officer rank just below a one star general. Likewise the insignia on a colonel's uniform is the national bird with the U.S. shield on the torso, and an olive branch and bundle of arrows in the talons. In stark contrast, the white of Illinois's flag resembles a flag of truce or surrender, and oddly, the national bird is unarmed. Usually, the war arrows of the bald eagle are juxtaposed to the olive branch, as it is with the original quarter, the modern dollar bill, and the presidential flag. But this is a rare instance when the national bird solely presents the olive branch of peace.

Geography

North Dakota is at an inflection point between the cultural divides; North Dakota inflects with Canada, while Illinois inflects with the South.

As states are often a mix of their neighbors, North Dakota's recipe is composed of two cups of South Dakota, one cup each of Montana and Minnesota, plus a cup of Manitoba and half a cup of Saskatchewan. Consequently, North Dakota has a slight Canadian aftertaste.

As for Illinois, her recipe is one and a quarter cup of Missouri mash, one cup Indiana dough, a half cup each of Iowa corn and Wisconsin beans, three teaspoons of Kentucky butter, and one drop of Michigan bitters. This recipe gives Illinois a strong upper south fragrance. Note that persons from South Carolina may not be able to detect this southern flavor, but when leaving the Chicago metro area, it can be sensed. Professional geographic experts will recognize that Illinois bears an oddly similar taste to old Virginia—reason being, Illinois has a Virginia tilt. Further, Illinois was secured into the American fold by a Virginian, George Rogers Clark (1752-1818), who captured Kaskaskia on July 4, 1778.

A Virginia tilt indicates a state is both at the latitudes of Africa and Europe, with a tilt toward Europe. In local Illinois terms, the southern portion of Illinois is known as "Little Egypt," and the most southern city is called Cairo. But this region of Illinois does not quite reach to the latitude of Cairo, let alone anywhere near Egypt. A more appropriate name for southern Illinois would be "Little Carthage" since southern Illinois is on par with the ancient North African city of Carthage, which was the ancient rival of Rome. After Ancient Rome conquered the Carthage Empire during the Punic Wars, it became a conquered territory known as the breadbasket of Rome. Likewise, southern Illinois can be considered America's Carthage, because it is a breadbasket as well.

But getting back to the U.S.—Cairo, Illinois, is at the same latitude of Newport News, Virginia. At the opposite north end, Illinois is at the same latitude as Boston, Massachusetts. This gives Illinois unique powers, since she is the only state in the Union to have latitudes equal to both Boston and Richmond. Consequently, a fighting Illini' can throw fast, gray matter Yankee jabs to the cranium like a proper *Braintree* of Boston, and also give powerful, prayer-worthy southern slugs to the gut like Richmond.

Illinois's southern streaks in her hair are comparable to Virginia, while North Dakota has a slight Canadian perm. In fact, when we dig into North Dakota's history, we learn that half the state has deep roots to Quebec and Canada (more on that later). Suffice it to say, North Dakota knows what cold winters on par with Ottawa, Montreal, and Toronto are like. Illinois also knows southern summers as they are in Richmond, Louisville, and Cape Girardeau.

Perhaps the most famous American roadway is Route 66, which has a start point in Chicago, Illinois. Due to John Steinbeck's *Grapes of Wrath* (1939) and Hollywood, this road became enchanted as an American icon. Like the Oregon Trail, Route 66 is no longer an official primary route, however it retains the pole position as America's Iconic Roadway for the combustion engine age, and there are tons of roadside attractions. Finally, its fitting moniker is "The Mother Road."

To balance this supposition, North Dakota is hereby granted the title of having a terminus of "The Father Road" with Route 52, which starts in Portal, North Dakota. Portal is a special city because it has a secret portal of sorts; the Gateway Cities Golf Club is built along its international border. It is the only place where one can cross into the Deep North of Canuck territory (north of the 49th) under the radar without informing either border agency. Further, one will not receive a $5000 fine if caught crossing the northern 49th parallel, so long as one does not chase any balls that land off the property of the Gateway Cities Golf Club. The clubhouse and final hole are in the U.S., but most of the course is in the province of Saskatchewan. Route 52 begins at this quirky border of the Canadian Confederation and ends at the original "house" of the Confederacy in South Carolina.

Like a perfect East Coast/West Coast rivalry, the end of the "Mother and Father Roads of America" end upon opposite shores. Route 66 starts east of the Mississippi and ends in California, at the Santa Monica Pier along the Pacific Ocean; while Route 52 begins west of the Mississippi and ends at Charleston, South Carolina upon the Atlantic shore. Although the end and the beginning of a road are relative to an observer, regarding the beach as the final destination provides a more festive and celebratory atmosphere, for would be "cannonball runs."

Unlike Route 66, Route 52 was never the star of a socially conscious book nor had the spotlight in television shows, *Route 66* aired from 1960-1964. However, Route 66 crosses Route 52 at Shorewood, Illinois. Thus, one could argue that Route 52 made an unofficial cameo TV appearance when Tod Stiles and Buz Murdock drove through this part of Illinois. Lastly, both roads start at Canadian latitudes and end at declinations that match Mexico. However, the crossroads of Route 52 and Route 66 meet in the All-American Belt, which is wholly a private latitude and declination of the USA, beyond Mexico and unknowable to Canada.

History

The written histories of North Dakota and Illinois begin in Canada. Illinois's rudimentary beginnings stem from Quebec, while North Dakota's formative roots are linked to the Hudson Bay Company. French traders from Quebec and Montreal established a network of trading posts during the 1600s, but the first permanent settlement was near the massive Indian Mound complex at Cahokia, Illinois. Since the eastern half of North Dakota was a part of the Hudson Bay watershed, it was a component of Prince Rupert's Land. Prince Rupert (1619-1682) was a German-English royalist/cavalier officer during the English Civil War (1642-1651). Rupert was the iconic action hero of the mid-1600s. He served in the Army and Navy, plus he fought in the second and third Anglo-Dutch Wars. He was also a military employee of the famous and most extravagant Sun King of France, Louis the XIV (1638-1715), who put the divinely reasoned absolute rule of the monarch in perfect practice, as echoed by *Sir Mel the Books* who had saith in 1981, "it's good to be the king." Consequently, with his abundance of fortune and glory, Prince Rupert was chosen as the first governor of the Hudson Bay Company in 1670. Thus, the Hudson Bay Company is synonymous with Prince Rupert's Land. And from 1670 until 1818, North Dakota was at the center of the lucrative fur trade, as the most southern and warm portion of the Hudson Bay Company, established 1670.

The first permanent settlement of North Dakota was set up by Thomas Douglas, 5th Earl of Selkirk, shortly after 1811. The Earl of Selkirk was granted a land concession from the Hudson Bay Company, which became known as Selkirk's Grant. Selkirk essentially bought his way onto the board of directors. Selkirk's Grant for a new colony included the lands of the Assiniboine and Red River Watershed. This land grant of "Selkirksylvania" became known as the Red River Colony. Most of Selkirk's pioneers were farmers displaced during the Highland clearances in Scotland.

Since eastern North Dakota was "Canadian" for over a century until 1819, she has the ability to see things from the Canuck perspective. Consequently, North Dakota had a front row view of the 1816 Canadian Civil War of Corporations. This conflict was a rivalry between the North West Company and Hudson Bay Company. They did not fight over taxes or representation, nor did it have anything to do with slavery. The root cause, as with any modern-day gang, had much to do about the bottom line—profits.

It all started when Selkirk wanted to give his Red River Colony an economic advantage and sought to corner the pemmican economy. Pemmican is a type of processed meat, usually buffalo, that became a key food source of protein and was especially important during the long cold winters. You can think of pemmican as an artisan buffalo spam/beef jerky. Selkirk's economic restrictions on the trade of pemmican affected both the North West Company and the Hudson Bay Company. Nonetheless, Selkirk wanted all traders in the area to become dependent on the food produced by his Red River Colony instead of the ubiquitously available pemmican.

From 1812 until 1821, these Canadian fur trading companies were in a dog fight for economic supremacy. The North West Company was based in Montreal and generally allied to the Métis, a hybrid group of Natives and Newcomers, with a French tilt. The Hudson Bay Company was allied to the mostly Scottish people of Selkirk's Colony in the Red River, with a British tilt.

Eventually the hostility built up and the epic Battle of Seven Oaks became the key note of this "War Between the Corporations." On June 19, 1816, near Winnipeg, Manitoba (then a part of the Red River Colony), the NWC trounced the HBC. Compared to the fighting in the American Civil War it was only a skirmish; nonetheless, it was an extreme event for Canadian history. Of the fatalities was the death of the Yankee-born governor of the Hudson Bay Colony, Robert Semple from Boston.

It's interesting to note that the Battle of Seven Pines in Virginia was also a domestic conflict but for the U.S., as was the Battle of Seven Oaks for Canada. It was in the aftermath of Seven Pines that Robert E. Lee was given a chance to prove his worth. Union forces would have to wait another three years to threaten Richmond again. Likewise, the open hostility between HBC and NWC continued for two more years after 1816.

Although the War of 1812 forged a core of Canadian identity, the subsequent *Buffalo-Jerky, Pemmican War Between Canadian Companies* was the start of a small, yet thorny issue for Canadian Métis and White Canadians. In the aftermath of the Battle of Seven Oaks, the British legislated a forced corporate merger of the two parties, simply as the Hudson Bay Company, in 1821. Today, the legacy of the Hudson Bay Company lives on as a department store akin to Sears, more commonly known as The Bay. Imagine if Congress forced McDonald's and Burger King to unite due to profit driven violence as Donald McBurger King?

To balance North Dakota's connection to the Canadian Deep North (North of the 49th), Illinois has a connection to slavery akin to a southern state. Illinois has a Virginia tilt after all. Although the Great Lakes region of the Northwest Territory was declared as free soil by the Northwest Ordinance issued in 1787, slavery found a way in "Little Carthage."

Settlers in the Illinois country arrived long before it became a state. When the ban on slavery was made in 1787 under Articles of Confederation President Arthur St. Clair, born in Scotland, a few settlers in this region were allowed to keep their slaves because they were grandfathered in or "vital to the economy." Most importantly, they threatened to relocate if forced to free their slaves. In 1805, when Illinois was still a part of Indiana Territory, the Indiana legislature permitted slaves to work "within the tract of land reserved for the use of salt works near Shawneetown" on a limited time basis. When Illinois became an official state in 1818, the state constitution outlawed slaves in the territory—except under a special contract. Slaves could only be contracted for one year and could only be kept in bondage near Shawneetown. Shawneetown is next to Kentucky across the Ohio River. Thus, Shawneetown rings true the modern adage of returning to difficult, unsatisfactory work is like going back to the salt mines.

The 1818 Illinois constitution also stated that after 1825 no slaves could legally be brought into Illinois—otherwise they would be considered free, until the California Compromise of 1850. Generally, before then, when slaves reached the border of free soil on the underground railroad, they could become free. However, after the fugitive slave act of 1850, the freedom end zone was set to Canada since free soil states were legally obliged to return runaway slaves. Canadians of course did not have to follow the regulations of the fugitive slave act, since they had, and still have, the ability to give a one finger salute to U.S. law, and vice versa.

A major historical connection between North Dakota and Illinois is the Lewis and Clark Expedition—a three-year trek from May 14, 1804, to September 23, 1806, across the newly acquired lands of the Louisiana Purchase. Besides investigating the Louisiana Purchase, they pushed on into the disputed North Pacific, which was claimed by the U.K., Spain, and Russia. In 1819, Spain essentially handed off its claim over the North Pacific to the U.S. with the Adams- Onís Treaty of 1819, which was also the year the most valuable chunk of Rupert's Land fell into the lap of North Dakota. Like *Star Trek*, the Lewis and Clark episode had a military structure and scientific order, as it was known officially as the Corps of Discovery Expedition. Coincidentally, North Dakota and Illinois played starring roles in this pilot episode of American history. The first winter stop took place in McLean County in the heart of North Dakota—specifically at Fort Mandan. Like any big production, a practice run was in order before the official launch. Providentially, it took place in Madison County, Illinois, at Camp Wood. This full-dress rehearsal took place during the winter of 1802–1803. And don't forget, it was thanks to an older brother of William Clark that Illinois brought into the fold of America, George Rogers Clark.

Of the many Natives to cross a path with America, North Dakota and Illinois gave America two middle school teachers who left their mark on American consciousness: Sacagawea and Black Hawk. Black Hawk was born in Illinois

Territory. However, Sacagawea's birthplace is a mystery. It is generally considered to be in Idaho. Nonetheless, when the Lewis and Clark Company was wintering at Camp Mandan in present-day North Dakota she was "born" into American consciousness when she was chosen to join the expedition.

It just so happened that intertribal warfare between the Shoshone (Aztecan Family) and Hidatsa (Sioux Family), paved the way to Sacagawea's historical destiny. Sacagawea was born into the Lemhi Shoshone Tribe around 1788. She was captured by the Hidatsa Tribe (circa 1800) and held as a captive near Washburn, North Dakota. About a year later she was sold into marriage with Toussaint Charbonneau, a French Canadian explorer from Boucherville, Quebec. She then had their first child, Jean Baptiste Charbonneau (born February 11, 1805), as recorded by Meriwether Lewis. This was the first birth certificate of a North Dakotan, long before North Dakota became North Dakota. Her son can be seen on the Sacagawea dollar coins that are in circulation.

It was positively providential to the mission that Lewis and Clark recruited Sacagawea. When tribes came into contact with leaders of the expedition led by a Red woman with babe, it was an affirmation of peace and evidence that Lewis and Clark Expedition was not a war party. A Native mother with a child leading a band of White men certainly calmed the various chiefs and sachems.

Sacagawea's fame came much later when she was adopted as a national heroine in the women's suffrage movement. Only then would her shadow become illuminated in American memory, long after her death.

Like Sacagawea, Black Hawk also bore witness to the dawn of the United States and watched their lands fall into the hands of European civilization.

Black Hawk (1767-1838) was the first Native American to have his life recorded from his own perspective. His autobiography was first published in 1833 with the help of a French Canadian American from Michigan, Antoine Le Claire (1797-1861). Black Hawk describes the American people in a vivid, honest color. He acknowledges the good, bad, ugly, and brave of America, providing the first non-Eurocentric portrait of America.

Black Hawk became a warrior by age 16. He earned his first scalp by killing an Osage Brave. Black Hawk led several battles against the Osage; in one encounter he killed six, with one being a woman by accident. Black Hawk enjoyed the thrill of ultimate victory, but when he was forced to feel the opposite, the bitter end of the War Club, he was devastated and filled with genocidal rage. When Black Hawk's father was killed by a Cherokee, in his mourning Black Hawk admitted to wishing for the annihilation of the Cherokee race.

Black Hawk fought against America as an ally to the British during this war. But Black Hawk is hardly remembered for his participation during the War of 1812. Instead, he was remembered for the war, eponymous to his name, the Black Hawk War. As was the pattern with many Red-to-White conflicts, it stemmed from poorly informed and poorly executed treaties, poor communication, and the fact that many Natives were not included in the proceedings. Black Hawk previously made several attempts to return home and was escorted to the west side of the Mississippi. But in 1832 he became an American legend when he stood up for his right to return home. After his surrender Black Hawk would gain further fame and respect.

Black Hawk was able to travel eastward and met President Jackson. Back east, he was warmly welcomed by the cities of America as a folk hero. A man born of the stone age bore witness to the cutting-edge tech of the railroad and industrial revolution. Black Hawk and his band even saw the first of American aircraft, when a balloon flew into the heavens. Memorable and awesome was the way of White man's strange and peculiar magic—science.

His autobiography included his honest and warm description of his ancient cousins from the East Sea, laid plain to the people of America. It was not a glowing tale, made to shill for the almighty dollar. Rather, Black Hawk's legacy was a sermon and love letter to America. He was able to point out problems and grievances, yet he ended with a frank, friendly, and uplifting hope. Unlike Natives before him, whose stories and motivations were fabricated by alien eyes, Black Hawk was able to tell a Native American story with his own voice for posterity.

Curiously, Abraham Lincoln and Jefferson Davis were united as brothers in arms during the Black Hawk War. Although neither man saw combat, at the end of the war, First Lieutenant Jefferson Davis was assigned to escort Black Hawk to prison in St. Louis, according to Black Hawk. Black Hawk describes

Lieutenant Davis as a kind, respectful, and honorable officer.

Private Lincoln served in the Illinois State Militia. He was later elected to the position as militia captain until his first term ended. Lincoln then re-enlisted as a private once again until he was mustered out at the end of the war. The only clear record for Private Lincoln's participation was that he was present for a burial detail at the Battle of Stillman's Run in northern Illinois. It is also recorded that he lost a wrestling match to another man in front of his own company.

Neither Black Hawk nor Lincoln ever mentions meeting the other. But with a little stretch and sparkle of imagination, a creative per chance meeting between Lieutenant Davis and Private Lincoln is in the realm of quantum possibilities. Perhaps it was just in passing? Imagine a youthful Jefferson Davis standing next to or bumped into by a lanky Lincoln. Neither knew of each other's destiny at this time, and if they had passed by, who would remember such an inconsequential passing of two ships in the night? Perhaps they shared a mess together? Or maybe Lincoln washed Lieutenant Davis's dishes without knowing so?

Perhaps they had a speechless, comical encounter at the latrine? Lieutenant Davis approaches a tall man standing near an oak tree to ask for directions, unaware that Private Lincoln is relieving himself. Davis is 15 paces from the private and is about to speak, but then a thunderous roar falls upon the prairie. Lieutenant Davis does a quick about face, and the only witness to this collision of Promethean titans is a prairie dog who ducks for cover upon the reverberations across the land. Nevertheless, it is a subtle irony that a generation later these essential sons of Kentucky were each other's political adversary since during The Black Hawk War of 1832, Lieutenant Davis was an officer for federal forces, while a bootstrap, scrabble Private Lincoln was fighting on behalf of the state militia.

Coincidentally, North Dakota and Illinois became the adopted states of two iconic American presidents: Theodore Roosevelt and Abraham Lincoln. On most lists of the best presidents, Lincoln and Roosevelt place in the top five. So honored and beloved is their memory that the shadow of their lives literally moved a mountain. Mount Rushmore features Lincoln and Roosevelt in addition to two others.

There is a weird systemic harmony between Lincoln and Roosevelt that's connected to Illinois and North Dakota. First, a look at geography: Lincoln was born in a state with a Virginia tilt, namely Kentucky. Later, he would become his own man when he moved to Illinois, which also has a Virginia tilt. Teddy was born in New York, a state on the border with Canada, and became his own man when he became a rancher in North Dakota, which also has a border with Canada. In Illinois, Lincoln met his wife, Mary Todd, served in the Illinois Militia, practiced law on the prairie in a little house, and most importantly, entered politics in the Illinois General Assembly in 1834. In Illinois, Lincoln cut his cloth to become a leader among men.

In North Dakota, Roosevelt became a fully rounded man, healed by the serenity of the frontier. Roosevelt was born in the core of the Big Apple, Manhattan borough, on October 27, 1858, at 28 East 20th Street, NYC. He was a sickly, assumedly socially awkward, rich kid who was able to graduate from Harvard in 1880. Although spoiled, Teddy seems to have been the good spoiled as opposed to the obnoxious, self-entitled, bratty spoiled variety of the *Charlie and the Chocolate Factory* type. At Harvard, Teddy overcame his relatively weak asthmatic condition, leveling up from a socially awkward nerd to a rough-and-tumble jock by joining the boxing and rowing teams. Roosevelt dove into politics in 1882 and immediately made his mark as an anti-corruption reformer. However, tragedy struck on Valentine's Day 1884. Two days earlier, his first wife, Alice Hathaway Lee, gave birth to his first daughter, Alice Lee Roosevelt. However, Alice's pregnancy masked her failing kidneys, and she died on February 14 mere hours after his mother, Mittie Roosevelt, passed away. Perhaps due to the underhanded political issues of 1884, combined with a broken heart, Roosevelt dropped out of politics and pursued ranching in North Dakota. It was there at the Elkhorn Ranch that Roosevelt's broken heart was sewn back into place. Note that in 1884 North Dakota did not yet exist, as it was still a united south and north Dakota Territory. Besides learning the ways and means of the cowboy, Roosevelt received a firsthand respect and education and love of the wild and natural realm of North America. It was here that Roosevelt changed from an arrogant, big city New Yorker to a salt of the earth man of all classes. But destiny had other plans for Roosevelt when he was offered a position on the board of the NYC police commissioners. This led to his becoming an assistant secretary to the Navy. When war broke out with Spain, he became a national hero as the colonel in the rough rider's outfit, which paved the way to his presidency.

Also note the regimental flag of the Rough Riders matches in nearly perfect form to the flag of North Dakota, the major difference being the background, which is a field of yellow, instead of the traditional blue. And U.S. regiments are usually led by a colonel, in this case it was Colonel Roosevelt, Theodore.

Lincoln and Roosevelt were men of opposite means. Lincoln was born in a log cabin on the frontier, while Roosevelt was born in a well-to-do family in Manhattan. Lincoln only had a short military stint in the Illinois State Militia during the Black Hawk War, while Roosevelt rose to the rank of colonel in the Spanish-American War. Roosevelt made every effort to clear out corruption, put a bridle on powerful corporate entities, and preserve America's natural wonders for future generations. Lincoln had the harder task of ending the millennial scourge of humanity at the cost of his own life.

Roosevelt and Lincoln were the middle presidents who performed a kind of miraculous surgery upon America. Lincoln took office as an ancient cancer was eating away at the U.S. A malignant tumor was bleeding in Kansas and had metastasized at Harpers Ferry, Virginia.

On Monday, March 4, 1861, President James Buchanan handed the fairly elected Lincoln a broken America. Seven states had broken away; thus, it became Lincoln's destiny to begin radical reconstructive, lifesaving surgery.

Roosevelt was the last surgeon of the middle presidents. As Lincoln was destined to cut a state in half, with the northwestern region of Virginia becoming West Virginia, Roosevelt was fated to suture two territories as one—with Indian territory and Oklahoma Territory merging to become the 46th state in 1907. The formation of Oklahoma meant the map of modern America was complete. As Lincoln's predecessor gave him a broken map of America in 1861, Roosevelt handed to his successor, William Howard Taft, a finished map of America in 1909, as it remains today, for its borders and shapes.

Thus, the first adopted sons of North Dakota and Illinois, Roosevelt and Lincoln, are the presidential bookends of America's middle passage, who earned their seats next to Washington and Jefferson at Mount Rushmore. Lincoln and Roosevelt are the latter-day founding fathers who added a secondary source code for America that runs her modern constitution.

Of leading ladies there is Hillary Clinton (1947) of Chicago, Illinois, and Cornelia Coya Genavive Knutson (1912-1996) of Edmore, North Dakota. Hillary Clinton may be a pioneer for women in politics, but before Hillary there was Coya. Coya was the first woman elected to U.S. Congress in Minnesota, and did so in the heart of the 1950s, counter to the media's promoted idea of the 1950s housewife. Coya was in federal office from 1954 to 1958. Coya was reared in a socialist American family to boot—her father was a part of the Nonpartisan League (NPL)—but she ran as a Democrat. Mrs. Clinton also broke new ground as the first female senator for New York.

North Dakota has yet to send a native daughter or son to the White House, but Illinois gave us Ronald Reagan (1911-2004). Reagan's rise to power as a Hollywood actor was a systemic shock to the political establishment. What's next? A stand-up *comedian*? A rap star? Perhaps someone from the WWE or from the adult entertainment industry? No doubt you can count on America to make the impossible possible. Generations born after Reagan missed that cultural shock wave. But Regan was no ordinary movie star. He earned his political stripes and proved his worth as the governor of California from 1967 to 1975, and like a real-life member of the X-Men, was gifted with a "mutant ability." He had a photographic memory, which came in handy for acting and being a leader. But Reagan is best remembered for America's deliverance during the Cold War.

The 1980s was the decade of Reagan. He was elected in 1980, won reelection in 1984, and left office in 1989. Reagan pursued a polite yet covertly aggressive policy to undercut the Soviet Union. Since then, Reagan became a symbol for freedom loving, flag waving, unabashed, guilt-free American patriotism. In a way, America was able to shine her brightest via her art, music, and storytelling in the face of tyrannical, perverted social justice of communism. The 1980s was a time when free market forces were in control of Hollywood, as there were no social agenda boxes to check. It was a time when the directors were free to create so long as the ships of the imagination soared with maximum economic efficiency. America had to dig deep on the social and spiritual front. This is part of the reason why the 1980s has such an enchanting afterglow. A man born in the tallest upright state with a Virginia tilt was at the helm during the closing phase of the Cold War—the Commander in Chief of the United States of America, Ronald Wilson Reagan. It was under his watch that the Berlin Wall fell and international communism died, under the punches and prayers of the most famous of fighting Illini.

On the opposite political polarity of Reagan, Illinois also gave the world its first American-born female leader of a nation. Janet Jagan from Chicago, Illinois, born 1920, became the leader of our mostly ignored South American English-speaking cousin down under in 1997, the nation of Guyana. Like Hillary Clinton, Jagan was originally the first lady of a nation and she was able to use her platform as first spouse, namely public recognition, to gain power and prestige. And a fun flag fact, it was an American who designed the flag of Guyana—Whitney Smith (1940-2016), the founder of vexillology as a discipline.

Culture

North Dakota and Illinois, like the flags indicate, are a contrasting class of states. This also happens with Virginia to Massachusetts. But differences aside, they make a balanced blend like salt and pepper, or sugar and spice.

A combo reflective of this interstate harmony is Peggy Lee and Benny Goodman. When Peggy Lee (1920-2002) of Jamestown, North Dakota, joined forces with big band leader Benny Goodman of Chicago, Illinois, they became an instant icon across the nation. Peggy's smooth vocals and Goodman's clarinet skills was a *Back to the Future* moment during WWII that hypnotized the nation with their duet of "Why Don't You Do Right" on July 27, 1942. It is a timeless tune that any generation can recognize.

Also of the big band era are Lawrence Welk (1903-1992) of Strasburg, North

Dakota, who is hereby paired with Gene Krupa (1909-1973) of Chicago, Illinois. Due to a nearly perpetual rebroadcast on PBS stations across America, Lawrence Welk is a generational phenomenon. Welk's genre is champagne, rated-G music that sings of sweet Sunday church kisses. At the other end of the big band is the drummer Gene Krupa, whose recording of "Sing, Sing, Sing" put American drumming on the map. "Sing, Sing, Sing" is an "Out of Sight, Out of Time" beat from 1936 that just reeks of the classical bright lights and big stage feel of Chicago, Illinois. It's one of the few big band songs to transcend time and is able to enchant each generation beyond. It truly is in the league of the Buck Rogers class, worthy to be played now or in New Chicago in the 25th century. Krupa is the founding father of the modern drum set and drum solo. Every modern drummer since has basically ricocheted off of Krupa's beats, taps, and rhythms.

On a modern note, two generational rap stars include Wiz Khalifa (1987) of Minto, North Dakota, and Montana 300 (1989) of Chicago, Illinois. Wiz and Montana rap with the hardest of hard-hitting lyrics that punch it to the gut, at the max. Montana 300 takes it all balls out, taking the Chicago gangster ethos to the next level, setting the bar to the speed of light that no rapper, White or Black, shall pass evermore.

On the country sunny side is Alison Krauss (1971) from Decatur, Illinois, paired with Lynn Anderson (1947-2015) of Grand Forks, North Dakota. When Lynn Anderson joined the cast of *The Lawrence Welk Show* (1995-1982) with her hit single "If I Kiss You, Will You Go Away," it thrust her into the stratosphere of big wide country spaces.

In 1956 two twins were born, the actresses Joan Allen of Rochelle, Illinois, and Janice Elaine Maxwell of Fargo, North Dakota. Allen starred in *Room* (2015) and *Death Race* (2008), while Maxwell was a star in *Brain Dead* (2016) and *Gossip Girl* (2007-2012).

A wonderful set of queens manifested in the 1970s: Tami Erin of Wheaton, Illinois and Leslie Bibb of Bismarck, North Dakota. Tami Erin broke through first in 1988, with *The New Adventures of Pippi Longstocking* (1988). Pippi Longstocking is a playful, Annie-like girl with random superpowers from Swedish folklore. Leslie Bibb popped on the Hollywood radar with the WB's *Popular* (1999-2001), a show about two teen girls on opposite ends of the social spectrum who are forced to interact when their parents marry. Leslie Bibb played the popular girl: straight-A, fashionable, and a cheerleader in the TV show.

As for the king of spades, from Wilmette, Illinois, we have Charlton Heston (1923-2008). After playing Moses in *The Ten Commandments* (1956), he became the bedrock of the American tough guy and was decorated further with his role in the thought-provoking *Planet of the Apes* (1968). During the 1950s and early 1960s, Heston was one of the minority of actors to stand up for Black civil rights. Later, Charlton Heston became the spokesman for the National Rifle Association (NRA) from 1998 to 2003. No star can match Heston, but another father figure born in 1923 who could exude that tough-guy exterior is Ray Boyle from Lisbon, North Dakota. He was a part of the Greatest Generation, serving in the U.S. Marine Corps in WWII. He later became a major star when he played the iconic *The Life and Legend of Wyatt Earp* TV series from (1955-1961) during the heyday of black-and-white Westerns.

As for the queen of hearts, we have the White star, or rather Betty White. White was born in 1922 and would shine continuously across the generations. In fact, it was nearer the time frame when many stars lose a certain luster that White's star began to shine in even more brilliant colors, when she became a gold star on *Golden Girls* (1985-1992). Even past the mandatory age of retirement of many companies and careers, White's zesty and sparkling light was able to reach past the generations to X, Y, and Z, as a love letter of guidance from the Greatest Generation. White's loss for America was sorely felt due to her timeless charm and role as our collective grandmother, sister, and mom. There is perhaps no match to the sparkle of White, but all things are relative. Paula Winslowe of North Dakota, born in 1910, fills this role for her essential performance as Bambi's mother in the animated classic *Bambi* (1942). Ergo, White and Winslowe are two stars who leave us with a maternal afterglow of love, reminding us of what is important, and that love continues.

And on matters of love, two lovely places that have manifested on planet earth that echo the call for peace and harmony are the humble Peace Chapel of the International Peace Garden in North Dakota and the illustrious Bahai House of Worship in Illinois. Souls are drafted without consent into a nation and a particular religion—from a certain point of view. For the vast majority, a person's long-forgotten familial predecessors from long ago bravely chose a path. As a consequence, each person is blessed with a particular nationality and reared in the communal warmth of a certain religion. But for a special garden in North Dakota, the strict and codified division between Canadian and American lands established by the dead from long ago are partially halted, such that the 49th parallel north loses its power to divide and is empowered to unite, whereby Canada and the United States have created a unique garden planted between two worlds. In particular, the International Peace Chapel straddles the 49th parallel north. As for Illinois, the Bahai House of Worship is the first of its kind in the Americas. It is a monumental house of worship that acknowledges the divinity of all previously established religions. This house of worship is decorated with symbols from Hinduism, Buddhism, Judaism, Christianity, and Islam. Thus, as the International Peace Garden of North Dakota unhinges an imaginary line that divides two nations on paper, the Bahai House of Worship of Illinois embraces all the prayers from previously established religions, regardless of which document of divinity they were written.

Two dashing kings of the semi-cowboy king of hustler hearts are Clint Ritchie (1938-2009) of Grafton, North Dakota, and Harrison Ford (1942) of Illinois. Clint cast the mold as Clint Buchanan in TV with *One Life to Live* (beginning 1979) and *Centennial* (1978-1979), as well as the movies *Patton* (1979) and *Bandolero!* (1968). Clint was a true cowboy who taught actors how to ride a horse and was your standard Hollywood cowboy of the 1960s to 1970s. However, Harrison Ford took the cowboy mythos to the next level when he broke the mold as the penultimate space cowboy, starring as the beloved Han Solo in the *Star Wars* saga. Harrison Ford further extracted that intangible academic cowboy by blazing a completely new trail as the intelligent action adventurer in the *Indiana Jones* movies.

Of Generation X, Josh Duhamel (1972) of Minot, North Dakota, and Michael Peña (1976) of Chicago, Illinois, are two American men who successfully blended action and drama. Josh became an action star in the *Transformers* films, starting in 2007, while Peña landed comic action roles in the fantastic 2010s Marvel movies. Kellan Lutz from Dickinson, North Dakota, is a temporal twin to Christopher Denham of Blue Island, Illinois, and both men were born in 1985. Kellan became a star at sunset with *The Twilight* films (2008-2012). He was on the vampire side of the family. Christopher Denham rose as a star in *Shutter Island* (2010)—a neo-noir psychological thriller.

Of the boomer generation, Shadoe Stevens (1946) of Jamestown, North Dakota, is as close as you can get to the star power of Bill Murray (1950) of Evanston, Illinois. Bill Murray is the king of deadpan and the thinking man's comedy. Bill Murray is a walking paradox; his acting range is small, yet his performance is large. He is a master of Zen who does everything by doing nothing. The Master of Chillax, Foreman of Funny, the Duke of Deadpan, chances are he is not quite all human. On the flip side is Shadoe Stevens. Shadoe is the ultimate wingman's wingman. Shadoe has a distinct voice that let him hit it big in radio, and he has starred in *The Kentucky Fried Movie* (1977), *Shadoevision* (1986), *Dave's World* (1993-1997), the *Clueless* TV series (1998), and *The Tick* (2019). Shadoe's voice is perhaps more recognizable than his face. Another dynamic duo that crossed upon the electric stage in 1990 in the movie *Awakenings* is Robin Williams (born 1951) from Chicago, Illinois and Gordon J. Weiss from Bismarck, North Dakota (born 1949). The essence of carpe diem is a strong theme in this soulful film as well as an overarching theme in Williams's life. Williams and Weiss sparkled at different and unequal magnitudes—and that is how our lives go. Sometimes we are the star of a situation, and sometimes we are just an uncredited member of the cast in the background. In the end, it's good to cherish our roles as they transition between the soloist and the chorus.

As for storytellers, Robert Zemeckis (1952) of Chicago, Illinois, is a mainstream success matched to a side-stream director, Ronnie Cramer of Bismarck, North Dakota (1957). Zemeckis released a string of top tier movies that ensnared the world's attention: *Romancing the Stone* (1984), *Back to the Future* (1985), *Forrest Gump* (1994), *Contact* (1997), and *Cast Away* (2000). Zemeckis has a knack for bottling lightning, with soulful stories that transcend demographics and national borders. Ronnie Cramer, on the other hand, is an art house director creating unique, offbeat, and wholly creative movies that challenge the mainstream like *Highway Amazon* (2001)—a documentary about a real-life female bodybuilder who wrestles men in hotel rooms. Other peculiar titles by Ronnie Cramer include *Even Hitler Had a Girlfriend* (1992) and *The Hitler Tapes* (1994), which are wacky-o-ball funny movies that can only be enjoyed by the smallest slices of America.

In 1984, a man from North Dakota gave critical artistic support to a performer from Illinois, and the result was endless soulful enchantment—*Ghostbusters*. Richard Edlund (1940) from Fargo was the special effects director for this epic film, while Harold Ramis (1944-2014) starred as the scientific exorcist Dr. Egon Spengler. Both men were endowed by the most mysterious of creative muses. Edlund was the master cameraman on *Star Wars* (1977). He also worked on quintessential Hollywood hits *The Empire Strikes Back* (1980), *Raiders of the Lost Ark* (1981), *Poltergeist* (1982), *Big Trouble in Little China* (1986), *Die Hard* (1988), *Ghost* (1990) and more recently *21 Jump Street* (2012). Ramis made his mark in America with *Caddyshack* (1980), *Stripes* (1981), *National Lampoon's Vacation* (1983), and *Groundhog Day* (1993). As for the many imaginations of the 1980s, Edlund of North Dakota helped set the style, while Ramis of Illinois gave it substance.

One of the key souls that seals the unequal relationship between North Dakota and Illinois is Phil Jackson. A youthful Phil Jackson went to high school in North Dakota at Williston High School, where he played football, baseball, track, and of course, basketball. In college, Jackson played basketball at the University of North Dakota. And it was during the 1990s that he became the head coach of the Chicago Bulls, becoming a legend in Illinois.

For companies, the Bobcat company came into existence at West Fargo, North Dakota in 1947. Bobcat specializes in excavators, loaders, and engines. On a larger scale, a match for Bobcat is the John Deere company, which also makes heavy equipment and other machinery. Over the years, John Deere has become synonymous with effective lawn care. John Deere got its start in Grand Detour, Illinois, in 1837.

On the more personal side of places where you can get a taste and feel for each state are UNO Pizzeria & Grill for Illinois, and Space Aliens Grill and Bar for North Dakota. UNO began as a franchise in 1943 in Chicago. It became famous for the Chicago deep-dish pizza that is something akin to pizza quiche. One slice of this heavy body pizza can usually satisfy the average man. For North Dakota, an alien themed restaurant with classical arcade is a family fun zone with a bar for the big kids. Two Gen X/Y restaurant chains that came to be in Reagan's decade were Jimmy John's sandwich shop in Charleston, Illinois, in 1983. During Reagan's second term, North Dakota put Burger Time on the map in 1987.

As for Gen Z places that allow one to sample the spirit of North Dakota and Illinois, we have Argo Tea and The Vault coffee shop. Argo tea was founded in 2003 at 958 West Armitage Avenue, Chicago, Illinois. Its mission was to become the "Starbucks of tea." While at Valley City, North Dakota, The Vault created a unique coffee shop that is an unmanned, self-serve bakery, coffee shop, and bookstore, which opened for business in 2009. It started up operations in a former bank, thus it is a bit of an oxymoron as the vault is unlocked to the public.

Long ago, the Old West's iconic general store was the original all-purpose place to get dry goods. But 200 years later, these general purpose dry goods stores would evolve into brick-and-mortar retail outlets. As shopping is a certain kind of national pastime, it led to the rise of the modern retail chain store. And the one store to literally rise to the top in the 20th century was Sears. So profitable and powerful, the Sears Tower became an iconic illustration of wealth and shopping. The Sears Tower held the title as the tallest building in the world for 25 years from 1974 until 1998. But here is the sweet coincidence: before 1974 the U.S. had the title of the tallest structure on Earth, the KVLY-TV mast. Providentially, the tallest structure in the world just so happened to be Illinois's essential wingman, North Dakota, in the wee city of Blanchard.

Thus North Dakota, like Illinois, had a stint as the undisputed reigning sky structure champ of the known universe. North Dakota held the title of tallest structure from 1968 until 1974. Just as Illinois gave birth to the tallest building, the Warsaw radio mast unseated North Dakota with a Soviet pride project that snookered in the tallest man-made structure title in the world by 21 extra feet. However, the Warsaw Tower oddly collapsed the same year the Soviet Union fell. Four months before the Soviet Union would fall, the Warsaw Tower collapsed on August 8, 1991. The Soviet Union entered the hallowed halls of the history books on Christmas in 1991. Thus, North Dakota got a second run as the tallest structure in the universe well into the next millennium.

Illinois and North Dakota are a dynamic duo of contrasting flavors. Their contrasting forms make a delightful essential whole like the Wonder Twins Zan and Jayna, Batman and Robin, Ren and Stimpy, or best of all, Han and Chewie. They are an eye-catching supercouple of the tall 'n small, thick 'n slim, or the shy and congenial. Although their backgrounds differ like midnight and noon, they are essential elements of the nation who put a spotlight on the national bird, centered on the North American bald eagle in its glorious fullness. The eagle rests on the ground next to a solid rock upon Illinois's banner, while she is in flight next to a stellar aurora with North Dakota, truly … a union of *Heaven and Earth.*

thirteen

INDIANA & RHODE ISLAND

The Alchemy of Fire and Water Hidden in Plain Sight

THE FLAG REVELATION

INDIANA

A golden circle of 13 stars is the primary point of concord between Rhode Island and Indiana. Their flags' backgrounds differ like day and night. Rhode Island is yang, because in the philosophy of the Tao the color white and other bright, hot colors are associated with yang. Indiana is yin; yin is associated with cool, dark colors and night.

These flags also echo the essential dichotomy found in all cultures, as water is arbitrarily assigned as the opposite of fire. Indiana has a golden torch, while Rhode Island has a golden anchor. The torch is a man-made tool that demonstrates man's mastery over the ancient element of fire. Essentially, it is a flaming sword that banishes the darkness. The torch is basically a primitive level one Jedi Knight sword. Likewise, the anchor is a woman-willed object that allows womankind to hold her ground, independent of the ebb and flow of the tide or river's current.

When you look at the inner stars of Indiana's flag, they outline the design of the anchor found on Rhode Island's flag. From 1882 and 1897, Indiana and Rhode Island had nearly identical state flags because the background field of Rhode Island was navy blue. Both flags have a single word written. Indiana has

RHODE ISLAND

its name in the top crest position above the torch, in between the larger 19th and 12 o'clock top star, while Rhode Island has the word "Hope" written on the blue ribbon in the downward compartment area under the anchor.

The tilt of the stars differs. The stars of Indiana are in the same alignment as if in aircraft formation. Indiana's stars are oriented as they are on the modern 50-starred flag. However, the stars of Rhode Island are oriented as if they are dancers holding hands in a circle. Thus, each star has its own unique tilt, as it is with the Betsy Ross flag.

Indiana's flag was adopted in May 1917, after the Indiana Society of the Daughters of the American Revolution held a contest for a state flag. The winner was Paul Hadley of Mooresville, Indiana. Officially, the torch represents liberty and enlightenment, and the rays represent their far-reaching influence. The current flag for Rhode Island is the third version adopted on November 1, 1897. The word "Hope" is linked to Hebrews 6:19: "Hope we have as an anchor of the soul."

Geography

Indiana and Rhode Island are primarily grounded to contrasting bodies of water, the marine waters of the ocean or the fresh waters of the lake. Rhode Island is a member of the "salty dog den" as a coastal state, while Indiana is a part of the "peppery feline pride" of the Great Laker club. Indiana is the smallest member in the band of six that made up the Northwest Territory, and Rhode Island is the smallest member in the chorus of six that makes up New England.

Rhode Island and Indiana even have a similar shape to each other, if you ignore the eastern isles of Rhode Island. Rhode Island looks like a miniature version of Indiana, or rather, Indiana is a super-sized version of Rhode Island. The Pawcatuck River for Rhode Island is the counterpart of the Wabash River for Indiana. And just as Rhode Island's northeastern corner juts into Massachusetts, the northeastern corner of Indiana juts into Michigan.

Indiana and Rhode Island have a somewhat intense love-hate rivalry with a larger neighbor. For Indiana, the bossy brother is Chicago in Illinois, and Gary in Indiana is a roommate with Chicago. They sometimes fight, but they get along when they need to, or rather, have to. For Rhode Island, Boston in Massachusetts is the loud and proud "know it all Jan" on the top bunk. When they don't see eye to eye, they give each other the silent treatment.

For the most part, the Six Sisters of the Northeast have a relatively cozy relationship, compared to the somewhat distant Six Brothers of the Northwest Territory. And you can also thank the patriotic, pigskin on-goings that occur every fall for the tight-knit relationship with the New England Six. But for the Six Laker Brothers, it has the opposite effect.

Along their southern border, a body of water separates them from their southern cousins. The Mississippi River separates Indiana from Kentucky. Their family traditions do differ a bit, but they vacation with each other from time to time. Block Island Sound separates Rhode Island from New York. Again, their accents and manners do differ just a bit, but they enjoy family visits over the holidays.

History

To banish or not to banish, that is a perpetual theme across society, history, the first garden, space, time and now, social media. Rhode Island and Indiana are states consecrated in the afterglow of a ban. The genesis of Rhode Island came about due to the perpetual battle for the soul. The Puritan mandates of Massachusetts Bay Colony saw that Roger Williams was cast out from a shining theocratic city on a hill, not to return upon the penalty of death. Rather than becoming a martyred footnote for religious liberty of conscience, Williams became its honored founding father. After Roger Williams was expelled from the "holier than thou" community of Massachusetts in 1635 for spreading *"Newe and dangerous opinions"* little did he know he was laying a foundation for the 13th state of the United States and the nation's core value for freedom of religion, under the first amendment.

The ban related to the birth of Indiana was of a different sort, with even more profound consequences. The ban that shaped the destiny of Indiana and the nation was the Northwest Ordinance of 1787. It was arguably the most important piece of government programming under the Articles of Confederation, American Gov. 1.0. It was signed into law by the Confederation president, President Arthur St. Clair, born in Scotland in 1737. Article 6 of the Northwest Ordinance of 1787 established that "There shall be neither slavery nor involuntary servitude in the said territory." As a consequence, Indiana was the 19th overall, sixth of the second 13, and the third state born free.

It is easy to take religious liberty and the end of slavery for granted. Before the birth of the United States, the idea that the government or one of royal blood had the right to tell one how to worship and subjugate one as property, under penalty of imprisonment, torture, or death was the status quo for much of humanity's history in every nation and tribe.

But tribalism is an ancient specter that transcends time in various forms today. The Northwest Indian War of Indiana and the Pequot War in Rhode Island are the tragic opening acts of hostilities between colonists and aboriginals of America.

The Pequot War was the first race war to truly embroil the colonies of America and set the pattern of conflict between Natives and Newcomers. Thousands of lives on both sides were lost. Native villages were erased off the map and frontier settlements abandoned. This was the initial ugly baptism of the Native American suffering that would eventually catch fire from sea to shining sea. Before Wounded Knee, Little Bighorn, the Black Hawk War, and Tippecanoe, there was the Pequot War.

The Pequot War traces one of its roots to the murder of John Stone. Captain John Stone was born in England around 1573 and became a trader/pirate in the New World. John Stone had a reputation as a rowdy loudmouth who took well to drinking, fighting, and womanizing. Suffice it to say, by today's standards John Stone had a toxic personality to the ire of the Puritans and Natives alike. Nonetheless, when he was murdered, his death was virtually the first American "No Justice, No Peace" protest. John Stone's murder was most likely justifiable. However, the Whites would give no peace to the Pequot unless the murderers were handed over for Puritan justice, an eye-for-an-eye style of justice via public execution. John Stone was murdered on the Connecticut River after he captured two Pequot and forced (or enslaved) them to work for him on the Connecticut River in 1634.

Previously, the Pequot leaders wanted to maintain a trade monopoly with the Dutch in the area for precious advanced "alien technologies." However, the Dutch were inclined to the free market style of trade, eager to deal with anyone who had the goods. In order to corner the market with the Dutch traders, a Chief Tatobem of the Pequot discouraged other tribes from dealing with the Dutch, via murder and intimidation. After Chief Tatobem killed several rival Natives, the Dutch arrested him and promised to release him back to the Pequot for a ransom—a mother lode of Indian currency known as Waupun. The Pequot paid the large ransom. However, the Dutch returned a lifeless Tatobem back to the Pequot. Consequently, the Pequot avowed retaliation against the Dutch. That call for revenge fell upon his son Chief Sassacus, the new leader of the Pequot.

The spark that ignited the Pequot War was when another White man, John Oldham, was mysteriously murdered in July 1636, along with several other sailors on Block Island, Rhode Island. The Pequot were the prime suspects due to the promised blood vendetta by Chief Sassacus. But John Oldham was English, and the plan was to deliver a cold dish of revenge upon the Dutch. Like John Stone, John Oldham had a reputation as a troublemaker. Suffice it to say, nice guys would have little chance of being a successful colonial trader back in the early 1600s. But the death of a second White man at the hands of non-Christian "heathens" became the perfect catalyst to fire up the Puritan calls for justice. Consequently, a war party of White men were sent to Block Island, Rhode Island, with orders to kill Native men, and steal away the women, children, and plunder. The Pequot War had begun.

It is likely the English colonists would have lost the war except for one secret weapon. This weapon was previously discovered by Hernando Cortés with his conquest of Mexico in 1521. The English were able to enlist the help of the rival tribes to make war upon the Pequot. The tribes allied to the English colonists were the Narragansett and Mohegan, both bitter rivals of the Pequot. Almost as bitter as it was between the rival White tribes in the area: the English, Dutch, and French.

The most memorable battle of the Pequot War was the Mystic Massacre on May 26, 1637. It was here that English colonists effectively used total war. The Pequot were protected by a wooden palisade in Mystic. After a hard fight, the English and Native allies set the encampment on fire. Any civilians, including the elderly, women, and children who ran from the flames, were gunned down as they tried to escape. This type of egregious genocidal murder disturbed the Mohegan and Narragansett allies of the English. It is hard to put a number on the number of dead Pequot, but it's estimated that somewhere between 400 to 700 Pequot civilians were either burned alive, shot as they fled the flames, or were sliced down by cold English steel.

The Pequot were defeated. The last independent leader of the Pequot, Chief Sassacus, son of Tatobem, attempted to find refuge with the Mohawk Nation in New York. Instead of offering sanctuary, the Mohawk leaders thought it wise to cut off his head and sent it back east to curry favor with the English.

The treaty that put a period on the Pequot War was the Hartford Treaty of

September 21, 1638. It divided up the remaining Pequot among the Mohegan and Narragansett as slaves, and some were shipped off to the Caribbean at top market prices. The Hartford Treaty of 1638 also stipulated that the Pequot could no longer use "Pequot" to describe themselves, and they were banned from ever returning to their home territories.

As the Pequot War was the harbinger of things to come for Native Americans, blame can be partially grounded to English, rather than to the United States. However, soon after the birth of the United States, the defeat and divide of Indian lands by U.S. agency, following its sad and forlorn course, began in earnest with what was to become Indiana.

Two centuries later, the similar situation that arose in colonial Indiana became known as the Northwest Territory Indian War. Shortly after the end of the American Revolution, colonists were eager to settle lands of the Northwest Territory. However, the Natives living here were, for the most part, allied with the British during the revolution since they had promised to keep colonists out of the area. Since most colonists had little to no respect for Native culture and their claims to this land, conflict followed its tragic pattern.

As torture and murder between Natives and colonists flared up along the northwest frontier, the new *U.S. Government 2.0* under President Washington, was forced to take action. The first campaign to pacify the Indians of the Northwest Territory was the Harmar Campaign, which took place in the fall of 1790. In October 1790, a series of battles raged near Fort Wayne, Indiana. The natives were led by Little Turtle and Blue Jacket. The Natives delivered several punishing defeats to U.S. forces, which ultimately became known as Harmar's defeat. The U.S. had yet to wholly embrace the use of turncoat Natives as scouts as standard protocol.

As Harmar's defeat shocked the American public, the worst was yet to come. The ultimate defeat of U.S. forces during the colonial era took place the following year on November 4, 1791. Arthur St. Clair, the former president of Confederation Congress who had previously banned slavery in the Northwest Territory led the charge. The humiliating defeat of St. Clair took place in Ohio at Fort Recovery, and this blow was dealt by an Indian from Indiana, Chief

Little Turtle. It was an even match of numbers between Native and Newcomer, but the Indian Confederacy walloped the American forces. Of the 1,400-plus members of the U.S. force, fewer than 200 were able to escape being killed or captured. The infamous Battle of the Wabash, also known as St. Clair's Defeat, went down as one of the greatest victories for Native Americans and the worst defeats for the U.S. until Little Bighorn in Montana. However, this Native American victory was short-lived. The U.S. would gain the upper hand three years later at the Battle of Fallen Timbers on August 20, 1794, when Mad Anthony Wayne crushed Native American resistance. The Northwest Indian War closed when the Treaty of Greenville—which opened up the southern half of Ohio, a small southeastern sliver of Indiana—was signed on August 3, 1795.

Coincidentally, a generation after each war, as it was with WWI and WWII, the pattern would repeat itself again. In round two, Native resistance attempted to purge themselves of all things Western and European; it truly became a race war. The Race War of the Northeast is best known as King Philip's War or Metacomet's War. It took place in the pre-centennial 1676, officially from 1675 to 1678. King Philip's War is another overlooked tragedy that laid the foundation for the American psyche. King Philip's War was a race war where opposing forces sought to wipe each other out. It was fought all across New England, including Massachusetts, New Hampshire, Connecticut, Maine, and Rhode Island.

The chief sachem of the Wampanoag Confederacy, King Philip the Metacomet, became disillusioned by the colonists because of their ever-expanding appetite for land and less than respectful attitudes toward Native American traditions and religions. As Puritans were hostile to the various denominations of Christianity (including the Church of England), one can only imagine the vicious and abhorrent revulsion that they harbored toward Native American religions. When King Philip recognized the waning power of the Indian and dominance of colonists, he resolved to make a pan-tribal alliance between Native tribes to oust the European colonists. The spark of the war began as King Philip's plans to attack colonial settlements were revealed to the colonists. In January 1675, a Native convert to Christianity known as a Praying Indian, John Sassamon, warned Plymouth Colony of the looming hostilities from "non-praying Indians." The colonists then delivered a message to King Philip the Metacomet: should they hear any more planning of war; they would confiscate more Wampanoag land and seize their guns. Shortly afterward, John Sassamon the praying Indian, was found dead in an icy pond. In June, a jury convicted three Wampanoag men of this murder, and they were swiftly executed on June 8, 1675. King Philip, the Metacomet, was indicted as the mastermind.

Fighting began in earnest in late June 1675 in Massachusetts at Swansea, where several colonists were brutally killed. The first reprisal was upon King Philip's home village of Mount Hope in modern-day Rhode Island. As war fever gripped New England, colonists united and declared war on King Philip the Metacomet. Soon, other tribes were drawn into the conflict, and this war would rage for the next three years. Colonist arrogance and Native resentment mixed with a rift in understanding led to its bloody conclusion.

A high battle mark took place in Rhode Island at the Great Swamp Fight in December 1675. Previously, the Narragansett Tribe had welcomed Roger Williams with the genesis of Rhode Island. But with the broad-brush strokes of the perennial "us versus them" mentality that arises with every political conflict (even in the year 2020), many colonists saw all Indians as a threat and sought to wipe them out like a terminator. Josiah Winslow from Plymouth Colony ignored the October 1675 Treaty of Neutrality and attacked the Narragansett, pushing them into the camp with King Philip.

The Great Swamp Fight took place on December 19, 1675, in South Kingstown, Rhode Island. In this battle, a Narragansett village was previously protected by the swampy waters, but a severe cold had frozen the natural, organic moat, allowing the colonists to easily hunt down the Narragansett, with allied Indian help. Once found, the colonists unleashed the might of the Western technologies, and a lopsided battle took place even though both sides were evenly matched with about 1,000 warriors.

This battle broke the backbone of the Narragansett, as their women and children were also killed. The Narragansett struck back a few times afterward and managed to burn Providence for its pre-centennial in 1676 and the home of Roger Williams. It was a tragedy that Roger Williams was the most tolerant of colonists who initially befriended the Narragansett, but at the end of his life, he found himself at war with his once landlord and protectors. Providentially, a kind of karmic blow back would visit the English when the colonists would fight a war against their sovereign landlord and protector a century later in 1776.

The last major battle of King Philip's War took place in the summer of 1676, at North Smithfield, Rhode Island, known as the Second Battle of Nipsachuck. It was here that the colonists famously used cavalry tactics against the Narragansett. Although most of the Narragansetts had fled to Connecticut, a band had returned to Rhode Island to (it is speculated) reclaim stashes of corn seed for the planting season. However, John Talcott—with about 300 colonial militia and 100 Mohegan and Pequot—was able to track down and destroy the foraging food party. When the Native queen of the Narragansett, Queen Quaiapen Magnus, and her chief engineer Stonewall John Nawhun were killed, they were all but finished. The surviving Narragansett of this battle were either executed or sold into slavery.

As it became clear that all hope was lost for King Philip the Metacomet, his braves began to surrender en masse. King Philip took refuge in the Assawompset Swamp just below Providence, but he was hunted down by a combined militia and Native force. King Philip the Metacomet was discovered on Mount Hope in Bristol, Rhode Island, and killed on August 12, 1676, by a fellow Native American, John Antoquan—a recent convert to Christianity from the Wampanoag Tribe with a chemically propelled, processed rock that burst from a long metal tube. Metacomet's corpse was then beheaded and drawn and quartered. King Philip's head was then mounted on a spike at Plymouth, Massachusetts. It remained there as a chilling reminder and warning for the next two decades.

Two centuries later in Indiana, another anti-American, or rather, anti-Western, purge movement reached a fever pitch with the rise of Tenskwatawa, better known as "The Prophet" of the Shawnee. The Shawnee prophet was born at the beginning of the American Revolution during the winter of 1775. His initial name was He Makes Loud Noise, and he was something of a weak child. The prophet showed no evidence of being a powerful spiritual leader. His father, Puckeshinwa, was killed before he was born at the Battle of Point Pleasant,

THE FLAG REVELATION

Virginia, on October 10, 1774. It was one of the last battles between British colonials and Indians before the British colonists miraculously transformed into Americans, while a lesser half would shape shift into Canadians. He Makes Loud Noise couldn't keep up with his more athletic brothers, who were skilled at activities like hunting. Eventually, it is assumed, his low self-esteem and low popularity was a catalyst for his alcoholism. He also lost his right eye due to a bow and arrow injury. Although He Makes Loud Noise was present at the Battle of Fallen Timbers in 1794, along with his more famous brother Tecumseh, he did not distinguish himself in the battle.

He Makes Loud Noise reached rock bottom sometime in 1804/1805, as he was widely known as the village drunk, but things started to turn around when he underwent a series of vision quests. He changed his name to Open Door as Tenskwatawa and threw off his self-destructive ways and cleaned up his act. Open Door was able to overcome his addictions and became a charismatic healer and spiritual leader. The medicine he preached was a return to the Old Ways, calling for a separation or segregation from White civilization and for the unity among Native Americans to resist the American and European civilizations. Calling for unity between Native tribes was a tall order. Ancient hatreds were long simmering between various tribes that festered as a perpetual state of war.

Things initially went well, and Open Door founded a new religious movement that resonated with various tribes resentful of unfair treatment from Euro-Americans and colonial hostility. Eventually he founded a new community known as Prophetstown, near present-day Lafayette, Indiana. Prophetstown became a place of Native revival where Indian traditions and religions would take center stage. As this new pan-Indian alliance movement grew, it gained the attention of the U.S. government. By 1811 Prophetstown became a stronghold, and its message became more militant. They fiercely advocated that land should not be sold to colonists, and accurately understood it would ultimately undermine the Native American way of life.

Prophetstown was led by two famous brothers who were a match of brawn and brains, Tecumseh and Tenskwatawa. Tecumseh earned a fierce warrior reputation and was attempting to bring more tribes to the cause. In 1811, Tecumseh went on a recruiting mission in the south. At that very moment, William Henry Harrison made plans to strike out at Prophetstown. However, Tecumseh left orders that Tenskwatawa was not to engage in any hostilities with the Whites until he returned.

But as Harrison's forces approached to investigate Prophetstown, the pressure mounted and Tenskwatawa decided to strike first. On November 7, 1811, the U.S. Army was within one mile of Prophetstown. The Natives led a surprise attack at dawn. After several hours, it was clear that Harrison had the upper hand at what is known as the victory at Tippecanoe. The next day, Harrison was able to shatter the dreams of the Pan-Indian Confederacy and burn Prophetstown to the ground. The Prophet and Tecumseh eventually retreated into Canada. When the War of 1812 broke out the next year, Tecumseh fought bravely on the Canadian side but lost his life at the Battle of the Thames in Ontario on October 5, 1813. Tenskwatawa later returned to the U.S. and settled on a reservation in Kansas, passing in obscurity in the mid-1830s. William H. Harrison was elected president in 1840, but caught pneumonia shortly after inauguration day, and died weeks later, having been president for one moon.

During the American Revolution, Indiana and Rhode Island earned their battle scars and are a reminder that American independence is perpetually indebted to the Frenchman's pride. Much of the hard fighting during the American Revolution was along the eastern seaboard but fighting on the frontier is best noted by George Rogers Clark (1752-1818), who was the older brother of the famous William Clark (1770-1838), of the Lewis & Clark expedition. The older Clark's campaign was the key that empowered the U.S.'s far-reaching claims to the east bank of the Mississippi River. George Rogers Clark led the militia that captured Kaskaskia in Illinois 1778 and Vincennes in Indiana 1779. Illinois was captured without firing a shot, but Vincennes was a bit of a challenge. It was captured by a British force from Detroit on December 17, 1778.

If Vincennes in Indiana were left in British hands, the U.S. would have had a weaker hand at the peace table. It is likely Michigan would have remained in British hands, and now be a part of Canada. But the timeline of a "Canadian Detroit" was severed when George Rogers Clark led a daring winter campaign march to recapture Vincennes. Nearly half of the American force was composed of French militia from Illinois country—former subjects of forlorn New France. After a 180-mile hard march in the dead of winter, George Rogers Clark was able to lay siege to Loyalist forces and retake Vincennes (Fort Sackville). Vincennes was officially surrendered by the British on February 25, 1779. This victory—with ex–pat, ex-French Canadian help—solidified U.S. claims to Michigan Territory.

In Rhode Island, the Battle of Rhode Island took place on August 29, 1778. It was the first battle in which French and American forces cooperated as a unit. The British had taken Newport, Rhode Island, and the combined U.S. and French forces attempted to retake the city. The first French naval officer to work with American forces was Charles Henri Hector D'Estaing. However, due to bad weather and lack of confidence, the British were able to repel the Franco-American attempt to take Newport.

D'Estaing did not have a clear victory when working with American forces during the siege of Rhode Island in 1778 and later with the siege of Savannah in 1779. However, he did receive injuries that required him to walk with a cane for the rest of his life. Nonetheless, D'Estaing provided essential interference to frustrate the British Navy around Rhode Island and elsewhere. Without French assistance, Canada could have become the most powerful nation on Earth, but that timeline was severed with the help of Frenchmen like D'Estaing.

What's in a name? Would guns and roses by any other name be just as seductive and or destructive? Two names that echo with a profound power across the boundless reservoir of American memory are Jefferson Davis and John Brown. Of matters concerning wars between brothers, like Abel and Cain, the wakes of their lives have fundamentally altered the mystic chords of memory and shall nevermore be forgotten. Rather, John and Jefferson of the Brown and Davis clans are two emissaries from the past that represent two ends of a rose, be it the soulful sweetness of the flower or the painful pinch of the bloodletting thorn. John Brown and Jefferson Davis are connected to an undying wellspring of perpetual curiosity that has generated a deep, voluminous, and ever-increasing ocean of reflection.

INDIANA & RHODE ISLAND

By a peculiar Providence, there is a lesser John Brown and a lesser Jefferson Davis of historical fame who stand in the shadow as the counter to the grander mountains of their respective names. They are the counter-color disc within the yin and yang symbol, as to the gravity that's bound to the names of John Brown and Jefferson Davis. In Rhode Island, John Brown was born on January 27, 1736, and his high birth allowed him to give aid and comfort to the ugliest beasts sown by man, to the American style of race-based slavery. In Indiana, Jefferson Davis was born on March 2, 1828, but of low birth and was an element who quickened the destruction of the Confederacy—a government with a foundation squarely mounted on a racial caste system.

The John Brown born in the Year of the Dragon and sector of Aquarius in the city of Providence, Rhode Island, became an American patriot, merchant, statesman, and notorious slave trader. A year before several patriots summed up the courage for a secret costumed tea party in Boston, John Brown led a group of patriots to attack the *HMS Gaspee* on June 9/10, 1772. The *HMS Gaspee* was torched, but no one was killed. One British officer was reported injured, William Duddingston, after being shot in the groin. In 1772, the *HMS Gaspee* was basically a U.K. colonial American coast guard ship, enforcing the rule of law of the port authority. John Brown was a zealous, out and proud patriot, long before the Declaration of Independence was declared, and a key officer in the secret Sons of Liberty.

Like the latter-day John Brown of anti-slavery fame from 1860, the John Brown of the American Revolution was a firebrand partisan, dedicated to the cause. In contrast to the latter-day John Brown, the John Brown of the American Revolution wholly embraced of slavery, especially the White ownership of Blacks. But on March 22, 1794, U.S. congress passed the Slave Trade Act, which prohibited the making, loading, outfitting, equipping, or dispatching of any ship to be used in classical human trafficking. John Brown ignored that law and became the first American persecuted under the Slave Trade Act of 1794. Providentially, the name of the offending ship was "*Hope.*" John Brown was convicted and forced to sell "*Hope.*" He was a key patriotic founding father, and he and his family were instrumental in founding Brown University at Providence, Rhode Island, where he set the cornerstone of this prestigious Ivy League University.

However, John Brown had a younger brother with another powerful and providential name, Moses. Moses the younger Brown was born in the Year of the Horse in the month of the Balance, September 23, 1738. Like the grandest Moses from collective memory, Moses Brown was a liberator for mankind who sought to put an end to slavery. Moses, who held abolitionist views, was the black sheep of the patriotic Brown family. He became a Quaker and helped found the Providence Society for abolishing the slave trade, standing in opposition to the older brother, John Brown, in principle and action since the younger Moses took his slave trading brother to trial over Hope. Should there ever be a call to rename Brown University due to John Brown's zealous love of slavery, the counter of Moses Brown and the latter-day John Brown from Connecticut are names that will always buffer such an impulse.

As for Indiana's dichotomy of names to cut at the soul "Jefferson Davis" sits on the front page of American history. Jefferson Davis was born in Clark County, Indiana, in the Year of the Rodent in the month of Twin Fish on March 2, 1828. This lesser "twin fish," Jefferson Davis of the North was born 20 years after the more famous Jefferson Davis of the South. Unlike the synchronicity bound between the John Browns of posterity, these Jefferson Davises lived concurrently.

What is the significance of one's birthplace? Does the cosmic geography of the heavens play a role in shaping one's destiny? No doubt, the heavens are the ultimate timepiece that allows for the calibration of the calendar, such that a civilization can find its place in space and time, regardless of the world one should manifest upon. But the sky is more than just a clock. It has only been recently revealed to the civilized mind that oceans, mountains, and alien clouds of amber and azure fill up the collective, communal ceiling across the heavens. Destiny has a certain sense of humor, and its punchline is often revealed over the course of history. One funny footnote randomly planned to manifest during the American Civil War was placed upon the Davis clan. A sordid twin fish, a Jefferson Davis born in a land bathed in bondage in the year 1808. A single score later, another Jefferson Davis was born in 1828 in a realm christened in liberty in the year 1787. But were these two Jefferson Davises simply a product of their environments?

The stars may or may not have our destiny written in them, but it was the peculiar destiny of Jefferson Davis from Indiana to become a successful Civil War general for the North. Jefferson Davis of Indiana was born within the military—meaning he didn't go to West Point, unlike the highborn Jefferson Davis of Kentucky, who graduated West Point class of 1828.

Jefferson Davis of Indiana was 19 when he enlisted with the 3rd Indiana Volunteers to fight with Mexico. He rose to the rank of sergeant and was promoted at the Battle of Buena Vista in Coahuila, Mexico for his bravery. When the Civil War broke out, Jefferson Davis was providentially stationed at Fort Sumter and bore witness to the official opening of hostilities between the Union and Confederacy, as ordered by his senior Pisces-twin, Jefferson Davis. The lesser Jefferson Davis was also the commanding general who worked with Grant and Sherman during their Southern campaign and took part in the Sherman's March to the Sea.

But men are never simply a black-and-white issue of good versus bad. This lesser Jefferson Davis infamously deserted a party of recently freed slaves at the crossing of the appropriately named river, Ebenezer Creek. He deceptively told that trailing party of refugees that they needed to wait on one side of the river and would only be allowed to cross after the Army secured the area. However, as soon as the last portions of the Army cleared Ebenezer Creek, Jefferson Davis—like the unreformed Ebenezer Scrooge of Charles Dickens fame—ordered his men to quickly pack up the pontoon bridge before the refugees could cross. Shortly afterward, a Confederate unit arrived to recapture the slaves with an untold cruelty. Many newly freed slaves attempted to cross the river but drowned. After the war, Jefferson Davis became the first Commander of the Department of Alaska in 1867, which was the administrative position that evolved into the governorship of Alaska.

Perhaps the greatest Civil War general to tie the knot between Indiana and Rhode Island was General Ambrose Burnside. He was born in Liberty, Indiana on May 23, 1824, but later moved to Rhode Island, where he eventually became its senator. Most importantly, the smallest state became his final resting place on September 13, 1881, at Bristol, Rhode Island, just in time for the first U.S. Open. Burnside is famous for having very large sideburns, which is where this facial hair feature gets its name. For a short while, he was the commanding general of the Union army but was savagely beaten back by Lee at the Battle of Fredericksburg. In 1871 he also became the first president of the National Rifle Association.

Two Civil War generals who made their marks during and after the civil war are Lew Wallace (born 1827) and William Sprague IV (born 1830). Lew Wallace from Brookeville, Indiana, fought in the Mexican American War and rose to the rank of two-star general, major general. He helped stave off defeat at the terrifying battle of Shiloh and helped establish a foothold in the Confederacy with the Battle of Fort Donelson. After the War he went on to write *Ben-Hur: A Tale of the Christ* (1880). Before the publication of *Gone With the Wind*, *Ben-Hur* was an all-time best seller in the U.S. *Ben-Hur* is the fictional story of a Judah Ben-Hur who was a prince in Jerusalem who lived in the first century. Every generation has a movie adaptation of *Ben-Hur* starting in 1907, then 1925, 1959, and 2016. The 1959 version stars Charlton Heston and is the most famous classical movie-to-perpetual-TV broadcast version.

William Sprague IV, the wingman of Lew Wallace, distinguished himself as the rare acting governor to participate in a war while still in office, talking the talk and walking the walk. Governor Sprague of Rhode Island saw action at the First Battle of Bull Run at Manassas Junction, Virginia. Although Sprague never went on to write a book, the story of his father's death is stirring, as the original unwritten Dark Knight story. When William Sprague was 13 his father, Amasa Sprague, was murdered on New Year's Eve in 1843. The man convicted of the murder, John Gordon, was the last person executed in Rhode Island on Valentine's Day 1845. However, it is generally believed that the culprit was someone else. Apparently, John Gordon was railroaded by law enforcement due to anti-Irish Catholic sentiment of the time. Thus, the true killer, or "Joker," got away. Like the caped vigilante of comic lore, William Sprague IV was born into a politically powerful and wealthy business family. After his career in politics, William Sprague worked on several innovative devices, akin to the legendary Tinkertoys of Wayne Enterprises.

Culture

Who knew the Hoosier and Quahog could make a pair? Indiana and Rhode Island link the two original hemispheres of the colonial region, from the Northwest Territory to New England. This region of the U.S. is doubly linked via the fraternal flag twins of Maine and Wisconsin. Unlike Maine and Wisconsin, they are not border states, making them free from any sort of Canadian influence.

What exactly is a Hoosier? Is it any person who can clam up his hand, then blow into it and make an owl/dove call? If so, the most famous American to bring the "Hoosier call" to the attention of America was David Letterman on his late-night TV show. This top 10 Hoosier was famous for doing this on TV with his off the wall, wacky beat humor. But the state to actually embrace the clam as its state symbol is Rhode Island, via rocky shelled Quahog clam.

Both states brag about corn. For Indiana corn is the virtual religion of the taste bud temple, likewise Rhode Island is not ashamed of her sweet varieties of corn. A match of the small tasty clams from Rhode Island are the morels from Indiana. Indiana is infected with a certain kind of morel madness every year. The morel mushroom breaks with the standard cadence of the umbrella style fungus fruiting body plan. Instead, morels opt for a spongy, skeletal-like structure, looking more like some kind of coral reef or sponge than a parasol. For some odd reason, many a Hoosier is enchanted with these flavors provided by these modern art, non-conformist mushrooms. Likewise, Quahogs have fallen in love with a bivalve mollusk, the hard-shell clam, also known as the Quahog. As many Hoosiers are masters of the morel hunt, true-blue Quahogs are keen clam diggers.

Due to an aspect of geography, Indiana and Rhode Island are the perfect marriage of the farmer's daughter who fell in love with the fisherman's son. Harvesting the bounty of the sea is a major source of income for Rhode Island, while netting large bushels of fruits and vegetables from the Earth is a way of life for much of Indiana.

The ultimate heritage of racing on land and sea made a comfy home in Indiana and Rhode Island. Car racing and racing sails can be done anywhere across the world. But Indiana and Rhode Island ingrained these contests into their state ethos.

The Indianapolis 500 is billed as "The Greatest Spectacle in Racing" and is a part of the Triple Crown of Motorsport. The other two crowns are the 24 Hours of Le Mans in France that started in 1923, and the Monaco Grand Prix that was first held in 1929. But the Indianapolis 500 was the first—held in 1911. Typically, the Indy 500 is held over Memorial Day, which originally began as a day of remembrance to decorate the graves of fallen soldiers of the Civil War, as it was originally called Decoration Day. Then, in 1971, U.S. Congress standardized its observance as Memorial Day, and it recognized all the soldiers who fell while serving in the U.S. military.

Coincidentally, Indianapolis is cut by the Mason-Dixon Line at 39°43'. The beltway that surrounds Indianapolis rides around the Mason-Dixon line. When a city reaches a certain size, a ringlike structure composed of a highway, usually dubbed the beltway, will form out of necessity. Thus, I-465 in Indiana is the Mason-Dixon beltway. Likewise, Indiana is the one state that is evenly cut in half by the Mason-Dixon line. Most states along this line are tilted one way or the other. Indiana's northern half is square and artificial, while her southern half follows the natural contours of a river.

As the fire of engines roars in Indiana every Memorial Day, sails swiftly steal breezes to slice across the water in Rhode Island every summer. From 1930 until 1983, America's Cup was held off the coast of Newport, Rhode Island. This most famous of yacht races started in 1851 when the British Royal Yacht Squadron held a race in 1851 around the Isle of Wright off the southern coast of England. The winner was a schooner called *America* from the New York Yacht Club. Then in 1857 the trophy from the race in 1851 was deeded as a trophy gift after the first winner and was open to perpetual international competition. It was held in American hands until 1983, when Australia won America's Cup, which shocked the nation's formerly perfect string of wins since 1851.

Although America's Cup is an international two boat race that is now held at various locations across the seven seas, Rhode Island is host to hundreds of boat races, small and large, every season. Whether one races in a car or boat, a highly trained crack crew is needed to attain maximum speed and efficiency. The captain of the ship and the driver of the racing car must command a special type of intelligence that relies on years of experience and long hours at the helm. Again, these two racing sports providentially reflect the core aspects of their flags that are tied to fire and water. Likewise, the fanfare of regattas and atmosphere of car races are a delightful attraction themselves, as an excuse to watch, eat, drink, and celebrate.

Indiana and Rhode Island are also court kings of different sorts. The basketball court in Indiana is holy ground, while the tennis court in Rhode Island is of historical heritage. Both courts are nearly the same size, utilize nets, and involve the proper bouncing of balls. However, these courts differ like yin and yang, as the difference of the plebeian and patrician.

The first U.S. Open was held in August 1881 on the grass courts at Newport, Rhode Island. It was won by Richard Sears. The venue has since moved to NYC, but Rhode Island has perpetual first bragging rights as the birthplace of competitive tennis in the United States. As for Indiana, although basketball was not founded here, basketball put its soul into this state after the Milan High School Indians won the Indiana High School Boys Basketball Tournament in 1954. So beloved was this story that the movie *Hoosiers* (1986) was made, inspired by this amazing achievement. Likewise, Larry Bird from West Baden, Indiana, would further cement this lore, and later excite the basketball player spirit across Rhode Island, forevermore as honored player number 33 of perpetual Celtic's pride in New England.

As mentioned earlier, David Letterman (born 1947) from Indianapolis, Indiana, is the ultimate boomer buddy of America who extracted jokes straight from the corny callosum of the funny bone. His late-night talk show popularized the top 10 list thematically. Letterman also oozed that humble and silly Indiana persona that is the hallmark of a would-be Hoosier. The equivalent

Quahog to make par on the humorous hillside of Letterman's score is none other than Harry Anderson born in 1952, another jokester who was able to reach amazing heights upon Mt. Giggle-Boomer. Harry Anderson from Newport, Rhode Island, was famously known as Judge Harry Stone on the TV show *Night Court* (1984-1992). But before becoming a TV mainstay he was able to combine stand-up with magic. Like Letterman, Anderson brought a wack-a-doodle humor that skated along the edge of edgy without being offensively edgy. Harry Anderson and David Letterman were the classic classroom clowns who had the special ability to hug all of the sordid segments of America under the guise of a joke. Although Harry and Dave are retired from the spotlight, be sure to know that this quirky power to dish out a joke and hug simultaneously is an elemental ability of every man, woman, and child of Rhode Island and or Indiana, of that "just messing with ya' way!"

Two serious antihero action stars are Steve McQueen and David Hedison. Steve McQueen from Beech Grove, Indiana (born 1930), was the Tom Cruise of his generation. During the rapid change of culture of the 1960s and 1970s, Steve McQueen was the king of cool. David Hedison (born 1927) is the memorable match from Providence, Rhode Island. David Hedison was launched into the front row of Hollywood in 1958 as the original star of *The Fly*. He later starred in *License to Kill* (1989).

Shelley Long from Fort Wayne, Indiana (born 1949), pairs with Joyce Jillson from Cranston, Rhode Island. Jillson starred in TV's *Peyton Place* (1964-1969) and cult movie *Superchick* (1973). Shelley Long from is the iconic midwestern girl who became famous on *Cheers* as Diane Chambers. She went on to star in a string of hit movies like *Night Shift* (1982), *The Brady Bunch Movie* (1995), and recently starred in *Modern Family* (2009-2020).

And speaking of *The Brady Bunch*, the original Carol Brady of the Bunch was Florence Henderson from Dale, Indiana, born in 1934. Her contemporary partner is Ruth Buzzi from Westerly, Rhode Island, born in 1936. Ruth Buzzi, best known for her funny roles on *Rowan & Martin's Laugh-In* (1967-1973) and all across TV with spots on *You Can't Do That on Television* (1979-2004), and *The Bearstein/Berenstain Bears* (1985-1987), as the original mama bear.

Brendan Fraser and Christopher Stanley are the Gen X fire-water team alpha. Brendan Fraser from Indianapolis (born 1968) has starred in several generational fun-time films like *Airheads* (1994), *Furry Vengeance* (2010), and *Doom Patrol* (2019-2023). Christopher Stanley from Providence, Rhode Island (born 1965), has starred in *Mad Men* (2009-2015), *Waco* (2018), and *Narcos:Mexico* (2018-2020).

Jama Williamson (born 1974) from Evansville, Indiana, matches with Mena Suvari (born 1979) from Newport, Rhode Island. Mena Suvari starred in *American Beauty* (1999), *Sugar & Spice* (2001), and *You May Not Kiss the Bride* (2010). Jama Williamson has starred in *Hollywood Heights* (2012), and *School of Rock* (2016-2018).

Two rising stars that are not yet in full effulgence are Claudia Lee (1996) and Olivia Culpo (born 1992). Claudia Lee from Lafayette, Indiana, has starred in *Hart of Dixie* (2011-2015) and *Kick-Ass 2* (2013). Olivia Culpo took her Miss Universe Crown of 2012 and pitched into Hollywood. She has starred in *I Feel Pretty* (2018) and *Reprisal* (2018).

America has cornered the market on out of the world entertainment. American science fiction has enchanted audiences across the known galaxy, and two stars to put a human touch out there, are Avery Brooks (born 1948) and Taaffe O'Connell (born 1951). Avery Brooks from Evansville, Indiana, became the first Black, lead captain on *Star Trek: Deep Space Nine* (1993-1999) as Captain Benjamin Sisko. The ideas of identity, religion, and politics were handled with care on the mature and uniquely addictive show. Taaffe O'Connell from Providence, Rhode Island, was able to ignite her star in the classical cult, old-school, campy style of sci-fi with the film *Galaxy of Terror* (1981), produced by Roger Corman. Taaffe O'Connell stars as Dameia, the ship's technical officer. *Galaxy of Terror* has some technical expertise as it can be considered James Cameron's high school movie project, since he was the production designer. These two stars are from opposite quadrants of sci-fi's galactic entertainment. The fine wine that is of a Shakespearean sci-fi stars Avery Brooks. In the opposite wing of the galaxy is the hypnotically horrific, grotesque, alien action-packed star of Taaffe O'Connell.

Two authors who cast an enchanting spell on a cosmic level with letters and words over the imagination of the nation were Kurt Vonnegut from Indianapolis, Indiana, and H. P. Lovecraft from Providence, Rhode Island. Kurt Vonnegut's *Slaughterhouse-Five* (1969) rode the wave of anti-war sentiment sweeping the nation. The story was a fictional account of the firebombing of Dresden, whence aliens intervene. But in real life, Vonnegut was a veteran of WWII who fought at the Battle of the Bulge, where he was captured by German forces. As a P.O.W. he witnessed his allies killed by friendly fire. Most importantly, Vonnegut was taken to Dresden where he bore witness to the actual firebombing himself, where 25,000 civilians were killed during Valentine's Day in 1945. It is truly a cosmic miracle that he survived, but it's best to read the book for oneself. Although science fiction, it may be loosely based on events that actually happened. Previously, Vonnegut was already in harsh headspace because upon his arrival home on leave in 1944, his mother committed suicide ("or accidentally") by overdosing on sleeping pills. Other works of Vonnegut include *The Sirens of Titan* (1959) and *Cat's Cradle* (1963).

A generation earlier another writer to write where no writer had written before was H. P. Lovecraft (born 1890) in Providence, Rhode Island. Although he was born in a wealthy family, both his parents were institutionalized by 1919. Lovecraft was able to establish himself with the original pulp fiction—fiction written on "cheapo" pulp paper that centered on weird, fantastic, and horror fiction. However, H. P. Lovecraft broke into new areas of science fiction with the creation of the Cthulhu Mythos. Basically, Lovecraft was the astro-thinker-naut who was able to conceive of varied hostile alien forms and imagine if non-terrestrials interbreed with earthlings. Such ideas were taboo fiction at the time, but a generational battalion later, this idea was made popular with the most famous fictional miscegenated hero of Star Trek lore, Spock, who is half human and half Vulcan. It was only after he left the mortal platform that Lovecraft work was rediscovered for its trailblazing artistry.

Two superstars who lit the torch and dropped anchor on the American soul, as the bond between Rhode Island and Indiana's flags indicate are James Dean (born 1931) and Otis Young (born 1932). James Dean from Marion, Indiana, is an American immortal of the big screen, who was the godfather of non-conformist rebellious youth. James Dean's most iconic role was *Rebel Without a Cause* (1955). It was the classic story that anyone who had to change schools during high school can relate too, having to deal with new social webs and compete and establish oneself as the new kid on the block. James Dean tragically died in a car crash just as his star started to soar. Nonetheless, he became an immortal icon for the spirit of the 1950s. Otis Young of Providence, Rhode Island, who was born on the 4th of July 1932, became another legendary king of cowboys. He starred in the *The Outcasts* (1968-1969), *The Clones* (1973), *The Last Detail* (1973), and *The Capture of Bigfoot* (1979).

Two boomer-Xer men who unite the flame and wave are Dean Norris (born 1963) and Mark Morettini (born 1962). Dean Norris from South Bend, Indiana, starred in *Breaking Bad* (2008-2013), *Total Recall* (1990), and *Starship Troopers* (1997). Mark Morettini from Providence, Rhode Island, starred in Fox's *Prison Break* (2005-2017) as correctional officer Rizzo Green. These guys bring the bucks and tough-guy bricks from each state.

Two boomer queens of the legacy news media are Jane Pauley and Meredith Vieira. Jane Pauley from Indianapolis, Indiana (born 1950), has a nose for news and hosted on *Dateline NBC*, *The Today Show*, and *CBS Sunday Morning*. Meredith Vieira from Providence, Rhode Island (born 1953), is another classic newsy who was able to platform on *The View* (1997-2006), *Dateline NBC*, *Rock Center with Brian Williams*, and *NBC Nightly News*.

Another contrast of fire and water but on the familial musical front are The Jackson 5 from Indiana and The Cowsills from Rhode Island. Both family bands exploded big with bubble gum pop. Jackie, Tito, Jermaine, Marlon, Michael, Randy, and Janet Jackson are all from Gary, Indiana. Just as the American cultural revolution kicked into high gear in 1969, they released a string of hits such as "I Want You Back," "ABC," and "I'll Be There." All through the 1970s they carried on with happy jingles that just tickled the feet, to make one want to dance. On the flip side is the Cowsills family from Newport, Rhode Island. Hits from the Cowsills include "The Rain," "The Park and Other Things" (1967), and "Indian Lake" (1968). Eventually mom joined the band, and this group was the inspiration that led the TV show "The Partridge Family." Although not impossible, before the end of the decade a Jackson family crossover with the Cowsills would be a miraculous moment for the halls of pop music.

Adam Lambert (born 1982) and Stevie Aiello (born 1983) are two singers from the millen-Xer sort. Adam Lambert from Indianapolis rose to fame after a run on *American Idol* in 2009 and has since been a consistent chart topper. Stevie Aiello, from Cranston, Rhode Island, rocked it real with the band Thirty Seconds to Mars.

Coincidentally, both states have two Johns who put a pulse on the heartland of rock and roll in the 1980s: John Cougar Mellencamp and John Cafferty. These rockers were launched to famous heights whose music defined the key sector of the 1980s. John Cougar Mellencamp from Seymour, Indiana (born 1951), was able to make it rock with just a dash of a southern flavor. Mellencamp's hits include "Jack and Diane," "Pink Houses," and "R.O.C.K. in the U.S.A." John Cafferty from Narragansett, Rhode Island (born 1950), broke into music in 1980 with songs like "Wild Summer Nights" and "Tender Years." But John Cafferty's massive hit came with the score to the movie *Eddie and Cruisers* (1983), which opened the door to score songs in the movie *Cobra* (1986) and *Rocky IV* (1985). John Cafferty has been MIA since, but maybe a day shall come to pass that Mellencamp and Cafferty unite for a short tour—it would be a magical nostalgia '80s rock star dream come true.

William Bruce Rose Jr. and Richard Michael Barrett are two boomer-Xers who made rock history. Will Rose, better known as Axl Rose from Lafayette, Indiana (born 1962), was the front-man for Guns N' Roses and is the king of hard rock. The proper wingman of stature to Axl is Dicky Barrett from Providence, Rhode Island (born 1964). Dicky Barret is the front man of The Mighty Bosstones and took rock in a different direction as the prince of ska punk.

Two artistic comic kings are Jim Davis and Don McGregor from the class of '45. Jim Davis from Marion, Indiana, was able to sit in the lap of America with an imaginary orange cat by the name of Garfield. Before the Internet was rife with cat videos, we had Garfield, starting in 1978. Don McGregor from Providence, Rhode Island, is another Comic Royal best known for his work with

Marvel comics. He wrote and popularized one of the first graphic novels, *Sabre: Slow Fade of an Endangered Species* in 1978. It is the story of a swashbuckler in a dystopian future. But it should be noted that the future will be dystopian no matter what. When looking into the past, the customs and rules for society are quite alien and absurd to the modern world. It's also true that modern society as of today is already a dystopian nightmare for some who grew up in the customs and rules of society of the 1950s, as it will be for those who grow up in the 2090s.

As Indiana's torch represents fire, Rhode Island's anchor represents water. Coincidentally, when the ancient alchemical symbols for fire and water are combined, they make up King Solomon's seal. An upward triangle represents fire, while a downward triangle represents water. This pattern is essentially another fundamental permutation of yin and yang. Fire is yang and water is yin. This reflects the essential dichotomy of the dominant male principle, which contrasts with the submissive female principle. Lastly, the union of these alchemical symbols, coincidentally, represents the Jewish people.

By the mysterious path of Providence, Rhode Island, is home to the oldest synagogue in the United States, the Touro Synagogue in Newport, Rhode Island. The congregation was founded during the experimental republican era of Oliver Cromwell in 1658.

As for Indiana, when you combine the anchor and torch, like a quirky *Mad Magazine* fold up, it makes up the figure of a cross: anchor on top, torch underneath. The cross is a somewhat controversial symbol within some schools of Protestant Christianity that has gone through phases of being expounded or muted—especially within the Puritan perspective. However, the cross has always been embraced as a paramount symbol of faith by the Catholic Church. Coincidentally, the most famous of American Catholic institutions that garners the nation's attention with pride or resentment every fall is Notre Dame at South Bend, Indiana, whose name is synonymous with the de facto holy trinity of modern America: God, country, and football.

But on a note of soulful synchronicity, the cross within the Catholic Church is symbolically topped with the letters INRI. The banner on the top of the holy cross is Latin shorthand for *Iesus Nazarenus, Rex Iudaeorum*. This translates as Jesus the Nazarene, king of the Jews. INRI is an abbreviated version of what was written two millennia ago in Western Asia at Golgotha/Calvary when Israel was a part of the Roman Empire.

And by the way, when the official state abbreviations of two fraternal flag twins combine, it spells out INRI. Coincidentally, one state has a capital name that perpetually honors the concept of "sacred synchronicity" better known as Providence, while the other means the "City of Indians" also known as Indianapolis.

fourteen

WYOMING & WEST VIRGINIA

Sacred Synchronicity upon
the 50th Year of Jubilee

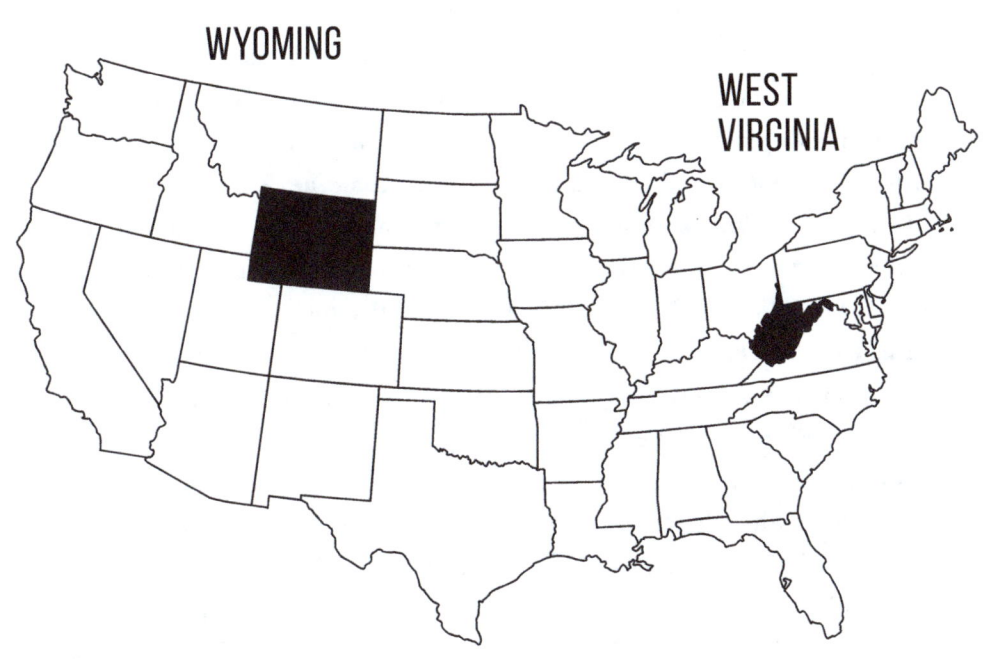

WYOMING

Wyoming and West Virginia are the pair of sister states to feature a framed flag. The red ribbons, flowers, and bow of West Virginia are the harmonious counter to the red frame of Wyoming. Likewise, the negative blue silhouette space of Wyoming matches the blue frame of West Virginia. Another essential alignment is the miner with pickaxe, who is the right-side supporter of both flags. The Wyoming miner holds his pickaxe in his left hand like a cane, while the West Virginia miner has his pickaxe slung over his left shoulder. The other supporter of Wyoming is dressed in the iconic cowboy uniform with a hat and handkerchief and is holding a rope. The cowboy represents the livestock industry on a whole that includes sheep, cattle, and hogs. But for West Virginia the man dressed in yellow is a farmer and on his right is the bounty of the earth that includes a stalk of corn and sheaf of wheat.

Another point of concord are the watershed dates of profound historical impact. West Virginia's flag has the date of June 20, 1863, carved into the central rock. Officially it represents the date of West Virginia's entry into the Union as the 35th state. That year also heralded the end of slavery. The Emancipation Proclamation was issued in the fall of 1862 and was legally effective on

WEST VIRGINIA

January 1, 1863. Slavery limped along as a protected institution in the border states until the ratification of the 13th Amendment on December 6, 1865.

The end of slavery in the United States was truly a year of golden jubilee that is providentially aligned with the end of the second war of independence, better known as the War of 1812. The year of jubilee is an idea that stems from ancient Israel concerning the 50th year of slave ownership, as is written on the Liberty Bell of Pennsylvania. As a reminder, the inscription on the Liberty Bell reads "PROCLAIM **LIBERTY** THROUGHOUT ALL THE LAND UNTO ALL THE INHABITANTS THEREOF," a quote from Levi 25:10 from the King James Bible, but it is important to note the full context of the verse. The full verse reads "And ye shall hallow the **fiftieth year**, and—PROCLAIM **LIBERTY** THROUGHOUT ALL THE LAND UNTO ALL THE INHABITANTS THEREOF—it shall be a jubilee unto you; and ye shall return every man unto his possession, and ye shall return every man unto his family."

The year of jubilee was originally celebrated ever 50 years with the release of slaves and prisoners, and debts would be forgiven with a general evocation for the mercies of the divine. The War of 1812 ended in 1815; and 50 years later, through a fateful alignment of history, all the slaves of the former British colonies were free.

Another amazing alignment occurs with a date found upon the flag of Wyoming. There are two years that can be seen on Wyoming's flag. On the cowboy side is the year 1869 and on the miner's side 1890 is written. The year 1890 refers to Wyoming's entry in the union as the 44th state on July 10, 1890. However, the year 1869 refers to women's suffrage for Wyoming. Wyoming was the first state to fully and permanently entitle women the right to vote. Through some quirky twist of history and time, it was upon the subsequent year of jubilee after 1869 that women gained the right to vote across the nation, 50 years later, as a connection from 1869 to 1919. Nearly half the states already gave women full suffrage before 1919, many gave partial, while a few gave none, and were legally forced by federal law to impart full suffrage for women with the passage of the 19th Amendment. West Virginia was a part of the jubilee bunch that enfranchised women by federal law, rather than by state law, 50 years after Wyoming.

The pillars with oil lamps on top of Wyoming's flag balance the symmetrical rhododendrons of West Virginia. The rock of West Virginia is something like a tombstone yet can be considered more like a birth stone since it has West Virginia's birth date carved into it. Regardless, the rough rock of West Virginia is in concord with the precisely crafted masonic pedestal of Wyoming, upon which a woman stands holding a banner with the official state motto on top reading "EQUAL RIGHTS." West Virginia's motto is also present, but at the bottom of the seal reading "MONTANI SEMPER LEBERI" which translates to "Mountaineers are Always Free." Also note, the rough rock being shaped into an elegant stone has top tier symbolism in Freemasonry.

The state name appears on each flag. The name of Wyoming is present on the circular seal, while West Virginia's name is on a large red ribbon in the crest. Wyoming and West Virginia are the only pair of fraternal flag states to bear arms. Two crossed rifles are clearly visible on West Virginia's along the compartment, bottom half area with a Phrygian cap resting at the center. Wyoming's gun is a bit harder to detect. Just the handle of a revolver is visible on the cowboy's right pocket area. Depending on how the seal is drawn, sometimes the cowboy's gun is impossible to notice.

Geography

Wyoming and West Virginia represent the Western Rockies united with the power of eastern Appalachia. Being so mountainous has led to a powerful connection with mining, especially with coal. No doubt, a coal miner worker exchange program could serve to benefit both states at all levels—from the grunts on the front line to the suit and tie support staff who keep the operation going.

Wyoming and West Virginia both have unique genesis stories. In a way, they are both cabooses of their respective leagues: east Mississippi versus west Mississippi states. West Virginia is the last state of the original eastern area to form, while Wyoming was the final note on the western frontier. By the election of Abraham Lincoln, the states and territories east of Mississippi had all formed with sub-federal governments who bore witness to the upcoming rebellion—except for West Virginia. In contrast, Wyoming is the only part of the United States whose territorial government formed after the Civil War ended. Thus as West Virginia is the penultimate state drenched in the sufferings and scars of the Civil War, Wyoming is at the polar opposite as an unborn entity "in utero" as a completely detached observer of the Civil War. This makes Wyoming a virgin to the experience of the Civil War. In a way, Wyoming is a proverbial "Far West Virginia."

Wyoming is the only state with both Canadian and Mexican heritage. Reason being, the southwestern corner was a part of Mexico from 1821 until 1848, while the northwestern corner of Wyoming was a part of the British Columbia claim during the joint occupation period from 1818 until 1846, while West Virginia is the only state born out of the Confederacy.

Of American heritage, Wyoming and West Virginia have a unique outlook. Wyoming is the undisputed winner of attending the most "territorial universities" than any other state, while West Virginia has a concordant history with Virginia since 1607. Wyoming received a panoramic education because several states were able to give Wyoming their two cents on matters of how to be American, starting with the Louisiana Purchase. Thus, for American schooling, Wyoming was taught by New Orleans in Louisiana, St. Louis in Missouri, Omaha in Nebraska, Yankton in South Dakota, Bismarck in North Dakota, Boise in

Idaho, Olympia in Washington DC, Oregon City in Oregon, Austin in Texas, Monterrey in California, and Salt Lake City in Utah.

For West Virginia, her history was synonymous with Virginia. Thus, West Virginia was ruled by Jamestown, Williamsburg, and Richmond. However, in 1861 Wheeling ruled as the restored government of Virginia until 1863. Thus, from May 13, 1861, until June 20, 1863, there were two competing capitals of Virginia. Legally speaking the restored governor of Virginia, Francis Harrison Pierpont of Morgantown, West Virginia, ruled as the federally recognized governor of Virginia from 1863 until 1868.

Over the course of U.S. history several dozen proposed states have come and gone, but only a select few were able to garner serious consideration and leave a mark. Wyoming's close but no cigar state was the nevermore 34th state of Jefferson, while a primordial West Virginia almost broke out as the 14th state of Westsylvania.

One of Wyoming's most famous natural phenomena is Old Faithful, a world-famous geyser with amazing consistency. Old Faithful puts on at least 12 shows per day. It takes her from 44 to 120 minutes to recharge her waterspouts. Old Faithful used to erupt every 61 minutes, until a few earthquakes broke her mojo in 1959, just as the make of America expanded beyond the contiguous, united core of 48 states, to include Alaska and Hawaii. Wyoming is also home to the largest geyser in the world, Steamboat Geyser. This geyser is not as predictable, yet when she goes, it's the tallest in the world with a waterspout that can reach up to 300 feet and last for a weeks. Old Faithful only reaches up to 185 feet, and shows can last anywhere from 90 seconds to five minutes.

West Virginia is also home to a famous hot spring, Berkeley Springs. Unlike the visually stunning geysers of Wyoming, the hot springs of West Virginia allow for an intimate and immersive experience with the naturally heated waters of America. The warm water mineral springs in Morgan County, West Virginia, have been known to Native Americans for perhaps several hundred centuries. Waters spring forth from the ground constantly at 74.3 degrees Fahrenheit. Today it is a public park that anyone can visit. One of the open baths or rather mini tubs were touched by fame when George Washington visited, and it retains its name as "George Washington's Bath Tub 1748." For the record, Berkeley Springs is the first spa of the nation in which warm water is fed at a rate of 1,000 gallons per minute.

Coincidentally, the Western Continental Divide crosses through Wyoming, while the Eastern Continental Divide crosses through West Virginia. The Western Continental Divide for Wyoming marks where water either falls in the Pacific Ocean or Gulf of Mexico, while the Eastern Continental Divide of West Virginia marks where water either falls in the Atlantic Ocean or Gulf of Mexico. For historical purposes the Eastern Continental Divide was the initial dividing point for the 1763 proclamation, which set a western limit on colonies just before the American Revolution. Likewise, the Western Continental Divide marked the western limit of the Louisiana Purchase in 1803. The bottom line in the tub and sink is that Wyoming and West Virginia are at the western and eastern fringes of the Mississippi Watershed.

Bear Scratch Mountain and the Seneca Rocks are natural wonders on the bucket list for each state. Bear Scratch Mountain is famously known as Devils Tower, made famous by the movie *Close Encounters of the Third Kind* (1977).

An enchanting story of its own is associated with the Seneca Rocks—the betrothal of the Princess Snow Bird. As this story goes, long ago Chief Bald Eagle and consort White Rock gave birth to the most beautiful maiden among the Senecas, Snow Bird. Upon the day when she was to choose a husband, suitors across the kingdom came to court her. Eventually seven suitors were selected as finalists, and they were to face off in an endurance rock climbing contest to see who could match Snow Bird's strength and stamina.

Snow Bird waited at the summit of the Seneca Rocks, which looks like something like a skinny craggy wall piercing the sky. Not going to spoil it here, but there is a link with the online footnotes to the original story. You can get there by following the footnotes QR code at the end of this book.

The above story was based on the story written by Harry Malcom Wade in 1932. However, the Seneca's homelands are in upstate New York. But during the Iroquois Beaver Empire of the 1600s, the Iroquois may have expanded into this area. Wade's story may have some basis upon stories handed down by Native American tradition. As this story was first written in 1932 long after the Natives were expelled from the region, who really knows? Regardless, the Seneca Rocks are a majestic set of towering rocks that make up a craggy wall that pierces the forest canopy of West Virginia. It is located in the lower arm of West Virginia in Pendleton County. It looks out of place and is a typical rock formation fit for Wyoming. The wall of rocks reaches over 900 feet straight up from their base stream level and the public is allowed to climb and reach the summit at their own risk. Nonetheless, the summit is a dangerously romantic place to propose a marriage.

The Wyoming rock formation to match the Seneca Rocks is Bear Scratch Mountain, aka Devils Tower. The summit of this surreal rock formation reaches nearly a mile above sea level at 5,112 feet, shy by 168 feet from being a mile (5,280 feet). From its base, its prominence runs 867 feet for this organic skyscraper, which is equivalent to the Transamerica Pyramid of San Francisco or Trump World Tower in NYC, plus or minus a few feet.

Unlike the story of Snow Bird's betrothal, Devils Tower has several distinct Native American stories connected to its genesis. The Arapaho tells of seven children who found a magical bison bone that turned a girl into a bear-girl. The bear-girl eventually climbed a rock that she made big scratches upon, and this became the Bear Scratch Tower. The Cheyenne tells of a giant bear jumping from a magical rock and leaving scratches upon it. The Crow version tells of two little girls who were being chased by bears and escaped by climbing a rock. Then the Great Spirit raised it higher and higher so the bear would not get them. The bear ended up leaving scratches on the rock, while the girls remain to this day on the summit. The Kiowa have a similar story, but it involves seven girls. But the seven girls got stuck in the sky when the rock grew to its current height and girls were smooshed into the firmament and became the Pleiades.

Two nationally famous parks are Yellowstone National Park and Harpers Ferry. Yellowstone was the first of its kind in the U.S. and even signed into law before Wyoming became a state. Yellowstone was established on March 1, 1872; Wyoming became a state 18 years later, on July 10, 1890. Harpers Ferry National Historical Park, which was founded on West Virginia's centennial in

1963. Also note the national parks of Yellowstone and Harpers Ferry cross into several states. The vast majority of Yellowstone lies within Wyoming, but the park slices into Idaho and Montana. Likewise, Harpers Ferry is mainly seated in West Virginia, but a wee portion of Maryland and Virginia compose the park.

History

The historical events at Harpers Ferry were the harbinger of the upcoming Civil War. This American "October Revolution" took place in 1859 from October 16th to 18th and is better known as John Brown's raid. It was the final and most famous slave revolt before the Civil War. The friction created by the unjust economic system based upon the federally protected policy of human-on-human ownership would literally rip Virginia apart, with repercussions that continue today. Although Virginia officially joined the Confederacy, there was an element within Virginia that knew this course was folly. The more civilized half of Virginia broke away from the Confederacy and reconstituted herself as the 35th state of West Virginia.

John Brown, by a certain synchronicity of circumstance and his first name, became the John the Baptist figure for the final destruction of the satanic-like economic system of human bondage. If there ever was a version of Hell on Earth, the system of slavery that evolved in the United States was arguably the best example. Slaves were hounded by demonic overseers from cradle to grave and subject to whippings and other forms of cruel and unusual punishment that included rape. But the coming of John the Brown preceded the ultimate messianic figure and final martyr to put an end to slavery, Abraham Lincoln. Abraham Lincoln's name is also aligned with another figurehead: the Patriarch of Abraham. The Patriarch Abraham is regarded by many across the world as the ultimate "source code" prophet to initiate and accept the terms and conditions of divine protection and guidance in perpetual contract, a covenant, with the Architect of the Universe. Note it is thought that the Patriarch Abraham was born in what is now considered modern Iraq and lived several centuries before the paramount figure of the original testament, Moses.

The biblical Patriarch of Abraham is a recognized prophet by the three primary religions to arise out of Western Asia: Islam, Christianity, and Judaism. Ergo the term Abrahamic refers to all three paths. Consequently, there is a worldwide recognition and an invisible power bestowed upon the name of Abraham, which is a common name for men in all three branches. In order to illustrate this phenomenon, the names of the ruthless tyrants to arise during the 20th century from Austria and Georgia are perpetually cursed with a negative connotation. Such is the kingdom of names whose governance and existence are ethereal yet very real.

The powerful and lauded lens of history is destined to perpetually focus upon John the Brown at Harpers Ferry, West Virginia, and as well with the great American patriarch, Abraham of LaRue County. Similarly, Christians attest that John the Baptist baptized Jesus in the Jordan River, heralding his powerful role in human affairs. John the Baptist also became a martyr and was executed by King Herod for criticizing his marriage to his niece. Nearly two millennia after these events took place, Baptist churches became a powerful and ever-present force in America—North and South as well as Black and White. On a side note, there is a small congregation from the Middle East who regard John the Baptist as the final and ultimate prophet, excluding any later teachings. Thus, from a certain point of view, the Mandaean Baptist congregation of Western Asia built a temple/church positioned in between Judaism and Christianity.

Regardless of one's faith or lack of it, the series of events that follow the story of John the Baptist at the River Jordan had quite a profound effect upon world history and was the beginning of a story that would enrapture the attention of every king and queen affected by its wake and eventually reshape Rome and Western civilization. Likewise, the story of John the Brown at the Shenandoah River is a concordant American story that would reshape the course of civilization for the American hemisphere.

It is a matter of synchronicity that the federal forces ordered by Yankee-born President Buchanan from Pennsylvania to put down the slave revolt at Harpers Ferry were led by Robert E. Lee. Another soon-to-be famous cavalry officer from the South who participated in this hallmark event in U.S. history was

J.E.B Stuart, who was sent to offer the insurrectionists the option of peacefully surrendering. Stuart was the penultimate cavalry officer who was basically the Buck Rogers of the South. But when the freedom fighters rejected "Confederate Buck Rogers" offer, J.E.B. Stuart signaled with his hat for federal forces under the command of a U.S. Colonel, Robert E. Lee, to crush the rebels. In the ensuing violence one U.S. Marine was killed and a handful were wounded, while nearly a dozen freedom fighters were martyred. Seven insurgent, abolitionist rebs were captured alive only to be executed by the Buchanan government. One died in jail awaiting execution, yet five were able to escape. John the Brown was injured in the melee, being struck by a sword but only later to be publicly executed on December 2, 1859. Consequently, John Brown became the primary martyr or patron saint for the abolition of slavery for the duration of the Civil War. Abolitionist Julia Ward Howe later wrote lyrics of John Brown's body in 1861 to the tune of "Battle Hymn of the Republic."

No other state can hold a candle to West Virginia's connection and intimate link to the War Between the States. Rather it was more like a War Between the Counties for the Virginias. Initially, the Loyalist counties that broke away from Confederate Virginia did so with the intention of becoming the restored government, hoping to reunite with all of Virginia after the Confederacy was defeated. However, as the situation evolved and bodies piled up, such a reunion with "East Virginia" became untenable. The political dividing line between the Virginias is a permanent scar and token reminder of America's greatest war of wars.

If West Virginia had a front seat view of the Civil War, then Wyoming was not even in the parking lot. Wyoming missed all the action and entered into U.S. history after the entire Civil War cast and audience had left the theater. Reason being, Wyoming did not exist as a state or a territory. Wyoming was "in utero" as a part of Dakota Territory for the duration of the war. Three years after the war had ended, in 1868, Wyoming Territory was finally created. This gives Wyoming a unique charge from a neutral-outsider point of view. Wyoming is like a young whippersnapper born after a major historical event has passed and has to believe what her elders say about a profound generational event like Pearl Harbor, JFK's assassination, landing on the Moon, 9/11, or Covid-19. Arizona,

THE FLAG REVELATION

New Mexico, Colorado, Utah, Idaho, Washington BC, and the Dakota Twins were all territories as "underage states" who all had living governments to bear witness to the genesis of West Virginia. Further, Arizona, New Mexico, and Oklahoma/Indian Territory were active participants in the clash of sisters between the South and North.

Although Wyoming may be the youngest, she was a quick learner. She graduated to statehood quite early for her territorial age. Wyoming leap frogged over older territories like Arizona, Utah, and New Mexico. Note that Wyoming Territory was a competitively driven classmate with Idaho Territory. However, Idaho crossed the "statehood finish line" one week ahead of Wyoming on July 3, 1890. Even though Idaho had a five-year head start, Wyoming nearly made up the distance, losing out by one week whence she became a state on July 10, 1890. It seems that Idaho could not bear the thought of the sassy whippersnapper Wyoming cutting ahead. It would have been like having a gifted, smarty pants 13-year-old "Sheldon Cooper" uppity bratty little sister graduate high school with the "on track" older sister of 18. But in this case, big sis Idaho was able to maintain her lead over her talented little sister, Wyoming.

Also, if West Virginia were a Transformer, she'd be Skyfire. Skyfire, also called Jetfire, was originally a Decepticon. Decepticons are the militant, badass Transformers who lust after energy no matter the consequence. Their emblem features a purple catlike insignia, and they usually hide their identity of sentient robots as aircraft. Their rival brethren are the Autobots, who usually transform into road vehicles. The emblem of Autobots is red and is more dog-like. Because Skyfire couldn't jibe with the cruel and brutal policies of the Decepticons, he became a turncoat and joined the Autobots. Ergo West Virginia is Skyfire. To balance this association, Wyoming's match is Grimlock. Grimlock is the extraordinarily brawny Transformer who changes into a Tyrannosaurus Rex. For the record, South Carolina is the perfect match for Megatron, the leader of the Decepticons.

As West Virginia is tattooed with the end of slavery, Wyoming is hot iron branded with the issue of equal rights for women. For much of human history, strict gender expectations locked society into a rigid framework, from the technologically primitive illiterate societies to complex communities grounded with a massive bureaucracy of literate bean counting middlemen charged with regulating the lives of the national tribe. The ancient law of the jungle provides an environment for complex life to evolve and adapt. The overwhelming *modus operandi* of Mother Nature's decrees seems to nurture a division of labor and behavior between the sexes as seen within the insect and animal kingdoms.

However, the original '60s was an intense time of change. The magnitude of change during the '60s of the 20th century cannot hold a candle to the change of the '60s of the 19th century. The 1960s has a better marketing team and videos to push its narrative of profound change forward. But in 1869, an understanding that a common element in humanity exists in every person regardless of race and gender took hold in Wyoming. The daring and novel concept of allowing women to partake in the governance and vote was a revolutionary step. It was one small step for women, yet one wonderful leap for all of womankind. The territorial governor of Wyoming, John A. Campbell, signed the bill that enfranchised women on December 10, in 1869.

The first rose to bud from this revolutionary legislation for gender equity was the story of Esther Hobart Morris (1812-1902) from Spencer, New York. She providentially became the first female justice of the peace in the United States on Valentine's Day 1870 in South Pass City, Wyoming. Also of note, South Pass is at a geographic nexus between the Atlantic and Pacific, allowing her to claim the first woman in all of the Established East and Wild West to become a government official. Esther Morris's term lasted a perfect pregnancy of nearly nine months.

Esther Morris moved to Wyoming when it was still a part of Dakota Territory, just months before it became a territory in 1868. This put Esther at ground zero for the genesis of Wyoming. Esther Morris was able to become justice of the peace due to the efforts of an activist judge, John W. Kingman, who appointed her. As it is today, once the news went online by telegraph, the world was either shocked, tickled, or inspired. The old-school tweet read: "Wyoming, the youngest and one of the richest Territories in the United States, gave rights to women in actions as well as words."

No doubt Esther Morris held the law over many a man and woman in the frontier that included surly and sassy miners, gamblers, prostitutes, and other delightful scoundrels. Morris was the first of American women to take the reins and show the world that women were indeed qualified to lead, judge, and dish the law to would-be evildoers. Although not as famous as Amelia Earhart, Queen Elizabeth I, Maya Angelou, or Joan of Arc, Esther Morris is officially the first of female American leaders, and one whose universal ubiquitous bouquet of fame is long overdue.

Like John the Brown, Esther's book of life ended before her oppressed sisters gained the right to vote across the nation. Nonetheless, Esther became the first of the first patron saints for women's suffrage. To balance out John Brown's parallel to John the Baptist, the Book of Esther is a fine match. According to the Book of Esther, the original Esther was an orphaned Jewish girl whom the Persian King Ahasuerus fell in love with due to her stunning beauty, akin to Gal Gadot—DC's Wonder Woman as of 2017. Basically, when King Ahasuerus ordered Queen Vashti to show off her beauty at the court, she refused, so he divorced her and looked for a new queen. When his eyes fell upon a gal, who may have looked like Gal Gadot, with the name of Esther, he was smitten. However, King Ahasuerus did not know his new wife was Jewish until long after his betrothal.

Later, when Queen Esther was the Queen of Persia, her cousin Mordecai overheard two gender-neutral eunuchs plan to assassinate her new husband, the king. With the plot foiled by her cousin, Mordecai, or Morty in today's modern English, was honored and earned the right to become of service at the court as an advisor to Queen Esther—like a scene taken out of *Game of Thrones*. But, one day the chief secretary to the Persian king, Haman the jealous Agagite, ordered everyone to bow down to him; Morty refused on the account of his faith. Consequently, an enraged and indignant Haman bribed the king to issue an order to exterminate all the people of Morty's faith from the kingdom.

Long story short, the king is reminded that Morty saved his life by foiling the assassination plot and learns that his fairest queen is actually Jewish. Upon this revelation, the king is distraught since he cannot rescind a royal order, but with the advice of Esther and Morty, they issue another order that allows the Jewish people to strike out against anyone who poses a risk. What follows is basically a violent scene as if taken from the animated *The Rick & Morty Show* (since 2013).

Bottom line, the name Esther at its essential genesis is a heroic love story between an Israelite queen and Iranian king. Likewise, the twisted synchronicity is the story of an American Esther who was destined to lead the way on an auspicious day, Valentine's Day 1870. As for the Jewish community in general, the spirit of Esther is hallowed with the celebration of Purim, which is akin to a Hebrew Halloween, but not quite. Usually during March, if celebrated, costumes and masks are worn because the story of Esther is associated with the mysterious nature of Divine Will, as if the Grand and Divine Architect of the Cosmos is able to wear the masks or is the ultimate puppet master of the friend and foe alike, such that good things happen in the end, which mere mortals cannot possibly comprehend. Sadly, today Israel and Iran are at odds like Hatfields and McCoys.

And speaking of feuding families, two historical feuds tied to Wyoming and West Virginia have since become a part of American folklore. In Wyoming there was the Johnson County War that inflamed their region from 1889 to 1893, while in West Virginia there was the aforementioned feud of the Hatfield and McCoy families that erupted from 1878 to 1891.

The Hatfield's were mostly from West Virginia, while the McCoy's were from Kentucky. The bad blood began to flow during the Civil War when Asa McCoy was killed. There are conflicting reports concerning how exactly he died, but whatever the case the Hatfield family was held responsible. After the Civil War, the conflict began in earnest over a pig in 1878. A dispute arose over the ownership of a pig that went to courts in favor of the Hatfields, whilst the judge was a member of the Hatfield family. No surprise there. The witness who supported Hatfield's claim, Bill Stanton, was later killed by Sam and Paris McCoy and avoided punishment since it was done in self-defense. Later in 1882 Ellison Hatfield was killed during a drunken fight by three McCoy brothers. In retaliation, the Hatfield's formed a posse and killed the three McCoy brothers in vigilante justice. Soon afterward Lark McCoy was killed; the assumed killers were the Hatfield posse. As the two sides aimed to get the upper foot, tensions reached a climax with the 1888 New Year's Night Massacre, when a posse of Hatfields surrounded a sleeping McCoy cabin and fired away. Two children were killed trying to escape and Sarah McCoy was nearly beaten to death. This event led to the final clash at Battle of Grapevine Creek in West Virginia on January 19, 1888. The two families formed militant bands and clashed. Eight Hatfields were captured and put on trial in Kentucky. Seven were sentenced to life imprisonment and one, Ellison Mounts, was hanged.

The feud attracted national attention and had all sorts of sordid details as a real American *Romeo and Juliet* story. However, the feuding along the Tug River in West Virginia was the real McCoy. In 1881, Roseanna McCoy was to marry John Hatfield, but was later jilted when John married Nancy McCoy. Eventually the fighting and tension eased in the early 20th century. Since then, their last names are now a metonym for bitterly feuding rivals; instead of fighting like cats and dogs, one can say they *fight like Hatfields and McCoys*. In the modern era, their descendants appeared on the *Family Feud* for a week in 1979. They hammed it up, as a pig was kept on stage, and guns were playfully toted on the set. The McCoys ended up winning more cash. The Hatfields won $8,459 while the McCoy's won $11,272. However, the officials decided to even the winnings so that both families received $11,272. In 2003, an official truce was declared and signed by more than 60 descendants of the two families. And Governor Bob Wise of West Virginia signed a proclamation that June 14 would be known as Hatfield and McCoy Reconciliation Day.

As for Wyoming, the Johnson County War is an equivalent match of misery, which like the Hatfield and McCoy feud would become a wellspring of drama for storytellers and modern movie day magic. The Johnson County War reached a climax at nearly the same time from 1889 to 1893, but instead of feuding families, this war of White-on-White violence pitted powerful business interests versus small family homesteaders. But the root of the fight was over a cow rather than the pig. The situation evolved such that large ranching outfits formed a cattle cartel as the Wyoming Stock Growers Association (WSGA), that comprised Wyoming's wealthiest elite. All during this time, cattle rustling was the spark that was used to justify killing off the competition, literally, and anyone else who got in the way. The powerful cattle interests were able to put the law in their back pocket, and it's assumed they hired hitmen called Regulators from Texas to clear out the local small-time homesteader resistance.

One of the main causes of the problem was the policy of maverick cattle claiming. As the Whites replaced the Indians, cattle replaced the bison. On the wild frontier, cattle were allowed to free range all across Wyoming. Ownership was maintained by branding of the beasts. The problem arises with new calves born on the open range. Those not attached to a mother were known as mavericks and were fair game for anyone to claim as their own. This was the nominal policy for a while. Consequently, this allowed people who owned no cattle to get a fresh start. As hired cowboys learned of this process, they figured out they could keep the mavericks for themselves or sell them off at great profit.

By the mid-1880s, the cattle barons changed the law such that mavericks were to be rounded up and auctioned off to the highest bidder at the pleasure of the WSGA. However, something like a $3,000 fee/bond was required to get a seat for bidding, which in today's value is something like $80,000. This kept out small-time folks and assured that only the cattle barons were the bidders. If a small-time homesteader were able to put up the entry fee, the cattle barons would collude to squash the small potato.

Ella Watson was one of many, but she was infamously the first woman to perish from this big business gestapo justice when she and her husband were lynched on a tree. They hanged her on trumped-up charges of being a cattle rustler and alleged prostitute. It is also more likely that all her male visitors came by for her sewing shop side hustle.

The most heroic underdog to stand up against the big ranchers was Nate Champion. He was one of the outspoken leaders of the small family homesteaders to stand up to the cattle elites. Doing so put him in the crosshairs of these special interests, and he was soon facing charges of cattle rustling.

The gunfight at the KC Ranch was the real deal, Wild West show of deadly consequences. The hired guns tracked down Nate and ambushed him at the KC Ranch. There were also three trappers on the ranch. Two got away while getting water but Nick Ray was killed in the hallway. Nate Champion was able to barricade himself in the cabin and hold out for several hours, making journal entries all the while under attack. Champion was able to permanently retire four of the hired guns, but once the regulators set the cabin on fire, Nate Champion was forced to run out the back door with guns blazing. It had a tragic end and cinematic death, as his body was riddled with bullets. The invaders pinned a note on the chest that read "Cattle Thieves Beware" and ripped out pages of his journal, assuming to cover his testimony to hide the damning information.

However, two friends of Nate Champion were able to witness the event from a distance and alert the sheriff of Buffalo, Wyoming. An appropriately named Sheriff Angus raised a posse of 200 men to track and take down the invaders taking up space. However, the invaders got word that a homesteader posse was now after them, and they barricaded themselves at the TA ranch. This is where the homesteader posse laid a siege that lasted three days in April 1892. About 60 WSGA regulators were fighting off a posse of 200 angry homesteaders. Ironically the hired guns had previously cut (or planned to cut) the telegraph wires so they could murder all the named persons on the hit list. But even without the wire, words travel, and the siege ended when the U.S. military got wind of the situation.

Upon their arrival of the 6th Cavalry from Fort McKinney, the posse was forced to yield, and the fighting parties were taken into custody. After an initial investigation it was found that hired guns were to be paid $5 a day and $50 for each person killed on a list that had over 70 names. In today's numbers, this is like $170 per day and $1,700 per murder of each accused cattle rustler. There was enough incriminating evidence to take down quite a few cattle barons and public officials. However, due to the whims of frontier justice and power of the cattle barons, they were able to tip the balance of justice in their favor. The hired guns from Texas were able to drift away into the sunset, while the charges against the WSGA were dropped. The prosecution team ran out of money and bankrupted the county; thus, justice was not served due to a lack of insufficient funds. Things finally settled down after 1893. In the end, somewhere between 25 to 38 people were killed during the Johnson County War.

The bad blood between powerful barons and homesteaders would take time to heal, and it was by marriages and that forbidden Romeo and Juliet love that helped smooth out ruffled feathers. But it demonstrates back then, as it is now, money can have a powerful influence on the path of justice.

Wyoming and West Virginia are further united via the Algonquin family tree. By far the family tree with the most branches of Native Americans bands belong to the Algonquin. Their historical tribal lands reach the furthest across the states and provinces of North America, crossing into Canada and the U.S. At the beginning of the American Dream, this family welcomed and provided critical care for the genesis of Virginia and Massachusetts. Fatefully Wyoming and West Virginia were the original homes and hearth to this largest family of nations. In West Virginia, the Shawnee and Cono were the nations to live here upon first contact. In Wyoming, the Cheyenne and Arapaho were established upon the arrival of the Western wagon trains.

Two men who seal a bond between Wyoming and West Virginia are Thomas Jonathan "Stonewall" Jackson and Edward Lee "Rescue" Baker Jr. Their lives had no chance of intertwining because they lived in two different versions of America, separated by the year 1864. Stonewall Jackson (1824-1863) was a military officer who was the proverbial "punisher" of the Confederacy born in West Virginia, while Edward Lee Baker Jr. (1865-1913) was the first proverbial Black Captain America to arise from the Spanish-American War born in Wyoming. Stonewall Jackson lived during the American Era whence owning the children and wife of another man was the law of the land. He died at the deepest of inflection points of American history when this satanic policy was outlawed with the passage of the 13th Amendment in 1865. On the other hand, Edward L. Baker was born in a brave new world less than a fortnight after the 13th Amendment became legal in totality, effective across the nation. On December 18, 1865, Secretary of State Seward certified the 13th Amendment as valid to all "intentions and purposes" as a part of the U.S. Constitution after the required 27th state, Georgia, ratified it. Ten days later, Edward Lee Baker Jr. was born.

Stonewall Jackson was born on January 21, 1824, in a section of Virginia that is now part of West Virginia. Jackson was the right arm of Robert E. Lee who delivered punishing defeats to Union forces. He was basically an invincible opponent who appeared at the right moment and right time, like a heaven-sent angel. Indeed, Stonewall Jackson was a deeply religious man and faithfully observed the Sabbath through the war. He was a true-blue Bible thumper with Presbyterian views, and he followed the religious laws set by Moses to the letter of the law, with one obvious exception. He was a mystics warrior for the South and a miracle playmaker in nearly every battle he participated in and made it a point to thwart the Union's advance at every turn.

But there is a strange synchronicity of his passing, which was timed with the birth of Loyalist Virginia. West Virginia's birth was messy, to say the least. The secession of West Virginia was like the formation of a moon of a moon of a moon, the U.S. being the first moon-rebellion, the Confederacy being the second moon-rebellion, and West Virginia being the final moon-rebellion. Note too that not all of West Virginia wanted to leave the Confederacy. However, several ducks had to be lined up before complete separation. A new constitution was needed, and one was written in 1862. Then the people had to approve the move. Although West Virginia was signed in on April 20, 1863, by Lincoln, her official entry was delayed to legally take effect two moons later on June 20, 1863. Thus, the western regions of Virginia were given a unique two-month transition period.

It was during this two-month period that the northwestern counties of Virginia entered into a proverbial cocoon stage. Coincidentally, during this political metamorphosis, two profound watershed events for the South took place: the flag of the Confederacy underwent a radical change and Stonewall Jackson was recalled to heaven.

From 1861 until 1862, the war was officially sold to the public as a political contest between the right of the states to secede vs. the power of the federal government to deny this right. But when the Emancipation Proclamation went into effect in 1863, slavery became the primary uncloseted theme of the war. Likewise, the second version of the Confederate flag, it took on the modern-day look and notions of a truly divisive rebel flag. And more importantly, it became a symbol for the preservation of slavery, more so, than states' rights.

As flags and political aims of the Civil War changed, the northwestern half of Virginia was rearranging herself into a new state. Coincidentally, the unstoppable Confederate tour de force who just happened to be born in that region of Virginia that was fated to become the 35th state, was eliminated from the game. The emergence of West Virginia in some kind of wicked butterfly effect was in sync with the death of Stonewall Jackson. Rather than a butterfly flap causing the death of Stonewall Jackson, it could have been the flapping of a new Confederate flag that caused the wind to change and, just maybe, affect the path of a bullet. As Stonewall Jackson's hometown deserted the Confederacy, he too was drafted by mysterious forces to end his commission in the Confederate army during West Virginia's primordial transition phase. Stonewall Jackson was accidentally shot in his left arm by his own men on May 2, 1863. Due to complications, he died on May 10, 1863. A month and ten days later, the amputated northwestern arm of Virginia emerged from its cocoon, spreading her wings for freedom as the ultimate battle-born state, West Virginia, born on June 20, 1863.

As Thomas J. Jackson completed his divinely guided work on Earth, Edward L. Baker Jr. was just getting started. Edward Lee Baker, like Stonewall Jackson, was one of the lucky few born on the shifting sands of history. E. Lee Baker Jr. was born in Dakota Territory, but three years later, the name of his birthplace changed to Wyoming Territory. Unlike Stonewall Jackson, Captain E. Lee Baker would live to see his hometown transition into a new state in 1890. Captain Baker entered into the honor roles of American history during the Spanish-American War of 1898. While under enemy fire, Captain Baker rescued a wounded soldier from drowning at Santiago, Cuba. Likewise, the Spanish-American War is regarded as the point of healing when the states from the North and South were united again against a common foe. Although not as recognized as Stonewall Jackson, Captain Lee of Wyoming, of the first name Ed and last name Baker, has a legacy that carries on. He is the maternal grandfather of Dexter Gordon (1923-1990), a famous jazz saxophonist who jammed with the likes of Charlie Parker and Dizzy Gillespie.

The primary point of concordance between Wyoming and West Virginia is mining. Mining has long been practiced in both states—from the early days with a pickaxe and candle to the modern day with sophisticated million-dollar space age machinery. They are familiar with the whole range of mining for precious metals, liquid oil, and natural gas. It was during the Carboniferous Period that this abundant resource was created long, long, long ago when the Earth was in a different place of the galaxy far, far, far away. Coal is basically ancient sunlight captured by plants that lived more than 350 million years ago. By some peculiar earthly and cosmic alignment, Wyoming and West Virginia were destined to be Coal Country. Before nuclear, solar, and oil, there was coal. Coal was technology's first love and provided the first thrust that jump started the industrial revolution. The love continues, on a smaller magnitude, but it continues.

Wyoming and West Virginia are often stuck next to each other in books since they both start with the letter W. Coincidentally, the Chinese character for the word mountain looks like the letter W. And if you haven't yet noticed, the letter W itself looks like a mountain. Also, when their state abbreviations are considered, we get something that looks like a mountain range: WV-WY.

Miners may seem like a dying breed but hold your horses. When the space age truly kicks in, no doubt corporations will lust after the men and women of Wyoming and West Virginia. The economic engine of the space age without a doubt will be grounded to the mineral wealth from the moon and other heavenly bodies. Perhaps in 2255, many of our great, great, great grandchildren on the moon will trace their family heritage to Wyoming and West Virginia? These states have a handle and intuitive knowledge with the best means and practices of extracting the mineral wealth from the upper layers of a planetary body. If they ever open the gates in Antarctica, Wyoming and West Virginia could also certainly lead the way to a self-sustaining economy.

Wyoming and West Virginia are a match of the king of cowboys with the queen of the mountains. Wyoming branded herself as the cowboy state, and indeed this is true. Wyoming even has the historical cojones to back up this claim. Since Wyoming was a part of Mexico, she retains the source code of the cowboy spirit that began out of Spanish Mexican tradition. Also, Wyoming was a part of the Republic of Texas, thus she inherited the strength and proud

Texan showboat sparkle. Wyoming also retains as an element of U.K.-Canada heritage, since she was a part of British Columbia. Thus, she has a bit of that refined equestrian elegance. Finally, Wyoming has a concentrated cache of the all-American Yankee hustler, Han Solo mojo. Consequently, no other state can keep up with her wild rodeo show. Wyoming is the perfect all-American cowboy state who can handle the range in all four seasons: winter, summer, fall, and spring, on the plains and mountain high, wet or dry, oh my, oh my, yes indeed Wyoming cowboys do fly high.

On the other hand, West Virginia represents the welcome home party of America. She flirted with the rebellion but turned her back on such forlorn ways and took those first hard and humiliating steps to get back home. Should you lose your path in America, West Virginia can show you the way. Fractured hearts can find healing in her mountains, as she is no stranger to broken hearts. Her unique genesis has given her a special sadness—a sweet sadness that can mend a heart with patience and time. She is America's original mountain mama, patiently waiting with arms wide open, and has just set the supper table. It's no accident that the song "Take Me Home, Country Roads" (1971) by John Denver best captures this feeling. Likewise, "Rocky Mountain High" (1972) applies to Wyoming, since most of the state is in the Rocky Mountains.

Culture

On the cultural welcome crew are Mickey Daniels of Rock Springs, Wyoming, and Don Knotts of Morgantown, West Virginia. These men were born at the golden age of cinema and present a friendly smile you'll easily find in either Wyoming or West Virginia. Mickey Daniels (1914-1970) made America laugh as a part of *Our Gang* and *Little Rascals* (1922 to 1944) movies that started in the silent era. Mickey Daniels was the red-haired, freckled Norman Rockwell kid with a big smile. As Mickey Daniels's star dimmed down, Don Knotts lit up the sky and was able to shine across two centuries. Don Knotts was one of those ubiquitous actors that crossed into all media from cartoons to high-profile Hollywood hits. His resume includes *The Incredible Mr. Limpet* (1964), *Herbie*

Goes to Monte Carlo (1977), *The Andy Griffith Show* (1960-1968), *Scooby-Doo* (1969-1978), *Matlock* (1986-1995), and *That '70s Show* (1998-2006).

Jim Siedow (1920-2003) and Paul Dooley (1928) are another pair of American buckaroos. Jim Siedow of Cheyenne, Wyoming is best known for his role in *The Texas Chainsaw Massacre* (1974) as the Old Man, while Paul Dooley of Parkersburg, West Virginia, is best known as the dad in *Sixteen Candles* (1984).

Two boomer-Xers who were able to carry that mountaineer hunkiness to Hollywood are Darren Dalton and John Corbett. Darren Dalton (born 1965) from Powell, Wyoming, came to fame as one of the Socials in *The Outsiders* (1983) and may be best known as Daryl in *Red Dawn* (1984). John Corbett was born in 1961 in Wheeling, West Virginia, and rose to fame as Chris Stevens in *Northern Exposure* (1990-1995) and *My Big Fat Greek Wedding* (2002). As a special note to better understand synchronicity and serendipity, the movie *Serendipity* (2001), which stars John Corbett does a fine job.

Cecilia Hart and Joyce DeWitt are the two women on the welcome wagon of America. Cecilia Hart (born 1948) from Cheyenne, Wyoming, starred her finest on the police drama *Paris* 1978 to 1980 where cupid struck an arrow between her and James Earl Jones. Thus, she is also known as the wife of Darth Vader. Joyce DeWitt (born 1949) from Wheeling, West Virginia, became everyone's roommate in the sitcom *Three's Company*, which aired from 1976 until 1984. Two Gen Xers who were able to get a few stints in Hollywood are Arloa Reston and Devon Odessa. Arloa Reston (born 1978 in Cheyenne) starred in *Beneath the Eyes of God* (2018) and *Desperate Housewives* (2004-2012). Devon Odessa (born 1974) from Parkersburg, West Virginia starred in the TV show *My So-Called Life* (1994-1995) and the movie *Uncle Buck* (1989).

And speaking of famous spouses, from the silent era we have Mildred Harris of Cheyenne, Wyoming, and Virginia Fox of Wheeling, West Virginia. Mildred Harris was born in 1901 and was the first wife of Charlie Chaplin and starred in several movies. Virginia Fox (born 1902) was the fictional consort to Buster Keaton in the movie *Neighbors* (1920).

Two mountain papa heavyweights are the Beaver and Harvey. Jim Beaver (born 1950) in Laramie, Wyoming, starred in CW's *Supernatural* (2005-2020) and *Deadwood* (2004-2006). Harvey (born 1957) in Welch, West Virginia, has been all over TV and Hollywood. No mention of his resume is necessary due to his supernova status. But in case you didn't know, Steve Harvey is the host of the *Family Feud*, since 2010. If they ever make a buddy-something movie together, it'd power a rocket to the moon.

Two athletic Gen Xers to steal America's heart are Olympians Rulon and Retton. Rulon E. Gardner (born 1971) from Afton, Wyoming, unleashed an *Autobot* "grim lock" on his opponents when he won gold at the 2000 Sydney Olympics in wrestling, while Mary Lou Retton (born 1968) from Fairmont, West Virginia, "jetted like starfire" with her gymnastics routine for the gold at the 1984 Olympics.

Jackson Pollock and Charlie Harper are two artistic influencers whose art put the mod in modern art. Jackson Pollock was born in 1912 in Cody, Wyoming, and opened Pandora's box in the art world, whereby abstract, random, and literally off the wall themes forever changed the halls and walls of galleries across the world, pushing the frontiers of art into dimensions beyond convention, space, and time. Charlie Harper (born 1922) in Frenchtown, West Virginia, also bottled a bit of that abstract element, yet fused it to more conventional and stylistic art that has become a recycled baseline of art that has been used many times in the modern interpretations across the web.

George Clayton Johnson and Mary Alice Kemery are two writers who boldly typed where no one had typed before. George C. Johnson (1929-2015) was a science fiction writer whose pen expanded minds via *The Twilight Zone* (1960-1968, 1983), *Logan's Run* (1976), and *Ocean's 11* (1960). From the other hemisphere of the mind, Mary Alice Kemery (1925-1995) of Morgantown, West Virginia, opened another vista of the New Thought movement in the late 1960s. Kemery's unprecedented astrology book was providentially positioned to catch the new and groovy wave of the '60s counter culture movement, as echoed in the 1969's "Aquarius/Let the Sunshine In." Her recognizable pen name is Linda Goodman, and the book that sprung her to success was *Linda Goodman's Sun Signs*, first published in 1968.

Two writers closer to earth are Patricia "Patty" MacLachlan and Tom Wilson.

THE FLAG REVELATION

Patty MacLachlan (born 1938) from Cheyenne, Wyoming, basically won the lottery when her book *Sarah, Plain and Tall* (1985) won the Newbery Medal. The Newbery Medal is given once a year to an outstanding children's library book. Tom Wilson, born 1931 in Grant Town, West Virginia, captured a simple wonder in comics with his simply drawn character Ziggy.

West Virginia and Wyoming are framed fellows who have a matching caliber of mountains and men. Although separated by several thousand miles, their stories sometimes match with similar contours if you look with your heart or listen closely with your ears. They are each other's essential guardian angels who are charged with covering their opposite unseen mountain views. The hills of Appalachia and the cliffs of the Rockies are different, yet on occasion, so similar. By the quirky crumbling of a cosmic cookie in the sky, it seems that one half fell in West Virginia while the other half landed in Wyoming.

fifteen

NEW YORK & NEW JERSEY

The Big Apple and Zesty Tomato

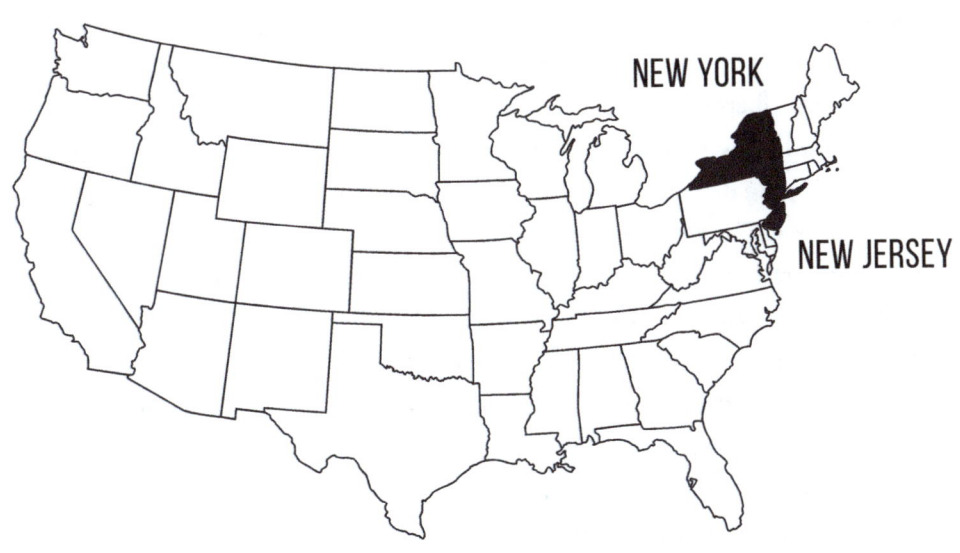

THE FLAG REVELATION

NEW YORK

The key element that unites New York with New Jersey's flag is the appearance of the Goddess Liberty. This Roman goddess seals the bond of synchronicity between these sister states. Either by happenstance, Providence, or purposeful intention, the Goddess Liberty is concordantly standing on the left, hoist-ward side. She is holding a liberty staff, which is the pole topped with a Phrygian cap. Also, like most Roman deities, the Goddess Libertas is derived from a Greek goddess, whose name is Eleuthera. Compared to New Jersey, the liberty cap on New York's flag is rather drab. It is a wrinkled brown rimless hat. But the liberty cap on New Jersey's flag looks like it was just sewn by Papa Smurf himself, with an added blue patriotic stripe with white stars. These types of hats do not have a brim but are something like knit hats worn by elves or the famous seven dwarfs.

So, what is the deal with Phrygian caps and freedom? Well, it all goes back to Ancient Rome. Certainly, many slaves were set free from their masters unceremoniously. But when certain slaves were set free and granted citizenship, a ceremonial proceeding was given. During the liberation ceremony a symbolic hat, sometimes called a pileus, was given to slaves who were promoted to the citizenship class. This is something akin to graduating seniors, like the gradu-

NEW JERSEY

ation cap. Thus, the Phrygian or liberty cap is essentially an Ancient Roman graduation cap to symbolize an end of bondage and granting of citizenship.

In contrast, the goddesses on the right differ. New York has the Goddess of Justice, while New Jersey has the Goddess of Abundance. Lady Justice is blindfolded and holding a sword, her Greek equivalent is the Goddess Dike. But Dike is not blindfolded and usually does not hold a sword. The symbol of the sword with Justice is appropriate, since disputes settled by court are the civilized means of going to war by having two parties fight with the pen, rather than the sword. Long ago and as it is still in the animal kingdom, and occasionally within the human kingdom, disputes are settled by force or violence. Usually, the strongest carried the day. But with civilized society, disputes can be won by words; the strongest and most intelligent mind is now able to carry the day. However, supporting this intelligence requires a vast supply of financial force. Consequently, rather than physical fitness tipping the scales of justice, it is the most economically fit that can tip the balance of justice to her side.

When justice is delivered, it cuts like a psychic sword into the ego. Thus, the sword on Lady Justice is appropriate and serves as a reminder that when justice shall fall, the consequences may result in psychological pain, a financial penalty, or imprisonment. In some cases when the death penalty is being meted out, the metaphor becomes literal.

As for Ceres with New Jersey, Ceres is associated with agriculture or wealth in general. Ancient Romans used to celebrate Ceres during mid-April with the return of spring. Her name is where the word cereal derives from. But her original Greek form was the Goddess Demeter. Both Demeter and Ceres are represented by the Cornucopia or horn of plenty. Upon New Jersey's flag it is filled with grapes, apples, greens, and a plum. Ergo, she is the perfect Goddess for the Garden State.

The dress of the goddesses differs. In New York, the robes with capes present a regal and formal attitude of a high priestess or ancient Roman official. In New Jersey, the dress is distinctly feminine, as something worn by a maiden or servant. Yet the women of New York wear headbands, while the women of New Jersey wear regal olive laurels.

Also note the robes of New York have a yin and yang counter where Liberty is wearing a blue robe with a yellow belt, while Justice is wearing a yellow robe with a blue belt. The common element is that both women are wearing red capes, and the tips of the belts are red as well. For the record the outfit of Liberty matches Superman, while the colors of Justice are the livery of Mighty Mouse.

The compartments of the two flags contrast like an innie and outie belly button. The plain white ribbon along the bottom of New York has the word "Excelsior" upon it that projects forward in a masculine outie belly button, while the elegant blue and reddish trimmed ribbon of New Jersey projects backward in an innie, feminine form belly button, with 1776 in the center. The final element of concord is the torse, which is basically a braided headband. New York's torse is holding up the planet, while New Jersey's torse is in the proper position on top of a knight's helmet. Torses are essential elements to any proper coat of arms.

The torse was a part of the distinct uniform of knights in shining armor. As they were covered in heavy metal, during warm days it could get rather stuffy under the armor. Knights would then wear a fabric over their armor like an Islamic sheik, which was held in place by the torse/headband. Also, as jousting became a popular sport, in order to distinguish a particular knight, the coat of arms acted as a jersey to identify at a distance who was who. The head dress became complex and distinct so that people could further discriminate. Thus, if New Jersey was a knight jousting in a tourney in England during the 1400s, he would be wearing a blue and gray headband with a blue and gray jersey, as these colors are indicated by the floral mantling flowing around the helmet, with his helmet topped with a horse head that would have been sewn from fabric. If New York were in the tourney, then he would have a blue and yellow headband with no jersey since there is no mantling present, and his headgear would be double stacked with the earth and an eagle on top. New Jersey would be at an advantage since New York would not be wearing a helmet, going true commando, as there is no helmet on New York's flag.

Oddly, it is only New Jersey that has a proper coat of arms. All the other coat of arms found on the other state flags break the rules of classical heraldry. Thus New Jersey sets the gold standard by having a regal heraldic coat of arms, which honorably maintains the prim and proper heraldic traditions from the motherland, the United Kingdom.

In stark contrast, as Jersey maintains the dignity of English heraldic traditions, York has an in-your-face element that goes the extra step with a disrespectful gesture. New York's flag directly insults the royal establishment. Did you already notice it? If not, see if you can find it before it's revealed here: New York's Goddess of Liberty is stepping on a formerly respected symbol of power, the royal crown, which is positioned under her left foot.

The insult to the crown can be variously interpreted, but one partially positive way to look at its message is, "We don't care who your daddy was. What makes you so freaking special?"

The background colors of New Jersey and New York are a perfect revolutionary patriotic alignment of buff and blue. Buff and blue were the distinguished colors of the uniforms chosen by George Washington to represent his bodyguard, generals, and aides to the executive camp. Most importantly here, the New York and New Jersey regiments under Washington's command in the Continental Army were also assigned blue coats with buff facings.

The coincidence that New York and Jersey echo the command colors of Washington is only a recent alignment. For over a century, from 1778 to 1901 New York and New Jersey both employed buff for the background. With that in mind, the flags would have looked nearly identical from a distance. The change to blue took place in 1901 for New York. And it is under these meanderings of serendipity that harken back to the original uniform of Washington.

At the moment buff is not a popular name for this color. In modern terms, it can be thought of as a mid-tone of khaki. But somehow this color has mutated to a yellowish color on many New Jersey flags.

By unintended happenstance New York's flag reflects the ancient conception of the four sacred elements of the Western tradition. *Fire* is represented by the Sun, *earth* is represented by the mountain on the riverside, *water* is represented by the river, and finally *air* is visible around the Sun and is filling the sails of the two ships on the river. In yin and yang concord, New Jersey does the same for the two extra ancient elements conceived from the East via the three plows upon its shield, which are made of *metal* and *wood*.

New York and New Jersey even have an official flag that combines the two. The Port Authority of New York and New Jersey uses a flag that mashes up the two designs. The flags are linked by rope, whereby the seals are enclosed in white as if looking through a pair of binoculars. New York composes the hoist half, which is closer to the pole for hoisting, while New Jersey gets the fly half, which flaps and flies along the open sky.

Geography

New York and New Jersey are key components of the middle colonies, not quite like New England or the South, and they were a part of New Netherlands. They are of the lucky few fraternal flag twins to have a line of scrimmage, like Alabama-Florida and Iowa-Missouri. Consequently, there are parts that look exactly the same geographically, as it is with their people. Like any good sport, having a line of scrimmage can result in a testy rivalry.

If New York is iconic of being the Empire State, then New Jersey is the perpetual Underdog State. New York loves to lord it over the other states about how great it is, and as a matter of fact, New York does indeed have the cojones to back up this claim.

Truly an Empire State, the rivers of New York reach far and wide. New York is a part of the Colonial Delaware Valley, Big Shot Hudson Valley, Federal Chesapeake Bay Valley, Elegant Quebec Lake Champlain Valley, and International Great Lakes Valley. On top of that, she has a private one on one lake with Canada via Lake Ontario. When you compare canals, New York has the grand Lake Erie Canal that runs across the state as a marvel for its time, while New Jersey has the smaller and quaint Raritan Canal that unites the Hudson with the Delaware.

New York borders several states while New Jersey is stuck to one, which gives New York the attitude that "Anything you can do, I can do better." New York borders Vermont, Massachusetts, Connecticut, Pennsylvania, in addition to Ontario and Quebec. This gives New York a well-rounded domestic and international awareness that leaves Jersey in the dust. Thus New York is the Big Skipper, consequently Jersey is the proverbial Little Buddy, Gilligan.

Basically, New York has cornered the market with New Jersey. As for Pennsylvania, New Jersey does not make land to land contact, further New York shares an even longer line of scrimmage with Pennsylvania. But New Jersey has one ace up her sleeve—New Jersey is not totally boxed in by New York, Jersey has a semi-secret, hidden land border with Delaware. The land border came about relatively recently and by artificial means. It arose because Delaware took possession of all the small marshes and islands in the Delaware River. But during the 1970s in Salem County, New Jersey, there was a land reclamation project due to the construction of the Salem Nuclear Power Plant. With all the extra dirt being moved about, two river islands of Delaware became attached to New Jersey. Thus, when New York gets too uppity and counters every move New Jersey makes, Jersey can buddy up with Delaware and get one over on New York, since New York cannot tap the power of the first state, Delaware, as New Jersey can.

Long before statehood, New York got one over on New Jersey when she pushed the line of scrimmage southward (to where it is now) during the New York-New Jersey Line War that lasted from 1701 to 1765. New Jersey's northern border was supposed to be at 41°40' north, along the Delaware River in Sullivan County, New York, in Cochecton Township. However, a map erroneously indicated a branch river was at this point when there wasn't. So, New York was able to aggressively argue the border down to where it is now, at Port Jervis at 41°21', shortchanging New Jersey 19 minutes of precious farming land. Thus, the lost tribes of New Jersey make up the southern communities of Rockland and Orange in New York. But the biggest lost tribe of New Jersey can be found on Staten Island. Staten Island is much closer to Jersey, but New York was able to snag this beaut for her very own. On the whole Staten Island is rather happy to join the "cool kids table" of NYC, even though she is much closer and bears a resemblance to a Jersey girl.

A similar situation happened with Fisher's Island, Connecticut. Fishers Island is closer by more than several miles to Connecticut and would have given Connecticut one good habitable island of her very own in Long Island Sound, and an international waterway. But nope, Connecticut was denied a worthwhile island of her own. Although New York had more than enough, with the king-size isle of Long Island and associated smaller isles, this demonstrates that the Empire State is not afraid to steam roll over the little guy and take every nickel and dime's worth of a widget to the legal limit of the law. After all, it is called the "Empire State" for a reason. New York takes no prisoners and has hard ball action on the permanent playlist. At first this may not seem fair, but New York plays on the hard, square and mostly fair; consequently, when one is able to get one over on New York, it makes the win so much more delightful, as any sports fan will testify. In fact, most of Long Island used to belong to colonial Connecticut, but New York was able to ensure a proper coastline for herself in the Atlantic and deny her what should have been a part of Connecticut, Fisher's Isle.

New York even had ambitions to snag Block Island from Rhode Island, plus Nantucket and Martha's Vineyard from Massachusetts. And from 1664 until 1691, Nantucket and Martha's Vineyard were officially under the rule of colonial New York, until a new charter was issued by the province of Massachusetts.

Every so often since 1937, Nantucket will threaten retrocession back to New York when Boston does not give her enough attention.

One geographic fact that New Jersey can lord over New York is that New Jersey is a core member of the all-American Belt. It is the region completely south of Canada and north of Mexico. On the other hand, upstate NY has a northern border along the 45th north monkey in the middle line and gets a blast of all four seasons, every year. And this truly is the case, as parts of upstate New York get snow falls that can put Canada to shame.

The one cardinal direction that New Jersey can lord over New York is south, and she has just a little something southern about her. New York can go further east, west, and north than New Jersey, but not south. When the Mason-Dixon line is extended completely as defined by the Pennsylvania-Maryland border, New Jersey has a significant chunk of land south of the extended Mason-Dixon line. New Jersey even dips so far south to have few points more southward than Virginia herself. Cape May, New Jersey is south of Harpers Ferry and Leesburg, Virginia, being on par with the northern half of Washington, DC.

Also, New York and New Jersey have unique shapes that look like important objects in the bathroom. If you rotate New York 90 degrees counterclockwise, she looks like a sink. Just imagine Long Island is the faucet. Likewise, New Jersey looks like an old-school toilet if you flip it 180 degrees. Together they make the perfect bathroom buddies of America, where America can relieve herself and wash up to look pretty; on second thought, New Jersey also resembles the bust of Nefertiti.

The most iconic geographic dynamic or dispute is with the Statue of Liberty. This is one of those quirky counterbalanced items whereby the Statue of Liberty is within New Jersey's maritime borders but is considered a part of New York. The same thing happens with Ellis Island. But there was a recent ruling that any artificial reclaimed land of Ellis Island would belong to New Jersey. Thus, this island is totally within New Jersey's waters, but the organic half belongs to New York.

As for old York and old Jersey, the original York is located in northeastern England and is the famous location for the House of York, represented by a white rose. Their most famous medieval rival was the House Lancaster, represented by a red rose. After decades of violent and petty infighting during the high middle ages for the crown of England, known as the War of the Roses, it was resolved with a fairytale ending. The feuding houses were united by marriage, which created the famous red and white rose of England, the Tudor rose. Now for old Jersey, it is a lovely southern English isle, just off the northern coast of France. Every summer ye' old Jersey shore is home to heaps of families and tourists having a fun go at the beach and whatnot, as it is with the newer Jersey shore of America.

History

The first permanent settlements within New Jersey and New York stem from the Netherlands. For a solid 50 years, the Dutch laid the first roots in the Garden and Empire States, starting in 1614 and ending in 1664, when the British acquired the region in a hostile merger. This makes New Jersey and New York the essential Dutch brothers of America. Unlike Quebec, the Dutch Americans or "Neder-quoi" were not able to prevent their assimilation into British culture. Dutch is the closest linguistic cousin to English, and switching over to English is not as much hassle on the brain as switching over to French or Spanish. Note, the Dutch returned for short stint in 1673, but the British retook it a second time.

    The Dutch have the stereotype of being the best on the square and fair traders who are not afraid to split the bill down to the penny and then cut that penny in half, and then cut into a quarter-penny if need be. The term "going Dutch" indicates that every person pays for their own meal at a restaurant, which stems from the wise business acumen and reputation of Dutch traders. There is nothing impolite or insensitive about deal making for prices and accounting for every dime, nickel, and penny. It's just business on an upright fair and square with no strings attached. The positive side of looking the market squarely in the eye is that you don't have to read between the lines, take hints, or beat around the bush for what is wanted. Thus, it should have been no wonder that the markets of the city formerly known as New Amsterdam would blossom into the mecca of finance, which is now known as Wall Street of NYC.

During the American Revolution, pivotal battles that turned the corner for the American Revolution took place in these states. After the initial victory at Boston in 1775, the American Revolution slowly lost steam as the professional crack troops of the British Empire would repeatedly punish the ragtag army of citizen soldiers and frontiersmen. At this early juncture, it was a battle of David versus Goliath. After the initial victory at Boston ended on March 17, 1776, the empire returned to strike back, and strike back it did, at NYC. Washington was whipped at every turn and came dangerously close to losing the war on more than one occasion. During the Battle of Long Island, the providential arrival of fog along the East River allowed Washington to escape to Manhattan for brief respite. However, the empire would continue to punish the Continental Army in a series of humiliating defeats.

The worst beat down came to pass at the Battle of Fort Washington Heights, New York. Fort Lee, New Jersey, and Fort Washington, New York, were supposed to be the conjoined guardians to hold back the tide of British forces. They were twin fortresses on opposite sides of the Hudson River, as the critical link between New England and the middle colonies. However, a traitor by the name of William Demont provided the British a layout that enabled them to deliver a blistering loss with the capture of 3,000 patriots, nearly all the troops at Fort Washington. The British then daringly crossed the Hudson at night and nearly snuffed out the rebellion at the Battle of Fort Lee, New Jersey. Washington was forced to turn tail and retreat across New Jersey to safer territory in Pennsylvania. Coincidentally, Thomas Paine composed his pamphlet "The American Crisis," which echoes this loss with the phrase, "These are the times that try men's souls." It was at this point that Washington's reputation hemorrhaged and political voices grew stronger to get rid of the "loser" Washington.

By December 1776, the rebellion was in dire straits. It was clear that the Continental Army was no match for Imperial Troops. But Washington did not give up, with the clock running down for the enlistments Washington desperately needed a win not only for his career but for the rebellion. The retreat from

THE FLAG REVELATION

NYC to Pennsylvania across New Jersey may have been the darkest hour of the rebellion. But the Continental Army persevered, and George Washington finally delivered on December 25, 1776, when he crossed the Delaware River to score the lauded victory at Trenton, New Jersey. It was a victory for Washington, a veritable do or die situation that replenished hope and kept his detractors at bay. Most importantly it caused the ranks of the Continental Army to swell, as Washington earned the confidence of his men and the nation.

The next battle that turned a critical corner was the Battle of Saratoga, New York, on October 7, 1777. If Washington's Victory at Trenton was Christmas, then the victory at Saratoga was the "Yom Kippur Battle" for the patriots. The holiday of Yom Kippur—the after echo of Jewish New Year is considered the holiest of holy days as a day of atonement—usually, though not always, takes place during the front half of October. It was at Saratoga that France was finally convinced that the Americans were worthy of helping. No longer would the U.S. fight alone, but a powerful ally, France, became the ace that was needed for ultimate deliverance. This required alliance paved a path to victory, which without, would have been virtually impossible.

As the battle at Trenton, New Jersey was the break of dawn after the long night of suffering when the Empire struck back at NYC. The victory at Saratoga, New York, was the high noon mark whence the chances for the rebels changed from a longshot to likely. New York and New Jersey became sanctified proving grounds for the American Revolution and George Washington himself, more so for New Jersey. These states were witness to tragic losses, soul searching defeats, and the long night of doubt; but ultimately, both gave uplifting victories. The mechanism or "the force" at work, ascribed by Washington himself, was due to a manifold manifestation of Providence. Although the American spirit may have been forged at a valley in Pennsylvania, it was in New Jersey and New York where its steely determination was tested and ultimately proved by Providence, or in modern nondenominational academic terms, by synchronicity.

The American Revolution can also be characterized as a Civil War. This was most effectively the case with New Jersey and New York whose population was bitterly divided and subject to hostile backwoods partisan violence. But two persons of high rank to side with the Loyalists were William Franklin and David Mathews.

William Franklin is the perfect person to frame the American Revolution as a civil war because he was the son of Benjamin Franklin. William Franklin was also the last Loyalist governor of New Jersey. It is quite an irony that the son of the ultimate founding father of the American Revolution was on the opposite side of the war. As the American Revolution pitted families and neighbors against each other, this revolution pitted the Franklin family against itself. No doubt, Benjamin Franklin's broken relationship with his son left a gaping wound in their souls. William Franklin was not content to sit on the sidelines and let his father's country go its separate way. William Franklin was an active Loyalist who planned partisan and violent raids against the "rebel fodder" of his father; it was a reversed Luke and Anakin relationship. Will Franklin's outspoken Loyalist views and actions led to his capture and imprisonment. He was left to rot in solitary confinement at Litchfield, Connecticut, for eight months, and it nearly ended his life. He was finally released in a prisoner exchange in 1778. Once free, William Franklin rejoined the ranks of the Loyalist side with a renewed spirit of vengeance. After the war, he moved to London and died there on November 17, 1813 in relative obscurity. Unlike Darth Vader and Luke Skywalker, Benjamin Franklin never reconciled with his firstborn son.

David Mathews was the last colonial mayor of New York City. Born in New York, he was one of the leading voices for the Loyalist cause. Mayor Mathews was indicted for conspiracy to assassinate General Washington and also captured by patriot forces. However, Mathews was able to escape parole and ran to British lines in NYC, where he was reinstated as the mayor. During the term of the last Loyalist mayor of NYC about 10,000 patriots died on prison ships in the East River, which is higher than the number who died in combat. These men were of the first batch of American POWs who miserably died in prison, often treated as mere criminals and pirates rather than proper prisoners of war. After the war, David Mathews moved to Nova Scotia and helped establish Cape Breton as a Loyalist community.

New Jersey and New York bore witness to some of the world's greatest modern tragedies. The Hindenburg airship was a marvel of the 20th century. These technological wonders were akin to an alien mothership that heralded the arrival of the modern age. Imagine if Columbus had landed in the Americas on such a vehicle in 1492. But the Germans made the mistake of using flammable hydrogen instead of helium. A spark ignited the flames on May 6, 1937, and the Hindenburg's destruction was captured on film in New Jersey. The horror of the Nazi ensign going up in flames was telling of the horrors that would soon envelop the world. For New York, another massive superstructure of the 20th century was destroyed in another spectacularly soul jeering fashion. On September 11, 2001, the World Trade Center towers fell when two U.S. civilian aircraft were hijacked and flown into the buildings by terrorists. Other planes crashed in Washington, DC, and western Pennsylvania. Nearly 3,000 people died in the horrible yet hypnotic spectacle of terror, which froze the attention of the world.

Both tragedies were half-time events between their respective wars. For the Hindenburg, it took place between WWI and WWII, as the world made war with Germany. For 9/11, it took place between the first and second Gulf Wars as the United States made war with modern Mesopotamia.

Two key founding fathers who pair are George Clinton and Aaron Burr. Coincidentally, both men were vice presidents under Thomas Jefferson. Aaron Burr from Newark, New Jersey is the original New Jersey tough guy. If New York brings the brass, then New Jersey brings the brass knuckles—starting with Aaron Burr. Burr became famous for killing Alexander Hamilton in a duel and is associated with a crackpot scheme to create a new nation out of Spanish Texas. George Clinton from New York was the first vice president to serve under two different presidents, Jefferson, and Madison. Aaron Burr was also a vice president under Jefferson's first term from 1801 to 1805, and Clinton was the vice president during the second term from 1805 to 1809.

Culture

America is divided along linguistic, ethnic, religious, and political lines. How the nation keeps herself together is quite a miracle. But one essential substance that binds the nation is the hallowed national love of sport. Football and baseball trace their roots back to these two—in particular New Jersey. Baseball has its origins in stick and ball games played in Europe. Baseball has a common ancestor with the game of cricket; but sometime in the early 1800s they went their separate ways. The exact history of American baseball is rather foggy, some say the New York Knickerbockers of 1845 are the first documented team to play under modern rules. No longer could the defense out a player by hitting them with a ball, as they were now forced to tag the runners. Likewise foul lines were established. With the new rules of "modern baseball" in place, the first official competitive game recognized as the official start of American baseball took place on June 19, 1846, at Elysian Fields in Hoboken, New Jersey. Modern baseball did not take off initially at this stage of its evolution, as cricket was more popular in the press. Only after the Civil War would baseball rise to becoming a voyeur's delight. As violent as the Civil War was, in between the fighting there were long periods of doing nothing. Consequently, the New York style of baseball caught on and spread across the nation during these long periods of hurrying up and waiting between battles. Hurry up and wait is also the *unofficial* motto of the U.S. Army: *Festina et Exspecta*.

Football, like baseball, also has a foggy history, as well as an evolutionary cousin that went in another direction which became rugby, capturing the market as the favorite tackle ball game of the world. (For the record, the British were able to ensure that rugby and cricket, rather than football and baseball, were spread across the world.) The rise of American football began with the first ever intercollegiate football game on November 6, 1869, when Rutgers University of New Jersey played Princeton University. At the suggestion of Rutgers captain William J. Leggett, the rules were based upon the London Football Association's current rules. But American football was not yet on par with the game as we know it today. Modern football was formalized with play familiar to the modern mind when Princeton, New Jersey University, and Columbia, a New York University, met with Harvard and Yale on November 23, 1876, and included some of the rugby touchdown rules used by McGill University. Thus New York and New Jersey were a part of the first Intercollegiate Football Association (IFA), and this game that took on certain Canadian rugby rules would eventually surpass baseball as the national sport a century later.

Since then, several other games have cornered the market on the public square of casual conversation. New York also demonstrates its Empire State character, since it is one of the few states to double up on franchises in each prime-time sports arena. Many states don't have a major league sports team, and consequently college teams and or the local high school is the connection point for a community. A few cities are able to maintain at least one within the big four of Major League Sports with MLB, NFL, NBA, or NHL. Some are strong enough to carry all four, like Philadelphia and Detroit. But NYC, or New York City metro, is the Big Mac, since it is double stacked with two teams in each of the majors. With baseball, NYC has the Yankees and the Mets; for football, she doubles with the Giants and the Jets; for basketball, there are the Knicks and the Nets; and for hockey the Rangers and Islanders. New Jersey has what? Just the Devils (New York snagged the Nets away from Jersey in 2012), and here is the rub that truly underscores the relationship between New York and New Jersey. The Giants and Jets actually play in New Jersey. Like the Statue of Liberty issue, New Jersey is a stepping stone that New York, with no guilt, steps on to receive fortune and glory. The name of New York gets the glory while the name of New Jersey gets the shaft. Imagine if the LA Lakers played in San Diego or San Francisco and referred to themselves as the LA Lakers? What if the Chicago Bulls played in Gary, Indiana? What if the Dallas Cowboys moved their stadium to Austin or somewhere in Mexico, yet kept the Dallas name? Nevertheless, it seems New Jersey is fine with this Kal El dynamic. Behind every super man of steel from New York who won a Super Bowl ring on the gridiron, there is a Clark Kent from New Jersey who made it possible.

New York and New Jersey are states that shamelessly lean blue. As Alabama and Florida like to competitively go more red than the other, New Jersey and New York compete against each other to see who is the bluest of the blueberry bunch. But like all states, there are smatterings of red communities in Jersey and York as there is a minority of blue patches in Florida and Alabama.

One of the factors that makes New York and New Jersey such hard left leaning states is their bountiful diversity, which is off the scale compared to most states. Ellis Island was the iconic New York-New Jersey port of entry from 1892 to 1954. Nearly 12 million immigrants entered through this gateway. It was here that other regions of Europe that were formerly eschewed would add to the American identity, mostly from Eastern and Southern Europe. On the national average, Italian Americans register at the same percentage of Asian Americans at around 5%, but in New Jersey and New York Italians make up a finer slice of American pie. New York is about 14%, while New Jersey taps 18% of Italian identity. Likewise, Asian Americans for both New York and New Jersey figure somewhere near 11%. But Asia is a big continent, and Asian statistics includes India and the Middle East. In the standard American mind set, Asian is erroneously thought of as from East Asia only: Japan, China, Korea, Vietnam, and Southeast Asia. But if one includes the Jewish population with Asia, since Israel is in Asia, the Asian population bumps up to 20% for New York and 17% for New Jersey. Note, the Jewish population of the U.S. is on par with the national average for Native Americans, somewhere around 2%.

Iconic American monsters of yore that match up are the Headless Horseman from New York and the Jersey Devil of the Pine Barrens. The first legendary American ghoul distinct from the classical pantheon of monsters from the Old World was established by Washington Irving's seminal classic *The Legend of Sleepy Hollow* in 1820. Another distinct American monster with a unique phenotype is the Jersey Devil. It arose organically via folklore as some sort of devilish beast that roamed the Pine Barrens of southern New Jersey. The Jersey Devil is purported to have bat wings but with the body of a kangaroo and a forked tail. Its face is a combination of a horse or goat. Some legends trace it back to the 1700s but others much later. Note that popular ghouls like the vampire, Frankenstein, mummy, and werewolf are not native to the American imagination. But the Headless Horseman and the Jersey Devil are of the first order of original American ghouls, established in New York and New Jersey.

As for the sexual revolution, New Jersey and New York have laid second note anthems with two blockbuster shows: *Jersey Shore* and *Sex in the City*. First, *Sex in the City* (1998-2004) is a Gen X show that has opened the floodgates with the good, bad, and ugly that comes with such lifestyles. Then, *Jersey Shore* (2009-2012) documented a new order of liberated personal relationships for younger generations to either aspire, copy, or outright reject. Both shows throw the traditional values of courtship out the window, to the ire of conservative families.

Two iconic American gangster sagas are rooted to these states. *The Godfather* (1972-1990) is based in New York, and *The Sopranos* (1999-2007) stems from New Jersey. They artfully highlighted the drama and rivalry between underworld economies. Additionally, *The Sopranos* made driving on the dismal and often congested New Jersey turnpike a must do magical experience with *The Sopranos* opening soundtrack.

Two jewels of American life that have iconic roots in these states are Broadway and the Boardwalk. Basically New York is the queen of the theater, while New Jersey is king of the Boardwalk. There are plenty of beaches, theaters, and boardwalks across America. But if you want to see the best of the best, Manhattan delivers the top tier class of song and dance performances. No stage can outshine the sparkle and pizzazz of NYC. Two iconic musicals that capture a generational spirit on Broadway are *Jersey Boys,* set in the early 1960s for New Jersey and *West Side Story* for New York set in the late 1950s. Likewise, the Boardwalk of Atlantic City is the original sidewalk of wood by the beach. This seaside town was the original McCoy that stole the heart of America, establishing the beach resort rhythm that has been copied many times over. A testament to the iconic status of Atlantic City is the game *Monopoly,* which is modeled after Atlantic City. Nearly every state, college, and pop cultural institution has taken note and imitated this classic, Jersey original. Although people are less than willing to admit, a tiny piece of New Jersey has embedded itself across America, at the fun spot, which is a summer ritual for most. It is with *Monopoly,* by no accident, that one learns about the cutthroat Wall Street wheeling and dealing in that old Dutch aggressive fair and square manner. As for many Americans, *Monopoly* is often the first time one gets to own a property, and or only time they can build houses and hotels.

One of the biggest rivalries between New Jersey and New York is the claim for best pizza in the USA. New York has a very loud and established claim with its unique, flat style pizza that is a triple A plus delight. But a grassroots counterclaim has been established in New Jersey with Manco & Manco Pizza, established in 1956 (original name Mack & Manco). The trouble with NYC pizza is that no one place owns the title for best of the best pizza. But in New Jersey, there are legions of Manco & Manco pizza lovers that make seasonal pilgrimages to the Jersey Shore. NYC style pizza is more like pizzas across the nation, but a whole lot better. Manco & Manco pizza has a fresh and distinct flavor that puts it on another level, whereby eating the crust is wholly communion with the spirit of America.

Likewise, it is important to eat each pizza at its given location. You must eat NYC pizza in NYC with that distinct NYC air and noise (it just tastes better) likewise for New Jersey, Manco & Manco pizza is best eaten at the Jersey shore, with salty seaside vapors that blend into each bite, while a crashing surf makes music in concert with soulful songs of seagulls of the Jonathan Livingston flock.

New York and New Jersey shine with the spirit of the bright lights of the big city. Frank Sinatra and Tony Bennett were two soul-stirring singers who captured that first-class sparkle of champagne culture. Frank Sinatra, from Hoboken, New Jersey (1915-1998), is the archetype of the high roller—full of jazz and class, with a touch of that nice guy charm, ready to put up his dukes for the little guy or a damsel in distress. Tony Bennett, from Queens, New York (1926-2023), was the founder of the Frank Sinatra School of the Arts located in NYC. Together, these men were the perpetual toast of the town, singing in that smooth, clear, and confident classy style that reflects the upper crust of American life without the haughty air of a snob. Rather, they operated with grace, a wink, and a friendly smile, with a finger pointing right at ya kid, telling you that you too, could have this as well. It is quite a perfect fit that a man from Hoboken, New Jersey, sang the iconic rendition of "New York, New York" (1977).

Another set of godfathers of American comedy are the Marx Brothers and Abbott and Costello. The Marx Brothers were the first set of influencers who made the transition from Vaudeville to early cinema. The Marxes were all born in New York at the turn of the century, and their comedy set the tempo of the first generation of TikToks to amuse the public. New Jersey's laugh track counter to Marx humor are Abbott and Costello, also born at the dawn of the 20th century and became the world-famous influencers who smashed the funny bone in the modern electric era. Abbot was born in Asbury Park, New Jersey, in 1897, and Costello was born in Paterson, New Jersey, in 1906.

Another pair of American jokers both born in 1926 to leave a legacy with the modern generations are Mel Brooks from NYC and Jerry Lewis from Newark. They are king jesters of wacky and off the wall slapstick.

Another pair of old-school kings of the one-liner are Rodney Dangerfield and Emil Cohen. Emil Cohen from Elizabeth, New Jersey, was billed as America's foremost American Jewish humorist. But Jacob Rodney Cohen (stage name Dangerfield) from Babylon, New York, crossed the comic streams in order to blast ectoplasmic jokes to all the people groups of America. With their self-effacing, jokes-on-me humor, these joke-busters were able to earn just a little bit of respect.

Two understated emperors of comedy are Emperor Don Rickles and National Jester, Ernie Kovacs. Ernie Kovacs from Trenton, New Jersey (born 1919), was the original artist of the bizarre off the wall, weird, visual comedy sketch that has gone on to inspire *David Letterman*, *SNL*, *The Muppet Show*, *Conan O'Brien*, *Ren and Stimpy*, and *Adult Swim*. Don Rickles from NYC (born 1926) made an art of roasting himself and the audience, with a full throttle acceleration as a double black belt master of joke-fu, or rather "judo," who can throw anyone to the ground in stitches with his seething, sarcastic delivery and one-liners. "Don Tickles" also maintained the highest JPM (jokes per minute) of any comedian since or afterward.

Two ancient kings of cinema preserved in black and white are Humphrey Bogart and Thomas Mitchell. They were two supernova stars of their generation, before the modern space age. Bogart from NYC (born 1899) has become a verb and icon due to movies like *The Maltese Falcon* (1941), *Casablanca* (1942), and *Sabrina* (1954). Thomas Mitchell from Elizabeth, New Jersey (born 1892) was the first triple crown winner of acting to win an Oscar, Emmy, and Tony. Mitchell starred in *Gone with the Wind* (1939), *It's a Wonderful Life* (1946), and *High Noon* (1952).

Two temporal twins (both born in 1916) were Kirk Douglas from Amsterdam, New York, and Sterling Hayden from Upper Montclair, New Jersey. Alan Arkin from NYC (born 1934), pairs with Roy Scheider from Orange, New Jersey (born 1932), as serious to funny men of the stage. When Roy Schieder was fighting *Jaws* (1975), Alan Arkin made America laugh with *The In-Laws* (1979). Two great Allens from the Lost Generation are Alan Alda and Allen Garfield. Alan Alda from New York star was launched with *M*A*S*H* as Hawkeye Pierce. Allen Garfield from Newark (born 1939) starred in *The Majestic* (2001) and *Beverly Hills Cop II* (1987).

Two drama kings who punched their passion with acting into the heartland are Al Pacino and Jack Nicholson. Al Pacino from NYC (born 1940) is a virtual demigod of American cinema who is the only one, qualified, to hold the stage with Jack Nicholson from Neptune City, New Jersey (born 1937). They are the true godfathers of American cinema who have yelled, cried, loved, and laughed with the American public.

Two men who exude the tough-guy-with-heart-of-gold energy are Sylvester Stallone and Michael Douglas. Stallone, from Manhattan, NYC (born 1946), was destined to complete his passion project, *Rocky* (1976). It was a movie that revived the American spirit after the loss in Vietnam, silently preaching to the heart that there was still something in America we can believe in, just in time for the bicentennial. Before *Rocky*, Stallone was a nobody with a dream. Michael Douglas, from New Brunswick, New Jersey (born 1944), is of Hollywood royalty, though this is no guarantee of success. Douglas finally made his sacred mark upon America with *Romancing the Stone* (1984), with a little help from a Greek "Demi-God" from planet Zemeckis, who has the uncanny ability to bottle the electric discharges of a forlorn deity from Mount Olympus.

A pair of passionate tough-guy twins (born in 1943) are Robert De Niro from NYC and Joe Pesci from Newark. When these two stars came together, they became money printing machines on demand. They have co-starred in *Raging Bull* (1980), *Goodfellas* (1990), *Casino* (1995), and *The Irishman* (2019). They are a deep multilayered cake of personality, with a refined richness that anyone, from any class, or any generation can appreciate.

THE FLAG REVELATION

Matthew Broderick (born 1962) pairs with Ian Ziering (born 1964). Ian Ziering, from Newark, was launched as a heartthrob in *Beverly Hills, 90210* (1990-2000) and was a lead in *Sharknado* (2013). Matthew Broderick, from NYC, became the universally likable classmate with his many roles as the humble, common-sense, nice yet cool guy that everyone can get behind.

Two more boomer tough guys are Mickey Rourke and Ray Liotta. Mickey Rourke, from Schenectady, New York (born 1952), is a star who has been up and down, but was able to get back up. Ray Liotta (born 1954) from Newark is another Jersey tough guy who oozes that ultimate crack-your-knuckles wingman who has your back. Two natural leaders who found that magic ratio of tough and nice are Bill Pullman from Hornell, New York (born 1958), and Ed Harris from Englewood, New Jersey (born 1950). These kings of cinema brought a dramatic and friendly flare to Hollywood that has resulted in a multitude of hit movies.

I don't know how it happens, but sometimes, when New Jersey and New York team up together, you get nothing but gold. This was the case when Jerry and Jason teamed up on *Seinfeld* (1989-1998), a show that had a charter monopoly on sitcom comedy during the 1990s. Jerry Seinfeld from NYC (born 1953) was a perfect match with Jason Alexander from Newark, born 1959.

As for the proverbial "little guy" of America, Steve Buscemi and Nathan Lane are a perfect pair of boomers who bring a package of silly and serious. Steve Buscemi from NYC (born 1957) has starred in hits like *Fargo* (1996) and *The Big Lebowski* (1998). Nathan Lane from Jersey City (born 1956) has starred in *The Producers* (2005). Their voices have been immortalized by Disney. Buscemi was immortalized in *Monsters, Inc.* (2001), while Lane hit a high note as Timon in the *Lion King* (1994).

Superstar A-list drama dudes who match are Alec Baldwin from Amityville, New York (born 1958), and John Travolta from Englewood, New Jersey (born 1954). Again, a path of gold and drama has followed these men.

The Fratelli Brothers are loveable bad guys who rolled the ultimate and iconic snake eyes in their starring roles in *The Goonies*! The slender, Luigi-like brother Robert John Davi from NYC matches with the mama's favored son, the Mario-like Joe Peter Pantoliano of Hoboken, NJ. "Mario" Pantoliano later starred as the "Judas" character in *The Matrix* (1999), while "Luigi" Davi stared in *Predator 2* (1990) and *Showgirls* (1995).

From the third Star Trek Anthology, *Deep Space Nine* (1993-1999), New Jersey and New York minted two iconic alien characters from fantasia: the slick yet loveable money-grubbing Ferengi whose religion is grounded to profit and abundance—Quark—played by Armin Shimerman from Lakewood, New Jersey, matches concordantly with the cold, scrupulous, law-and-order shape-shifting life-form from the Gamma Quadrant—Odo—played by René Murat Auberjonois from NYC. By serendipity, their respective alien species' values align with themes found on their respective state flags of their chosen "Earthly Emissaries." The values of "Quark" are honored and echoed on the flag of New Jersey via the goddess of Abundance and or Profit, the Goddess Ceres with a cornucopia in her left arm, while "Odo's" deep and resounding respect for law enforcement echoes of destiny with Lady Justice of New York, who holds the sword of righteousness in her right hand.

Here is a quick list of actors who match up, as time is money and space is limited, so this is going to go quick. Eddie Murphy from Brooklyn, New York (born 1961) matches with Bill Bellamy from Newark, New Jersey (born 1965). Tom Cruise from Syracuse, New York (born in 1962) matches with James Gandolfini from Westwood, New Jersey (born 1961). Alpha dog "Iron Man" Robert Downey Jr. from NYC (born 1965) matches with underdog "Ant Man" Paul Rudd from Passaic, New Jersey (born 1969). Jon Cryer from NYC (born 1965) matches Willie Garson from Highland Park, New Jersey (born 1964). Both from 1965, Charlie Sheen from NYC pairs with Peter Greene from Montclair, New Jersey. Highbrow Ben Stiller from NYC (born 1965) is the funny man partner of low brow humorist Kevin Smith from Red Bank, New Jersey (born 1970). Adam Sandler from Brooklyn, New York (born 1966) is the match to Artie Lange from New Jersey (born 1967) from *Mad TV* (1995-2016). Adrien Brody from Queens, New York (born 1973) is a match with Zach Braff from South Orange, New Jersey (born 1975). Billy Crystal born on π Day 1948 in NYC, matches with Floyd Vivino from Paterson, NJ born 1951. Finally, Macaulay Culkin from NYC (born 1980) and Jason Biggs from Pompton Plains, New Jersey (born 1978), are two *youthers* flung into the mainstream with *Home Alone* (1990) and *American Pie* (1999).

Two godmothers of cinema are Lucille Ball from Jamestown, New York (born 1911) and Joan Bennett from Fort Lee, New Jersey (born 1910). Joan Bennet's star has begun to fade from memory, as will happen with the superstars of today. Joan Bennet starred in *Woman in the Window* (1944), *Suspiria* (1977), and before her star would shine its last twinkle in 1990, she starred in *Guiding Light* in 1982, a long running TV series that lasted from (1952-2009). On the other hand, Lucille Ball's star has transformed into a long-lasting magnetar due to her iconic role in *I Love Lucy* (1951-1957). Generations yet to be born will still be drawn to her light of humor and grace. Lucille Ball's star went supernova in 1989, one year before her companion star from Fort Lee, New Jersey, turned into a white dwarf. When a star ends its life in a nova explosion, it can either become a humble white dwarf or something more powerful like a pulsar or magnetar. Due to Ball's smashing success, she is a magnetar.

Two women blessed with beauty and put to good use in Hollywood were Rita Hayworth from NYC (born 1918) and Vivian Blaine from Newark (born 1921). Vivian Blaine is known for her role in *Guys and Dolls* (1955), while Rita Hayworth is the queen of the black-and-white era of cinema. Two blond bombshells from 1937 are Jane Fonda from NYC and Loretta Swit from Passaic, New Jersey. Loretta Swit is best known for playing Major Margaret "Hot Lips" Houlihan on *M*A*S*H* (1972-1983). Jane Fonda started as a fashion model who also became a superstar of the movies. She has starred in *Barbarella* (1968), *The China Syndrome* (1979), and *9 to 5* (1980).

Two Hollywood queens royal par excellence are Sarandon and Streep. Susan Sarandon is from NYC (born 1946) and Meryl Streep from Summit, New Jersey (born 1949). Susan Sarandon has starred in a slew of hits beginning with *The Rocky Horror Picture Show* (1975). Meryl Streep is a star for her generation who has dished out the hits in Hollywood with movies like *Kramer vs. Kramer* (1979), *Death Becomes Her* (1992), and *The Devil Wears Prada* (2006). And they are still shining their golden light in their 70s. When these stars get together, they tap into the deepest wells of emotion and reality. They are virtual members of the all-American family.

Kerry Washington and Zoe Saldana make a deuce, Washington from NYC (born 1977) has starred in *The Last King of Scotland* (2006) and *Django Unchained* (2012). Zoe Saldana from Passaic, New Jersey (born 1978) has starred in *Guardians of the Galaxy* (2014), *Avatar* (2009), and *Avengers: Infinity War* (2018). Claire and Cypress are a magical pair. Claire Danes from NYC (born 1979) became a star on teen dramas and a golden ticket maker in Hollywood. Tawny Cypress from Point Pleasant, New Jersey (born 1976), starred in the TV series *Heroes* (2006-2010).

Sarah Michelle Gellar and Ali Larter make a perfect pair of blondes. Sarah Michelle Gellar from Long Island, New York (born 1977) has starred in *Swans Crossing* (1992) and the *Scooby-Doo* movies (2002-2004). Ali Larter from Cherry Hill, New Jersey (born 1976), has starred in *Varsity Blues* (1999) and *House on Haunted Hill* (1999).

Loken and Laura are another sweet pair. Kristanna Loken from Ghent, New York, has starred in *Terminator 3: Rise of the Machines* (2003). Laura Prepon from Watchung, New Jersey, was the bombshell redhead on *That '70s Show* (1998-2006). And speaking of *That '70s Show*, Danny Masterson from Long Island, New York (born 1976) who played the counterculture 1970s stoner perfectly matches Jason Mewes from Highlands, New Jersey (born 1974). Jason was the vocal and amusing sidekick in *Clerks* (1994) and *Jay and Silent Bob Strike Back* (2001), who played to perfection the counterculture stoner of the 1990s.

From 1982 two sparkly superstars are Anne Hathaway from NYC and Kirsten Dunst from Point Pleasant, New Jersey. Two stars of the millennial sort are Scarlett Johansson and Emma Bell. Emma Bell from Weehawken, New Jersey (born 1986), has starred in *Frozen* (2010), *Breaking Wind* (2012), and *Final Destination 5* (2011). Johansson from NYC has starred in *Black Widow* (2021) of Marvel Comic fame.

Two core Gen X TV personalities who are hosts with the mostest, are Alfonso Ribeiro and Kelly Ripa. They have crossed the line as TV stars and TV show hosts. Alfonso Ribeiro from NYC (born 1971) starred in *The Fresh Prince of Bel-Air* (1990-1996) and became a host of *America's Funniest Home Videos*, the original YouTube before YouTube, which was on the Boob-Tube. Kelly Ripa from Berlin, New Jersey (born 1970), had her star first lit on *All My Children* (starting 1990) and *Marvin's Room* (1996). But in 2001, Ripa became a core TV talk show host, starting with *"Live with Regis and Kelly."*

Whoopi and Wendy are the talkers of the town. If you appear on their radar, you are sure to get a boost. Whoopi Goldberg from NYC is a key star on the daytime talk show *The View* (starting 2007). As her stage name indicates, nearly everything she touches turns to gold. She has starred in blockbusters like *Sister Act* (1992), *Ghost* (1990), and *The Color Purple* (1985). She was also a queen of stand-up comedy back in the 1980s. Wendy Williams from Asbury Park, New Jersey is another TV talk queen. Before her daytime show she was a shock jockette and like Whoopi has done a comedy show. Somebody get these girls together now for a smart and wonderful comedy!

Kristen and Kate are a pair of joking queens with flair for the dramatic. Kristen Wiig from Canandaigua, New York (born 1973), pairs up with Kate Micucci from New Jersey (born 1980). These women can do comedy and drama or dramedy, whatever is needed. Kate Micucci got a big lift from *The Big Bang Theory Show* (2007-2019), while Wiig was launched by *SNL* in the mighty 20-ohs, in 2005.

The little guy typically gets the short end of the stick with life, women, respect, career, and is perpetually fowled and subject to harassment for a physical trait that he has no control over, like skin color and race. However, Mickey Rooney and Danny DeVito are exceptions to the rule. Mickey Rooney from Brooklyn, New York, was a national treasure for much of his life. Likewise, Danny DeVito from Neptune, New Jersey, is another treasure, and we are blessed to be alive while he is here with us.

Two guys who echoed the anthems of Generation X are Christian Slater and John DiMaggio. Slater born in NYC (1969) was a teen heart throb and loaded up all over movieland. John DiMaggio from North Plainfield, New Jersey (born 1968), was a rep for AI in *Futurama* (since 1999) as the robot with attitude "Bender."

NEW YORK & NEW JERSEY

The American pop star became a thing whence radio was invented. At the moment two reigning royals of the American popper-verse are Lady Gaga from NYC (born 1986) and Kevin Jonas from Teaneck, New Jersey (born 1987). No descriptor is needed, as their fame continues to sparkle and enchant the masses.

Heavy rocks from KISS and Danzig unite via Paul Stanley and Glenn Danzig. Paul Stanley from NYC (born 1952) is a co-founder and front man for the band KISS, while Glenn Danzig (1955) was the founder of the Misfits, Samhain, and Danzig. Their dark imagery with sound blends like hypnotic rocker trance. Two Gen X rappers to carry on with hip-hop are 50 Cent and Shaq. 50 Cent from NYC born (1975) rose up from the rough ganglands of New York to rise to the top of the game, while Shaquille O'Neal from Newark (born 1972) took the athletic route to rise through the NBA to later cut rap albums. Eventually both men would score hits in Hollywood. Two artists to leave a grand legacy to reach across America are Tupac Shakur from NYC (born 1971) and Lauren Hill from Newark (born 1975). Their songs would become generational anthems during the 1990s. Another pair of rapper royalty is Jay-Z from NYC with Ice-T from Newark. Both men were reared on the rough streets of the city yet were able to turn that energy into classic street rhymes and rhythms.

Singers minted in 1941 are Neil Diamond from NYC and Paul Simon from Newark. These singer-songwriters created a library of songs that generations down the road can perpetually enjoy. But the two master tracks of New Jersey and New York belong to the Boss and the "Piano Man." Billy Joel from NYC (born 1949) is the uptown artist. Bruce Springsteen from Long Branch, New Jersey, also born in 1949 is America's soulful rocker. Both men were born in the USA and are demigods in the music world. Their music is universally recognized across the generations and are anthems of America for the modern 50 starred flag of the U.S.A. Two hair metal rockers who defined a generation are Steven Tyler from NYC and Jon Bon Jovi from Perth Amboy, New Jersey. They both prove that age ain't nothing but a number with their ever-youthful energy.

Chart toppers for Generation X are Whitney Houston and Mariah Carey. Whitney Houston from Newark, New Jersey (born 1963), has hits all concerning love. Mariah Carey from Huntington, New York (born 1969), is another distinguished singer who was able to express the ultimate value of love with her songs. Two queens who were present for the birth of rap and hip-hop were Mary J. Blige and Queen Latifah. Mary J. Blige from NYC (born 1971) is known as the queen of hip-hop while Queen Latifah from Newark (born 1970) is the queen of rap. Since the launch of their musical careers, they have crossed over into Hollywood land. Although they have crossed the 50-yard line, their stars shine brightly evermore with a soulful luminesce.

Barbra Streisand and Dionne Warwick. Streisand from NYC (born 1942) is a top charting singer and actress known to all generations, while Dionne Warwick from Orange, New Jersey (born 1940), is another top charter of the singing of song. It'd be nice if Barb and Dionne could come together for a classic duet.

Two men who have transcended time and as the front men of America are John Williams and Frankie Valli. From the extreme end from the Empire State, we have John Williams from NYC. His classical score has enchanted America as well as the world, most notably with scores with *Star Wars* (since 1977) and *Harry Potter* films (since 2001). Frankie Valli of the Garden State from Newark, New Jersey, has written more earthy songs that were synchronized to the new inclusive colors of America after 1960 of the 50-starred American flag. His hits include "Sherry," "Big Girls Don't Cry," "Oh What a Night," and a timeless ditty "Grease." As John Williams wrote high minded classical music that tapped the spirit of galactic wonders, Frankie Valli wrote timelessly familiar songs localized to youth and having fun, here now on Earth, with a loved one. Valli and Williams were two of the lucky few to write music to transcend generations.

Two late-night hosts who rule the late-night talk are Jimmy Fallon and Chelsea Handler. Jimmy Fallon from NYC (born 1974) is the host of *The Tonight Show Starring Jimmy Fallon* (since 2014) while Chelsea Handler from Livingston, New Jersey (born 1975), is the host of the late-night show *Chelsea Lately* on E! (2007-2014). When it comes to foodies Anthony Bourdain and Martha Stewart are legends in the kitchen. Anthony Bourdain from NYC was an experienced chef who later beefed up the love of food with the public. Martha Stewart from New Jersey became a leader in the happy house, Jersey girl style, by pushing easy bake recipes in the kitchen. A combo of talk and comedy are

Jon Stewart from NYC (born 1962) and Marc Maron from Jersey City (born 1963). Both men got their first legs with stand-up, have become talk show kings, and have dabbled in movies. Marc and Jon have successfully blended the lines between news, commentary, and comedy.

Powerful businessmen who captured a pharaoh's wealth to become superstars in the "Game of CEOs" are Donald Trump from NYC (born 1946) and Steve Forbes from Morristown, New Jersey (born 1947). Both men were privileged to high birth, with fathers who laid the foundation and bridge to the top tiers of high society. Unlike many rich and pampered children, both men were able to avoid the pitfalls of established money and maintain "a lion's share of a Lannister's wealth." Trump was able to use his influence to punch a hole in Hollywood and then into the Oval Office. Forbes attempted to punch a hole in politics, but he forgot the necessary step of putting himself in the media with the common folk as Trump did with his appearances in movies and TV. Basically, Forbes and Trump were born on *Park Place and Boardwalk* and were able to stay in the game and expand their respective financial monopolies. Nonetheless, being rich comes with its own set of burdens that most mortals cannot handle or understand and could easily lead to one's own self destruction, but both of these men have handled this burden/blessing rather well.

Two directors who bombed the public with multiple blockbusters are Martin Scorsese and Brian De Palma. Martin Scorsese from Queens, New York (born 1942), puts the arts and sciences in cinema. His movies include *Taxi Driver* (1976), *Raging Bull* (1980), *The Last Temptation of Christ* (1988), *Casino* (1995), *Gangs of New York* (2002), and *The Wolf of Wall Street* (2013). De Palma, born Newark on September 11, 1940, directed the original *Carrie* (1976), *Scarface* (1983), and *Mission Impossible* (1996).

Two great writers who earned universal greatness behind their names for a time are Woody Allen from NYC (born 1935) and Judy Blume from Elizabeth, New Jersey (born 1938). Woody Allen is a legend for this unique look at the world from that epic New Yorker perspective. Blume is a children and young adult writer who has become a touchstone for kids in American classrooms. Both writers are followed with a bit of controversy that has put off many of their work.

Bill Maher and Joe Piscopo are two comedians who won in the gambit of Hollywood, later to be key talking heads of America. Bill Maher from NYC (born 1956) is currently an alpha dog talking head on the topic of politically touchy and taboo talk. Joe Piscopo is another comedian-actor turned talker from Passaic, New Jersey (born 1951), is on the air with *Piscopo in the Morning*, on talk radio in NYC: *AM 970 The Answer*.

Two men who walked the walk and talked the talk are the original shock jock king, Howard Stern from NYC, and Joe Rogan, the podcast king from Newark. Stern and Rogan are two voices from New York and New Jersey that have withstood outrage of the moral mob and powerful corporations. They were able to wing it as American exemplars without bending the knee, doing it their way, on their terms, with backbones made of steel. Stern paddled against the mainstream when it had a conservative current in the 1980s and 1990s, while Rogan held the line when the media took on a powerful liberal lean in the 20-teens.

Before the decade is out an illusionist team up of David Blaine and David Copperfield is hereby ordered. David Copperfield from Metuchen, New Jersey, put a spell on the public with his sleight-of-hand mastery. David Blaine from NYC is the secondary heir to these masterful manipulations of attention and space. If these two ever worked together, David and David could easily make a million dollars magically disappear and reappear in their banks.

It must be noted that Christopher Reeve is a superstar to both New York and New Jersey. Christopher Reeve was the first full-color American comic book hero to establish the genre as more than just a kid's story in 1978. Reeve was born in NYC in 1952, but after his parents divorced, he grew up in Princeton, New Jersey. Also note Superman lent out his spare capes on permanent loan to Liberty and Justice, on the New York state flag.

Another paramount figure who casts a sparkling shadow to be recognized in science classes ad infinitum is J. Robert Oppenheimer, "The Father of the Atomic Bomb," who was the director of the Manhattan Project. His spirit by the law of synchronicity entangles NJ and NY via a spooky and groovy kind of historical fusion, since he popped into existence in NYC in 1904 and then tapped out in Princeton, New Jersey in 1967. Within that smallest time frame relative to civilizations, Oppenheimer was able to make a mark on world history, like a magical quantum Pop-Tart—(Jersey humor).

Talk of nuclear weapons requires a bit of levity, and Pop-Tarts were created in 1964, originally called "Country Squares" and in 1967 frosting was added. A generation later, after the attacks of 9/11, the U.S. military "bombed" Afghanistan with 2.4 million Pop-Tarts. As for Oppenheimer, he may or may not have eaten a Pop-Tart, and if he did, it is likely it did not have any frosting, since this sweet aspect was added the same year he died.

The ultimate aldermen of American comedy that stem from the Empire and Garden State are George Carlin (born 1937) and Flip Wilson (born 1933). Flip Wilson Jr. from Jersey City became "TV's first Black superstar" by being a master of storytelling comedy—kind of a lost art these days. Both men had a stint in the USAF before their transition to stand up. Flip Wilson was on permanent call on comedy as an all-star who was able to star on *Charlie & Co.* (1985-1986) , *Living Single* (1993-1998), and *The Drew Carey Show* (1995-2004). But George Carlin was in a league of his own. His thought-provoking, linguistically witty style darkened as he aged, as he dished his over-the-top analysis about stupid people and stupid situations. In the end, his routine evolved into a mind-expanding metaphor as the penultimate New Yorker middle finger to the system, whose middle finger continues to inspire and provoke a riotous bounty of laughter long after his death. But if you look closely at Carlin's middle-finger philosophies, there is always an aura of love hidden underneath. As Flip Wilson was the king of the corny from the Garden State, George Carlin gave us the most Excelsior single finger salute of the Empire State.

Two men who are aligned in a trifecta of concord are Michael Jordan and Dennis Rodman. They typify the stereotypes of their birth states and extremes of culture. Jordan's style is sharp, with a suit and tie sparkle of those on the square and fair. Rodman on the other hand is iconic of the counterculture movement who is covered in tattoos, body piercings, and has at one time or another adopted colorful hair styles of fun and fabulous, long before it became commonplace.

Michael Jordan was born in Brooklyn, New York, on February 17, 1963, while Rodman was born in Trenton, New Jersey, on May 13, 1961. Like the old drawing simple card game of War another flag match happens whence they moved away from their birth states. Michael Jordan moved to North Carolina where he grew up, while Dennis Rodman moved to Texas. Note, Texas and North Carolina are fraternal flag partners, as can be seen on the cover. And their stories are covered in the next book!

The final triple crown of synchronicity was made evident from 1995 to 1998, when "The Worm" and "Air Jordan" were united under the flag of the ox, when they helped the Chicago Bulls win three NBA championships in 1996, 1997, and 1998. Coincidentally, the coach who led them during the 1990s played on teams that match their birth states. Chicago Bulls coach Phil Jackson only played for two teams in the NBA, the New York Knicks from 1967 to 1978 and the Nets, when they were in New Jersey, from 1978 to 1980.

But Jordan and Rodman enjoyed the fruits of the labor and expressed their American Dreams in two drastic styles. Every American follows their style at some level, being like The Worm or like Mike, or somewhere in between. Even in 1776, the dress of most aboriginals was akin to the style of The Worm, while much of colonial society was more like Mike.

Jordan is the shining clean-cut knight in a conservative suit, while Rodman has the colorful style of a court jester. Both men are American legends who are exemplars of the classy side of New York and the sassy side of New Jersey. But note, things are always like yin and yang, since there is plenty, with mucho sass with a capital "F" for Funky, in New York on Team Rodman, as there are loads of classy people, with a capital "S" for Sharp, on Team Jordan from New Jersey. Jordan and Rodman represent the polar ends of American culture from the A to the Z of America. They are the epitome of the *Big Apple* of New York and *Zesty Tomato* of New Jersey.

So, where do you fit on the spectrum between Sir Rodman and Sir Jordan?

sixteen

VIRGINIA & MASSACHUSETTS

The Alpha and Omega at the Genesis of America

VIRGINIA

In heraldic terms, the side-by-side comparison is akin to a counterchange. The white field with a blue center of Massachusetts is a counter to the blue field and white center of Virginia.

Coincidentally, ancient weapons can be found on both states' flags. Virginia's spear is a tool known to all the tribes of the Old and New Worlds, which is in stone age concord with the bow and arrow of Massachusetts. Also, swords appear on both flags but in different fashions. Virginia's sword is sheathed while being held by the Goddess Virtus dressed in sky blue. The sword of Massachusetts is the cresting element on the coat of arms, being held by a colonist's hand. Coincidentally, there are two contrasting personalities found on both flags. Virginia has a man and women, while Massachusetts has a Native and Newcomer, albeit an eighth of a colonist. The arm holding the sword is derived from the seal of the first patriot congress at Massachusetts, which formed in 1774. The royal governor Thomas Gage dissolved the provincial assembly to punish the unruly colonists. Afterwards a "patriot" congress formed without Royal consent in an act of insubordination.

The patriot congress of Massachusetts employed Paul Revere to design a seal

MASSACHUSETTS

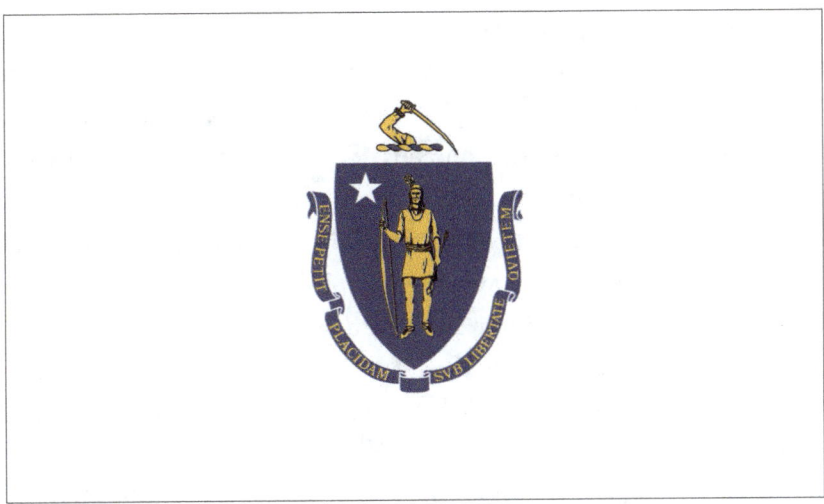

for the legislative body, which featured a man in colonial dress holding a sword in his right hand and the "Magna Carta" on a scroll in his left. Either on purpose or by accident, this design reflected the expression "the sword versus the pen." The first patriot seal of Massachusetts stood in stark contrast to the royal seal that featured an Indian standing in front of two smaller pine trees while holding a bow and arrow. The first patriot/rebel congress of Massachusetts dissolved when the state constitution went into effect in 1780. Consequently, a new seal was requested, and the modern flag is based upon this hybrid version that harkens back to the Native American from the old colonial seal, and it also uses the right arm of a patriot holding the sword from Paul Revere's design. However, gone is the Magna Charta and two pine trees.

Unfortunately, the bit about the Magna Carta was thrown into the trash bin of history. Too bad, since the Magna Carta was seen as the first step toward democratic and representative government in the English-speaking world. It was the first baby step in the formation of Congress, or, as the British call it, Parliament. There are several major technical differences between Parliament and Congress, but it is nearly an analogous law-making body. The Magna Carta limited the power of the king and spelled out English liberties for the aristocracy. The founding fathers of the U.S. were well aware of this document and often cited it in their fight for liberty, as demonstrated when Massachusetts incorporated it into the first congressional seal.

For Virginia, Virtus is stepping on a tyrant dressed in purple. The color purple is shown on purpose, Tyrian purple—the rarest of dyes. Its high cost was due to the laborious extraction from thousands of predatory sea snails. Consequently, only the very wealthy could afford such luxurious fabrics, making it a status symbol of power and wealth. Over the years the seal has changed slightly, but it consistently shows a male tyrant being trampled on by a woman. The tyrant's chains are broken, and a whip is in his right hand.

In older versions of the seal for Virginia, Virtus is sometimes wearing armor, of the medieval sort. Likewise in older versions of Massachusetts's seal, the arm holding the sword is sometimes depicted in armor.

The final element of concord between Massachusetts and Virginia is the pairing of the white star of Massachusetts with the wreath of Virginia. Those are not flowers in the wreath of Virginia; her state flower is the dogwood. Instead, the wreath is composed of the Virginia creeper, which is an indigenous ivy plant of North America. The leaf pattern of the Virginia creeper is five pointed, like the most popular design for stars found on the state and national flags. In the fall, this Virginian ivy turns a bright red. The Virginia creeper is often confused as being poison ivy, but poison ivy is three leafed. But like poison ivy, there are a minority of people who are allergic to the creeping ivy of Virginia, *Parthenocissus quinquefolia*.

Geography

Father of the North, Massachusetts, is shaped like a protruding phallus into the Atlantic, while Virginia's Chesapeake Bay is invaginated with respect to the open sea, which is where the first colony of the English people successfully germinated.

The womb of Virginia is located within the inter-continental belt where Africa, Asia, and Europe all see eye to eye. This geographic alignment echoes the wholeness of the United States, as a future home to the tribes of Europe, Asia, and Africa. It is within this region that the climate, Sun, and constellations of the New World are analogous to the cosmic rhythm of the stars, planets, and weather of the Old World. While Massachusetts lies wholly within the *American Sphere of Continental Concord*, where the American continents are due north and south of each other. Note, the western tip of Virginia is not due north of South America, whereby Virginia's Lee County is due north of Antarctica, instead of the South American Mainland as is most of the U.S.

Coincidentally, both states had major cesarean sections, where another state budded off to make a new state due to the political friction over slavery. The separation of Maine from Father Massachusetts took place during the Missouri Compromise of 1820, so as to keep the balance between slave and free-soil states. But when West Virginia was violently torn from Mother Virginia, it occurred during the Civil War.

Sadly, when West Virginia was forcibly amputated from Virginia, Virginia would no longer snuggle the back side of Pennsylvania, nor would she reach into the north across the Mason-Dixon line. When Maine was removed from Massachusetts; Massachusetts would lose the secret kissing corners with Canada and would no longer touch the international "magical four seasons circle" of 45° north.

Both states are alpha dogs of their regions, surrounded by an entourage of six. For Massachusetts the entourage is composed of New Hampshire, Rhode Island, Vermont, Connecticut, New York, and Maine. For Virginia, her posse is composed of Kentucky, North Carolina, Maryland, Tennessee, DC, and West Virginia. They also have one major "frenemy" in the group who likes to compete for leadership. For the Massachusetts posse, New York is the competitive Kelly, and for the Virginia entourage, DC is the black sheep that sometimes shows up, but more often than not, flakes out or takes a dump on the southern gang.

Virginia and Massachusetts also have detached parts. The counties of Accomack and Northampton of Virginia on the Delmarva Peninsula pair with the isles of Nantucket and Martha's Vineyard. Both states have secret panic belly buttons that can get them excited or put them in sleep mode. Massachusetts has an outie belly button, the "Southwick jog," that juts into Connecticut, while Virginia has the innie belly button, the "White Mountain skip," with Tennessee. Lastly, Virginia and Massachusetts are, pedantically speaking, not states. They are commonwealths.

History

Of the founding fathers, the ultimate match is George Washington and Benjamin Franklin. These two men are the alpha and omega of America's founding fathers. Washington is the alpha who took on the burdens of the warrior to strike at the heart of the self-righteous elitist empire with a sword, while Franklin is the omega who fought with the power of the pen to unshackle the colonies from tyranny. They are immortalized on American currency with the lowest and highest forms of common legal tender. The $1 bill contains the portrait of George Washington, while the $100 bill has the likeness of Benjamin Franklin.

Benjamin Franklin was born January 17, 1706, in Boston, Massachusetts, while George Washington was born on February 22, 1732, at Popes Creek, Virginia. Coincidentally, their rise to fame commenced within the King's Quaker Colony of Pennsylvania. It was here that Washington was at the tip of the spear that resulted in the final French and Indian War of 1754; likewise, Franklin would rise as a printer whilst living in Philadelphia.

Franklin became the voice of America, won through years of dedicated work in the press, when it literally required pressing. Before the *New York Times*, *Wall Street Journal*, and *USA Today*, there was Benjamin Franklin. Franklin sits at ground zero of the American matrix in media, philosophy, science, and poetry. Franklin distinguished himself from other colonial voices as a renaissance man, whose inquisitive nature expanded into the sciences. Franklin was not satisfied with the comfort that riches brought, but he was able to dedicate his life to further study the natural world. His iconic Dr. Emmett Brown moment that allowed his name to recall itself into the future took place in 1752. Unlike the fictional Dr. Brown, *Dr. Franklin* truly tapped the power of a lightning bolt, to the astonishment of the world. Consequently, Franklin was able to transcend time—not with a DeLorean but through the power of the written word.

Lightning is a deadly yet spectacular force of beauty that can easily remind the human ego of its meekness and small place within the scheme of grander things. It was June 1752 in Philadelphia, Pennsylvania, when Benjamin Franklin tested his theory that lightning and electricity were of the same nature. It was near Christ Church that Benjamin Franklin ran his famous kite experiment. He flew a kite into a storm with a metal key attached as a lighting lure. Before 1752, lightning was a random and mysterious phenomenon, ascribed to the understanding of the Gods and or God alone. But after 1752, mankind rose one step closer to understanding this wickedly spectacular process. Benjamin Franklin coined a slew of terms that are still in use today like battery, charge, condenser, conductor, plus, minus, positively, negatively, and armature. Additionally in 1752, Betsy Ross was born, and the American/English-speaking calendar lost 11 days, whence the day after September 2, 1752, became September 14, 1752, adding fuel to the notion that time is simply a man-made construct.

Washington's rise unto the stage of history's fame also occurred in Pennsylvania, but at the opposite end, near Pittsburgh. It was here that Washington was able to make the cut into the highlights of history. His expedition in the spring of 1754 ignited the final episode of colonial wars between France and England. It is debated that Washington preemptively attacked a French force at the Battle of Jumonville Glen as the French were building at what was later destined to become Pittsburgh, called Fort Duquesne. The leader of the French party, Joseph Coulon de Jumonville was according to some reports gruesomely killed by the Native warrior known as the Half-King, who split open Jumonville's skull with a tomahawk and proceeded to wash his hand in Jumonville's brains. Apparently, the Half-King's rage was due to a story that a group of starving French soldiers had murdered and cannibalized his family when the Half-King was a youth.

After the French and Indian War, it was in Pennsylvania at Valley Forge that the Continental Army was forged into a force to be reckoned with. The army was upgraded from ragtag militia to a professional army, under the guidance of Friedrich Wilhelm Baron von Steuben. As the British Empire was able to recruit

German muscle with the Hessians, the patriots countered with skilled German gray matter via Baron von Steuben. Basically, the training at Valley Forge, Pennsylvania, was the original action hero montage. The action hero montage is when a movie shows a bunch of non-verbal cut scenes of how our hero or team of heroes is whipped into shape, as it is in every *Rocky* (1976) movie and films like *The Karate Kid* (1984).

Washington was the leader of America's Braun, while Franklin was the leader of America's brains. Washington put in the hard work of the sword to wrestle down the Empire, while Franklin was the chief diplomat who pencil pushed the French into the patriot's corner. Washington spent the majority of his presidency in Philadelphia, Pennsylvania, while Franklin rose to his heights of fame while living in Philadelphia, Pennsylvania. It was in the Keystone State that a man from Massachusetts and another man from Virginia would imprint their spirit and shape on the essential ideals of the American way.

No doubt, Franklin and Washington are two of the few founding fathers who would embrace the modern world. There was something deeply curious to both Washington and Franklin, as both were renaissance men. Surely, they would be amazed by the modern wonders and varied personalities that constitute the modern identity of America. Modern history has transformed them into supernatural beings, but be assured, they were flesh and blood whose countless mistakes are untold.

Both men would suffer as fathers somewhat. Benjamin Franklin would lose all bonds of affection with his firstborn son, who sided with the Loyalists. Likewise, Washington would never know the invisible and intimate joy of fathering children of his own flesh and blood.

True to the title of an alpha and omega relationship, the beginning and the ending of the American Revolution is linked to both states. The draw of first blood of the American Revolution began at Lexington and Concord, Massachusetts. It was during the month of Aries under the proverbial God of War, on April 19, 1775, that fighting between the colonies and Empire began in earnest. Tensions reached a boiling point around Boston as the Empire sought to punish Massachusetts for its unruly behavior. Although there were more qualified men with more experience, the politically correct thing was to hire a Virginian to bolster support in the South. Nearly three months after the first shots took place at Lexington and Concord, Washington took command of the Continental Army on July 3, 1775.

The British occupied Boston and were surrounded, as the patriot army laid siege to the royal army. The armies were at a stalemate, and it wasn't until the capture of Dorchester Heights that the rebels gained the upper hand and unleashed the power of the rebellion upon the Imperial forces. The British evacuated on St. Patrick's Day, March 17, 1776. This was the first taste of victory as the British were expelled from Boston. They fled to Halifax, Nova Scotia and to England. Washington's middle years were rough, as the bulk of fighting with the Continental Army took place in the middle colonies. It was in New York where the Empire struck back the hardest and nearly captured the rebel commander on several occasions. Finally, the Battle of Yorktown in Virginia in 1781 was the ultimate victory of the rebel alliance that secured independence.

Using a *Star Wars* analogy, the 1776 victory at Boston was like the explosion of the first and original Death Star, when the British were kicked out of Boston. The middle chapter in the middle colonies was like *The Empire Strikes Back* that took place in NYC, where Imperial forces did indeed strike back, and is best remembered by the Hoth-like environment of Valley Forge. Lastly the *Return of the Jedi* element is sealed when Admiral Akbar, played by Admiral Francois Joseph Paul de Grasse, was able to pin down the Imperial Navy while "Han Solo," i.e., Washington's army, took down the Imperial Commander Cornwallis at Yorktown. The fictional Battle of Endor, like the real-life Battle at Yorktown of 1781, spelled ultimate doom for Imperial forces and two years later, peace was granted in 1783. Providentially fifty years later, on another proverbial year of jubilee, slavery ended within the U.K. in 1833, whence the British *let go & let God*, of matters concerning the 13 colonies.

As for this chapter, it's important to note that the American Revolution began in Boston, Massachusetts on April 19, 1775—the "alpha moment." The final, conclusive battle took place at Yorktown, Virginia on October 19, 1781—the "omega moment." It was a perfect revolution that ended in the autumn when leaves surrendered their leaves in the month dedicated to Balance of Libra. Also, note the long and winding path of peace took a while to settle. The Treaty of Paris between the U.S. and U.K. was drafted on November 30, 1782, signed on September 3, 1783, and ratified on January 14, 1784.

Two leaders who primed the colonies for the revolutions were Ruggles and Randolph. Timothy Ruggles from Massachusetts was the chairman for the Stamp Act Congress that met in New York City at Federal Hall from October 7 to October 25, in 1765. This Congress was the embryonic formation of the U.S. government. It issued the first of pre-constitutional ancestral documents that eventually led to the formation of the U.S. government. The first of rebellious documents was the Declaration of Rights, issued on October 19, 1765. The Stamp Act Congress of 1765 issued 13 points for the king and Parliament to recognize colonial rights. Some of these rights were formally established with the U.S. Constitution of 1787. Points included from the Declaration of Rights were a right for "trial by jury" and "no taxation without representation."

The next 12 years resulted in some accommodation from Parliament, but it was a mixed bag of results that would properly simmer for a decade. After the Imperial government sought to punish Massachusetts after the Boston Tea Party of 1773, the repressive measures from the Crown resulted in the formation of the First Continental Congress, and this Congress was chaired by Peyton Randolph. This Congress met at Carpenter Hall Philadelphia from September 5 to October 26, 1774. It was here that the backbone (or notochord) of the American government started to form as more documents were issued in the name of the colonies. The Articles of Association, also called the Continental Association, was the primary document of power. It called for a trade boycott against British merchants. Likewise, the beginnings of a nervous system formed when the committees of correspondence formed in the colonies after 1774, as they sought to keep in touch with each other over these mounting tensions. Finally, the muscle began to form as the Articles of Association, which was an illegal union made up of committees who were granted the power to enforce the boycott.

Thus, the "essential simmering period" between 1765 and 1774 is gated by two insubordinate congresses, before the official outbreak of hostilities. At one end is the Stamp Act Congress, chaired by Timothy Ruggles of Massachusetts in October 1765, while at the "other bookend" is the First Continental Congress, chaired by Peyton Randolph of Virginia in October 1774. When the revolution broke out in April 1775, Randolph and Ruggles did not side with the rebel cause. Timothy Ruggles became a dedicated Loyalist, while Randolph would watch from the divine sidelines. The first president of the First Continental Congress was escorted to the pearly gates beyond when the Second Continental Congress was in session during the month of October in 1775.

It is likely that Peyton Randolph would have signed the Declaration of Independence. He was the highest-ranking political officer of the American Revolution when fighting broke out at Lexington and Concord in April 1775. Part of the reason Randolph was chosen as the face of insubordinate, on the cusp of revolution colonies is that he had previously petitioned the Crown over unfair taxes, nearly two decades before the Stamp Act Crisis of 1765. In 1748, Peyton Randolph was the attorney general of colonial Virginia. Basically, Randolph was the top Jedi Supreme lawyer of Virginia, who possessed a special kind of lightsaber (that all attorney generals possess) that could slice through and make sense of the nearly impenetrable mumbo jumbo bedrock of law. And like the fabled Jedi Masters from fantasia, it takes years and years of practice and proper dueling to get proficient at cutting through big business and government red tape to attain Jedi Supreme attorney general status. But back in the 1750s, when Royal Governor Dinwiddie enforced a tax fee on new land grants in the colony that was approved by the British Board of Trade, many in Virginia were outraged at this new tax. Consequently, Randolph was chosen to sail to London in order to petition the king's Privy Council (which is the semi-equivalent to the modern-day executive cabinet) to reconsider the tax imposed by Dinwiddie. Randolph's mission failed; nonetheless, it was a pre-seasoning effort that breathed life into the idea of taxation without representation, at least in Virginia.

Although Timothy Ruggles was the presiding officer of the Stamp Act Congress of 1765, after the 1773 Boston Tea Party, Ruggles sided with the Loyalists. As it was for many brothers in Kentucky and Maryland during the U.S. Civil

War, it truly was a divided house for the Ruggles family. His younger brother, Benjamin Ruggles, was a steadfast patriot, and their last encounter on a bridge is iconic of something out of a dream, movie, or epic saga. The two brothers would meet one last time as a family united in the summer of 1774.

In the aftermath of escalated tensions of the Boston lockdown, the older brother was chosen to serve on the *loyalist* Governor's Council. One can imagine the gravity of their last encounter, where the weight of an uncertain future would make wives widows, brutally and permanently injure men, and seed a barrier between families. Just after the ultimate tea party of tea parties of 1773 and before a shot was heard around the world in 1775, the former chair of the Stamp Act Congress, Timothy, said to his brother upon a bridge, "I shall come back at the head of 500 soldiers." Benjamin retorted, "If you cross this bridge today, you will never cross it again alive." On that assuming hot and muggy summer day in the August of 1774, upon the gathering of war clouds, Timothy Ruggles crossed the proverbial *Rubicon of American Rivers* and never looked back. Nearly nine months later, shots were heard around the earth at Lexington and Concord. The older brother, General Ruggles, became one of many founders of a northern dominion *from sea to sea*, while the younger, Captain Ruggles, became *one out of many* founders of the United States of America.

Additionally, the children of Timothy Ruggles were divided. His sons followed his lead and settled in Nova Scotia after the war, while his daughters remained in the U.S. But his daughter, Bathsheba Ruggles Spooner, lived up to the famous Bathsheba of biblical lore when she became entangled in a murderous plot against her husband. Bathsheba was found guilty of plotting the murder of her husband and was executed by hanging on July 2, 1778, along with three other conspirators. Bathsheba petitioned the U.S. government to delay her execution because she was pregnant. Her petition was ignored, and on July 2, 1778, in Worcester, Massachusetts, she became the first woman executed by the U.S. government. The postmortem examination discovered that she had been telling the truth about her pregnancy; she was five months pregnant with a male child. Thus, one can consider, in some manner, this as the "first abortion" in the United States.

As for the biblical Bathsheba, according to the *Abrahamic Path*, she became the Queen of the Jews when King David stole her away from her husband Uriah the Hittite in an adulterous affair. After King David got the beautiful Bathsheba preggers, he sent her husband to the front lines in war to increase his likelihood of being killed, and it worked. However, their passion child born out of wedlock died. Nevertheless, King David was the second king of the United Kingdom of Israel and moved the capital from Hebron to Jerusalem a millennium before the birth of Christ. David later married Bathsheba, and a later son born under the sanctity of marriage became King Solomon. It was during the rule of the third king of Israel, King Solomon, that the First Temple of Jerusalem was built.

But for America's foundation, John Hancock and Richard Henry Lee make a perfect pair of Articles of Confederation presidents. Richard Henry Lee of Stratford Hall, Virginia, was selected as the fourth president of the Congress of the Confederation from November 30, 1784, to November 4, 1785. Lee was the first head of the American Republic to be fully recognized as an American leader by the U.K. after the Treaty of Paris was ratified on January 14, 1784. This concordantly matches with John Hancock of Massachusetts, since Hancock was the highest-ranking political officer of the United States for the entirety of 1776. John Hancock was the chair of Congress on July 4, 1776, making him the face of the revolution, which explains why his signature is so large—not because of an overinflated ego.

Fatefully, a month before the famous Declaration of Independence was issued, Richard Henry Lee is keenly remembered as the prime catalyst for this egregious and profound impulse. Richard Henry Lee became famous for "Lee's Resolution," issued on June 7, 1776, where he put forth the motion to declare independence from Great Britain. Lee was the first officer to put on paper what everyone was mulling over, committing his name, reputation, and life as a prime mover on the path to independence. Thus, Richard Henry Lee and John Hancock make a perfect pair of statesmen from Virginia and Massachusetts who sit at the zero hour, minute, and second for independence.

Samuel Adams and Patrick Henry were firebrand American patriots whose work for the revolution can never be understated. Adams, from Boston, was the lodestar of the American Republic, while Patrick Henry was one of the brightest stars of the southern constellation, shining from Studley, Virginia. Both men's words are relived, repeated, rewritten, and echoed in honor, school reports, and, every so often, in jest, Patrick Henry's most famous line being "Give me liberty or give me death!" One of Samuel Adams's many quotes was "Our contest is not only whether we ourselves shall be free, but whether there shall be left to mankind an asylum on earth for civil and religious liberty." Many leaders of the early continental congresses were wishy-washy about American independence, but Sam and Pat the Patriots were political rams who ran at full ramming speed from the time of the Stamp Act Crisis of 1765. Both men were iconic members of the Sons of Liberty, the secretive and elite patriot organization that was dedicated to the rebel cause, founded 1765. After the American Revolution, both men became governors of their respective states.

James Otis of Barnstable, Massachusetts, carries a weight with James Madison of Port Conway, Virginia. James Otis had a fundamental role in fanning the revolutionary flame in Massachusetts with the court battle *Paxton v. Gray* that was thrust into his lap. This court case challenged the idea of "writs of assistance" whereby the authorities had the right to enter any home with no advance notice, no probable cause, and no reason given. The legacy of this case would echo across time and movies, as authorities would need a search warrant to enter the private property of an individual. Of further and *most excellent* value, James Otis was one of the few founding fathers to promote rights for the all hues of humanity, whether Black or White. Otis asserted that Blacks also had inalienable rights when he wrote that slavery was an unnatural condition in 1764 "The colonists are by the law of nature freeborn, as indeed all men are, white or black." However, Otis had the most peculiar death; he was struck by lightning at the war's end in 1783.

Madison jumped on the patriot side early and was able to serve on the Committee of Safety, which was a patriot organization. Further, James Madison is considered the "Father of the Constitution." Madison was one of the prime movers who organized the Constitutional Convention in Philadelphia in 1787, and he was president during "America's Second War of Independence." Consequently, Madison was the prime author, or rather the primary programmer of the source code, for the U.S. government, *American Gov. Operating Systems 2.0,* the U.S. Constitution.

The essential iconic horsemen of the American Revolution are Paul Revere from Boston and Light Horse Henry Lee from Leesylvania, Virginia. Paul Revere's perpetually reimagined midnight horse ride to forewarn the patriots of the impending imperial march on Lexington and Concord marked the beginning of hostilities between the patriots and the British, since his ride took place on April 18, 1775. Whether or not he actually shouted on the hilltops that "The British are coming, the British are coming!" is not known for sure; nonetheless, this phrase has become attached to his legacy.

The southern horseman who has the historical right to trot alongside Paul Revere is Light Horse Henry Lee. Light Horse Henry Lee was the original top gun, cavalry officer of the American Revolution. Henry Lee started out as captain and slowly worked his way up the ranks with his wily lightning strikes and always-winning cavalry raids. As his reputation grew, his name struck fear into the hearts of British officers. His most daring Han Solo moment took place at the Spread Eagle Tavern near Valley Forge when the Queen's Rangers had him boxed in, as in any action hero shootout sequence from Hollywood. However, with Lee's careful plan of defense, Lee was able to thwart their attacks and escape. Much later, after Lee took down the British at Paulus Hook, New Jersey, he was awarded a gold medal from Congress. Lee also fought in the south, participated at the Guilford Courthouse Battle, and was present for the final victory at Yorktown. However, Lee never actually received that Congressional gold medal, as it got lost in the governmental bureaucratic sauce—along with a supposed lost ark, some say.

After the war, Light Horse Henry Lee became the ninth governor of Virginia and was an ardent Federalist, just like Paul Revere. However, when the War of 1812 rolled around, Henry Lee was attacked by a fierce anti-Federalist mob, since Federalists were "peaceniks" who did not want to pick a second fight with Mother. Lee was attempting to defend the editor of the Federalist newspaper, but he was severely beaten in the melee, such that he never recovered from his wounds. Even though Lee was a national hero, his reputation could not save him from an angry mob charged with political passions—as it is today, as it will be always. The injuries sustained permanently handicapped Lee for the rest of his life. As for Paul Revere, he became rich and successful, building off his silversmithing industry, while Lee "lost the farm" due to a lack of money smarts and his bad investments.

Both Lee and Revere would have grandchildren who fought in the Civil War. Also, Lee's most famous son became the legendary General Robert E. Lee. Although Lee and Revere made a united front between Virginia and Massachusetts in 1776, by 1861, their offspring would be fighting each other, on a much grander scale. Of Paul Revere's grandsons, Edward H. R. Revere died at the Battle of Antietam and Paul Joseph Revere died at the Battle of Gettysburg. However, all three of Henry Lee's grandsons from Robert E. Lee, who fought for the Confederacy, would live to the conclusion of this most costly of interstate wars.

It is the established narrative that Paul Revere had the opening words of the American Revolution with his semi-legendary phrase "The British are coming!" on April 18, 1775. Consequently, it can be said that Light Horse Henry Lee put a period on it. If Paul Revere waved the green flag of the American Revolution, then Henry Lee waved the checkered flag, as Lee was chosen to give George Washington's eulogy on December 26, 1799, at the German Lutheran Church in Philadelphia. Lee gave a rousing, soul-stirring speech, but his eulogy is best remembered for one particular line, now hallowed in the halls of history, that described Washington as "First in war, first in peace, first in the hearts of his countrymen …"

By mere happenstance and/or as written by Destiny, both Paul Revere and Light Horse Henry Lee would cross over in 1818, the year that the essential character of the American flag was established. The current algorithmic design of the national flag was established not by Betsy Ross nor by Francis Hopkinson. The lion's share of the architecture for the "flag formula" goes to a man from Connecticut—Captain Samuel Chester Reid (1783-1861). The one scant record of the adoption of the U.S. flag dates to June 14, 1777. But it was not precisely clear what the flag should look like in terms of the shape of the stars and specific lengths. When a new state joined the Union, a star and a stripe were added. This is why the Star-Spangled Banner, made famous during the War of 1812, has 15 stars and 15 stripes. Officially, Congress acknowledged only two major stripe patterns: 13 stripes and 15 stripes. There were unofficial, de facto flags with 14 and 16 stripes or more. By 1817, there were 20 states in the Union. Although these flags were not "official," they were de facto. People started to notice that the flag was getting unwieldy, and something had to be done. Captain Samuel C. Reid came up with the idea to keep the stripes constant and the stars fluid. This gives the flag an elegant dichotomy because the stripes permanently represent the past as "retro," while the stars represent the future-now as perpetually "modern." Congress adopted this framework as the Flag Act of 1818 on April 4, 1818; ergo, April 4 is U.S. Flag Coming of Age Day. Light Horse Henry Lee died the month preceding, on March 25, while Paul Revere passed a month succeeding, on May 10. Thus, by a certain kind of synchronicity, Lee and Revere are the penultimate horsemen of 1776 and legendary color guards of the American flag, at its genesis of being both a perpetually modern constellation and forevermore an ancient order of 13 stripes since 1818, as it was at the beginning.

George Mason and Elbridge Gerry are two men who had fundamental roles in shaping the course of political events, even unto this modern day. George Mason, from Fairfax County, Virginia, was the father of the U.S. Bill of Rights, which was derived from the Virginia Declaration of Rights from June 1776. Mason was a complex character who advocated for an end to the slave trade, believing that it was an unhealthy institution. Nonetheless, he was one of the most powerful slave owners in Virginia. But George Mason is regarded as the most vocal opponent to the modern U.S. government under the Constitution. Mason did not want the states to surrender their power to a federal government. Nonetheless, he was present for the Constitutional Convention and acted as a buffer to keep power within the states. Mason's fraternal flag partner, Elbridge Gerry of Marblehead, Massachusetts, is famous for the seedy political process of redistricting legislative districts, such that parties in power can remain in power by fixing the voting precincts. Elbridge Gerry, like George Mason, was opposed to the 1787 Constitution and both men refused to sign it since it lacked a bill of rights. After the Constitution was adopted, Elbridge was elected to Congress and was a strong advocate for the passage of the Bill of Rights, which is typically known as the numbered amendments. The first 10 Amendments/Bill of Rights to the Constitution were passed on September 25, 1789, and became the legal law of the land when they were ratified on December 15, 1791, during Washington's first term as president.

Two lesser-known Articles of Confederation presidents are Griffin and Gorham. Nathaniel Gorham from Charlestown, Massachusetts, was the sixth Confederation president, and his term officially lasted from June 6, 1786, to February 2, 1787. However, Gorham was the acting president of the Confederation for six months previous, acting in John Hancock's stead due to Hancock's ill health. When Gorham was "President of Confederation," he put out a pre-proposal to the King of Prussia to become the King of the United States—reason being, the outbreak of Shays's Rebellion (1786-1787) indicated to some, including Gorham, that a royal figurehead could be useful. Cyrus Griffin, from Farnham Parish, Virginia, was the last elected "President of the United States in Congress Assembled"—who had the right to use a presidential seal that was made up of 13 six-pointed Star of David–shaped stars in a constellation of the likeness found upon King Solomon's seal, as it is with the official obverse of the 13 five-pointed stars on the Great Seal of the United States, which would have been legal under U.S. Gov. version 1.0/The Articles of Confederation. His term began on January 22, 1788, and ended on November 2, 1788.

But a century before the Declaration of Independence, two different wars would rage across Virginia and Massachusetts in 1676. Bacon's Rebellion would etch its pre-centennial memory in Virginia, while King Philip's War would simultaneously leave a parallel pre-century's scar in Massachusetts before 1776.

Nathaniel Bacon was born in England, but upon his arrival in Virginia, tension between backwoods frontiersmen and colonial Governor Berkeley was steadily growing. Bacon and his allies were upset that Governor Berkeley was overtaxing the colonists and doing little to protect colonists against hostile Natives, along with several other issues. As a result of this tension, the first Civil

War within the American colonies took place. Nathaniel Bacon was branded a rebel by the colonial Governor in this summer of '76.

The Civil War within Virginia began in earnest in June 1676 when Governor Berkeley bowed to public pressure to make Bacon a general and authorized him to lead a military campaign against the hostile Indians so long as Bacon bent the knee to Governor Berkeley. However, Governor Berkeley flip-flopped and revoked the initial commission given to "General Bacon." Upset, Bacon returned with about 500 armed militants on June 23, 1676, and held the assembly of burgesses as virtual hostage. Bacon was then able to extract a commission. During his summer campaign against hostile and friendly Indians, General Bacon issues several declarations that would echo in the minds of the Virginians, unto the American Revolution. On July 30, 1676, Bacon issued his famous Declaration of the People. This declaration railed against excessive taxes, the corrupt law system, failure to protect colonists, the need for the people's consent, and corrupt business practices.

Thus, during summer 1676, Virginia was divided into factions loyal to the established government under Berkeley and those who sided with the rebel leader General Bacon. Governor Berkeley had finally had enough of Bacon's insubordination and sent a force to cook Bacon's army, but General Bacon was able to counter the governor and attacked the capital at Jamestown. General Bacon was able to burn the capital to a black crisp on September 19, 1676. However, the rebellion of 1676 ended when Bacon suddenly died on October 26, 1676 from dysentery. And, being without its charismatic leader, resistance began to melt. The Loyalist faction gained the upper hand in December 1676, and by January 1677, the remaining rebel holdouts were put in their place. Some were pardoned, while others were executed.

As Bacon's rebellion raged in 1676 Virginia, King Philip's War would rage in 1676 Massachusetts. Both wars hinged on the racial tensions between Natives and colonists. King Philip's War was in fact the deadliest war of the colonial period. As in Virginia, colonists were able to effectively utilize "praying Indians" against their "traditional path" brethren, with a policy of divide and conquer.

The end result of King Philip's War or King Metacomet's War, which lasted from 1675 to 1678, was that Native power was utterly smashed in New England. Many captured Indians were sold off as slaves to the Caribbean. Coincidentally, slavery was embraced in Virginia after Bacon's Rebellion. The reason being, slaves could not compete for land rights as did indentured servants, who were typically freed after seven years of service and wanted land for themselves. Bacon was able to tap the resentment of freed indentured servants who were forced to borderlands closer to tribal lands. Native Americans made a poor choice as a slave since they could easily run away and blend with their own or another tribe. African slaves could be more easily tracked down and would have a harder time being accepted into a Native American tribe.

Two centuries after the English Civil War of 1640s, Virginia and Massachusetts were the essential matriarchal states on opposing sides of the American Civil War of the 1860s. The main contest between the two armies took place between the capitals of their respective nations. In between Richmond, Virginia, and Washington, DC, the greatest loss of life would take place as the soul of America was tested to its core.

Both states would produce two top tier generals who would square off upon this deadly octagon in the east. Robert E. Lee from Stratford Hall, Virginia, became the paramount general for the army of Northern Virginia. Of the generals to lead the Army of Potomac, Joseph Hooker was the one from Massachusetts.

Of the many rounds fought between these two armies, the epic Battle of Chancellorsville was the perfect battle royal of Virginia vs. Massachusetts. For General Lee, it was his crowning achievement, and for Hooker it was the most humiliating defeat. Lee was able to defeat an army more than twice its own size with cunning and sheer wit. Lee made a daring gamble of splitting his smaller army against the Northern Leviathan, and it paid off, but at the cost of his most competent lieutenant, General Stonewall Jackson. Although Virginia gave Massachusetts a spanking at the Battle Chancellorsville, in the bigger picture, it would lead to Lee's ultimate defeat and paramount Battle at Gettysburg, Pennsylvania. Like the old Chinese proverb of good luck leading to bad luck, whence a blessing becomes a curse. The devastating defeat of the Union at Chancellorsville set into motion a series of events where General Lee was cursed with a deadly spell of overconfidence, which lead to his providential defeat on the 4th of July 1863. General Hooker bore the heaviest and most humiliating of burdens that would finally reveal the Achilles heel of General Lee, his propensity to take risky gambles, which allowed the Union army to strike back with extreme prejudice when this fratricidal conflict was taken to the realm of free soil.

Perhaps the most difficult type of medicine to receive is the taste of one's own medicine. Native Americans, Mexicans, and the British/Canadians were fated to feel the opposite end of the proud and powerful boot of the U.S. military, as they were forced to swallow several teaspoons of American medicine. But from 1861 to 1865, Americans were finally able to sample these bitters previously dispensed to their neighbors. Perhaps the flavor of one's own medicine is the harshest and hardest of recipes to swallow? Robert E. Lee of Virginia and Joseph Hooker of Massachusetts were forced to swallow lethal doses; it's a miracle that either man was able to carry on. But the soul-crushing sting of this medicine did not destroy them.

As time is the ultimate healer, with the passing of time, Massachusetts and Virginia were able overcome their differences and restore their most ancient and oldest of kinships between states. The memory of war provides a certain type of intangible medicine. If these memories, like a certain metaphysical soma, are passed on in the correct dosage and proper supervision, it can impart a certain health and wisdom for the soul of society. As with any kind of powerful medicine—like shame, pride, or guilt—there is potential for abuse, thus care must be advised, upon its prescription. In order to become a well-balanced adult, it is wholly appropriate that children experience and come to an understanding with the powerful medicines of shame, pride, loss, and guilt. But note, there are perennial voices that abuse or refuse to take these medications, which can lead to unhealthy and destabilized levels of mental health.

The dominant narrative of the Civil War pits Virginia as the ultimate champion of the South for states' rights, against Massachusetts as the leading voice of the North for the abolition of slavery. But in reality, communities all across America were sharply divided. Like the yin and yang symbol, things were not a cut and dry, us versus them situation. Many officers from the North chose to serve the South, as there were many Southerners that fought for the North.

A short list of Confederate generals from Massachusetts includes General Adams, Charles from Boston, who was the grandfather of Helen Keller; General Blanchard, Albert from Charlestown, who was a West Point classmate of Robert E. Lee, class of '29; General Perry, Edward from appropriately named Richmond, Massachusetts; General Ruggles, Daniel from Barre, Massachusetts who married a niece of George Mason, Richardetta B. Mason Hooe Ruggles, and their son, Mortimer, helped John Wilks Booth temporarily evade capture; General Sears, Claudius from Peru, Massachusetts, who was wounded twice in combat and captured during the Siege of Vicksburg; finally there is General Pike, Albert from Boston, Massachusetts, who held the notion that only Whites should be allowed to vote and later became associated with the Klan after the war.

As for Virginians who fought to preserve the Union, there is General Cooke, Phillip of Leesburg, Virginia. General Cooke was known as the father of the U.S. Cavalry since he wrote the manual. John Wynn Davidson from Fairfax County turned down a commission in the Confederate army to serve under Lincoln and after the war, was nicknamed "Black Jack." General Dyer, Alexander from Richmond, Virginia, was fatefully given command of the Springfield Armory in Springfield, Massachusetts, when the war broke out. The Chief of the Corps of Engineers for the Union army, General Newton, John was from Norfolk, Virginia.

General Prentiss Benjamin from Belleville, Virginia, was the first division to be slammed by the Confederate tsunami at the Battle of Shiloh, in Tennessee. General Prentiss led the defensive delaying action at the Hornet's Nest and was captured. The holding action of the "Hornet's Nest" gave General Grant precious time to regroup and fight another day at Shiloh. After returning to the Union line in a prisoner exchange, General Prentiss was able to win the Battle of Helena on July 4, 1863, which was synchronized to the Union victories at Gettysburg and Vicksburg. The 4th of July 1863 was a triple crown, providential patriotic victory for the Union in the north, south, and west.

General Denver from Winchester, Virginia, helped Grant during the Vicksburg campaign. James Denver was also the governor of Kansas Territory when it was trying to make up its mind to be free soil or a slave state. Additionally, the city of Denver, Colorado, gets its namesake from the Virginian, James Denver. This all works well in the grand scheme because Colorado has a Virginia tilt after all.

The most famous Southern-born pro-Union Virginian was General Winfield Scott from Dinwiddie County, Virginia. Born in America BC (before the genesis of the U.S. Constitution), in 1786 Winfield Scott carried a special kind of intangible "Autobot matrix of American wisdom" since he took part in the War of 1812, Mexican American War, and initial phases of the Civil War. His anaconda plan to strangle the ports of the South was carried out, and he lived to see the final conclusion of the Civil War. He died one year after hostilities ended in 1866, rested in peace knowing that the Union was preserved.

As for the most famous of cloak and dagger tales of spying upon the enemy, Virginia and Massachusetts produced two legendary heroines. Belle Boyd from Martinsburg, Virginia, matches keenly with Laura Secord from Great Barrington, Massachusetts. Belle Boyd is the most famous female spy of the American Civil War. She was of the lucky generation to witness her birthplace change places. Up until she was 19, she was from Virginia, but after age 19 she was from West Virginia. Nonetheless, Belle Boyd has become a romantic icon of cloak and dagger lore. Belle Boyd operated out of Front Royal, Virginia, and fed vital information to Stonewall Jackson after crossing posted lines with forged letters. She was later awarded the Southern Cross of Honor for her actions. Belle Boyd was a slippery spy who was arrested several times but was able to evade incarceration each time. As her name popped up on Union intelligence services, Allan Pinkerton assigned three men to work on her case. In 1864, with the gathering heat of being a spy, she fled to England. However, her ship was captured, but she was able to assert her romantic charms on a Union officer, Sam W. Harding, and they were later married in England. Shortly afterward, her Yankee husband died, and she took up acting in London. Eventually she returned to the U.S. after the war and married a British Army officer who fought for the Union. He died and she once again toured the country, on the old-school TED Talk circuit, giving lectures about her dramatic life as a spy, in the bed with all sides.

Laura Secord from "West Massachusetts" is a Canadian national heroine due to her actions during the War of 1812. Laura Secord was born in His Royal Majesty's Province of Massachusetts in 1775, but when she turned nine, she was born in the state commonwealth of Massachusetts. Although her father, Thomas Ingersoll, fought on the side of the patriots during the American Revolution, his fateful move to Ontario in 1795 would fatefully leave an epic mark on the collective memory of Canada. Laura Ingersoll married a Loyalist, James Secord, and she was able to gain information that Southern aggressors were marching to attack British positions. She delivered this critical information to Lieutenant James FitzGibbon, and it proved essential to repulse the American attack at the Battle of Beaver Dams on June 24, 1813, near modern day Thorold, Ontario. Since then, the legend of Laura Secord has been honored and grew to mythic status. As every good Southerner keen on the issue of states' rights knows about Belle Boyd, every proper Canadian knows the story of Laura Secord, the female Canadian patriot par excellence to none.

Of America's founding mothers, Martha Washington and Abigail Adams are the ultimate prime pair of first ladies. They make a perpetual cross-stitch of cultures between the North and the South.

George Washington's marriage to Martha Dandridge Custis was a power play for George Washington that brought wealth and influence for the young upstart. However, the couple did not bear children of their own. Martha Washington was the first first lady to stand in the background as her husband commanded the stage. No doubt in private, Martha was the ultimate sounding board who could test and challenge Washington's ideas, shaping the course of America in private. In contrast, Abigail Adams, from Weymouth, Massachusetts, was an outspoken wife of the north who was not shy about making her opinions known. She was the first first lady to take an active role in politics and was a leader ahead of her time, since she spoke out for women's rights and Black rights. It would only take the nation a little less than 150 years, a sesquicentennial, to catch up to her ideas. Some in the press referred to Abigail as "Mrs. President" at times.

In the end, Martha Washington and Abigail Adams represent the two roles of the first lady: a first lady can be a supportive, secretive second fiddle while her husband steals the limelight of the political stage, or she can play alongside her husband in a duet, asserting her voice in the public mind as a veritable BOGO deal, two executives for the price of one.

Before Texas became a state, Virginia and Massachusetts each seated a native son to become president of the Lone Star Republic. Anson Jones from Great Barrington, Massachusetts, came to Texas in 1833 and opened a medical practice. During the 1836 Texas Revolution, he became a judge advocate and surgeon in the Texas army. Later, Anson Jones's "term" in the Oval Office of the Republic of Texas lasted from December 9, 1844 until February 19, 1846. It was during his term that the Mexican War began. But the first president of the Texan Republic was a Virginian, Sam Houston from Rockbridge, Virginia.

Coincidentally, Virginia and Massachusetts would send leader-heads whence California became a rebellious pro-American republic, but the state order was reversed. A man from Massachusetts, William B. Ide of Rutland, was the first president of the California Republic. His title was Commander of the California Republic. However, William B. Ide was the only executive of the California Republic before it was annexed by the U.S. Nevertheless, the last American leader of a disputed California was from Virginia; Richard Barnes Mason of Lexington Plantation in Fairfax County was the sitting U.S. military governor of a disputed Alta California when peace was officially signed with Mexico on Groundhog Day, February 2, 1848. Richard B. Mason's term lasted from 1847, until 1849.

Of the highest magnitude of latter-day founding fathers, look no further than to W. E. B. Du Bois and Booker T. Washington. Du Bois and Booker represent the essential Black forefathers of America, who took on the burdens of a reformed Union during the harsh and trying era of the Reconstruction Era and beyond. Their voices captured the precursory themes of the Civil Rights Era when Martin Luther King was on the peaceable side, who contended with the militant axis led by Malcom X. In pop-culture terms, it was like the fictional rivalry between the two mutant leaders of the X-Men comic books. W. E. B Du

Bois and Malcom X were something like the militant Magneto, the Master of Magnetism. Thus, Booker T. Washington and Martin Luther King were akin to Professor Charles Xavier, the most talented psychic of "mutant-kind" bound to a wheelchair, who fought for equal rights along a peaceful path.

Neither Du Bois nor Booker was given a manual on "How to Assert the Rights of Previously Enslaved and Oppressed Minorities for Dummies." W. E. B. Du Bois from Great Barrington, Massachusetts (1868-1963) pushed hard for equal rights, such that no adjustment period was necessary for White society. On the other hand, Booker T. Washington from Hale's Ford, Virginia (1856-1915), was the compromise leader who advocated a slower approach to racial equity. In 1895, Booker was able to strike a deal with southern White leaders, such that Blacks would tolerate the current state of discrimination and segregation so long as they gained a basic education and justice within the legal system. Washington advocated for the long game and understood that racial equity would not be won in one year, or one generation, but several generations. Rather than demanding immediate respect from the White community, Booker Washington professed that Blacks could prove and earn it by merit. On the other hand, Du Bois wanted to accelerate the process immediately. As the left-wing factions of the 20th century evolved, Du Bois found welcome support within the communist party. At the nadir of the Cold War, Du Bois received the Lenin Peace Prize in 1960. The Lenin Peace Prize was an award given by the Soviet Union for notable communists and socialists. But for Booker T. Washington, his honor within the U.S. matches George Washington. As George was the first White Virginian on a U.S. stamp, Booker was the first Black Virginian on a U.S. stamp in 1940, matching the original value of George's 10¢ stamp of 1847. W.E.B. Du Bois was recognized much later by the U.S. Post Office with a 29¢ stamp in 1992.

Two voices that echo the passions of poetry from Mother Virginia and the pizzazz of prose from Father Massachusetts are Ruby Altizer Roberts from Alum Ridge, Virginia, and Jack Kerouac from Lowell, Massachusetts. Ruby Altizer Roberts became the first Poet Laureate of Virginia of the fairer sex. She got her big break when her poems appeared in *The New York Times* and *The Washington*

Post. During the 1950s she became the editor of The Lyric, the oldest literary magazine in North America devoted to formal poetry since 1921, established in Norfolk, Virginia. It was also during the 1950s that Jack Kerouac was able to burst on the scene with his second novel, *On the Road* (1957), which defined the first impulse of the counterculture spirit that would reach its apex in 1969, the year Kerouac died.

Two women to lead the charge for women's suffrage are Susan B. Anthony from Adams, Massachusetts (born 1820), and Orra Langhorne from Rockingham County, Virginia (born 1841). Susan B. Anthony is the Optimus Prime of women's suffrage who made gallant efforts to bring the vote for women. However, Ms. Anthony never lived to see women gain the vote—at least on the national level. She was able to enjoy some of the fruits of her labor when several states and territories provided full voting rights before her death in 1906: Wyoming, Idaho, Utah, and Colorado. In Virginia, Langhorne was among the state's leading advocates for women's suffrage and also pushed for racial reconciliation a century before it became fashionable.

As the oldest pair of states, Virginia and Massachusetts have the clearest and privileged memories of the 1600s. Further, their memories are in crystal clear English. This is where Virginia and Massachusetts sit in a class of their own above the other 11 original colonies. Virginia and Massachusetts are like the gifted pair of kids in the elementary classroom, as the advanced fourth graders who took seventh-grade middle school math, while the rest of the class is borrowing numbers and figuring on fractions.

They have the natural advantage of seniority. Massachusetts also loves to lord it over Virginia and the nation that he is home to the oldest university established in the English colonies. Harvard was established in 1636—initially as an institution to educate professional clergy of the Puritan church. Although the Puritanical Christian aspect of Harvard is set to the wayside, the Harvard degree maintains a modern latter-day secular puritanical authority. Harvard graduates are no longer schooled in the Puritan teachings, yet their power to preach has simply transformed into a modern form. Virginia's answer to Harvard is her own institution of the College of William and Mary. It is the second oldest university in the U.S., founded in the year 1693, which also makes it the oldest university in the South.

But one thing Virginia can lord over Harvard is that she is home to the oldest fraternity in the United States, Phi Beta Kappa, which was founded on December 5, 1776, at William and Mary. This organization is no longer a traditional fraternity but is more like a well-endowed honor roll for select universities. Instead of being hazed by big brothers & sisters, one is hazed by the university itself to maintain a high GPA. Usually, students who fly above a 3.8 GPA and excel in other social skills areas are invited. Thus, the elites of society who have either a Harvard degree or who were allowed to join Phi Beta Kappa are destined to become leaders in business and government. Today, Phi Beta Kappa is open to both men and women, and persons with these Greek Letters on their resume usually get a leg up during an interview and have access to a vast network of high octane, get the job done professionals, for assistance and or comradery.

Massachusetts may have the oldest university, but Virginia is the only state to bear witness to the life and tales spun by the quill of Shakespeare. Virginia, established in 1607, was the only colony online, concurrently when the living spirit of Shakespeare inked its enchanting words of romance and drama to paper. Shakespeare's final curtain call on the grand globe of civilization took place on April 23, 1616, whence this lauded playwright took a bow and exited stage left, unto the great and most mysterious of frontiers. Although Massachusetts can lord it over with Harvard, Virginia alone, is the singular witness of the English colonies who can rekindle the authentic and living flame of Shakespeare's sonnets.

Both of these collective memories harken back to King James I, mostly famous for his version of the Bible and the genesis of the United Kingdom, whence England became united with Scotland under one crown in 1603. The first born of American colonies under His Majesty King James I of the freshly minted U.K. was a daughter; 13 years before the *Mayflower* was conceived, Virginia was born May 13/14, 1607. This settlement was heralded by the arrival of a new species to the Americas. Unbeknownst to the passengers of the *Susan Constant*, *Discovery*, and *Godspeed*, they were laying the foundation to a nation—later to be born within one span of Neptune's rule, of its cyclical passage through the heavens. In 1607, King Neptune had finally permitted the English permanent passage to the Americas. Neptune's cycle is set to a rhythm of 165 years, and after 165 years of a wise rule, Neptune returned to his throne in the heavens in 1772, and the American Revolution would commence in 1775.

King James I's second born was a son, Massachusetts. But there is a quirky twist to the history of Massachusetts. Its oldest region was founded as the Colony of Plymouth in 1620. A decade later Massachusetts Colony was established in 1630. Sixty-one years later, the colonies united in 1691. Consequently, the heritage of Plymouth was subsumed by Massachusetts as his own and Massachusetts reclaimed his age to 1620. Also note, the Virginia Company's third 1612 charter included Bermuda. And it was the wreck of the *Sea Venture* in late July 1609 upon Bermuda that inspired Shakespeare to write *The Tempest*. Thus, *The Tempest* is a play about Virginia. So how do you like dem apples, Harvard? Virginia was a part of Shakespeare's soul, while Massachusetts and Harvard were somewhere between nothing and never, as far as William Shakespeare was concerned.

Also note, Virginia and Massachusetts were online during the 1650s, which was the decade when the British colonies did not have a monarch, but instead were a part of a republic—albeit a theocratic Puritan republic officially called a Commonwealth, with Oliver Cromwell as its chief executive, titled as the Lord Protector. This phase of American history is fundamentally ignored in classrooms and cinema as if the idea of discarding the monarchy was an American invention. The English Civil War of 1642 to 1651 was foundational to the political gestalt of the founding fathers, which no doubt added fuel to the revolutionary spirit of 1776. As modern America views the Civil War of 1861 with passionate attachment, it is a near certainty the founding fathers would have viewed the Civil War of 1642 in a similar manner.

Thus, the English Civil War of 1642 to 1651 is the mostly forgotten great-great-grandfather Civil War of the United States. And note, the two cornerstone colonies of the north and the south were online to bear witness, Massachusetts and Virginia. Since Massachusetts already had a Puritan tilt, it totally embraced the Roundhead/Parliament, anti-monarchy side, while Virginia favored the Cavalier/royalist, pro-monarchy side. Virginia had stronger roots to the Anglican/English Church and in an act of insubordination, proclaimed the son of the executed monarch as king. Cromwell's government consequently punished Virginia with a naval blockade to bring "rebel Virginia" to heel. Thus, a century before the birth of Betsy Ross, on March 12, 1652, a 45-year-old Virginia was forced to surrendered to a "federal/republican style of government" for the first time.

The citizens of the British Empire suffered a decade from a puritanically woke republic that canceled, imprisoned, and executed problematic persons of the New World Puritan Order. It quietly quitted when the monarchy was restored in 1660 with King Charles II, who took the idea of chillax to the next level—the likes of which would even make William Clinton blush with embarrassment, as in the wise words of Sir Books the Mel, "It's good to be the king!"

The founding fathers were intimately aware of the divisive political themes that arose from the English Civil War. It can be summed up in a postmodern extract of Shakespearean paraphrasing as, "To kill the king ... or not to kill the king ... that is the lauded question for history to judge us by!" Also note, Shakespeare died in the poetically mirrored year of 1616, along with his quill-master wingman of the ages, Cervantes. Shakespeare and Cervantes are hereby partnered as supreme guardians of the quill. Cervantes (1547-1616) is the paramount *prince of prose*, while Shakespeare (1564-1616) is the penultimate *page of poetry*. For clarification, poetry is the creative-artful form of writing, while prose is the logos-functional form of writing. This book is mostly prose, with hints of poetry sprinkled throughout.

Note, the original congressional body that ruled over the British colonies, in fact, voted to "kill the king" a century before the 13 colonies forcibly divorced themselves by the cold, calculating, cruel, and yet inspiring, unwritten, and understood rules of war. On January 30, 1649, King Charles I was beheaded by the vote of the ancient colonial order of congress, better known as Parliament. Thus, the government of the collective English-speaking ego had its first go at a republican form of government, without a monarch, to the astonishment of

Europe! But this experimental form of government only lasted a decade, the 1650s. Yet, a generation later after the restoration of the monarchy, the power of the rebooted royal establishment was further reduced when the king was essentially fired and replaced by a more "socially suitable" and less "problematic" candidate. King James II was the royal giant who was "impeached," mostly due to his religious persuasion of being Catholic. The "appropriate" replacement was the duel Protestant monarchs of William & Mary, where Virginia's oldest university gets its namesake. Oddly they were first cousins, as King Charles I was their common grandfather.

A perfect duo that matches the theme of Father Massachusetts and Mother Virginia singing in harmony can be found with Edgar Allan Poe and Susan Archer Weiss. Edgar Allan Poe (1809-1849) is a double superstar who unites the spirit of Virginia with Massachusetts, as he was born in Boston, Massachusetts, and moved to Richmond, Virginia, before he was two. Poe attended the University of Virginia but dropped out due to lack of money. Likewise, he was drummed out of West Point, ironically it was this crushing failure that fatefully set him on his majestic destiny. Finally, his poem "The Raven", first written in 1845, took the nation by storm and secured his front row seat in the collective memory of America. A few rows back, Susan Archer Weiss is a fitting match for the "Bostonian," but she was from Hanover County, Virginia (1822-1917). Weiss was the heroine born of tragedy. She became deaf at age nine; nonetheless this handicap, she became a black belt in literature, allowing her to enter the literary circles with Edgar Allen Poe and wrote *The Home Life of Poe* in 1907. During the Civil War, she was imprisoned by the Union on the accusation of being a spy for the Confederacy. There she fell in love with an officer of the Union army, and after the war moved to NYC. But the marriage ended badly. But Ms. S.A.W. put her writing talent to use until her eyes were afflicted.

Archer and Allan, Weiss of the Susans and Poe of the Edgars, authorized the proverbial source code for the original "Jack and Sally" who were drafted by the dark gravity of lonely midnight sojourns, unto the darkest valleys of memory. Rather than being swallowed up by the abyss of despair, they were able to steal away sparkling seeds of beauty from the tree of melancholy and nurture an effervescent vine of wisdom for the soul, forevermore.

However, the most prominent pointer for the evidence of Providence is tied to the wake of Thomas Jefferson and John Adams. Their relationship captures with maximum majesty, the bonds of wisdom and affection between Virginia and Massachusetts. Their lives ended on a fateful note of synchronicity when they passed unto the great unknown on July 4, 1826, upon the lauded year of biblical Jubilee, the 50th anniversary of the Declaration of Independence. It is calculated that Jefferson died hours before Adams, and it was upon Adams's passing that he said, "Jefferson lives on." In the logical view of things, this makes absolutely no sense, since Jefferson by all objective measures, died first. However, with a Jedi-George Lucasian view of things, perhaps something of Anakin, Obi-Wan, or Yoda's last appearance on Endor could illuminate Adams's final words ... but that, my friends, requires a leap of faith.

[{(❤)}]

Adams and Jefferson encapsulate the divisions between the north and south. They were colleagues who became the best of friends during the Revolution. Their fundamental contribution to the incipient American Revolution makes them essential founders, whose efforts can never be overstated. After the presidency of Washington, they became the second silver and third bronze presidents. Thus, if Washington was the colonel of the American Republic, Adams was the lieutenant colonel and Jefferson was the major. Or in naval terms, Washington is the captain of the Republic, Adams is the commander, and Jefferson is the lieutenant commander of the American core.

When Adams was president, Jefferson was vice president. However, as political realities hit the concrete, there was a fallout between the two. Adams pressed for a strong central government of elites, while Jefferson went the opposite direction pressing for a weaker federal government. This was where they became estranged from each other. However, in their twilight years, their relationship was rekindled by time and maturity. This relationship is captured in the multitude of letters where they debated endlessly about the issues and destiny of the republic, and once again found common ground. In the end, they were able to overcome their differences and restore their friendship, having built the strongest and most magical of bridges between Massachusetts and Virginia, properly tested by time and sealed by the mysterious power of synchronicity on a verily, special 4th of July.

The beginning of America also heralds the ending of the ancient, unwritten America. For millennia, the first nations lived off the land in a legendary era, where the magic of oral tradition carried the sum of a nation's knowledge and known abilities. Of the 10,001 tribes to have lived and lost in the Americas, two were nations chosen to welcome their long-lost, ancient, and most clever cousins unto the New World. The chosen tribes were the Powhatan of Virginia and the Wampanoag in Massachusetts. This makes Chief Powhatan of Virginia the consort Chief Massasoit of Massachusetts. These elder and original kings of the indigenous American oak tree nations sealed their bittersweet fate whence they secured an alliance with the English. It was the beginning of the American apocalypse, where a new chapter of people from the East Sea would supplant the power of the elder peoples of Americas.

Of the peoples at the point of contact, at the genesis of the English saga within this hemisphere, Squanto and Pocahontas are penultimate emissaries, chosen by the mysterious hand of history to bring about the foundation of the American Dream. Like the two sacred pillars of King Solomon's temple labeled Jachim and Boaz, Squanto and Pocahontas are fundamental pillars of the great spirit of America.

As the permanent English arrival of America begins in Virginia, it was the fateful life of a Powhatan princess by the name of Amonute that herald's our beginning. Amonute would gain several names along her life's journey. Her English name was given after she was baptized as Rebecca, becoming Rebecca Rolfe. She married John Rolfe in 1614 and gave birth to Thomas Rolfe. Her marriage to John Rolfe was more than just a romantic affair—it was the consummation of a political alliance between the Powhatan kingdom and the English tribes. It would provide the necessary and peaceable pause, which enabled England to plant deep roots in Virginia that would blossom into greater and more complex permutations. Pocahontas later journeyed to London, England, and met the king James I and became a sensation. However, she fell ill after one year's visit and died, one year further than Shakespeare, in 1617. Pocahontas is buried in England at St. George's Church, Gravesend, on the eastern side of the Prime Meridian.

Squanto was born as Tisquantum of the Patuxet Nation. Although he is associated with the younger colony of Massachusetts, his story begins before the arrival of the *Mayflower*. Tisquantum was abducted by an unknown race of hostile aliens and taken to Europe. It was there that he bore witness to a marvelous technologically advanced alien civilization. Somehow, he was able to make his way to England, and it is thought he may have even crossed paths with Pocahontas while she was in England around 1616. Like an epic fairytale, Tisquantum was able to learn English and make his way back home. Sadly, when he returned, his village was decimated by smallpox. Squanto was able to find refuge with Chief Massasoit, which would prove providential when the *Mayflower* arrived in the autumn in 1620. The English were shocked to see a Squanto speak such good English. Thus, Squanto's destiny was written to welcome the Pilgrims, as a wicked twist of serendipity, or rather, the hallmark of Providence.

In closing, Virginia and Massachusetts sit at the two heads of history's long table of the 50 states sitting opposite their fraternal flag partner. At one end, Pocahontas is seated as Mother Virginia. At the other end, Squanto is seated as Father Massachusetts. Together, their enchanted lives and epic stories seal, enshrine, and protect the core and foundation of the American spirit. They were fated to literally and proverbially cross the ocean of time and are forevermore recognized as the Great Mother and Father of America, a constant lode star of the south for she, as well as it is for he, of the north.

Culture

Massachusetts and Virginia are the keystone species when it comes to American ideas and patriotism. Massachusetts has Harvard, Boston College, and the Massachusetts Institute of Technology, while Virginia puts many of those fancy ideas to good use at the Central Intelligence Agency (CIA) headquarters at Langley in Fairfax County, Virginia. Quantico is another training center where American brains and brawn merge in Virginia. Quantico is host to several major U.S. patriot organizations like the FBI Academy, Marine Corps Base Quantico (which is the largest Marine Corps Base), D.E.A training academy, Officer Candidate School (OCS), and Internal Affairs Operations for the Navy, Army, and Air Force.

Virginia and Massachusetts are the ultimate match of a Master Blaster relationship—an alliance between the smartest and strongest. Master Blaster in this case refers to the *Road Warrior* lore, where the fictional Barter Town is dominated by an ultra-smart dwarf-Massachusetts, who rides on top of super strongman-Virginia. In the movie *Mad Max Beyond Thunderdome* (1985), Master Blaster works as one unit to control the lifeblood of the city in a fictional post-apocalypse Australia.

Two heavyweights that have collided in the Hollywood Hills are Leonard Nimoy (1931-2015) and Warren Beatty (born 1937). Leonard Nimoy from Boston, Massachusetts, became a world icon with his portrayal of Spock—a half human half Vulcan hybrid. Anyone of two different religions and ethnicities can easily relate to Spock, if they grew up in between two cultures. Warren Beatty from Richmond, Virginia, was a star in *Bonnie and Clyde* (1967), *Heaven Can Wait* (1978), and *Dick Tracy* (1990).

A perfect pair of comedic boomer kings forged in 1957 and 1954 are Denis Leary from Worcester, Massachusetts, and Rich Hall from Alexandria, Virginia. Leary is known for his high energy ranting with stand-up comedy, while Hall will always be remembered as the *"Sniglet King."* Hall's *Sniglet* segment was a kind of creative forerunner to the Urban Dictionary. A *Sniglet* is a made up word that should be a word but does not exist; and note this book is full of *Sniglets*. James Spader, from Boston, Massachusetts (born 1960), matches with Wes Johnson from Arlington, Virginia (born 1961). Spader broke out with his role on *Sex, Lies, and Videotape* (1989) while Wes Johnson has had small roles in *A Dirty Shame* (2004) and *For Richer or Poorer* (1997).

Two funny kings are Steve Carell from Concord, Massachusetts (born 1962), and Patton Oswalt from Portsmouth, Virginia (born 1969). These average men have gone well beyond average, with super skills for tickling the funny bone of America. They have been all over comedy, TV, and movies. Somehow, they have taken the worst points of life, and framed them in nationally recognizable situational humor, so that we can laugh at the many little and big problems of life.

Two Gen X super dudes from the class of 1971 are Mark Wahlberg and David Arquette. Mark Wahlberg from Boston, Massachusetts, started as a musician but was able to express his never give up, positive energy in Hollywood, assuring a hit with nearly every other role that he played in films like *The Basketball Diaries* (1995), *Ted* (2012), *Daddy's Home* (2015), and many more yet to come. David Arquette from Bentonville, Virginia, also busted out in cinema as told on *Scream* (1996) and *Eight Legged Freaks* (2002). Matt Damon and Patrick Wilson are a perfect patriotic American pair of aces. Damon from Cambridge, Massachusetts (born 1970), pairs perfectly with Wilson from Norfolk, Virginia. Pat Wilson (born 1973) has starred in *Watchmen* (2009) and *The A-Team* (2010), while Damon (born 1970) is, well ... you know, Matt Damon! Do I really need to explain?

A patriotic power punch can be delivered by John Cena and Alex Riley. Cena from West Newbury, Massachusetts (born 1977), matches with Kevin "Alex Riley" Kiley from Fairfax Station, Virginia (born 1981). Cena was able to pin down Hollywood with his charms and smile, while Riley has just begun to make a small dent in Tinseltown. Chris Evans from Boston, Massachusetts (born 1981), matches Zach Cregger from Arlington, Virginia (born 1980). Chris Evans starred as *Captain America* (2011), while Zach Cregger rose to comic fame with the troupe *The Whitest Kids U'Know* (2007-2011).

Geena Davis from Wareham, Massachusetts, is a clean kosher match to Sandra Bullock from Arlington, Virginia. These women are class 10 superstars of the 20th century. Their hits are too numerous to recount but include *Beetlejuice* (1988), *The Fly* (1986), *Speed* (1994), *The Blind Side* (2009), and *Gravity* (2013). No doubt a few more blockbusters are getting ready to unload in their twilight years.

Elizabeth Banks from Pittsfield, Massachusetts (born 1974), is a virtual little

VIRGINIA & MASSACHUSETTS

sister to Jennifer Aspen from Richmond, Virginia (born 1973). Aspen starred in *Party of Five* (1994-2000), *Glee* (2009-2015), and *A Very Brady Sequel* (1996). Banks starred in *The Hunger Games* (since 2012), the *Pitch Perfect* (since 2012) movies, *Magic Mike XXL* (2015), and *The 40-Year-Old Virgin* (2005).

Two boomer queens to give a sweet wink to America are Allison Janney from Boston, Massachusetts (born 1959), and Jane Brucker from Falls Church, Virginia (born 1958). Brucker is best known as Baby's older sister in *Dirty Dancing* (1987), while Janney is master of fun-o-drama with movies like *American Beauty* (1999), *The Hours* (2002), *Juno* (2007), and her prime-time role as the modern mom on sitcom American TV show *Mom* (2013-2021).

Two women who put a permanent smirk and smile on America's face are Madeline Kahn from Boston, Massachusetts (born 1942), and Joyce Bulifant from Newport News, Virginia (born 1937). Kahn was able to throw a fury of funny fists to gut and keep on smiling with movies like *Young Frankenstein* (1974) and *Blazing Saddles* (1974), and at the end of her career with *A Bug's Life* (1998) and *Judy Berlin* (1999). Bulifant launched into the family of American memory with *The Mary Tyler Moore Show* (1970-1977) and later made the world chuckle with her part on the classic parody of *Airplane!* (1980); she was the mother of the sick girl during the "One River of Jordan" of humanity song. Joyce was also a recurring cast member on the original *The Bill Cosby Show* (1969-1971).

Two women who became giggle masters of the game are Amy Poehler (born 1971) from Newton, Massachusetts, and Wanda Sykes (born 1964) from Portsmouth, Virginia. Both women had recurring roles on *SNL* and were able to land gut busting silly sidekicks across Hollywood with movies like *Mean Girls* (2004), *Evan Almighty* (2007), and *Pootie Tang* (2001).

Paige Turco from Boston, Massachusetts (born 1965), is a match made on the Atlantic with Veanne Cox from Norfolk, Virginia (born 1963). Turco landed in the American imagination when she got the gig of April O'Neil and has been all over TV and movies since. The Virginian Veanne lit the stage with movies like *Miss Firecracker* (1989), and like Turco, made many a movie and TV show.

Two semi-lost legends at the dawn of talkies or moving pictures with sound are Bette Davis (born 1908) and Margaret Sullavan (born 1909). Sullavan from Norfolk, Virginia, was a star-powered actress who parlayed with Henry Fonda and Jimmy Stewart in movies like *The Mortal Storm* (1940) and *Shop Around the Corner* (1940). Bette Davis was nominated many times over for her performances with movies like *Jezebel* (1938), *Little Foxes* (1941), *All About Eve* (1950), and *What Ever Happened to Baby Jane* (1962). Bette Davis also received a a revival when her name became the focus of a song: "Bette Davis Eyes" hit the charts in 1981.

Jack Lemmon from Newton, Massachusetts (1925-2001) and George Campbell Scott from Wise, Virginia (1927-1999), were superstars of the black-and-white era. Lemmon starred in *Some Like It Hot* (1959) and *The China Syndrome* (1979). George Scott played iconic roles in *Dr. Strangelove* (1964) but is best known for playing George S. Patton in *Patton* (1970). Even at the end of their careers they were able to touch the millennial generation with movies like *Grumpy Old Men* (1993) and *New York News* (1995).

Two fantastic stars still shining a light upon us in 2024 of the Lost Generation are Shirley MacLaine from Richmond, Virginia (born 1934), and Leslie Parrish from Melrose, Massachusetts (born 1935). Parrish was a constant source of stardom all through television and movies with the likes of *The Manchurian Candidate* (1962) *For Love or Money* (1963), and the original *Star Trek* (1967) series. MacLaine from Massachusetts is a class 10 star who shined so bright that she turned night into day across the generations, starting in 1955 with *The Trouble with Harry*. Other classics include *Can-Can* (1960), *Sweet Charity* (1969), *Terms of Endearment* (1983), *Bewitched* (2005), and *The Little Mermaid* (2018). Besides entertaining America, both women were active on the social front. MacLaine dove deep into spiritual seeking while Parrish became an advocate for the environment.

Mindy Kaling and Will Yun Lee are two Asian American stars. Mindy Kaling from Cambridge, Massachusetts (born 1979), is a superstar with roots to India, while Will Yun Lee from Arlington, Virginia (born 1971), has roots to Korea and starred in *Die Another Day* (2002), and *The Wolverine* (2013).

Ed Norton who starred in *Fight Club* (1999) from Boston, Massachusetts (born 1969), matches with Scott Cooper from Abingdon, Virginia (born 1970). Cooper has starred in *Get Low* (2009) and *Austin Powers: The Spy Who Shagged Me* (1999). Two special stars from the funky 1970s are Uma Thurman from Boston, Massachusetts, and Sabrina Lloyd from Fairfax County, Virginia. Uma Thurman was immortalized in *Pulp Fiction* (1994), while Sabrina Lloyd starred in one of the original multiverse parallel realities sci-fi shows in the 1990s called *Sliders* (1995-2000).

News, news and more news, there is never enough news! The boomer king and queen of the news generation are George Stephanopoulos from Fall River, Massachusetts (born 1961), who is a perfect match to Katherine Anne Couric from Arlington, Virginia (born 1957). They have talked the talk and walked the walk with the famous to infamous.

Coincidentally, a musical Brown rose to fame from each state. Bobby Brown from Boston became a hitmaker in the 1980s and 1990s, while Chris Brown from Tappahannock, Virginia, carried the flame of soul further during the mighty 20-ohs. James Taylor from Boston, Massachusetts (born 1948), makes a harmonious whole with Wayne Newton from Norfolk, Virginia (born 1942). Wayne Newton's hits include "Daddy, Don't You Walk So Fast" (1972). The king of lounge, jazz, and pop also hit the top of the charts in the 1970s with songs like "Fire and Rain" and "You've Got a Friend."

Donna Summer from Boston, Massachusetts (1948-2021), was the queen of disco while Yvonne Fair from Richmond, Virginia (1942-1994) is another page from the '70s with the hit "Should Have Been Me" in 1975.

Between the stars of New Edition, five stars of Massachusetts match with the rhythm and blues talents stars from Virginia. Ricky Bell (1967), Michael Bivins (1968), Bobby Brown (1969), Ronnie DeVoe (1967) and Ralph Tresvant (1968) are all from Massachusetts and are the older soul siblings to the Virginians Missy Elliot (1971), Pharrell Williams (1972), and D'Angelo (1974). Perhaps they can all get together and make a *Supreme Gen X Edition* album for the record books.

A creative mix of north and south who went their own special way with music is John Flansburgh from Lincoln, Massachusetts (born 1960) and Bruce

Hornsby from Williamsburg, Virginia (born 1954). Bruce was a part of the band Bruce Hornsby and the Range, while John Flansburgh was one of the original duo members of They Might Be Giants. Both musicians broke away from the mainstream style of music to make distinguished audio tracks.

Robert Gerard Goulet from Lawrence, Massachusetts (1933-2007), is the smooth northern singer who matches with the southern icon Patsy Cline from Winchester, Virginia (1932-1963). Rob G. Goulet starred in movies and TV. Notable works include *Beetlejuice* (1988) and *The Naked Gun 2 ½: The Smell of Fear* (1991). Patsy Cline was the mother of modern country with several hit songs like "She's Got You," "When I Get Thru with You (You'll Love Me Too)" and "Crazy." It was during the peak of her career that she tragically died in a plane crash on March 5, 1963.

Two inventors who are the founding fathers of American ingenuity are Robert McCormick, from Rockbridge County, Virginia, who was born in 1780 and died on July 4, 1846, and Eli Whitney from Westborough, Massachusetts. Eli Whitney, who was born at the outbreak of the Stamp Act Crisis in 1765 and died in 1825, is famous for his cotton sorting machine that was supposed to hasten the end of slavery. His mechanical "cotton sorting engine," better known as the cotton gin, would, by his account, reduce the need for slaves. But, like many good ideas, it viciously backfired, and his cotton contraption made cotton cultivation a rather lucrative industry. On the southern side of ingenuity, Robert McCormick is famous for building the mechanical reaper that revolutionized agriculture. His son Cyrus McCormick further improved and patented his original design in 1834, and the McCormick reaper became legendary within the farming community. By cutting the costs of labor with mechanized harvesters, the McCormick family became the first of the "Reaper Kings" in America. The McCormick reapers led to the genesis of the iconic International Harvester Company, which ruled the farmlands of America until the 1980s, when the company imploded on itself and reformed as the Navistar International Corporation.

At the core of each state are several flavors, and it just so happens that peanuts became an American essential thanks to their first commercial cultivation in Virginia in 1842, Sussex County near Waverly, Virginia. Since then, goobers, monkey nuts, or cardboard encased mud-beans have become an essential anthem of the south. Nobody knows for sure who invented the forked peanut butter cookie, but it makes sense to pin this one on Virginia thanks to her part in putting the peanut on the American menu—with a little push from George Washington Carver. Consequently, the sugar sprinkled peanut butter cookie rooted to Virginia pairs perfectly with chocolate chip cookie, formally established in Plymouth County by Ruth Grave Wakefield around 1938 at the Toll House Inn in Whitman, Massachusetts. Thus, a simple and sweet way to commune with Virginia and Massachusetts with body, mind, and soul can be adjudicated via two easy bake items—two cookies sprinkled with a certain kind of magic that can put a spell over the heart and tummy.

In the end, Virginia and Massachusetts go together like peas and carrots, or like a can of pork and beans. As Massachusetts is famous for its Boston baked beans, smoked sweet Virginia ham is a delight. Together, they make the perfect pair. In conclusion, pork and beans are hereby required on every 4th of July.

CLOSING THOUGHTS

The big question to address is, "Why does this happen?" Synchronicity aptly describes it, but why is this twinning phenomenon taking place? One answer can be found within Freemasonry, which is discussed in detail with the Nevada and Alaska chapter. This leads one to the idea that Freemasons had a hand in making the flags appear as such—as a collusive process. Although the flags were adopted in a random fashion with a decree here, a committee there, and a contest over there, one could argue that the Freemasons put on the facade of a random process but were pulling the strings all along—like the grand Wizard of Oz.

Well, that idea is nigh on impossible. There is just too much going on across the nation to maintain such an array of organized conspiracy, and a secret as such would have already slipped out. Instead, it seems that the ideas concerning the duality of the Masonic teaching board may reflect a fundamental level of truth. It seems the Masons may have built their philosophical foundations on an essential aspect of creation. Masons, from a certain point of view, believe that a force, of divine extract, binds us all and permeates all aspects of life.

Another reason for the emergence of this structure may be due to the collective unconscious. We have a conscious, unconscious, and some believe another level of mind called the collective unconscious. There may be several layers to the collective unconscious; as communities make up regions, that make up states, that make up the nations, and finally the world—all of which have their realms of consciousness. At the moment, the idea of the collective unconscious is far out, on a limb for most. The collective unconscious may explain why so many math and science discoveries happened at the same time, which is known as simultaneous or multiple discovery. This happened with the invention of calculus, discovery of oxygen, the periodic nature of the elements, and even the theory of evolution. Perhaps when we sleep, we are connected to an invisible Internet-like layer of matter/energy that the five senses cannot perceive? But as we sleep, we gain access to this transcendental and irrational realm of existence, which has its own fluctuating rules of reality and consequences. Life is strange after all—especially dreams.

For example, there may be a bias toward symmetry in the collective subconscious. Thus, the reasoning goes something like this: after Texas chose a flag, there was a need to balance this pattern within the collective unconscious. Several decades later, when North Carolina was deciding on a flag, perhaps there was a collective, unconscious impulse to choose a flag that reflected the schematic established by Texas, as needed for some sort of visual balance.

Regardless of the causes behind this fraternal flag phenomenon, the essential revelation is; when the state flags are ordered in this manner, a new narrative underscored by synchronicity arises. Also note, the indigenous peoples who connected to the sacred, before the genesis of the divinely ordained document, were keenly aware that synchronicity was a powerful phenomenon and taken as a means of sacred communication—but much of those methodologies have been lost. Apparently, gaining the skills to read synchronicity properly requires something akin to a long and tutored period of Jedi Knight training.

Further there are religious and spiritual seekers who regard synchronicity as the hallmark of something divine, which is usually termed as "Providence" within the sphere of written religions.

Essentially, this manuscript provides object proof of synchronicity at work rather than relying on personal testimony. The object proof being the flags themselves, which are the objective, object evidence that can be observed, felt, and measured. A few have noticed flag similarities between certain flags here and there, but this is the first book to put it all together revealing a coherent and emergent pattern amongst the flags of the United States.

But here is the challenge and pitfall—there is a fine line between genuine synchronicity and gross superstition. Ascertaining authentic synchronicity is a

CLOSING THOUGHTS

nearly impossible puzzle to objectively quantify, in a similar quandary of free will vs. destiny. No doubt the purity of one's heart can act as a compass to overrule the desire of the mind's ego. The ego can easily be deceived and be led astray, while it is much harder, if not impossible, to deceive the heart. Perhaps it is good that synchronicity cannot be wholly understood? Otherwise, corporations and governments would have already harnessed its power, and use it to manipulate the masses for self-destructive profit margins and control of society, as they already do with the recent revelations of technology underwritten by science.

Flags are hardly permanent. They are always under the scrutiny of the public, and there is always some volume of pressure to change a flag, due to the shifting winds of politics, pride, and personal preferences. For example, in 2020 the New York flag was modified when the governor added unnecessary words on the ribbon in the compartment. Governor Cuomo basically "tagged" the New York state flag, not with a spray paint can, but rather with the power of his office. And note, this book uses the centurion aged, pre-2020 version of the New York state flag, which does not have Andrew Cuomo's mark of pride. As 20/20 indicates perfect vision, it is fitting that the state flags as they were in the year 2020, as presented in this book, provide Providential evidence of synchronicity.

Any future changes of a state flag cannot subvert the fraternal flag relationship established in this book. This book is the first to recognize in totality this emergent pattern with the state flags of the United States. Essentially a Rubicon has been crossed, where the knowledge of this relationship is akin to opening Pandora's Box or Thomas Young's famous double slit experiment. Now that the public is aware of the fraternal twinning flag phenomena, no one can make a flag without this bias and may purposefully design a flag that counters this fraternal flag pattern. Or on the contrary, design flags that maintain the partnered flag symmetry of an assigned pair. Essentially, the organic synchronicity and unfettered path of Providence may be lost upon the next generation of flags designed in the aftermath of this flag revelation.

This book looks back to the year 2020 as a focal point. Since then, much change has come, as it has been said and will always be said, change is inevitable. Nonetheless this emergent pattern, made evident by the colors above, creates an

THE FLAG REVELATION

intangible, unbreakable bridge of connectivity. Ergo, as flags change through the ages, this book will become a lighthouse that will forevermore illuminate the mysterious and ghostly phenomenon of synchronicity. Whereby in the far distant future, *The Banners of the Ancient Fifty States of America were in Precise 20/20 Alignment* can or shall be recognized as a perfect fraternity of flags for all of eternity, as a codex that can be used to educate and inspire.

SELECTED BIBLIOGRAPHY

This bibliography is by no means a complete record of the works and sources I have consulted in the writing of this book. However, it does serve to indicate the substance and range of reading and research that informed my ideas, and I intend it to serve as a convenience for those who wish to pursue their own study of American history, flags, and the topic of synchronicity.

 For more detailed footnote style end notes, please visit my online site here

INTRODUCTION

Pirto, Jane. "Synchronicity and Creativity." In *Encyclopedia of Creativity*, 2nd ed. Edited by Mark A. Runco and Steven R. Pritzker. London: Academic Press, 2011. 409-13. https://doi.org/10.1016/B978-0-12-375038-9.00210-7.

Jung, C. G. "Introduction." In *Synchronicity: An Acausal Connecting Principle*. Princeton, NJ: Princeton University Press, 1973.

CHAPTER 1

Pine, Leslie Gilbert, and Frederick Hogarth. "The Scope of Heraldry." *Encyclopedia Britannica*.

September 20, 2023. https://www.britannica.com/topic/heraldry/The-scope-of-heraldry.

American Swedish Historical Museum: Yearbook 1962. Edited by Henry Goddard Leach (Philadelphia: American Swedish Historical Museum, 1962), 27-28.

"Virginia-Pennsylvania Boundary." Virginia Places. Accessed July 23, 2023. http://www.virginiaplaces.org/boundaries/paboundary.html.

"Charter for the Province of Pennsylvania—1681." The Avalon Project. Accessed July 16, 2023. https://avalon.law.yale.edu/17th_century/pa01.asp.

Monmornier, Mark. *Drawing the Line: Tales of Maps and Cartocontroversy*. New York City: Henry Holt and Company, 1995.

Craig, Neville B. *Lecture upon the Controversy Between Pennsylvania and Virginia, About the Boundary Line: Delivered at the University Building, December 5th, 1843*. Pittsburgh: A. Jaynes, 1843.

Galbreath, C.B., ed. *Expedition of Celoron to the Ohio Country in 1749*. Columbus, Ohio: F.J. Heer Printing Company, 1921.

Hazard, Samuel. *Colonial Records of Pennsylvania*, vol. 5. Harrisburg, Pennsylvania: T. Fenn & Company, 1851.

Leyland, Herbert T. *The Ohio Company, A Colonial Corporation*. Cincinnati: The Abingdon Press, 1921.

"A Treaty Held at the Tow of Lancaster, by the Honourable the Lieutenant Governor of the Province, and the Honourable the Commissions for the Province of Virginia and Maryland, with the Indians of the Six Nations in June, 1744." Center for Digital Research in the Humanities. University of Nebraska–Lincoln. Accessed July 16, 2023. http://treatiesportal.unl.edu/earlytreaties/treaty.00003.html.

Washington, George. "The Diaries of George Washington, Volume 1, 1748-65." Library of Congress. Accessed July 17, 2023. https://www.loc.gov/collections/george-washington-papers/about-this-collection/.

Forbes, John. "General Forbes Describes His Route to the Forks to William Pitt, July 1758." ExplorePAhistory.com. Accessed July 17, 2023. http://explorepahistory.com/odocument.php?docId=1-4-29.

SELECTED BIBLIOGRAPHY

Bayliff, William H. *The Maryland-Pennsylvania and the Maryland-Delaware Boundaries.* Maryland Board of Natural Resources, 1959.

"Father Marquette National Memorial." Michigan History Center. Michigan Department of Natural Resources. Accessed November 20, 2023. https://www.michigan.gov/mhc/museums/father-marquette-national-memorial.

"1769—The Pennamite Wars." The Society of Colonial Wars in the State of Connecticut. Accessed November 20, 2023. https://www.colonialwarsct.org/1769.htm.

Gilbert, Bil. "The Dying Tecumseh and the Birth of a Legend." *Smithsonian Magazine.* July 1995. https://www.smithsonianmag.com/history/the-dying-tecumseh-97830806/.

"Fallen Hero." PBS. Accessed November 20, 2023. https://www.pbs.org/wgbh/americanexperience/features/lindbergh-fallen-hero/.

Gallagher, Danny. "Hurst Resident and Creator of The Crow, James O'Barr, on the Comic That Made Him Famous." *Dallas Observer.* August 5, 2016. https://www.dallasobserver.com/arts/hurst-resident-and-creator-of-the-crow-james-obarr-on-the-comic-that-made-him-famous-8561547.

Crumrine, Boyd. "The County Court for the District of West Augusta, Virginia: Held at Augusta Town, Near Washington, Pennsylvania, 1776-1777 / An Historical Sketch by Boyd Crumrine. With an Account of the County Courts for Ohio, Yohogania and Monogalia Counties, Virginia, Held 1777-1780." Washington, PA: Washington County Historical Society, 1905. Accessed July 17, 2023. https://catalog.libraries.psu.edu/catalog/39307131.

James, Alfred P. "The Role of Virginia and Virginias in the Early History of Southwestern Pennsylvania." *The Western Pennsylvania Historical Magazine* 34, no. 1 (March 1951): 51-63. https://journals.psu.edu/wph/article/view/2367/2200.

Cranmer, Gibson Lamb. *History of the Upper Ohio Valley.* Vol 1. Brant & Fuller, 1891.

Friar, Stephen, and John Ferguson. *Basic Heraldry.* London: W. W. Norton & Company, 1993.

Slater, Stephen. *The Complete Book of Heraldry: An International History of Heraldry and Its Contemporary Uses.* London: Hermes House, 2003.

"Betsy Ross and the American Flag." USHistory.org. Independence Hall Association. Accessed November 20, 2023. https://www.ushistory.org/betsy/flagtale.html.

◼ The core of this book is in perpetual gratitude to Pennsylvania. There are too many people and places to list for gratitude. Places that made this book possible include Lansdale, Doylestown, Lancaster, Newtown, University Park, Harrisburg, and Philadelphia; Likewise, I had a warm, welcoming, magical one week's stay in Michigan where I received a bounty of invisible spiritual gifts in Michigan that solidified this fraternal flag relationship. Basically, Michigan rolled out the magical red carpet. Therefore, the small chapter of my life in Michigan is embroidered in pure gold. Perhaps in time, like the heartfelt scenes from *The Crow* and *RoboCop*, in some distant future, the spirit or a soul from Michigan may become the ultimate guardian of this fraternal flag relationship, should its light ever become occulted. And, believe it or not, a person from Michigan, Renee Harrison, was fated by mere chance to work with me as I went through the cover design process. Synchronicity checkmate!

CHAPTER 2

"The Iron Brigade & the Black Hat." Wisconsin Veterans Museum. April 7, 2014. https://wisvetsmuseum.com/the-iron-brigade-the-black-hat/.

Bishop, Charles A. "5—Process Diagnostics and Coating Characteristics," in *Vacuum Deposition onto Webs, Films and Foils*, 2nd ed. Oxford: William Andrew Publishing, 2011. 81-114. https://www.sciencedirect.com/topics/chemistry/hall-effect.

"Kinetic Energy." *Encyclopedia Britannica*. October 17, 2023. https://www.britannica.com/science/kinetic-energy.

"Leavenworth Constitution." Kansas Historical Society. Accessed November 20, 2023. https://www.kshs.org/index.php?url=km/items/view/90817.

"Battleship Photo Archive." NavSource Online. Accessed July 18, 2023. http://www.navsource.org/archives/01/09a.htm.

"USS Wisconsin (Battleship #9, later BB-9), 1901-1922." Naval History and Heritage Command. Accessed July 18, 2023. https://www.history.navy.mil/our-collections/photography/us-navy-ships/battleships/wisconsin-bb-9.html.

"USS Wisconsin BB-9." USS Wisconsin BB-64. Accessed July 18, 2023. https://www.usswisconsin.org/wp/uss-wisconsin-bb-9/.

Sacquety, Troy J. "Colombia's Troubled Past." *Veritas* 2, no. 4 (2006). https://arsof-history.org/articles/v2n4_troubled_past_page_1.html.

Skretteberg, Richard. "Colombia's Bloody History." Norwegian Refugee Council. Last modified December 1, 2015. https://www.nrc.no/perspectives/2015/nr-4/colombias-bloody-history/.

Davidovicz, Sylvia. "A Prize for Warlike Ambition: The 1885 Panama Crisis and the Rise of an American Power Complex." Undergraduate thesis. Columbia University. April 10, 2019. https://history.columbia.edu/wp-content/uploads/sites/20/2019/05/Davidovicz-Thesis-2019.pdf.

▌ Of all the states to back me up, Maine has been my right-hand flag. I have never been to Wisconsin, but the lovely memories generated from *Happy Days, Laverne & Shirley, That '70s Show*, and Red Letter Media provided a special warmth and cheer.

CHAPTER 3

Bartels, Diane. "Sharpie: The Life Story of Evelyn Sharp – Nebraska's Aviatrix." The Ninety-Nines. Accessed July 22, 2023. https://www.ninety-nines.org/sharpie-life-of-evelyn-sharp.htm.

"Evelyn Sharp." National Park Service. Last updated August 2, 2021. https://www.nps.gov/home/learn/historyculture/evelyn-sharp.htm.

"Marker Monday: Evelyn Sharp." History Nebraska. Accessed November 20, 2023. https://history.nebraska.gov/marker-monday-evelyn-sharp/.

CHAPTER 4

"Constitution of Virginia – July 8, 1778." The Avalon Project. Yale Law School. Accessed July 22, 2023. https://avalon.law.yale.edu/18th_century/vt01.asp.

Anderson, Mark R. "Remember Baker: A Green Mountain Boy's Controversial Death and Its Consequences." *Journal of the American Revolution*. May 4, 2023. https://allthingsliberty.com/2023/05/remember-baker-a-green-mountain-boys-controversial-death-and-its-consequences/.

Ford, Thomas. *History of the Church*. Edited by B. H. Roberts. Vol. 6. 533-37. http://law2.umkc.edu/faculty/projects/ftrials/carthage/fordletter.html.

Finkelman, Paul. "A Look Back at John Brown." *Prologue Magazine* 43, no. 1 (Spring 2011).

https://www.archives.gov/publications/prologue/2011/spring/brown.html.

Smith, D.S. "We Started It All, Captain Kirk." Scale Reproductions. 1998. Archived December 5, 2004, at the Wayback Machine. https://web.archive.org/web/20041205181907/http://seafarer.netfirms.com/2-enter.htm.

Schenawolf, Harry. "Battle of Groton Heights and Massacre of Fort Griswold's Garrison." Revolutionary War Journal. Last modified July 16, 2021. https://revolutionarywarjournal.com/battle-of-groton-heights-and-massacre-of-fort-griswolds-garrison/#_edn1.

Kelly, Christina. "The Border War: New York and Vermont." History of the Town of Schaghticoke. September 13, 2011. https://schaghticokehistory.wordpress.com/2011/09/13/the-border-war-new-york-and-vermont/.

"The Green Mountain Boys." Vermont History Explorer. Accessed July 22, 2023. https://vermonthistoryexplorer.org/the-green-mountain-boys.

CHAPTER 5

Klein, Christopher. "When Japan Launched Killer Balloons in World War II." History.com. Last modified February 6, 2023. https://www.history.com/news/japans-killer-wwii-balloons.

"Michigan." History.com. Last modified February 10, 2023. https://www.history.com/topics/us-states/michigan.

"First Emigrants on the Oregon Trail." Oregon-California Trails Association. Accessed July 22, 2023. http://octa-trails.org/articles/first-emigrants-on-the-oregon-trail/.

"Life and Death on the Oregon Trail." Oregon-California Trails Association. Accessed July 22, 2023. https://octa-trails.org/articles/life-and-death-on-the-oregon-trail/.

Robbins, William G. "Oregon Donation Land Law." Oregon Encyclopedia. Last modified August 17, 2022. https://www.oregonencyclopedia.org/articles/oregon_donation_land_act/#.Wh8gerpFw5s.

Lang, William L. "Oregon Trail." Oregon Encyclopedia. Last modified November 22, 2022. https://www.oregonencyclopedia.org/articles/oregon_trail/#.Why4N7pFw5s.

"Historical Trails: Trail Basics – The Starting Point." National Oregon/California Trail Center. Accessed July 22, 2023. https://oregontrailcenter.org/starting-point.

"Historical Trails: Trail Basics – The Wagon." National Oregon/California Trail Center. Accessed July 22, 2023. https://oregontrailcenter.org/the-wagon.

"Where Did the Oregon Trail Go?" Oregon-California Trails Association. Accessed July 22, 2023. https://octa-trails.org/articles/where-did-the-oregon-trail-go/.

"The Great Migration." History.com. August 30, 2022. https://www.history.com/topics/black-history/great-migration.

Hill, William E. "Oregon Trail." *Encyclopedia Britannica*. Last modified May 22, 2023. https://www.britannica.com/topic/Oregon-Trail.

"The Ox-Bow Trail." Digging In: The Historic Trails of Nebraska. University of Nebraska–Lincoln. Accessed July 22, 2023. https://cdrhsites.unl.edu/diggingin/trailsummaries/di.sum.0003.html.

Cozzens, Peter. *Eyewitnesses to the Indian Wars, 1865–1890: The Long War for the Northern Plains*, xlvi. Mechanicsburg, PA: Stackpole Books, 2001).

CHAPTER 6

"US Flags." US Flags. Accessed July 22, 2023. https://usflags.design/.

Spartz, India M. *Eight Stars of Gold: The Story of Alaska's Flag*. Juneau, AL: Alaska State Museums, 2001. https://museums.alaska.gov/EightStars/src/exhibit_catalog.pdf.

Salisbury, Gay, and Laney Salisbury. *The Cruelest Miles: The Heroic Story of Dogs and Men in a Race Against an Epidemic*, 263. New York: W. W. Norton & Company, 2003.

Rocha, Guy. "When Is a State Flag Official?" Nevada State Library and Archives. April 1997. Archived February 23, 2004, at the Wayback Machine. https://web.archive.org/web/20040223122522/http:/dmla.clan.lib.nv.us/docs/nsla/archives/myth/myth16.htm.

Rocha, Guy. "How Nevada Went 60 Years Without an Official Flag." *Reno Gazette Journal*. Last modified October 22, 2017. https://www.rgj.com/story/life/2017/10/22/how-nevada-went-60-years-without-official-flag/789460001/.

Howe, Randy. *Flags of the Fifty States: Their Colorful Histories and Significance*. Guilford, Connecticut: Lyons Press, 2002.

"Chapter 235 – State Seal, Motto and Symbols; Gifts and Endowments." Nevada Legislature.

Accessed July 22, 2023. https://www.leg.state.nv.us/nrs/nrs-235.html#NRS235Sec005.

MacNulty, W. Kirk. *Freemasonry; Symbols, Secrets, Significance*. London: Thames & Hudson, 2006.

CHAPTER 7

"Hudson's Bay Company Archives – HBC Fur Trade Post Map." Archives of Manitoba. Accessed July 22, 2023. https://www.gov.mb.ca/chc/archives/hbca/post_maps/index.html.

"Webster-Ashburton Treaty." Wikipedia. Accessed July 22, 2023. https://en.wikipedia.org/wiki/Webster%E2%80%93Ashburton_Treaty.

Weiser-Alexander, Kathy. "Utter-Van Ornum Massacre, Idaho." Legends of America. Last modified November 2021. https://www.legendsofamerica.com/utter-van-ornum-massacre-idaho/.

Vrchoticky, Nick. "Inside the Utter-Van Ornum Massacre on the Oregon Trail." Grunge. Last modified March 27, 2023. https://www.grunge.com/247969/inside-the-utter-van-ornum-massacre-on-the-oregon-trail/.

Shannon, Donald H. *The Utter Disaster on the Oregon Trail*. Caxton Press, 1993.

"Dr. C.K. Ah Fong, 1893." Washington State University Libraries Digital Collections. Accessed July 22, 2023. https://content.libraries.wsu.edu/digital/collection/imls_3/id/69/.

"Edward Bing Kan: The First Chinese-American Naturalized After Repeal of Chinese Exclusion." U.S. Citizenship and Immigration Services. Last modified July 28, 2020. https://www.uscis.gov/about-us/our-history/history-office-and-library/edward-bing-kan-the-first-chinese-american-naturalized-after-repeal-of-chinese-exclusion.

Finn, Harold R. "Skip." Minnesota Legislature Reference Library. Accessed July 22, 2023. https://www.lrl.mn.gov/legdb/fulldetail?id=10179.

"The Largest Mass Execution in US History." Death Penalty Information Center. December 31, 2000. https://deathpenaltyinfo.org/stories/the-largest-mass-execution-in-us-history.

Khrushchev, Nikita Sergeevich. *Khrushchev Remembers*, 226. Vol. 1. Translated and edited by Strobe Talbott. Little, Brown & Company, 1970.

Lawrence, J.P. "'Peanuts' Creator Charles Schulz's Experiences in WWII Shaped the Character of Charlie Brown." *Stars and Stripes*. December 25, 2020. https://www.stripes.com/theaters/

us/peanuts-creator-charles-schulz-s-experiences-in-wwii-shaped-the-character-of-charlie-brown-1.656415.

Jim Northrup Quote from YouTube. PBS Wisconsin. LZ Lambeau: Jim Northrup. January 1, 2024. https://www.youtube.com/watch?v=URastjiT2is.

CHAPTER 8

Merriam-Webster.com, s.v. "Solidago." Accessed July 22, 2023. https://www.merriam-webster.com/dictionary/solidago.

"Delaware Declares Independence." History.com. June 12, 2020. https://www.history.com/this-day-in-history/delaware-declares-independence.

"Learn About Lake Barkley." KentuckyLake.com. Accessed July 22, 2023. https://www.kentuckylake.com/lake-barkley/.

Adelman, Garry, and Mary Bays Woodside. "A House Divided: Civil War Kentucky." American Battlefield Trust. Last modified December 21, 2021. https://www.battlefields.org/learn/articles/house-divided-civil-war-kentucky.

Hutton, Paul Andrew. "Kit Carson's Rescue Ride." HistoryNet. Last modified June 26, 2007. https://www.historynet.com/kit-carsons-rescue-ride/?f.

Trimble, Marshall. "Kit Carson: History and the Myth." *True West*. Last modified June 2, 2015. https://truewestmagazine.com/article/kit-carson-history-and-the-myth/.

"Sam Calagione." Live – Love Delaware. Accessed July 22, 2023. https://www.livelovedelaware.com/sam-calagione/.

▪ This book would not have been possible without Delaware. Delaware has a first-place position in support, friendliness, and overall achievement. Delaware was first to affirm my path on vexillology and give a blessing. Gratitude is due to Winterthur, the Du Pont Corp, the cities of Ellendale and Wilmington, and, most importantly, the Kalmar Nyckel Foundation. Indeed, Delaware provided many of the first feathers of friendly faith for the creation of this book.

CHAPTER 9

Green, Joey. *Dumb History: The Stupidest Mistakes Ever Made*. London: Penguin Books, 2012.

Hoig, Stan. "Land Run of 1889." Oklahoma Historical Society. Accessed July 22, 2023. https://www.okhistory.org/publications/enc/entry.php?entry=LA014.

Hoig, Stan. "Boomer Movement." Oklahoma Historical Society. Accessed July 22, 2023. https://www.okhistory.org/publications/enc/entry.php?entryname=BOOMER%20MOVEMENT.

Willis, Chuck. *Destination America: The People and Cultures That Created a Nation*. London: DK, 2005.

Hartvigsen, John M. "Correcting the Utah State Flag." *NAVA News* 210 (April-June 2011).

CHAPTER 10

"The Heraldic Pelican." Internet Sacred Text Archive. Accessed July 22, 2023. https://www.sacred-texts.com/lcr/fsca/fsca41.htm.

Davidson, Lee. "Time to Fix 88-Year Mistake in Utah Flag?" *Salt Lake Tribune*. Last modified December 25, 2010. https://archive.sltrib.com/article.php?id=50931358&itype=CMSID.

Wright, John D. *American History, Timeline of the Civil War: The Ultimate Guide to the War That Defined America*. London: Amber Books, 2007.

Brown, George W., and Elanor Harman. *The Story of Canada*. London: D.C. Heath and Company, 1949

Miller, Madeline S., and J. Lane Miller. *Harper's Bible Dictionary*. 6th ed. New York: Harper & Brothers, Publishers, 1959.

Pineschi, Anastasia. "The Pelican, Self-Sacrificing Mother Bird of the Medieval Bestiary." Getty. May 11, 2018. https://blogs.getty.edu/iris/the-pelican-self-sacrificing-mother-bird-of-the-medieval-bestiary/.

Murray, John. "Summum Philosophy: A Cosmic View." *Daily Utah Chronicle* 87 (May 8, 1978).

Heriot, Drew, dir. *The Secret*. San Francisco, CA: Gravitas Ventures, 2006.

CHAPTER 11

"Official Symbols of Canada." Government of Canada. Last modified June 16, 2023. https://www.canada.ca/en/canadian-heritage/services/official-symbols-canada.html.

Lang, William L. "Robert Gray." Oregon Encyclopedia. Oregon Historical Society. Last modified April 3, 2023. https://www.oregonencyclopedia.org/articles/gray_robert/#.YYv13E7MJPY.

Flora, Stephenie. "Captain Robert Gray." Oregon Pioneers. Accessed July 23, 2023. http://www.oregonpioneers.com/gray.htm.

Oldham, Keith. "Captain Robert Gray Becomes the First Non-Indian Navigator to Enter the Columbia River, Which He Later Names, on May 11, 1792." HistoryLink.org. Last modified January 13, 2003. https://www.historylink.org/file/5051.

Lockwood, Martha. "Hazel Ying Lee: Showcased Asian-American Involvement in War Effort." Air Force. March 19, 2015. https://www.af.mil/News/Article-Display/Article/580998/hazel-ying-lee-showcased-asian-american-involvement-in-war-effort/.

Crowther, Linnea. "Mike Mitchell (1944-2021), 'Louie, Louie' Guitarist with the Kingsmen." Legacy.com. April 20, 2021. https://www.legacy.com/news/celebrity-deaths/mike-mitchell-1944-2021-louie-louie-guitarist-with-the-kingsmen/.

Note that you can easily eat the inner trunk of the tree on South Carolina's flag at your local Bonefish Grill if you order their house salad, which includes hearts of palm. They look like little white hockey pucks. In this preparation, they taste like if a water chestnut and bamboo root had a baby.

▌ South Carolina is another state that rolled out the red carpet. This book is perpetually indebted to South Carolina, which provided sacred and spiritual positive feedback and protection for the first steps of this venture. Without South Carolina, this book would have been a thin shadow of itself, showing me the hidden sadness and glory of the American flag.

CHAPTER 12

"10. French Settlement in the Illinois Country." Illinois State Museum. Accessed July 23, 2023. https://www.museum.state.il.us/RiverWeb/landings/Ambot/Archives/vignettes/people/French_20Settlement.html.

"The Prince and his Poodle." Beyond the Book: A digital journey through the treasures of the Emmerson Collection. December 30, 2023. https://beyondthebook.slv.vic.gov.au/stories/prince-and-poodle/

Smith, George W. "The Salines of Southern Illinois." In *Transactions of the Illinois State Historical Society for the Year 1904*, 250. Springfield, IL: Illinois State Historical Society, 1904.

"Rivers, Edens, Empires: Lewis & Clark and the Revealing of America." Library of Congress. Accessed July 23, 2023. https://www.loc.gov/exhibits/lewisandclark/lewis-after.html.

Degregorio, William A. *The Complete Book of U.S. Presidents*. 4th ed. New York: Wing Books, 1993.

Hayden, Bree. "History of the Rough Riders Flag." Gettysburg Flag Works. August 10, 2021. https://www.gettysburgflag.com/blog/history-of-the-rough-riders-flag/.

CHAPTER 13

"October 9, 1635 Roger Williams Banished." Mass Moments. Accessed December 30, 2023. https://www.massmoments.org/moment-details/king-philips-war-breaks-out.html.

Church, Benjamin. "King Philip's War Breaks Out." Mass Moments. Accessed July 23, 2023. https://www.massmoments.org/moment-details/king-philips-war-breaks-out.html.

"King Philip's War." History.com. Last modified July 11, 2023. https://www.history.com/topics/native-american-history/king-philips-war.

Hudson, Myles. "Battle of Fallen Timbers." *Encyclopedia Britannica*. August 13, 2022. https://www.britannica.com/event/Battle-of-Fallen-Timbers#ref1273952.

"Anthony Wayne." *Encyclopedia Britannica*. January 1, 2023. https://www.britannica.com/biography/Anthony-Wayne#ref205449.

"American Frontier." *Encyclopedia Britannica*. October 27, 2023. https://www.britannica.com/topic/American-frontier#ref1262415.

"Saint Clair's Defeat." *Encyclopedia Britannica*. October 28, 2023. https://www.britannica.com/event/Saint-Clairs-Defeat#ref273816.

Ray, Michael. "Treaty of Greenville." *Encyclopedia Britannica*. September 14, 2023. https://www.britannica.com/event/Treaty-of-Greenville.

"The History of the Pequot War." Battlefields of the Pequot War. Accessed July 23, 2023. http://pequotwar.org/about/.

Jacobs, Timothy Lester. "John Stone, Hartford Founder." Society of Descendants of the Founders of Hartford. Accessed July 23, 2023. https://www.foundersofhartford.org/the-founders/john-stone/.

"In 1634 John Stone Is Lost in the Connecticut Fog of War." New England Historical Society. Accessed July 23, 2023. https://newenglandhistoricalsociety.com/1634-john-stone-lost-connecticut-fog-war/.

Pender, Caelyn. "Brown Changes Official Name to Remove 'Plantations'." *Brown Daily Herald*. September 3, 2020. https://www.browndailyherald.com/article/2020/09/brown-changes-official-name-to-remove-plantations.

"Memoir of Campaigns Against the British Post Northwest of the River Ohio." Indiana Historical Bureau. Accessed July 23, 2023. https://www.in.gov/history/for-educators/download-issues-of-the-indiana-historian/the-fall-of-fort-sackville/the-fall-of-fort-sackville-focus/memoir-of-campaigns-against-the-british-posts-northwest-of-the-river-ohio/.

CHAPTER 14

"Montani Semper Liberi: West Virginia State Motto." State Symbols USA. Accessed July 23, 2023. https://statesymbolsusa.org/symbol/west-virginia/state-motto/mountaineers-are-always-free.

"The Forgotten History of Westsylvania." *Observer-Reporter*. Last modified May 8, 2021. https://observer-reporter.com/publications/liwc/the-forgotten-history-of-westsylvania/article_41011b14-6ab5-11ea-bff9-57ff6679a38d.html.

"Sergeant Levin Wilcoxon: Settler of Westsylvania." Finding the Maryland 400. April 1, 2015. https://msamaryland400.com/2015/04/01/sergeant-levin-wilcoxon-settler-of-westsylvania/.

Blanco, Richard L. "Westsylvania Statehood Plans" in *The American Revolution 1775-1783: An Encyclopedia Vol. 2 in Routledge Library Editions: America: Revolution and Civil War*. Routledge, 2020.

"Legend of Seneca Rocks: The Betrothal of Snow Bird, Princess of the Seneca Indians." United States Department of Agriculture. Accessed July 23, 2023. https://mh3wv.org/wp-content/uploads/2018/10/Legend-of-Seneca-Rocks-Seneca-Princess-WV-Seneca-Rocks.pdf.

"First Stories." Devils Tower National Monument Wyoming. Last modified November 4, 2022. https://www.nps.gov/deto/learn/historyculture/first-stories.htm.

"Devil Places." Spooky Geology. July 30, 2018. https://spookygeology.com/devil-places/.

Alexander, Kathy. "Indian Wars List and Timeline." Legends of America. Accessed July 23, 2023. https://www.legendsofamerica.com/na-indianwartimeline/.

Davis, John W. "The Johnson County War: 1892 Invasion of Northern Wyoming." WyoHistory.org. Wyoming Historical Society November 8, 2014. https://www.wyohistory.org/encyclopedia/johnson-county-war-1892-invasion-northern-wyoming.

Karin, Marcy Lynn, Barbara Babcock, and Erika Wayne. "Esther Morris and her Equality State: From Council Bill 70 to Life on the Bench." *Women in the Legal Profession* (2002). (No longer available.)

CHAPTER 15

Hart, Albert Bushnell, ed. "George Washington Play and Pageant Book" in *History of the George Washington Bicentennial Celebration*, 192. Washington, DC: George Washington Bicentennial Commission, 1932.

"New York-New Jersey Line War." Academic Dictionaries and Encyclopedias. Accessed July 23, 2023. https://en-academic.com/dic.nsf/enwiki/1320746.

Karttunen, Frances. "The Nantucket-New York Connection." Nantucket Historical Association. Accessed July 23, 2023. https://nha.org/research/nantucket-history/history-topics/the-nantucket-new-york-connection/.

♠ New Jersey is the essential ace of spades in the creation of this book; likewise, New York is the ace of hearts. The contribution and precious years of life led in these states (the lion's share in New Jersey) provided critical care and support to make this book possible. Have no doubts about it, the experiences garnered in NJ are cherished as much as those in NY—for all the good, bad, ugly, beautiful, boring, angry, peaceful, sad, silly, weird, and fun.

CHAPTER 16

Anderson, Patricia Keppel. "But Did You Know…The History of Virginia Peanuts." Virginia Is for Lovers. Accessed July 23, 2023. https://blog.virginia.org/2020/10/virginia-peanuts-history/.

"George Washington Takes Command of Continental Army." History.com. November 13, 2009. https://www.history.com/this-day-in-history/washington-takes-command-of-continental-army.

Little, Becky. "How 22-Year-Old George Washington Inadvertently Sparked a World War." History.com. Last modified September 27, 2023. https://www.history.com/news/george-washington-french-indian-war-jumonville.

Klein, Christopher. "11 Key People Who Shaped George Washington's Life." History.com. Last modified October 10, 2023. https://www.history.com/news/who-was-important-to-george-washington.

"11 Little-Known Facts About George Washington." History.com. Last modified October 18, 2023. https://www.history.com/news/george-washington-little-known-facts.

Little, Becky. "The Worst Time in History to Be Alive, According to Scientists." History.com. Last modified August 1, 2023. https://www.history.com/news/536-volcanic-eruption-fog-eclipse-worst-year.

Blakemore, Erin. "The Revolutionary War Hero Who Was Openly Gay." History.com. Last modified June 22, 2023. https://www.history.com/news/openly-gay-revolutionary-war-hero-friedrich-von-steuben.

Mullen, Matt. "How George Washington's Iron-Willed Single Mom Taught Him Honor." History.com. Last modified March 27, 2023. https://www.history.com/news/george-washington-mother-mary-character-upbringing.

Jaicks, Fred. "Lightning and Benjamin Franklin." MJJ Sales. February 7, 2020. https://mjjsales.com/lightning-and-benjamin-franklin/.

Taver, Curtis. "Flags of Our Founders: A Study of Fraternal Organization Flags." Presentation at the North American Vexillological Association's 57th annual meeting, at Philadelphia, PA, October 8, 2023.

Daley, Bill. "Timothy Riggles – The Rise and Fall of a Massachusetts Loyalist." Sandwich Historical Commission. March 22, 2021. https://sandwichhistory.org/timothy-ruggles-the-rise-and-fall-of-a-massachusetts-loyalist/.

"Peyton Randolph." Colonial Williamsburg. Accessed July 23, 2023. https://www.slaveryandremembrance.org/Almanack/people/bios/biorapey.cfm.

DiCamillo, Michael. "'They Crucified Two Thieves': The Executions of John Bly and Charles Rose, Shays's Rebels." *The Histories* 5, no. 2. Accessed July 23, 2023. https://digitalcommons.lasalle.edu/cgi/viewcontent.cgi?article=1102&context=the_histories.

Lepore, Jill. *These Truths: A History of the United States*. New York: W. W. Norton & Company, 2018.

Wood, Gordon S. *Friends Divided: John Adams and Thomas Jefferson*. Penguin Press, 2017.

Gately, M.R. *Gately's Universal Educator: An Educational Cyclopædia and Business Guide*. 12th ed. Edited by Charles E. Beale. 1883.

Farid, Ronni S. "Peyton Randolph (1721-1775)." George Washington's Mount Vernon. Accessed November 30, 2023. https://www.mountvernon.org/library/digitalhistory/digital-encyclopedia/article/peyton-randolph-1721-1775/.

Daley, Bill. "Timothy Ruggles – The Rise and Fall of a Massachusetts Loyalist." Sandwich Historical Commission. March 22, 2021. https://sandwichhistory.org/timothy-ruggles-the-rise-and-fall-of-a-massachusetts-loyalist/.

McGaughy, J. Kent. "Richard Henry Lee (1732-1794)." Encyclopedia Virginia. December 7, 2020. https://encyclopediavirginia.org/entries/lee-richard-henry-1732-1794.

"Lee Resolution." National Archives. Accessed November 30, 2023. https://www.archives.gov/milestone-documents/lee-resolution

Tricky, Eric. "Why the Colonies' Most Galvanizing Patriot Never Became a Founding Father." *Smithsonian Magazine*. May 5, 2017. https://www.smithsonianmag.com/history/transformative-patriot-who-didnt-become-founding-father-180963166/.

Otis, James. "The Rights of the British Colonies Asserted and Proved" (1764). In *Pamphlets of the*

American Revolution 1750-1776, 439–440. Edited by Bernard Bailyn and Jane N. Garrett. Belknap Press, 1965. https://www.pbs.org/wgbh/aia/part2/2h18.html.

"Paul Revere." National Park Service. Accessed November 30, 2023. https://www.nps.gov/people/paul-revere.htm.

"The Two Grandsons of Paul Revere Who Fought in the Civil War to End the Compromise with Slavery." Walk Boston History. September 27, 2017. https://www.walkbostonhistory.com/history-blog/the-two-grandsons-of-paul-revere-that-fought-in-the-civil-war-to-end-the-compromise-with-slavery.

"Henry Lee III." American Battlefield Trust. Accessed November 30, 2023. https://www.battlefields.org/learn/biographies/henry-lighthorse-lee-iii

Woodward, Colin. "Henry Lee (1787-1837)." Encyclopedia Virginia. December 7, 2020. https://encyclopediavirginia.org/entries/lee-henry-1787-1837.

Broadwater, Jeff. "George Mason (1725-1792)." *Encyclopedia Virginia*. December 7, 2020. https://encyclopediavirginia.org/entries/mason-george-1725-1792.

"Elbridge Gerry." Miller Center. Accessed November 30, 2023. https://millercenter.org/president/madison/essays/gerry-1813-vicepresident.

Griffin, Cyrus. "Letter to George Washington from Cyrus Griffin, 10 July 1789." Founders Online. National Archives. Accessed November 30, 2023. https://founders.archives.gov/?q=-Author%3A%22Griffin%2C%20Cyrus%22&s=1111311111&r=20.

Sunshine, Daniel. "Leander James McCormick (1819-1900)." Encyclopedia Virginia. November 19, 2021. https://encyclopediavirginia.org/entries/leander-james-mccormick-1819-1900.

Adams, Samuel. "American Independence." August 1, 1776. State House, Philadelphia, PA. https://www.azquotes.com/quote/2046.

Henry, Patrick. "Speech to the Second Virginia Convention. March 23, 1775. St. John's Church, Richmond, VA., 23 Mar. 1775." https://www.azquotes.com/quote/130156.

Lee, Henry. "A Funeral Oration on the Death of General Washington." December 26, 1799. German Lutheran Church, Philadelphia, PA. https://www.nlm.nih.gov/exhibition/georgewashington/education/materials/Transcript-Funeral.pdf.

The First First Lady. Page Profile from George Washington's Mount Vernon, Website. https://

www.mountvernon.org/george-washington/martha-washington/the-first-first-lady/

Miller, Elizabeth Bissel. "Abigail Adams." George Washington's Mount Vernon. Accessed November 30, 2023. https://www.mountvernon.org/library/digitalhistory/digital-encyclopedia/article/abigail-adams/

▌ Visiting Virginia and Massachusetts is like visiting one's grandparents, and both states are major players in the genesis of this book. Grampy Massachusetts was fair and friendly and a little detached at times, while Grammy Virginia was able to bend the rules little so a favorite grandson got a little something extra. Thus, Virginia's contribution to this book is a bit thicker than Massachusetts's. A last thanks and grateful synchronicity is that the landlord of my residence where the majority of this book was written, Patrick Gorham of the DePaul Management Company, is a direct descendent of 6th Articles of Confederation President Nathaniel Gorham of Charlestown, Massachusetts. What are the chances?

Also note that some of the flags presented in each chapter are modified to a commercial format, and some flags have been modified for clarity to make it easier to make out the details on some of the more complex designs.

Table of Profound Coincidences or Synchronicities that relate to the 50th year of Jubilee

1783-1833	End of slavery across U.K. after peace made with 13 colonies
1815-1865	End of slavery in U.S. after second war of independence
1869-1919	Following Wyoming's lead, 50 years later all women can vote in U.S.
1919-1969	After equal rights established, 50 starred U.S. flag planted on the moon
1776-1826	Jefferson & Adams cross over 50 years after the Declaration of Independence July 4 , 1776-July 4, 1826

EPILOGUE

This is the first book in a trilogy, and part II is just around the corner. If you want to be first to read all about it, please sign up for the email list with this QR code

https://themanorebooks.blogspot.com/2023/09/join-our-reading-list.html

You can expect to get 1 email or less per month, as a newsletter. And with fingers crossed, book II should be ready for purchase for Christmas and the Holiday Winter Blitz of 2024.

Part II is written and undergoing post production. It will cover the flags for the other half of the nation, who tend to have abstract state flag designs. Fatefully, most of the states in book II are south of the Mason-Dixon line. As the state flags were chosen, most of the southern states picked flags that convey a "national identity" since they match in the thematic of other flags on the international stage. In contrast, the state flags of most northern states (mostly of book I) are more akin to local and county flags. Consequently, northern flags do not compete for "iconic attention" with the national flag. Ergo, the humble flags of the north allow the stars and stripes to garner the lion's share of adoration for collective identity, rather than allowing the state flags to compete or steal the limelight, as they do with Tennessee, Maryland, Colorado, and Texas.

In the meantime, if you want to read more about what I have written about flags please visit my blog, which has over a 10,001 short musing, facts, and insights; note some posts are incomplete, with lovely original artisan-spellings and on occasion, bizarre-original grammar sentence structures. The blog is perpetually "under construction" and best of all, you can leave a comment, subscribe, contribute, and do all that Internet jazz that they do, right here

Further, you can connect with me on my YouTube page here:

And this will take you to my official "X-Twitter" page, which does not have a blue or "whatever the color of the season" checkmark. Here:

This mostly non-fiction narrative shall be continued...

ABOUT THE AUTHOR

Christopher Maddish has belonged to the North American Vexillological Association since 2008; he joined the founding editorial board of *Vexillum*, its quarterly magazine, in 2017. He has also served as a delegate to several international congresses of Vexillology—in Yokohama, Japan; Rotterdam, Netherlands; London, U.K.; and Washington, DC.

Among his finest achievements was the vexillological discovery of a lost flag from the American Revolution, subsequently christened the "Martha Washington Flag." It has a blank field and a starburst of 13 stripes in the upper left corner that looks something like the flag of Imperial Japan, minus the central sun. More recently, Christopher was recognized by Her Majesty Queen Elizabeth II for his design of the Prime Meridian Flag, which was hoisted at the Royal Greenwich Observatory.

An alumnus of the Japanese educational JET Program, Christopher currently teaches Japanese, biology, and chemistry at a high school in suburban Philadelphia. Maddish volunteers on the Tall Ship of Delaware, the *Kalmar Nyckel*, and is an active member of the United States Coast Guard Auxiliary, where he recently supported its mission with U.S. Customs and Border Patrol along the southern border at Eagle Pass in Maverick County, Texas.

Ted Kaye, the author of Good Flag, Bad Flag

Printed in the USA
CPSIA information can be obtained
at www.ICGtesting.com
LVHW021222110624
782918LV00001B/44